BERTHA the Swiss Trader's Daughter

Based on a True Story

Love, War and Conspiracy in the Turbulent Past of Malawi – the little Jewel of Africa

Eleni Trataris Cotton

 New Generation Publishing

DEDICATION.

This is dedicated to the memory of my mother, Bertha, who was a true lady, gracious, wise and gentle in every way. Her love and generosity towards all and particularly those in need, were inspirational; she lit up her world with her ready laughter and love of life. Her light still shines on my path.

PROLOGUE

1964.

Her name was Berta. As far as she knew, it was a German name and the 'e' was pronounced like the 'e' in echo. Anyway, it wasn't really important because as soon as she started mixing with English people, they called her Bertha – and it stuck. Bertha Maria Deuss.

She was born in Central Africa, in Nyasaland, as it was known then. Of course, since independence, most names had been changed; she supposed that new governments made a point of doing this. Out with the old, in with the new! Nyasaland became Malawi and Fort Johnston, the town where she was born, became Mangoche. Names interested her; sometimes when she was daydreaming, which she often did, she pondered which name she preferred.

Fort Johnston had a military sound to her; that is, it evoked bold, colourful pictures of uniforms, rifles on shoulders, the thudding of booted feet marching on hard baked earth. It sounded exciting and, indeed, she felt that it should. The fort had a history; it was established to get rid of the slave traders who were terrorising the area. Oh yes, we're talking about the beginning of the twentieth century and, yes, slave trading was still rampant and profitable.

Her father, Ludwig, who was Swiss of German descent, was a business man, or trader as they were known: he was a very successful one, she learnt as she grew older. In later years when he was gone, what she remembered most about him were his vitality and playfulness. Her memories of him were filled with sunshine and laughter and the sure knowledge that he loved his little family totally and unconditionally. Her mother, Victoria, or A Mayi, as the children called her, was different: she was born of a wealthy, entrepreneurial African family in Portuguese East Africa. Berta remembered her calm, her serious demeanour and her dedication to her home and family. She was always there for them. Together with Ludwig, Victoria formed the bedrock of their children's secure and happy existence.

The family had a sprawling, colonial-style house in Fort Johnston and a small farm nearby, outside the town limits. They were quite close to Lake Nyasa – now Lake Malawi – where they spent many happy hours swimming and picnicking on the sandy beaches, always keeping a wary eye open for the predatory crocodiles which prowled amongst the clumps of reeds, bellies on the sand beneath the warm, clear waters.

There were four children, a son and three daughters. Berta was the youngest, indulged in many ways and in awe of her elder siblings. Richard,

1

the eldest child, was good-looking and full of charm and energy. He took after Ludwig while Elsa, the second eldest, had more of the look of seriousness that she had inherited from A Mayi, although, particularly as the girls grew older, her dry wit would often have them in gales of laughter. She was very protective of Berta and, since Berta started at boarding school at the age of seven, Elsa slipped easily into the role of surrogate mother. Paulina, the third of the children was, it often seemed to Berta, quite different from the other three, clingy with A Mayi and inclined to complain a lot about just about anything. Berta, the last in line, skinny and endlessly active, and with a giggle switch which was easily turned on was, according to the sisters at the Convent, a handful, albeit a loveable one.

The girls went to school quite a long way away from home, to a place in roughly the centre of Nyasaland, Nguludi, an exciting week's journey, as Berta recalled it. The girls walked or rode their bicycles and when they tired they were carried on *machilas,* which were a type of hammock carried by four bearers. Berta toyed with that name – Nguludi – happy that it had been left unchanged by the changing political scene. She once wrote in an essay that it sounded to her like a babbling brook dancing over the shiny stones and bright green plants in its bed. Berta smiled as she recalled how the nuns had loved that and decided that Berta was definitely artistic.

Now, sitting comfortably in an armchair on the veranda of the home where she and her husband had lived and brought up their children, embroidery on her lap, her needle still, she thought about that as she gazed around at the vibrant tropical garden she had created. Brilliant sunshine caressed an acre of lawns, winding paths and bougainvillea, purple, scarlet and white, tumbling over the pergola and up the columns of the verandas. Flower beds were a dancing sea of colour: dahlias, gladioli, cleome, zinnias, roses and carnations joyfully jostled for space. Gardeners trotted to and fro, digging, weeding and planting, calling out to one another and laughing with little outbursts of song. Shrubs, chosen not only for their beauty but also for their cooling shades of green, stood alone at intervals on the green lawns or in clusters forming restful backdrops for the flower beds.

She started suddenly, sat up and looked at her watch.

The United Kingdom's representative, Prince Philip was arriving today to share in the Independence celebrations, a big moment for the country. She and her husband, and their son as Deputy Mayor with his wife, had been invited to join the small welcoming party of prominent citizens for the British royal guest at the airport and then be part of the motorcade into town. She looked forward to the luncheon on the following day; the prince was well liked and one never knew what he would say next!

Another glance at her watch. No, there was still plenty of time.

Berta settled back in her chair and her mind flew again to those happy days, now long gone. She no longer saw her garden but the charming little red-brick building nestling in the tropical valley, sunning itself in the gentle mood of a summer's day.

It was only when she was much older that she understood that the convent, which was run by mainly French nuns, had been started for the children of the many nationalities of men who had married or cohabited with the local girls and could afford the fees. There was concern, apparently, that these children would be disadvantaged in the state education system, which was still in its infancy. When Berta looked back she remembered something that she hadn't really noticed at the time. What a selection of colours they were – every shade between rich, dark chocolate and sun-kissed gold. She recalled how, when she first met one of her daughters-in-law, the girl's eyes had widened and she'd said spontaneously, "Oh, what a beautiful colour you are, just like milk chocolate!" Berta smiled at the memory, remembering too the auburn mop on top, now more brown and streaked with grey.

What fun, she reflected, they had in those days, when knees didn't creak and backs didn't ache! During lesson breaks they played hopscotch on the dry brown earth of the quadrangle, where it was easier to mark out the boxes with a stout twig foraged for in the hedges that surrounded the playing fields. The girls played beneath the towering jacaranda tree which dominated the quadrangle; its blue blossoms would drift slowly on to them with each little breeze that rippled through its laden branches. Or they played on the grassy playing fields, netball, tennis, or simply catch. Sometimes it seemed to Berta that the sounds of the laughing voices and the slapping sound of the ball hitting home floated like twirling autumn leaves on the still warm air.

"You're too fanciful!" said Paulina, when Berta shared this thought with her.

Many of the older girls – whom Berta joined in later years – sat in groups on the grass in the shade of the loquat trees at the edge of the field. They chatted as they lazily pulled brightly-coloured zinnias apart: "He loves me, he loves me not…" Why, she wondered now, is so little made of teenage girls' rampant hormones? It's always the boys' that are talked about but she, for one, had never seen a group of teenage boys sitting cross-legged on the grass, holding flowers and chanting, "She loves me, she loves me not…"

Berta was nine years old when the First World War broke out, but it had little impact – that she recalled – on the children. The worst part, in her view, was seeing the wounded soldiers being brought back to the Fort

Johnston Hospital on the river steamers, from the fighting lines in the north. They were transported on stretchers from the steamers onto the waiting trucks, which were in themselves a new and exciting development, and the children were drawn against their will to watch the gruesome sight, which fascinated and repelled at the same time. The memory remained remarkably fresh after all these years; how frightened she and the other ten-year-olds were on seeing the pale, grey faces framed by bloody bandages, and the torn, bloodstained uniforms. Strange how both black and white soldiers' faces turned grey with loss of blood, she had thought at the time. And, oh yes, there was the excitement when the British steamer HMS Gwendolen on Lake Nyasa fought the first naval battle of the First World War and defeated the German vessel Herman von Wissman in August of 1914.

They prayed daily for the soldiers, all the soldiers, even the enemy because, said Mother Camille, they were all part of one human family and loved equally by God.

The comforting haze of nostalgia developed an edge of tension as Berta's thoughts turned to that last week. Everything had seemed so normal until then. Life continued as always, the strident brass bell being shaken enthusiastically by Sister Jeanne, ruling the children's lives, reminding them where to go and what to do. She remembered being in trouble frequently. "Berta! Come here!" "Berta! Go there!" "Berta, stop giggling!" "Berta, what a mess you're in!"

She was distracted by a sudden memory of the lavatory block that stood in the middle of the playground. It was small and consisted of two lavatories alongside each other with a shared veranda, and was reached by a small flight of steps. The lavatories were the old-fashioned "thunder boxes", that is a wooden throne beneath which was a hole in the concrete floor. Berta would always try to block her mind to the stories that Olga, an older girl, would tell them about the huge pythons that lodged in the murky darkness below. Olga's other favourite story was that she had seen a column of headless nuns, heads held at waist height, floating through the dormitory at midnight, each of them pausing and holding out their heads – which were skeletal – to peer from a distance of inches at the sleeping girls. The first story caused an epidemic of bowel irregularities and the second, many screaming nightmares.

Permission had to be requested to use the lavatory during play time; the drill was that when you needed to use the lavatory you went up to the nun on duty and said, "May I please be excused, Sister?" Berta remembered how hot and sweaty she would be from whatever game she was playing at the time and how she would hop from foot to foot as the nun scolded her for her dishevelled appearance. When she finally said, "Yes", Berta ran as fast as she could, because inevitably she had left things to the last minute.

A frown creased her brow as she thought back to that last day.

Suddenly made aware by the prick of her needle that she had forgotten her embroidery, she sucked her finger where a small drop of blood had appeared, lodged the needle in her pin cushion, put her work on the small table beside her and thought back. No, nothing had seemed untoward. The girls had played the usual games that day, gone to the usual lessons, worked, laughed, played and cried: everything had been normal. The nuns had seemed distracted, but Berta thought that it was probably because Lent was on the horizon, and they were busy thinking up ways to get the girls to give up the things they liked the most for Lent. Isn't it funny, she thought now, how when you're very young, rules seem to be made not for any good reason, but simply to curtail your enjoyment? Foibles of the adult mind, that's what they were perceived as.

Lost in the past, Berta was once again living that fateful night, when she went to bed tired and content, never imagining that her world was about to be turned upside down.

She now knew that that day, when it all started, was to go down in the history books as the day of the Chilembwe uprising. The date was 23rd January, 1915.

PART ONE

CHAPTER ONE

The jagged sweeps of blood-red sky fell below the hills, dusk melted into night and gradually, the clattering noises in the kitchens ceased. The nuns' voices died away and lamps were doused one by one until all was dark. The convent slumbered in the moonlight.

Berta was jolted from sleep by the tinkling dormitory bell, just after midnight.

Through the tumultuous sound of her heartbeat in her ears she heard Mother Camille, the Reverend Mother of the convent, saying insistently in a loud, clear voice as she strode up and down the aisles between the rows of beds in the dormitory: "Attention! Attention! Wake up, children. Wake up. I want you to listen to me."

The words were in French, the language of the school.

Berta struggled to rouse herself and open her eyes. It was pitch dark, except for the pale orange glow of the paraffin lamp that Mother Camille was holding in her left hand.

The other little bodies in the dormitory stirred, slowly at first then more quickly. Childish voices started to murmur; then as they became more fully awake they rose in intensity, querulous and questioning. Berta sat up, rubbing her eyes.

The nun's voice rose, became more authoritative; she stood at the top end of the dormitory where everyone could see her clearly.

"Listen to me, children. Listen very carefully because we do not have much time. We have to leave the school immediately. I repeat, we must leave immediately. When we reach the hills we will stop and tell you why. For now, just understand that we have to go as quickly as possible. Elsa, Lucy, Paulina and Dina, get dressed quickly and make sure that the little ones are properly clothed."

The voice of Mother Camille continued, allocating responsibilities, making sure that the children left the convent fully clothed and with enough food and drink to see them through the next several hours. Two more nuns came in, habits rustling, the rosary beads that hung from their waists clinking. They hung three lanterns on hooks on the walls.

Berta struggled out of bed; she felt an arm around her.

"Berta, hurry! Look, your socks are all screwed up. You'll get sore feet." Elsa was at her side, looking anxious, at sixteen more aware of the strange and sinister situation than her ten-year-old sister.

"Get your shoes on, collect the little ones as soon as they are dressed and wait for me on the veranda. Sister Jeanne will be there shortly."

And she was gone, chivvying and helping the younger children, many of whom were very young, between the ages of five and seven.

Berta threw the rest of her clothes on and scurried around doing her tasks, her mind in turmoil. She felt as though she were in a dream. The night was dark and the kerosene lamps made tall, dancing shadows on the walls and on the mosquito nets shrouding each bed; everything seemed alive. Faces in the flickering light were shadowed, the younger ones petulant at being awoken, the older ones questioning and afraid. A man's deep voice, close by, just on the other side of the wall, made her jump. Another voice in response lent her wings; she raced to the nun who was dressing the little ones at the other end of the room.

"Sister, I heard two men's voices outside my window." Her voice choked in fear.

Sister Jeanne straightened up quickly and bent to reassure her, holding both Berta's hands in hers.

"Yes, you're quite right, my dear," she whispered with a smile. "The farmers in the area have joined together to help us get to where we're going. They're waiting outside to help us on our way."

With a smile of relief, Berta returned to her duties. In a very short space of time the senior girls had the forty children milling around on the dark veranda, outside the dormitory building which formed one side of the quadrangle. Some of the very young ones were crying quietly, comforted by the older girls whose responsibility they were.

Berta crept to the edge of the veranda and peered around her. Despite the midnight hour, it was warm; and the night was as dark as only African nights can be. The moon was hidden behind a ragged shred of cloud, but the black sky beyond was littered with stars, like diamonds tossed carelessly onto a piece of black velvet. She shivered, despite the warmth of the balmy night. Even her beloved jacaranda tree, home of so many games, now looked huge, dark and menacing, no sign of its blossoms in the darkness.

Berta turned back. The nuns in their white wimples and grey habits were darting around, organising the children into groups, giving each a small bottle of water and little packs of biscuits, a word of support here, a quick hug there. Berta took her rations and stationed herself between two little five-year-olds, Maria and Eva, her arms around their shoulders. Just ahead, another little one, Alicia, stood separate from the others, gazing sleepily up at the stars.

"Alicia, what are you doing?" chided Berta. "You should be getting into line. Now, who should you be with? Ah, yes," and she moved her a few feet ahead, where she joined three other little ones. Berta returned to her two charges just as there was a call for silence and the name of each child was called out by Sister Jeanne and answered to.

Suddenly, Father Swelsen, their parish priest, his long white cassock floating around his legs, strode into view from the darkness, followed by six men dressed as though for hunting, in khaki safari suits and sturdy walking boots. Wide-brimmed felt hats hung on their backs from their chin straps. They each carried a rifle and a few had pistols hung in holsters against their cartridge belts.

Berta felt faint with relief as she recognised the priest; there was a general murmur of gladness and several greetings from the girls as he came and stood before them.

"Good morning, girls," he boomed at them, with a smile that even the darkness could not obliterate. "Yes, it is morning – just after midnight in fact. Not much fun getting up at this hour, is it?"

There was a chorus of "No, Father!" but everyone was now smiling too.

"There's been a bit of a problem and you'll be walking to a farm in Mikalongwe for a short stay. It will be quite tough going, but I know how strong you are, so I expect you'll be there in no time."

He turned to wave a hand at the six men.

"Here are six kind gentlemen, the volunteers, who are going with you, just to make sure that you'll be all right; so you have a lot of people looking out for you. Goodbye then, and I'll see you when you get back."

There was a chorus of goodbyes as the priest turned away with a wave and walked back into the darkness, in the direction of the priest's house half a mile up the road.

Mother Camille came to stand before the children. She was diminutive in size but her air of authority lent her height.

"Well, children," she said, "we're off on our adventure now. I want you to get into a line. The older girls will be close to you. And look, the moon is behind a cloud now. Let's see who'll be the first to see it come out."

Easily distracted, the children's mood lightened and Berta, with Maria and Eva on either side, joined the rippling crocodile as it moved off, each older girl holding onto two of the youngest ones, with the remaining ones sandwiched in between. At the head of the procession were two volunteers followed by two nuns; another two nuns were in the middle and a further two, together with six members of the convent staff, brought up the rear. The remaining four volunteers took up positions on the flanks and at the rear.

Three nuns at the front, the middle and rear carried a hurricane lamp each.

Now that she was moving, Berta felt the tension in her chest start to ease and she was able to tease and laugh with Maria and Eva as they slowly moved on. She was even able to notice the sweet perfume of the Pride of India vine that mingled with the other exotic smells of the plants that perfumed the African nights.

From the veranda, the line went through the broad quadrangle and round the huge jacaranda tree that was 'den' to so many of their games. The carpet of fallen blue flowers popped underfoot as the children passed by; Berta wished she had the time to collect some of the flowers to push onto her fingers so that she looked as though she had long blue fingernails. Their path took them through the playing fields and then along the gravel road that led past the kitchens to the back of the property. The convent guard dogs, large African Lion dogs, Simba Inja in Ndebele, rose to their feet beside their kennels and started to bay at the procession. A sharp command from Sister Magdalena, the animal lover and trainer of the convent dogs, and they subsided, growling and whining softly, the prominent ridges on their backs bristling. She had a sudden thought.

"Mother," she called softly as she ran towards her superior, "we cannot leave the dogs. They might be harmed."

"*Ma chere soeur*, you're right. The thought hadn't occurred to me." My dear sister; this was how the nuns addressed one another.

She paused for a moment to think.

"I can't see any alternative to taking them," she said finally. "Let them loose, will you, sister? They'll follow us."

The dogs were loosed and promptly took up positions on either side of the line of children. They were a reassuring sight, and many hands darted out for a quick stroke as the dogs passed by them.

From the back gate the road slowly narrowed until it was little more than a stony gravel path, as it left the convent grounds and headed for the hills, whose huge dark mounds loomed forbiddingly in the dark night.

As she held firmly to the hands of the two little girls, Berta looked back to the convent where she had spent most of the past three years. How dear it seemed at this moment, her home from home, a place of happy memories. How alone, how abandoned it looked, she thought.

"Goodbye," she whispered and she had a sudden, frightening moment of foreboding. But there was no time for emotion. Maria and Eva were talking to her and the climb had begun.

The long crocodile wound its way through the sleeping foothills past villagers' gardens, patches of cassava plants and through the tall maize harvest; the village dogs barked hysterically as they approached, yellow fangs glinting in the moonlight. The convent gardeners reacted swiftly, grabbing hold of the convent dogs by their collars and, by nature timid, the village animals soon backed off, growling and defeated at a shout from the convent servants. The sleeping villagers, if they heard sounds of the passage gave no sign of it; the doors to their huts were dark, hostile eyes. The path took the fleeing fugitives through dry river beds where the sand dragged at their feet and mosquitoes hovered ready to attack exposed arms and legs; the youngest children started to whimper.

With every step the walk was becoming more difficult. Peering ahead into the darkness, Berta could see that the path was taking them through tall grasses with razor sharp edges, and thorny little bushes and shrubs. As each child walked past, the grasses whipped back to sting the child following behind and scratch exposed legs. Berta flinched as a reed slapped her across her cheek. Her "ouch!" was involuntary and instantly she let go of the little ones' hands to try and protect them from the swinging lashes. They walked on, she with her arms outstretched to take the brunt of the stinging grasses, her eyes smarting with each little lash. But mercifully, she was soon oblivious to the myriad little cuts on her face, neck and arms.

The stones in the sandy path caused little feet to stumble, and soon many of the younger children were in tears and needing to be comforted. But no stopping was allowed. They must always move on; for much of the time the volunteers and kitchen staff had tired little ones on their shoulders.

It seemed interminable, that walk up the first hill. How strange it was, thought Berta, that this walk that they had done so many times on their nature rambles and that had shown them such delights, with each new discovery of flora and fauna, should now be so menacing. Arms still held out protectively for Maria and Eva where the grasses grew tall, she peered at the sides of the path to see if she could spot some of the wild flowers and grasses that she had seen during their rambles. No, it was too dark.

She guided Maria and Eva past some boulders that jutted into the path and wondered with a little shudder what they might conceal. At worst a snake, she thought and at best, scurrying inhabitants that darted off in all directions. She was diverted for a moment at the memory of drawing sketches of them in her notebook; that was fun! When they returned to school, the sketches were finished off and coloured and Berta was proud of hers. Only last week Sister had said that she was a talented artist. How she loved the nature rambles.

Things looked different at night, though, and her eyes swivelled nervously from side to side as she walked on. Plants that were familiar in daylight were now mysterious, unfriendly, darker even than the surrounding darkness. She faltered as she thought she saw a dark human shadow standing beside a bush, but before a scream could rise to her lips, she realised it was a huge cactus, arms reaching up to the sky. She shuddered and choked back a sob. The friendly grassy terrain, which she and her friends ran around as they searched for plants, had become a silent and sinister, dark world; she whirled around at every rustle of the branches of the shadowed trees, standing sentinel. Snakes were an ever-present danger, but Berta was reassured that the little procession made enough noise to frighten them away.

Sounds of scurrying in the dry grasses bordering the path caused shrieks of dismay. Bertha jumped as a hyena cackled suddenly from behind a rocky outcrop and brought fresh floods of tears from the little ones. It didn't help when the dogs gave ferocious chase and Berta tried everything she knew to calm her charges, although she herself was struggling to hide the increasing nervousness that was forming a lump in her chest. Who were these people from whom they were fleeing? Had they moved fast? Were they even now lying hidden in the darkness ahead? Was she going to die? *Oh God, please don't let us die. I don't want to die.* She realised that Maria was sobbing and pulled her thoughts together.

"Listen," she said to the tearful little girl. "The hyenas are laughing. That must be good news!"

Suddenly the moon came out from behind the cloud.

"*La lune*! The moon!" shrieked Maria in excitement and the words were picked up and shouted by the other little ones in a tinkling cascade of sound.

Now, in the bright moonlight, things looked much better. In the brightness even the trees threw a shadow and some of the children's confidence returned as they recognised landmarks. Berta's nervousness receded and in some excitement she joined the other children as they looked down into the valley where, clear in the moonlight, slept the convent they had just left.

A hundred yards away from the convent stood the beautiful stone church, still under construction, and further yet Berta was able to pick out the simple, modest "Fathers' house" where Fathers Swelsen and Anthony lived. The priests were of the Marist order and most of them were Dutch. Berta felt warm at the thought of Father Swelsen. He was a great favourite of hers, in some way standing in for her father, during the nine months of the year when she was at school and separated from her own father. She peered down, thinking that she might just see a flash of his white cassock but no, everything was still.

The excited chatter and pointing fingers of the children were soon stilled by the nuns; there was no time to dally. They must always keep moving.

Seeing the priests' house, Berta wondered where Father Anthony was. She had not seen him for a few days, but Father Swelsen was a regular visitor. The children loved his visits. He always had a joke and a laugh to share, his dark eyes twinkling and his white teeth sparkling in the middle of his big black beard when he tossed his head back. He invariably became involved in a game of catch and had complimented Berta on her speed in getting away from him the previous morning. "It must be something to do with that red hair," he had laughed, ruffling its springy abundance.

"Oh, Father," she had laughed shyly. "It's not red, just kind of reddy brown."

They were well up on the grassy slopes above the foot of the hill when Mother called a halt. The younger children needed to rest for a while, and Berta was only too happy to rest her scratched and weary legs.

Sister Magdalena, her big breezy form a reassuring presence to the children, swooped around in her customary manner, long grey skirts twirling, organising the setting down of blankets which had been carried by the kitchen staff. First, the grasses were pounded with the feet and when they were relatively flattened, the blankets were spread over. The children sat down cross-legged and unwrapped their first pack of biscuits. Mother said a brief prayer of thanksgiving to which they replied "Amen" and they started to munch the food. It was strange how delicious the biscuits were, eaten in this way, almost like a forbidden treat. There was a low contented murmur from the children as they began to enjoy what seemed to be a strange but very exciting treat. To them it was a picnic under the stars.

With the little ones distracted, Mother Camille and two of the volunteers had a hurried discussion, where they agreed to inform the older girls of what was going on, but to conceal the real seriousness of the situation.

They quietly called Elsa and the five other senior girls to the side of the company. Berta noticed Elsa moving away and immediately became anxious again. Unseen by the group, she crept behind a small shrub close to where they were sitting.

Mother Camille spoke slowly: "I am sure you're wondering what's going on," she said.

They nodded assent, tense, their dark eyes fixed on Mother. She paused for thought for a moment to order her thoughts.

"I'll be brief, because we need to move on. You may know that there has been a lot of talk about one John Chilembwe. He's a Baptist preacher and has recently travelled to Europe and America. He believes very strongly that Africa must be left to the Africans and that they should have independence from Britain. Well, he has now instigated a series of protests, some of which are turning out to be quite violent.

"Three farmers, including Mr Livingstone, have been killed in the Magomero area and Father Anthony, who is in Zomba at the moment, has written to Father Swelsen suggesting that we leave the convent for the time being, particularly since we are so close to Chilembwe's mission. Bishop Auneau has also instructed us to leave and has sent some guards to protect us. So we're heading over the hills to the nearest farm, and from there we plan to get on a train to Blantyre.

"Now, the farmers in the area have organised themselves into a group calling themselves the Mikalongwe Volunteers, and they're doing all they can to protect the people in the area. Thankfully, six of them are here to escort us and I would like to introduce you to two of them."

She turned and pointed to one burly European, his face shadowed in the moonlight.

"This is Mr John Taylor," she said. Turning to the other, who was standing slightly behind the first, she said, "And this is Mr Peter Hines."

The two men waved cheerily to the girls.

"We're heading for the Finch's farm in Mikalongwe, because we need to get you all to Blantyre and we can catch the train from there. The rebels have cut the telephone cable, but that is being repaired, and soon a train will be requested to pick us up. All the Europeans from the outlying districts are gathering at certain points for safety, and we shall join the Blantyre safe houses.

"I've sent Winston and Chipango ahead to reach Mr and Mrs Finch's farm and to tell them what has happened. We're hoping to sleep there tonight. Any questions?"

Fear choked Berta's throat and through the pounding in her ears she heard Elsa venture to ask, "Why would they want to harm us? We are a convent of young girls."

"They probably wouldn't want to," replied Mother. "But we prefer to be cautious."

"How big is the mob?" asked Theresa.

"Apparently, about two hundred men," said Mother, "but that could be an exaggeration."

"Why do you think they killed Mr Livingstone?" That was from Paulina, Berta's second older sister.

"I don't know, I honestly don't know. It might have something to do with the fact that he's a relative of David Livingstone. Remember, he was the explorer who discovered this part of Africa for the British." She paused and scanned the girls' faces. There was silence.

"Well," said Mother, "if there are no further questions we need to be moving on, don't you think? I have to repeat that you must not worry. We have no reason to think that they will harm us and all of this is just a precautionary measure. By the way, I don't think that the younger girls should know of this conversation."

There were more nods and murmurs of assent as the girls rose and walked slowly back to the main group, with Berta following at a discreet distance. She appeared nonchalant, but her head was reeling with what she had just heard. If those men had already killed, what was to stop them following the school girls and killing them too? She wanted so much to rush to Elsa – dear kind Elsa – who had always been like a second mother to her, and feel her arms about her, but she daren't let it be known that she had overheard the conversation with Mother Camille. She walked to the little ones and sat quietly amongst them.

As the time approached to continue their flight, Sister Magdalena circled the children and did a headcount. She paused and then counted again, this time from the opposite direction.

A frown creased the nun's forehead and she walked back to the group of nuns, bent down and asked Sister Pauline to follow her.

"*Ma chere soeur*, there appears to be a child missing," whispered Sister Magdalena. "I have counted twice. Can you count, please?"

"Of course," whispered Sister Pauline; she quietly and unobtrusively circled the little group, counting the small bodies.

Berta rapidly scanned the children close to her and saw with relief that both Maria and Eva were close by, playing cat's cradle with a piece of string that Eva always kept on her. *Who could it be?* she thought, trying to recall all the children.

Sister Pauline re-joined Sister Magdalene. "You're right," she whispered, her gentle face tense with concern. "We are one short."

There was a quick consultation with the other nuns and Mother rose.

"It's time to carry on our walk," she said to the children, her voice not betraying her anxiety, "but we need to check that you are all here, so I shall call out your names again."

Each name was called out into the still night and to each name there was a quiet, "Yes, Mother," until "Alicia!" was called. There was no reply.

"Alicia!" No response. Alicia was a little native girl, an orphan who had been adopted by the nuns when her mother died.

"Does anyone know where Alicia is?" No response.

At that moment a wave of sound like a muffled roar rose from the land below. Berta turned her head in the direction of the sound. All heads turned with her. Shock at the scene below them kept them still.

Where it seemed that only minutes before there had been nothing more than the convent, the church and the rectory sprawling in slumber, now Berta saw that there were hundreds of flickering lights. The roar became the pounding, angry chanting of hundreds of men wafting up towards them. The small children began to whimper with fear and Berta put her arms around Eva.

17

There was a whispered sound from Mother Camille: "*Mon Dieu*," she breathed, as she looked down at the scene before them. Abruptly she called out, "Sisters, blow out the lamps, quickly!" The volunteers leapt to help.

There was a flurry of movement and they were left with only the light of the moon.

Then, with a visible effort, she pulled herself together and drew the children's attention to her.

"Little ones. Do you remember we were talking about Alicia? Now, where do you think she can be? Has anyone got any ideas?"

There was a brief silence, then five-year-old Eva let out a wail: "She went back to get her bead bracelet and told me not to tell on her because she would be right back. I promised not to tell."

In the appalled silence that followed her words she burst into loud sobs and burrowed her head into Berta's chest. Berta quickly gathered her in her arms and rocked her, gently whispering reassuring words, wiping the tears from her cheeks.

Sister Magdalene plunged into the horrific moment. "Water!" she called out cheerfully. "Now that we've finished our biscuits, I think it's time for a drink and then off we go again." The children dutifully raised their water bottles to their lips and took an obligatory sip.

As Berta joined the reformation of the crocodile, two sticky little hands in hers, she was observing the nuns having a spirited consultation. She wondered what they were going to do. She heard Sister Jeanne urging quietly, "Someone must go back for Alicia. We cannot leave her there."

"We would be powerless against the mob," replied Sister Magdalena, "and we would then risk the lives of not only the rescuers but of all these children as well. I am sure that Father Swelsen will have found her, because he was sure to help Matonde and the other boys lock up after we left."

They were suddenly interrupted by Elsa: "Look! Look!" she cried, her arm rigid, finger pointing down into the valley.

There was a gasp. The priest's house was on fire. The blaze was lighting up the valley, throwing the church into relief and singeing the pines that circled the building.

The group stood transfixed, watching the flames rising higher, orange tongues of fire greedily licking the black sky. They gazed at the hundreds of little lights, torches held in the hands of men, running frenetically to and fro like fireflies. Mother Camille was the first to recover.

"Onward, everyone. Time to go."

Minutes later the shaky crocodile was on its way again, but everyone was silent, numbed by what was happening in the valley. Berta clutched the little ones' hands more tightly and struggled not to cry. Those burning buildings had been part of her second home environment for the past few years; she loved every nook and cranny, every squawking chicken, every tree. The delicious smell of wood smoke, reminiscent of camp fires, rose up and tinged the air, but now its ugly meaning robbed it of its flavour. This time it spoke of fear and darkness, and Berta felt terribly alone.

CHAPTER TWO

As Father Swelsen walked into the dark night, away from the convent, his face settled into grim lines. The message from Father Anthony had arrived just before midnight and had not said very much in terms of the extent of the uprising.

"News is filtering through of spots of rebellion, mainly around the Zomba area, but also an unsuccessful attempt to break into the arms depot in Blantyre," went the note. *"They say that three farmers have been killed – William Livingstone, Duncan McCormick and Robert Ferguson – and their families abducted. John Chilembwe, our neighbour, seems to be leading the uprising. No official confirmation yet of any of this. However, all expatriates are being urged to move into guarded safe houses around the south, and I strongly suggest that you evacuate the mission and take all to safety, to one of the Mikalongwe farms. From there you should be able to get everyone onto the train to Blantyre."*

A similar message had been received from the Bishop of the Diocese, Bishop Auneau; this had been brought by a detachment of six volunteers, whose instructions were to escort the mission inhabitants to safety.

The news was grim and, as he strode along the dirt track road, Father Swelsen asked himself whether killing was part of the plan. Perhaps it wasn't; maybe the three murdered men, reputedly racists, had been targeted for revenge by those who had suffered at their hands, he thought. He swiped irritably at a mosquito gorging itself on the back of his neck, and grimaced with distaste as his hand came away wet with his blood. He wiped it on a handkerchief, which he drew out of his capacious pocket on the right hip of his cassock.

He was surprised at Chilembwe, though. He was an educated man, a minister with his own church just a few miles away from the mission. He would not have expected this of him, despite his well-known, radical ideas.

There had been rumours for some weeks now that he had been organising a protest against British rule, but no one had been unduly concerned; there was nothing worrying about a protest in itself. It was thought that probably a march of his supporters would take place at the Zomba government offices and that would be that. He slapped at another mosquito.

Deep in thought, the priest slowly became aware that the night seemed unusually quiet; when the clouds intermittently hid the brilliance of the moon it was very dark indeed. The trees and thickets on either side of the road became inky, silent caverns, and he chided himself for the apprehension that shivered up and down his spine. Not even the village dogs barked as he passed and the cicadas, whose harsh melody was the accustomed background to the night sounds, remained strangely silent. He hurried on.

The children and the nuns were his concern and his anxiety for their safety had led him to move quickly, to get them onto the train to Blantyre, the capital – to safety.

A lump formed in his throat; he recalled their trusting, smiling faces as they looked up at him and quickened his step. The message from the bishop had been unclear as to what he, Father Swelsen, was expected to do. He preferred to stay at the mission; he felt sure that if the rebels approached he would be able to reason with them. After all, he knew the local people intimately, had lived amongst them for years. He must be ready for them if and when they arrived at the priests' house.

Suddenly he paused. If the insurrectionists came this way it was entirely possible that there would be looting. Undoubtedly Mother Camille would have arranged for some of her staff to lock up the buildings, but it would be wise if he returned to the convent to ensure that the buildings had been secured.

He turned on his heel and, walking very quickly now, made his way back to the convent. As he emerged from the shadows and walked towards the quadrangle he saw the convent gardeners, led by Matonde, holding a hurricane lamp and checking the doors of the numerous rooms and locking the ones that were open. They had half turned and were looking fearfully in the direction of his footsteps when they recognised him and greeted him with relief.

"*Bambo*!" they called out. Father, in Chinyanja. "We have almost finished," they informed him.

Father Swelsen thought a moment. "Look," he said. "I'll finish locking up; you go on ahead to the hills in case you are needed by the sisters."

The four men had a hurried conversation and decided that they would stay with him to see the outcome of any disturbance that might take place, and then go to join the nuns, bearing the latest news. The priest agreed and walked across to the dormitory side of the quadrangle to check those doors. A slight sound reached his ears and he stopped abruptly, trying to identify it.

Moments later it came again. It was the sound of a child, sobbing quietly, and it was coming from the dormitory. He opened the door and walked into the darkness, gingerly making his way towards the sound.

"Hello," he called out gently. "It's me, Father Swelsen. Who are you?"

The sobbing intensified. He moved closer and, after bumping his shins on a few pieces of furniture, came to the bed, where he could just see the form of a small child.

He sat on the edge of the bed. "Well, well, well, and who do we have here?" he asked, softly but cheerfully.

A little form leapt up, encircled his neck with its arms and laid its head on his shoulder.

"It's me," a little tearful voice said.

"Who is me?" he responded, holding her to him, although by now he had recognised her.

"Alicia."

"Alicia! And what are you doing here, may I ask?

Her reply was a shuddering sniff. The priest hid his appalled surprise at his find and kept his voice light and cheerful.

"Well, Alicia, I'm going to take you to our house for now, and then you are going to tell me all about why you are here and not with the others. Is that OK?"

He felt her head nod in the darkness.

"Now, I need you to help me lock up the convent, so I'm going to put you on my shoulders and you're going to tell me which door to lock next. OK?"

Another nod against his chest.

He stood up, settled her gently on his shoulders and, chatting jovially with her, finished the rounds, after which they met up with the four other men in the quadrangle.

"It's time to go," Swelsen told the four, and they set off at a fast pace towards the priests' house, Alicia by now fully recovered and humming to herself as she swayed and bumped on her rescuer's shoulders.

The priest's mind was buzzing with questions. How on earth had this child been left behind? She was an orphan, her mother having died in childbirth, and she had been abandoned to the sisters by her surviving relatives, who did not have the resources to look after a new-born baby. She had become the nun's adored child, the convent her home, and the pupils her playmates. There must be a simple reason, he concluded.

As they approached the house, the unnatural quiet once again struck the priest; he glanced around apprehensively, but there was nothing to be seen. They walked onto the front lawn and it seemed to him that he heard, in the stillness, a twig snapping amongst the shrubs on the perimeter. At that moment, four figures emerged from the shadows of the veranda and came to meet the small party. As they approached, it could be seen that they were armed, and the priest and his companions faltered in their tracks.

The four Africans came to a stop in front of them and the one in the lead addressed the priest quietly: "Greetings, *Bambo*," he said. "We have been sent by the bishop to escort you to safety in the hills."

Father Swelsen's response was hurried; he had sensed movement in the darkness around them. "Greetings. Let us get into the house and we'll talk there."

At a brisk pace he led the party to the house, up the front steps, across the veranda and into the hall. Here, the two gardeners, Tobias and Elias, were waiting.

They explained that rumours of "big trouble" were circulating thick and fast and that they had stayed up in case their priest was in danger.

"*Bambo*, you must go!" they urged him.

He hurriedly reassured them, telling them that he was certain that if the mob arrived, he would be able to reason with them. They looked down, shaking their heads worriedly.

"But I do think," he said, turning to Matonde, "that you should go now with Alicia to find the others. I think you should go now."

Suddenly, Tobias pointed through the windows to the front of the house. They all whirled around and there, where previously there had been immobile darkness, was a small sea of flickering lights along the perimeter of the garden.

Swelsen swung the little girl off his shoulders and handed her to Matonde.

"Take her through the back, Matonde, but hurry. Go!"

"*Bambo*," replied the man, taking Alicia into his arms. "It is too late. They will see us. It is better that they do not see the child."

His eyes feverishly following the progress of the lights as they came closer and began to encircle the house, the priest acknowledged the justice of Matonde's observation. He took Alicia back in his arms and hurried with her into the spare bedroom, saying over his shoulder, "Blow out the lamp, men, and go out quickly through the back. They must not see you with me."

To Alicia he said, with a crooked smile, "Now, I want you to hide under the bed and pretend we're playing hide and seek. As soon as I've finished talking to the people outside, I shall come back to you. Remember, no peeking and lie under there as quiet as a mouse. Can you do that?"

He felt her head nod vigorously in the dark and she chuckled quietly as she scrambled on her hands and knees to the far side of the bed, against the wall.

Swelsen straightened up and with a silent prayer walked out onto the veranda. The crowd was bigger than he had expected and, as they saw him, a low rumble of sound began, interspersed with sudden strident shouts.

"Go away!" they shouted. "Go back to your home. Leave our home to us!"

Swelsen held up his arms. "My brothers!" he called out. "I see you and I know you. You are my brothers and my friends. Let us talk."

The wave of sound broke, quietened for a few moments; but then the shouting began again, from here, from there, darting backwards and forwards as though rehearsed.

"Go away! Go back home! We do not know you. We do not want you. Go away!"

Twice he called out to them to talk with him. Twice the shouts drowned his voice and the rumble of sound rose again. The torches were brandished aloft and the crowd moved slowly forward. The priest, calm now that he was facing the danger, searched for faces he knew in the flickering light, but they were unrecognisable, mouths distorted, eyes red in the uncertain light, feet stamping the ground.

Then the priest recognised an odd shape that he had been unable to decipher, something that appeared to be a long pole with a ball at the top of it, carried by someone in the crowd. As it approached he realised in a moment of pure horror that it was the head of a man, a white man; and that a white woman, dressed in the African way, carried the pole on which it was impaled. The crowd was jostling her forward.

He stared, paralysed for a moment while the mob advanced inexorably, wooden clubs and scythes in their hands; as the frontrunners reached the bottom of the veranda steps and looked at him, with murder written on their faces, Swelsen knew that he had lost his gamble.

His one thought now was for Alicia. He must draw them away from her.

In a movement that caught the insurgents by surprise, he ran for the side of the veranda, leapt into the garden and made for the road leading to the church. As he dodged in and out of the shadows of the trees, it took them a few moments to realise what he was up to, and a few moments more to organise themselves to give chase. Then, yelling, they were after him.

The priest headed for the church, where he felt he might find shelter but, as he came to the turnoff to the cemetery, he made a split-second decision to turn down that road and hope that they had not seen this in the darkness. As he pounded down the road, his heart threatening to burst in his chest, he heard them go past the turnoff; but, almost immediately, they returned and came down the cemetery road. Feet slowing, and seriously hampered by his cassock, Swelsen realised that he could not go much further. Entering the cemetery, he made for the beautiful grotto the priests and nuns had built, with its statue of the Blessed Virgin crowning it. Perhaps he could hide amongst the boulders and shrubs at its back.

Then he stumbled and fell. As he struggled to rise to his feet he was overwhelmed by the ocean of sound that poured over him. He felt the first blows to his head and his body before he began to sink into darkness, but then he heard another set of voices a little distance away, on the fringe of the crowd.

A man laughed and said, "That's finished him. Let's go and burn the house."

The words gave Swelsen a strength that he didn't have any longer and he rose, arms flailing and shouting hoarsely. "No! No! Not the house!" There was pure anguish in his voice as the blows rained down and he continued shouting: "Alicia! No! Please, no!"

Then there was a shaft of excruciating pain in the back of his head. As he slid into oblivion he whispered, "Father, into your hands I commend our spirits."

CHAPTER THREE

It seemed to Berta that no matter how far they walked and how many hillocks they crested, they got no further. No sooner did they reach the brow of one hill than another appeared ahead of them.

Maria and Eva were very fractious by now, whimpering about the mosquitoes, about their sore feet and about how tired they were. Exhausted herself, Berta felt herself close to tears and was limp with relief when Mother Camille called out softly that they should rest for a few moments and have a drink.

The whole party sank gratefully onto the coarse grass; the very young children immediately nestled up against the closest older person and went to sleep.

The night had become an ally, its shadows a welcome camouflage, the cicadas a barricade of sound protecting them from the other noises in the dark, noises like the mob's roaring in the valley. The girls in their groups and the nuns in theirs conversed in low tones. As though by unspoken agreement, all eyes were averted from the glow of the leaping flames down in the mission.

"If only I knew that Alicia was safe," Sister Pauline was saying.

Sister Jeanne reached out and briefly squeezed her hand. "I'm sure that Father Swelsen has her safely with him," she said reassuringly.

There was a silence, each nun wary of voicing her thoughts and her fears.

Then suddenly, pounding steps along the path up which they had just come held them still. The smaller children woke up and started to cry and the older ones cradled them in arms, rigid with fear. Berta sat, transfixed with fear, eyes riveted on the bend in the path. Would it be friend or would it be foe? All eyes were fixed at the point in the bend where the arrivals would first be seen and recognised. The six volunteers stood, three on each side of the path and well to the side, rifles cocked and ready to fire.

A small group of men suddenly burst into view. When they were close enough to be recognised as four of the convent gardeners, together with four unknown but armed Africans, the fugitives slumped with relief. The head gardener, Matonde, was last; the other three made room for him to pass and run up to Mother. For a minute none of the men was able to speak as they struggled for breath, the sweat glistening on their bodies, the whites of their eyes shining in their contorted faces.

Mother motioned for Matonde and the nuns to follow her. She walked about thirty yards up the path, turned and waited calmly for him to speak.

Her arms were crossed and rested in her long, wide sleeves. "Don't hurry, Matonde," she said. "Get your breath back. When you are ready, we are listening."

In the stillness the muffled roar from below seemed to be very loud. Berta shivered convulsively.

"Mother, Father Swelsen is dead," he said at last, his voice hoarse.

There were gasps from the nuns; their eyes glistened with tears in the white light of the moon.

"Tell us, Matonde. What happened?"

"After you left," he continued, his voice slightly unsteady, "Father came to the convent to lock up."

And slowly, emotionally, the tragic story unfolded. There, under the light of the moon, with the noise of the cicadas around them, his little audience listened, unable to believe, praying that it was not so. Unnoticed, the children crept closer, fearful faces tilted towards Matonde.

As he described the burning of the house there were gasps from the nuns, and Mother Camille held out her arms as though to push away what she was hearing. Her voice was a little moan. "*Mon Dieu, non!*" My God, no!

Matonde's voice broke: "We couldn't save little Alicia."

There were a few moments of silence as the awful truth sank in, and then the wailing began. Grief and terror gave wings to their young voices, as the children stared down the valley to the raging inferno that had become Alicia's pyre.

Eva started to scream: "It's my fault, it's my fault..." and one of the nuns rushed to her and held her close.

"No. No, Eva. It wasn't anybody's fault."

The child clutched her hysterically. "Are they going to burn us all now?"

Close by, Berta cried, gasping sobs, aware only of a huge, devastating loss in her young life. In her anguish she could almost see and feel the priest before her, hear his carefree laugh, smell his pipe. Her heart crumbled as she faced the fact that she would never see him again, or Alicia. Her little body shook as her mind travelled on a futile journey. Why did I not keep Alicia near me? Why did I send her to another group? Sweet little dreamer, Alicia, always with her head in the clouds, so sweet, so loved by all.

She moaned, "Oh, Alicia. Oh, Father..." as she sat on the ground, her head on her knees, struggling to breathe through her sobs. Then strong arms gathered her up and she felt Elsa's wet cheek against hers.

"Hush, sweetie, hush," and she held her tight and rocked her. Both girls sobbed, clinging to each other, drawing strength from the nearness of the other.

"Oh, Elsa, why didn't I keep Alicia with me? I should have known... she was such a little dreamer."

"Shush, my dear, no one could have known."

"And Father Swelsen..." Her voice broke down completely and again sobs convulsed her little body.

Unable to speak, Elsa still held her close, her throat aching from the sobs that wanted to surface, to tear the night sky apart with screams. Just then, Paulina found them and quietly put her arms around Elsa from behind, laid her face against her back and silently wept, the three sisters at one in their grief on this dark night of their souls.

Silently, the nuns' tears ran unchecked down their cheeks. They clung briefly one to another, murmuring words of pain and comfort, moving then amongst the girls, offering consolation where they had none even for themselves, their faces wet masks of horror and despair. They reached for their rosaries, murmured prayers for the repose of the souls of their little daughter and the man who had offered his life for her.

But now was not the time to grieve. With the iron discipline that marked their lives, habit took over and, acting as one, the nuns and senior girls, although themselves numb with shock, hustled their charges and in a short time had them back on track, up the hill to safety beyond. No one noticed the cuts and scratches and whipping branches anymore. There was a far greater pain and fear in their hearts.

It was 3.30 a.m. on Tuesday the 26th of January 1915.

***

The rest of the night was a blur; nothing meant anything anymore and pain had turned into numbness. It seemed to Berta that the walk continued endlessly up into the hills, down into the valleys and up into the hills again. There was no fear any longer, not of the dark, nor of the sounds; the boundaries of fear and horror had been passed.

Dawn came and opened up into the heat of the new day. And still the cry was "*Marchez, mes filles.*" Walk, my girls. Keep moving was the message.

Anyone who could carry a little one did so; being carried on someone's shoulders gave the young children something to smile about. Although they were exhausted, they were momentarily diverted; their laughter and chuckles lightened the otherwise sombre mood of the by now bedraggled group of men, women and children. At all times, four volunteers walked on one side of the line, the bishop's men on the other, rifles at the ready, while two volunteers loped on far ahead, scanning the terrain and ensuring from every rise that they weren't being followed.

"We need to get as far away from Chilembwe's headquarters as possible," said John, the leader of the volunteer group, to Mother. "It is only five miles from the convent, and we have no idea where they have moved on to or what they plan next."

Soon after daybreak Mother Camille decided that it was time to stop for the remaining biscuits, which constituted breakfast. As they searched for somewhere to sit, they came upon several mango trees laden with plump ripe fruit.

"Thanks, Father," chuckled Sister Magdalena, with a glance heavenward. "Manna, indeed!"

The taller members of the party reached up for the fruit and soon all the little faces were buried in the sweet orange flesh of the delectable fruit. All too soon it was time to pack up and move on. Some of the children had developed blisters and Sister Jeanne suggested that they remove their shoes and walk barefoot. That, she told the children, would be less painful than having the shoes rub their heels more raw than they already were.

As they passed remote villages in the hills, the inhabitants came out and curiously watched them pass. They did not impede their progress, but neither did they offer to help. Their dogs, with their ribs showing through their fur, growled, bared their teeth and barked.

Despite their hunger and tiredness the children's spirits rose in the light of the day. They looked around them with interest and pointed out unusual huts and trees in the villages and the surrounding countryside. They tried to engage with the little native children but, for many who had never before seen anything other than black faces, this only served to terrify them, and they ran screaming to hide behind their mothers' *chirundus*. These lengths of material were wound around the body and had the added advantage of helping to hold a baby on their back in place and protect it from flies and mosquitoes.

As the blazing summer sun rose higher in the sky, Mother called Matonde to her: "We need water, Matonde. Do you know this area at all?"

He shook his head. "No, Mother."

She beckoned to the nearest volunteer and he trotted towards her.

"Mr Taylor, do you know this area?" she asked. "We need water."

"No, Mother, I don't," he replied. "The problem is that we have deliberately chosen trails that are rarely used, so as to avoid every chance of bumping into the rebels."

"Yes, I see," responded the nun. She turned to Matonde. "At the next village could you ask them where they get their water from? In the meantime, we need to keep our eyes open."

"That is true, Mother," he agreed. "I have been looking at those green reeds over there and I think that we will find water near them." He pointed to a broad line of lush green vegetation, snaking through the fields of golden corn and cassava a few miles further on.

"Also," he continued, "I am seeing many bananas on the trees in the village gardens. We must buy some at the next village."

It was midday when they approached the next village, and Mother called a halt under a cluster of mango trees at its outskirts. The blankets were once again laid out and the women and children sank gratefully onto their softness. Berta looked around for Elsa and went and sat by her, leaning against her and deriving comfort from her closeness. Elsa smiled down at her tenderly.

Suddenly, there was movement ahead of them and they saw a large group of men coming towards them from the village. Many were carrying hoes on their shoulders. The little party from the convent tensed and stared at the approaching men. Matonde, the other convent servants and the volunteers rose to their feet unhurriedly; each one had his hand on his rifle. The nuns moved to stand protectively in front of the children. Elsa put her arm around Berta and held her tight.

For long moments there was silence, as the villagers shuffled forward and finally stopped a few yards from the little party. Their spokesman stepped forward.

"*Moni*," he greeted them, good day. His face broke into a smile and he greeted each of the adults individually before returning to his position and squatting on his heels facing them. The rest of the men made similar greetings and finally they too squatted in the customary stance when settling down to a discussion. The servants and the volunteers followed suit, so that the men formed a circle, but the nuns and children subsided once more on to the blankets, their proper place in the background when men were talking. Berta slumped against Elsa, her knees feeling as though they were made of water.

In slow, measured tones the villagers enquired how it was that such a party was walking through the hills; Matonde told them only that they planned to visit a farm in Mikalongwe and hoped to reach it soon. With much shaking of heads, the villagers commented that none of the nuns or older girls were in *machilas*. How so? To which Matonde made a remark about these strange white people, *mzungu*, who suddenly, on a whim, decide they want to walk. There was more shaking of heads and grunts of surprise. Who would have thought to see such a thing? There were discreet chuckles from behind hands. Eventually, the conversation was brought around to asking about the possibility of buying bananas and finding water. The villagers clapped their hands in delight.

They would let them have as many bananas as they wanted and they would send some of the village girls with them to their destination, to carry gourds of fresh water from the river.

At this point the entire village descended and the women, with their children clutching their *chirundus*, shyly exchanged a few words with the travellers. They pressed boiled cassava roots and bananas on them and gave them clear, sparkling water to drink their fill. Following this feast, many of the little school children fell asleep and for a few hours the older girls and nuns sweltered in the heat, and dozed and chatted in a desultory fashion with the native women. It was clear that they had not heard of the uprising or, if they had, they had dismissed it as of no importance.

Three hours later, refreshed both physically and mentally, the little party gathered themselves for departure. They now had four extra members, two young girls and two male family members to escort them back, each with a gourd of fresh water perched on their heads.

There were greetings all around.

"*Pitani bwino*," called out the villagers as they set off: go well.

"*Tsalani bwino*," replied the travellers with a wave: remain well.

And they set off again. But now, there was a new spring in their steps. They had been shown kindness by the people whom they had feared the most and they were almost at the farm, where they would be safe at last.

Eventually, after several stops and as darkness closed around them, when limbs and minds were once again exhausted, a group of flickering lights appeared ahead of them in the darkness and the volunteers pointed them out excitedly.

"Look, Mother! That is the Finch's farm. We're almost there."

Mother Camille passed the message on to the children. "Look, children, the farm! Not much longer to go now. Courage! Courage!"

Just as she spoke, the sound of cartwheels and voices reached them and, within minutes, dark shapes could be seen coming towards them. Winston and Chipango were in the lead, running now to meet the exhausted, straggling party. Their joy was luminous. They clapped their hands softly and their faces were wreathed in smiles as they greeted the travellers, murmuring, "We have been watching out for you. God is good. God is good."

Berta felt herself hoisted into the air as little bodies were swung onto the two mule drawn carts and with the nuns, volunteers and servants walking alongside, a half-hour later they were at the farm, which was brightly lit and seemingly full of smiling welcoming faces.

The Finches were ready for them. The long hall and large sitting room floors were carpeted with blankets and any other linens that were available. The children were put to bed on the floor after a supper of sandwiches and a drink of milk, and blistered feet were bathed and bandaged. The servants were bedded in the servants' quarters and the nuns were crammed into the guest bedrooms, after they had given the Finches details of what they had witnessed the previous night.

The party from the village had been given room to sleep in the servants' quarters.

The volunteers meanwhile organised a sentry rota with the farm workers; two of them, with six workers, immediately started their patrol around the residential parts of the estate. The remaining four lay down wherever there was a space and tried to snatch a few hours' rest. As they confided to Sam Finch, there was very little information available about the uprising. Events had taken place suddenly and quickly, telephone wires had been cut and everyone had to be prepared for the worst.

Trying to get comfortable on the hard floor, Berta thought for a moment that she would not be able to sleep, but exhaustion had drained the children of their last reserves and there was no sound but the occasional hoot of an owl, a nervous dog baying at the shadows of the moon, and the distant laugh of a hyena, until late next morning.

***

Mother Camille tossed about restlessly, exhausted but unable to sleep. She glanced across at Sister Jeanne in the other twin bed and Sister Adelaide on the camp bed across the foot of their beds. Both were very still, breathing lightly and regularly, seemingly deeply asleep.

The past twenty-four hours had been the worst of her life. When Father Swelsen (*Mon Dieu*! Poor Father Swelsen) had come to raise the alarm just before midnight, she had immediately perceived the extent of the danger. Three men murdered and two families taken hostage. How terrible! And then she felt the weight of her responsibility for the students fall heavily onto her shoulders.

Once she had got moving and was completely awake, fear had receded and she had become engrossed in the arrangements for the evacuation. Very quickly, it seemed, they were all accounted for and moving away to safety. All accounted for, thought Camille, and pushed out of her mind the unspeakable events that followed the last roll call.

Her sisters had been wonderful. As always, Sister Magdalene cheered everyone up with her smiling, bustling presence and Sister Jeanne, so sweet and motherly, soothed little trembling fears. Sister Assumpta had rapidly brought the provisions from the kitchen, which was her domain, and distributed the food with her jolly smile. She and Sister Agnes, whose very reserve was reassuring to the children, took up their posts at the head of the line.

In the middle of the line, Sister Magdalene and Sister Jeanne had access to the children behind and in front of them, while Mother herself and equally diminutive Sister Adelaide brought up the rear. Mother had decided on this position because it meant that the volunteers could supply her with information and decide on strategy without the children being aware of every nuance and every huddled debate.

And how good the children had been! All of them so brave, and the older ones seeming older than their years as they soothed the younger ones – as though they didn't have troubles enough of their own

When the little party had looked down into the valley and seen the sea of lights, the danger in which they stood had been brought forcefully to her mind. Unbidden, stories of the torture and death that missionaries had endured in many parts of the world flashed into her mind. But worse, the possible fate of the children. Normally, she knew, the native Africans were a gentle, child-loving people, but who knew of what they were capable when inflamed by rhetoric in the midst of a crazed mob? She thanked God that the younger children, whilst frightened at times, nevertheless viewed the whole thing as an adventure rather than a threat.

When the children had been put to bed the nuns and their hosts, the Finches, had walked outside the farmhouse and there had been no mistaking the red glow in the distant sky. The burning of the mission could not have lasted that long; it was almost certain that the convent buildings had been burnt too. So many years of love and work and sweat and exhaustion – all gone, gone in one mad night of frenzy.

She roused herself from her reverie to think about the immediate future.

They had to live through the next thirty-six hours and hide from the children the possibility that at any moment a mob could arrive. All the villages through which, or close to which, they had passed were in a position to inform the rebels of their whereabouts. Unlikely it seemed, yes, but it only took one person to do the damage. Someone with a grudge maybe. The image of the flickering, massed lights came to her mind; she shivered, climbed out of bed and went to the window, parting the curtains to assure herself that she would not see them descending upon the farmhouse. No, all was still and peaceful outside. She stood there a while and, as her eyes adjusted to the darkness, she suddenly caught her breath and instinctively leaned back into the shadows; she saw movement in the darkness and the dull gleam of metal. A rifle? A panga?

Her heart pounding, she waited a moment, thoughts of escape whirling through her brain and, as she started to back away to call for help, the shadowy figures moved closer; she was able to discern the figure of one of the volunteers walking side by side with one of the farm workers, rifles on their shoulders. She slumped in relief, her lips whispering a prayer of thanks, and watched as the men walked slowly but purposefully towards the front of the house. As her agitation calmed down she kept her eyes on the disappearing men and mused that that must have been a senior farm worker, for him to have been trained to shoot.

***

Starting to feel sleepy, she went back to her bed and lay down. Thirty-six hours to go, she said to herself and reached for her rosary. Thirty-six hours to go until safety was reached.

Then the name she had been suppressing with every fibre of her being exploded into her consciousness. ALICIA!

Alicia. No, she couldn't block the thought of her out of her mind any longer. A sick devastation filled her and the tears rolled down her cheeks. A child so loved had had to face death alone and terrified, waiting for the help that never came. *She is at peace now*, she told herself, *safe in God's arms*. But still the tears came and she felt shuddering sobs that she could not control start to shake her chest. She slid out of the bed onto her knees and, fearful of awakening the two sisters, drew her pillow to her and buried her face in it. And still the sobs threatened to choke her. She held her head as dark, painful thoughts darted hither and thither, searing her mind ruthlessly.

I promised her grandmother that I would be responsible for her, that we would care for her, love her. And we did. She was the daughter that we would never otherwise have had.

Mother Camille pounded her forehead in desperate fury. *How did it happen then? Where were we when she was dying? Why did she die alone and frightened? Why wasn't I there? She must have been so frightened. She must have called and called for us. Oh, God, forgive me, forgive me. Oh, Alicia, my darling little girl, forgive me.*

Suddenly, there were two bodies kneeling on either side of her. Comforting arms came around her, on her left Sister Adelaide and, on her right, Sister Jeanne, who linked her arm in hers and whispered comforting noises.

She looked up at Sister Jeanne, eyes wide like blank caverns, her mouth trembling uncontrollably. She raised her arms and put them around her sisters on either side, and they sobbed as though their hearts would break.

They grieved for the little girl who had been a ray of sunshine in their lives, whose huge brown eyes had enslaved them from the first moment that they saw her, whose singing and playfulness had captivated them, their unutterably precious gift. A gift they would now have to learn to live without.

Eventually, in utter exhaustion, the paroxysms faded and the three women began to speak quietly, brokenly, their voices little more than hoarse whispers.

Mother Camille was the first to speak. Her voice was as soft as a sigh. "Such emptiness in my heart. How difficult to carry on living."

A shuddering breath from Sister Jeanne. "And Father Swelsen. He was like a younger brother to me, so like my Pierre back home…"

"God rest their souls…" whispered Sister Adelaide.

The other two nodded, heads bowed. In the bright moonlight their white undergarments had a pearl-like glow, their faces were ashen; tortured eyes like black holes stared out.

Then Sister Jeanne took the situation into her own hands. "Mother, it's time for you to sleep. You have a busy day ahead of you. Come."

She rose swiftly, helped Mother to her feet and led her to her bed. Both sisters settled her in and wished her goodnight. But she had fallen asleep as soon as her head hit the pillow and the two sisters followed suit. Exhaustion, physical and emotional, had taken over, to give them the blessed relief of oblivion.

35

CHAPTER FOUR

Berta awoke to bright daylight and a lifting of the nightmare; brilliant sunshine let hope raise its cautious head.

There was good news from the nuns to start off the day and they addressed the children, whom they called to sit cross-legged on the top garden terrace. It seemed that the telegraph lines had been repaired and so, despite its being a Sunday, telegrams were being sent to the children's parents to tell them that they were safe and should be collected as soon as possible either from the Finch's farm or from the safe house in Blantyre, depending on which was more convenient. Telegrams from the other end had let them know that an armed train would be on its way to pick them up at midmorning on the following day.

"And," continued Mother Camille as she addressed the expectant upturned faces, "we are going to be staying at the African Lakes Corporation compound in Blantyre, together with many other refugees from the rest of the southern region. Apparently, we are going to be staying in the rice warehouse!"

This was well received, with a cheerful titter, by the children, to whom the whole arrangement was exciting and different.

"Thank goodness everything seems well organised," said Elsa to Paulina as they walked away. Since their home was at Fort Johnston, some one hundred and forty miles distant, she knew that it would be a few days before their father could come to collect them. He faced an arduous journey, partly by river steamer and partly by motorbike.

For the first time since they had fled the convent there was an air of optimism amongst the party, and the adults joined in an unspoken aim to devote their efforts to helping the children to forget, at least for the moment, the traumatic events of the previous twenty-four hours.

They were given total access to the farm and after a brief introduction to the acres of growing tobacco, the Finch's main crop, they were taken to inspect the inevitable clutch of home animals. Fifty or so cows grazed contentedly in a field, while a herd of goats and sheep munched anything they could get their teeth into.

"Elsa," shrieked Berta, "the goat is eating my skirt!"

"*Arrete, arrete* !" scolded Elsa in French, coming rapidly to Berta's rescue and shouting at the goat to stop. "Silly," she said to her sister. "Surely you are used to animals by now? We have enough of them at home!"

Paulina ambled across, slow and moody as usual. "I'm bored," she announced. "When are we going to the station? And then we have the trip to Blantyre." She sighed. "I wonder when Papa will arrive to take us home."

"You know that it will take at least three days," retorted Elsa. "So, there is no point in being miserable. Just join in with everyone and look around the farm."

They were joined at that moment by another group of children and, together, talking and laughing, they set off for the house.

Berta liked the farm. She liked the broad shady verandas that circled three sides of the large farmhouse. She liked the big, high-ceilinged rooms and interesting outhouses, where one could find hens, ducks, geese and even a monkey. Most of all she liked the garden, which was a riot of typical African blooms, amongst which she recognised bougainvillea, zinnias, dahlias, carnations, exotic grasses, hydrangeas, hibiscus and many more that she wasn't familiar with. Papa was interested in gardening as he was in so many other things. He would have been interested to have a look around here, she knew, as she strolled through.

Suddenly she thought that she saw a tortoise disappearing into a bed of huge dahlias bordered by carnations. She bent down and carefully parted the plants. Yes! There it was, nose hungrily nuzzling the leaves, searching for something succulent to eat.

She squatted and delightedly scratched its back, moving deeper into the foliage to get a better look.

And so it was that a group of nuns walking around the garden with the Finches didn't see her as they slowly strolled past.

"You would have thought that Chilembwe would have some remorse for the evil that he did yesterday," Mrs Finch was saying. "But, no. He had to reinforce it today."

Sister Magdalene shook her head sadly. "But how could he preach the word of God at his church on Sunday, with Mr Livingstone's head on the pole beside him? It's too awful to contemplate."

Berta froze. She had tried hard not to think of yesterday's events; they had all but been submerged in her enjoyment of the change of scenery and playing with the animals. Now, the horror returned in full force and she screamed, still squatting, arms tightly encircling her knees as she rocked from side to side, eyes squeezed tightly shut.

Instantly, strong arms lifted her and she was held tightly in Sister Jeanne's motherly arms, while she sobbed away the horror of the last twenty-four hours.

Sister Assumpta murmured, "It is good that she cries. These children are so innocent, so sheltered, they have never been able to even imagine what they have experienced since yesterday. Last night must have been a waking nightmare for them. It will take time for all of this to be forgotten." And she stroked Berta's hair and her clammy forehead.

Berta calmed down slowly and allowed herself to be taken indoors and her face to be washed by Sisters Assumpta and Magdalena. Only then did she permit herself to be side-tracked by the offer of homemade biscuits and a glass of lemonade. When news spread of her upset, Elsa came hurrying to find her and she gave her a close hug, when she found her quietly eating on the veranda next to Sister Assumpta. The two farm dogs sat in front of her, gazing at her with rapt attention, eagerly awaiting a stray crumb or two.

The nun smiled at Elsa and stood up. "Now that you're here I'll go and give a hand in the kitchen," she said quietly to Elsa, a hand on her arm. And then, in almost a whisper, "I think she's all right now."

Elsa smiled back. "Thank you, sister."

"Elsa, how long do you think it will take Papa to get here?" Berta asked with a little hic, the legacy of the tears.

"I can't say," mused Elsa. "If he travels all day tomorrow, he could be with us in Blantyre on Friday evening."

"We won't be able to travel back straight away, will we? It'll be dark."

"Yes, you're right. We'll have to sleep there another night and then probably leave early on Saturday morning," surmised Elsa. She hastily added, "And I might be completely wrong, so don't pester me if Papa doesn't come when I have said."

"I like it here, but I shall be so happy to see A Mayi," sighed Berta.

She thought longingly of her mother's soft, black arms, where she would be held until she felt that nothing in the world could hurt her. And Papa. Good, strong Papa with his blond hair, green eyes that were such a rarity here, and sturdy, muscular figure. The sun rose and set on Papa in little Berta's eyes. And she was his baby, his particular weakness, although he would never have admitted it. Berta recalled how A Mayi had told her that he had delayed sending her to school until she was seven years of age. He and A Mayi had argued about it.

"Berta must go to school with Elsa and Paulina," A Mayi would urge, even though she dreaded the thought of the parting. "If we keep her back she'll be behind the other children. All the others start at five or six."

"Impossible!" he would retort. "You know how skinny she is. It's not normal. We need to keep a careful eye on her. I think she must be anaemic."

And he had ordered all manner of vitamin and mineral supplements for her to take.

"How can she be anaemic?" laughed A Mayi. "She is never still. She's into everything. She's constantly in one scrape or another."

"Ah, they are not scrapes," Ludwig would reply. "She isn't a naughty child, just very curious. She really isn't ready to be sent away."

And now, here they all were, mused Berta. Father Swelsen was dead and God only knew if their convent was still standing. A knot seemed to tighten in her stomach and she fought back the tears that welled up at the thought of the kindly priest.

"A penny for your thoughts," laughed Elsa, bringing her back to the present.

"Just thinking," Berta replied.

"Well, don't strain yourself," teased Elsa and they both giggled. Elsa could always turn Berta's tears into smiles.

Their kind hosts devoted their day to ensuring that the Nguludi children were kept busy and occupied. There was so much to do and see it was difficult to make a choice. Hens needed to be fed, the end of the milking could be watched, the cows, sheep and goats needed to be put out to pasture and there were endless interesting things to be done in the vegetable garden at the back of the house, and the beautiful front garden.

Sister Agnes joined Elsa and Berta as they watched some of the milking and then moved on to the chicken runs. A brood was hatching and they watched mesmerised as the last chick pecked its way out of the shell. Berta was enchanted. What a sight it was to see the tiny balls of yellow fluff shelter under their mother as they chirped and she clucked in response.

When the chicks had all disappeared under the hen they went to the goats, where the kids were having their breakfast. They had been separated from their mothers during the night so that the mothers would give more milk. Now that milking was over, there was a joyful reunion and the kids lost no time in suckling greedily from their mothers, butting the udders, forelegs rigid.

"Why do they do that – butt their mummies?" Berta asked Elsa.

"Probably to make the milk flow faster," replied Elsa. "Mind you, I'm guessing!" She gave Sister Agnes a questioning look.

"Don't look at me!" laughed the nun. "I really have no idea!"

"I wish Papa would hurry," grumbled Berta, quite forgetting that she was having a very enjoyable time. She and the other children had been able to forget their predicament for most of the time, despite the silent presence of the armed volunteers, who kept a ceaseless watch on the farm and its inhabitants.

Lunch was a quick meal and then the children were sent to rest, as was the usual habit.

"I think that we should keep to their routine as far as possible," confided Mother Camille to Nancy Finch. "The fewer shocks to their systems the better at this point."

The peace was not to last for long, however.

It was in the quiet of the afternoon when the children lay reading or snoozing and the nuns and the Finches read on the veranda, that there was a sudden shout followed by three shrill blasts from a whistle from one of the volunteers. There were pounding footsteps as the others, closely followed by the natives, ran up to him. Sam Finch joined them seconds later.

"Up there, look!" shouted the volunteer.

They turned to look in the direction of his pointing hand and saw, silhouetted against the sky in one of the tobacco fields, on a rise in the ground about a hundred yards away, the figures of fifty or more Africans. Time stood still as all the players stared at one another. Then, John Taylor spoke rapidly to his men: "Peter, take William and three of the farm workers and go to the other side of the house. Give two blasts of the whistle at any sign of an attack on that front. If it's clear and I whistle, come back again; it will mean that we're in trouble. Sam, go and tell the women and children that they are to stay inside. They must call Winston and Chipango to stay with them, barricade the doors and on no account come out until we give them the all clear. The rest of you, on my order choose your targets carefully and shoot to kill."

The named men slipped off and the rest stood, rifles at the ready under the blazing sun, sweat streaming down their faces as they faced the unknown.

Finally, the men on the rise made a move. Carefully stepping around the tobacco plants, they came slowly towards the house. As they came closer they could be heard talking to one another, and when they came close enough to make out faces they walked directly to the volunteers and, smiling broadly, greeted them. They were finally recognised as the villagers who had befriended them in the hills on the previous day.

Relief made the reunion heartier than it perhaps warranted, and there was much shaking of hands and expressions of surprise and awe at the size of the homestead. The men had come to accompany their young people home, they said, and Peter assured them that they had been about to leave. He sent a farm worker to call them and led the party to a shady tree, where they all squatted to exchange pleasantries. Biscuits and lemonade were brought from the kitchen and there was much chatter and expressions of delight at the novel tastes.

Soon the village girls and men arrived laden with their gifts: loaves of bread, jars of jam and cash prizes. Seeing that there were now many hands,

Sam also gave them a large sack of ground maize meal, their staple food. Again there were many expressions of gratitude and gentle clapping of hands. Finally, the bag of maize meal was hoisted onto a hastily contrived stretcher between two men and the other delicacies were spread out amongst the others. The party took their leave, obviously much gratified by the morning's events.

As they disappeared over the rise, everyone slumped with relief and walked wearily to the veranda, nerves shattered by the tension of the false alarm.

"You just never know, do you?" said Nancy, soberly, as she served cold beers. Then she turned to her husband, eyes wide with anxiety. "You will get these children home safely, won't you, Sam?"

"There is nothing more important to us at this moment," he assured her, putting his arm around her shoulder to the murmurs of assent from the men gathered there. The incident had emphasised to them all how very vulnerable they were, but it had also made them even more determined to face and survive whatever dangers should confront them.

CHAPTER FIVE

From the shelter of the trees in the little wood at the back of the priests' house, the priests' gardeners Tobias and Elias, together with Matonde and another of the convent gardeners, watched the drama unfolding in front of their horrified eyes. They could not hear what was being said, but saw Father Swelsen addressing the mob from the veranda, arms aloft as though imploring. A sudden stealthy footfall close by made them start in alarm, ready for flight.

"It is us," came a hasty whisper, "Daniel and Sixpence." The cook and the house servant had materialised out of the darkness.

"Where were you?" demanded Elias.

"Some men from Chilembwe's Mbombwe centre came and woke us at midnight. They said that we should leave, that things were going to happen. So we went to my brother's, but came back in case *Bambo* needed us."

The angry growl of the mob suddenly turned to exultant shouts. They saw the priest flying along the veranda, leaping off the edge and disappearing in the direction of the road. Some confused milling around of the crowd and then they were after him.

As one, the six men turned and followed, keeping parallel but about thirty yards to the side. They were oblivious of the lower branches of the trees whipping into their faces and the wiry grasses that cut into their legs. The sharp stones that gouged their feet went unnoticed as they ran to keep up with the mob. When Swelsen swerved into the road leading to the cemetery and the crowd followed him, the mission men suddenly found themselves very close to the rebels on the perimeter and flung themselves down, flat amongst the vegetation, unable to see what was happening but recognising with a sickening certainty that their *Bambo* had reached the end of the road.

They lay there for a few moments, numb with shock, grief and feelings of impotence that they had been able to do nothing to avoid the catastrophe. When finally the rebels moved off, their work done there, they called excitedly to one another of going to burn down the priests' house. On hearing this, the men were once again galvanised into action. They rapidly crawled on their stomachs to a safe distance, rose to their feet and ran as fast as they could in the inky darkness that enveloped them, as the clouds once again shrouded the moon.

Before they could see the house they knew they were too late; it seemed that some of the rebels hadn't joined the chase to the cemetery because the house was well alight, its thatched roof a blazing inferno. About fifty men stood in the garden looking at the flames, talking and laughing while a group started an impromptu dance.

The mission men dropped to their knees on the rough stony ground; they closed their hands in prayer and whispered in unison, "Hail Mary, full of grace… Holy Mary, mother of God, pray for us sinners now and at the hour of our death. Amen."

Finally, Matonde rose to his feet and the others followed. He spoke quietly and wearily, as though he were exhausted: "I must go and tell Mother what has happened," he said.

There was an instant chorus: "We are coming too."

He shook his head tiredly. "No, you must remain to pick up *Bambo's* body and look after it until the nuns and the children are gone and I can return with help."

He beckoned to his gardening mate: "*Tiyeni,*" he said. Let's go. He turned back to the others. "I'll pass by the huts of the other workers from the convent and take the men with me. We have seen what the rebels can do; those nuns are going to need every bit of help that they can get."

A small wave of the hand and they were lost in the darkness, leaving the small disconsolate group standing amongst the trees.

There was a long silence and then Tobias stirred. "There's a *machila* in the outside storeroom. We must see if the building is still standing and if it is, get the *machila* to carry *Bambo's* body." His voice was emotional; he had been particularly fond of *Bambo*, who had taken him on without any skills or experience and trained him to be a useful member of the mission staff.

The *machila* was a mode of transportation of people and goods and was made up of a piece of canvas slung between two poles. Either two or four men carried it at front and back. It would be appropriate for his mentor's last journey. The other men voiced their agreement softly and together they cautiously circled the back of the house until they could clearly see the storehouse. It appeared to be intact, probably because it had a corrugated iron roof. The area seemed to be deserted but, nevertheless, they approached with extreme caution. A faint glow in the east proclaimed the dawn and when they were certain that they were not being observed, they wrenched off the old, rusty padlock, opened the door, and, leaving Daniel as lookout, they found and brought out the *machila*.

When they emerged, Daniel was staring fixedly at a point to the east, in the direction of the convent, where there was an orange glare superimposed on the magenta hue of the dawn.

There was a sharp intake of breath, a quiet "Eh eh". There was no need to say more. The convent buildings were on fire.

A sudden and incongruous noise brought them to a standstill. Yes, there it was, the sound of singing. Massed voices singing a hymn. And it was coming from the partly completed stone church.

Shaking their heads in disbelief, they shouldered the *machila* and trotted to the cemetery, along the now deserted road. As they drew close to the church the singing became absolutely clear.

The mob was singing a hymn.

"It's blasphemy!" hissed Daniel as they turned off for the cemetery.

When they reached Father Swelsen's body they stared at it for a few appalled moments. Even by the light of the early dawn it was clear to see that his cassock had been ripped to shreds and what could be seen of his body was a bloody, mangled mess. The men stooped and, between them, they gently lifted the inanimate body.

A soft groan startled them and Elias dropped his part of the burden.

"Fool!" hissed Daniel. "Quickly now! Put him on the *machila*!"

The priest was laid down tenderly and Tobias gently probed the base of his throat. Presently he looked up, smiled jubilantly and said: "He lives!" But he continued soberly, "He is very sick, many bones seem broken and he is very cold. We must find help."

"But where?" asked the others. "We must be careful. The rebels must not see us."

Daniel took over. "Go to our houses," he told the other three. "Bring all the blankets we have and also water. He must have water."

The three men loped off and Daniel settled to wait, keeping a watchful eye on the lane leading to the road. The singing in the church had stopped and as the sun rose, he realised that everything was unnaturally quiet. No birds sang, no children played. No workers called cheerfully to one another as they made their early start to the day's work. And now, the smoke clouds could be seen over the mission and the convent, mute witness to the night's evil deeds.

The soft thumping of running feet announced the arrival of the mission men with all that they had been asked to bring. *Bambo* was lovingly and tenderly wrapped in the blankets and water was trickled drop by drop through his torn and swollen lips. A hurried consultation followed, and a decision was reached to go to the convent and see whether the dispensary had been spared. If it had, then they would go and search for Eselina, a young woman from a nearby village who worked at the convent as assistant to Sister Jeanne, who was a trained nurse in the dispensary.

With the utmost gentleness, the men lifted the *machila* and started the slow, careful walk to the convent. At first they walked fearfully, at the very borders of the road, so that they could dart into the undergrowth at the first sign of trouble. But it soon became clear that the area was deserted.

When they reached the convent grounds they paused in mute shock at the devastation. Every building had been gutted – the school, the nuns' and the children's quarters, the store rooms for the linen and the food, the kitchen, everything. As they walked closer they saw that even the poultry had been burnt alive in their coops. Only the remnants of the once beautiful flower gardens remained at the outer perimeter of the gardens, to show that something quite splendid had existed here.

"Why? Why?" they said to one another. "What did they gain by this?"

A gentle lowing from a field adjacent to the vegetable garden showed them that at least something had escaped the devastation. Two oxen stood contentedly chewing grass. At the far end of the field stood the ox-cart; fortunately, it had been left there by a careless gardener, instead of being stored in its shelter by the kitchen, and had escaped the holocaust.

Thoroughly disheartened and deeply anxious for their *Bambo*, they moved a little distance away and sat under a mango tree with the *machila* in the shade, protected from the already hot sun. They bathed Swelsen's face with the cool water and kept up a trickle of water into his mouth. Most of it trickled out again. *What now?* they wondered. *Oh God, what now?*

Suddenly, they became aware of sounds breaking the deathly silence, sounds of men, many men approaching the convent from the main road on the other side of the gutted buildings.

With startled exclamations the men leapt up as one, picked up each corner of the *machila* and moved as fast as they could further into the brush and away from the buildings. In a grove of poinsettias and oleanders which bordered the kitchen gardens, Sister Assumpta's pride and joy, they gently put down the *machila* and then lay on their stomachs, hearts pounding. Had the rebels returned? If they had, they were finished. They had no weapons, no means whatsoever of defending themselves.

As the newcomers approached the convent, they split up and darted into the bushes on either side of the road. Others leapt for fragments of wall still standing and hid, their rifles poised. The men were now close enough for it to be seen that they were Africans, and the mission workers looked at one another in despair.

Another wave of men appeared and then another.

And they were white! They were white!

Daniel and his friends leapt up, shouting hysterically. Then they bent and reverently picked up the *machila* and walked confidently towards the men they had now recognised as the Mikalongwe volunteers.

At first, the volunteers reacted warily, backing off and raising their rifles. After all, this could be a trap. But then some of the African cohort recognised the mission men, and rushed forward to greet them and relieve them of their burden.

"Daniel! Elias!" they called out their names joyfully. "We thought you were all dead when we saw what has happened here! God is good!"

The Europeans lowered their arms and joined the boisterous reunion, a reunion that suddenly quietened when they laid eyes on the pitiful state of Father Swelsen.

"Oh, my God!" was all there seemed to be to say.

"Can you help Father Swelsen?" asked the mission men.

"Yes, of course," replied one, coming forward with a First Aid kit slung over his shoulder. Others followed suit.

The volunteers, now reinforced by government troops as well as about a hundred African supporters, did their best, using their medical supplies, to ease the priest's more superficial injuries, but it was clear that there was probably serious internal damage. Some broken bones were protruding and it was a reasonable assumption that there was internal bleeding.

"We have to get him to the Mikalongwe Station," said the leader. The train will be arriving there at midmorning the day after tomorrow to collect the evacuees from the area – including the nuns and their wards – and we have to get him there."

"Which way shall we go, *bwana*?" asked Tobias, anxiously. He addressed the volunteer as 'sir'.

"The main road will be safe now."

But with the previous night's events fresh in their minds, the mission men demurred. Perhaps it would be safer over the hills, the way the nuns had gone.

The volunteer smiled. "Chilembwe is on the run," he said. "Our scouts have reported that his Mwombwe mission is deserted, the people who took part in the raids have dispersed and his supporters have deserted him."

Another thought occurred to him. "How are you thinking of transporting him?"

"With the *machila*, *bwana*," replied Daniel.

"Um," was the response. "Don't you think an ox-drawn cart might be more comfortable?"

The men gave it some thought. "The problem is," replied Daniel, "that the roads are very bad with the rains now. It would be very bumpy. At least with the *machila* we can try to give him a smoother ride."

The roads were indeed in very poor shape. They were little more than tracks, capable of taking ox-carts at the best of times, and only pedestrians at the worst.

Tobias contributed another angle. "It would be a good idea to take the ox-cart for provisions and tents. Usually, the villagers along the way would provide for us, but this is the third year of crop failure. Food is short."

The leader of the volunteers nodded his assent and turned to the large contingent he had brought with him; he raised his voice: "We need an escort of eight men for Father Swelsen to the Mikalongwe Station. Can I have volunteers, please?"

A small sea of hands shot up.

After a hasty conference, an additional sixteen men were selected to walk to Mikalongwe, taking it in turns to carry the *machila*. The others would rest in the cart with the provisions. If and where the road improved the *machila* would be taken into the cart.

The team swung into action and the fighting force offered from their supplies what would be needed for the rescue mission.

Elias, Tobias, Daniel and Sixpence volunteered to carry the *machila* for the first leg of the journey. They were tired, close to exhaustion in fact, but it seemed that there was a chance now that Bambo Swelsen could be taken to the medical centre in time to save his life. They felt new strength flooding into them as the rest of the cohort lined up behind them.

With broad smiles they picked up the *machila*. "*Tiyeni!*" Let's go, they shouted and moved off down the rutted winding road.

CHAPTER SIX

Berta was calm as she helped to replace the furniture which had been used as barricades against possible attack at the Finch's farm. When the alarm had first sounded she had been the first to run to the window, from where there was a clear view of what was happening. Sister Agnes had pulled her and the others back into the room and drawn the curtains.

"Get back, girls," she had whispered. She had shepherded them into the middle of the room and made them sit down. "Stay quiet and still." They immediately obeyed, mainly because her sternness was such a change from her usually reserved and quiet demeanour.

Then she, the other nuns, Winston and Chipango and the senior girls had quietly and quickly piled the heavy sitting room furniture against the doors. That done, they had all sat down cross-legged in a circle in the middle of the floor to wait. Outside there was silence.

Berta was tired. She was tired of trauma after trauma. She was too tired to be afraid; she was too tired to cry. She just wanted to go home. The other girls too seemed deflated. The youngest ones sat listlessly, a few of them sucking their thumbs.

But the threatened danger was over and the resilience of the very young soon asserted itself. The girls prepared to spend the afternoon looking around the farm.

In no time at all it seemed, dusk approached and they made their way to where the animals were being herded into the night stalls. The calves and the kids were separated from their mothers amidst much bleating and lowing, and the adult animals were called into their kraals, each one by its name.

"How can they tell them apart?" wondered Berta. No one quite knew.

As the girls stood there the setting sun lowered itself in the sky in an awesome eruption of every hue between pink, orange and scarlet, and the earth slowly quietened and prepared for sleep. The cattle and sheep herders lit log fires at intervals around the kraals; the smoke kept away the mosquitoes and flies and the flames kept away the prowling lions. In the growing quiet could be heard the howl of a distant dog, a woman's voice as she called to her children, the last of the birds as they returned to their nesting places. The perfume of the flowers intensified in the warm evening air and enfolded them in its sensual charm. *Could any night other than an African night be this beautiful?* thought Berta. She must ask Papa.

By eight o' clock the children were once again spread out on the floors, ready for sleep.

It wasn't a good night, however. The girls tossed restlessly in their sleep, some whimpering in their tormented dreams, others waking screaming or shouting from their nightmares. The nuns barely slept. Like ghosts in their white under-robes, they flitted from child to child, soothing, comforting, pressing cold water to quivering lips. It seemed to Berta that she only slept for minutes before another cry or whimper awakened her.

It was a relief to everyone when the roosters started to crow and the shy dawn coyly peeped over the mountains in a rosy blush.

Spirits rose after a wash and a hearty breakfast of porridge, followed by fresh farm eggs scrambled on toast. Then it was time to make their way to the railway station.

There was much laughter and excitement as two ox-drawn carts came around to the house and the children were lifted into them. The whole party could not fit, so half the nuns and the volunteers went with the first leg of transport. The rest would be collected shortly, since the railway station was only a mile or two distant.

It was a fresh and beautiful day, still cooled by the morning breeze. Later the heat would become oppressive. The hard-packed dirt road stretched ahead of them and wound its tranquil way through little woods, luxuriant after the summer rains, and tobacco fields rippling with the robust, green, leafy plants.

Soon they were at the railway station, which was little more than a shack with an Indian stationmaster in it and two native employees. Small though it was, it was delightfully attractive, with clumps of oleander and fragrant frangipane trees dotted around the perimeter. On guard at the entrance and around the embarkation area were stationed numerous volunteers, their rifles at the ready. It was unexpectedly busy; word had got around that a rescue train was being sent from the main town of Blantyre and farmers and their families had descended to travel to the safety of the town. The atmosphere was subdued, however, and only the children were their usual frisky selves. The parents were all too well aware of the possible danger that surrounded them.

The girls were offloaded and the cart began its return journey to the farm for the rest of the party.

The nuns wasted no time in finding space for themselves and their charges on a shady part of the platform, where they would be immediately at hand when the train arrived.

Sister Magdalena was unusually serious as she gave them their orders. "You can walk around the platform right up to the stationmaster's office, girls, but on no account must you go any further. You must be in full sight of us at all times."

There was a chorus of, "Yes, Sister," and the children ambled off, looking wide-eyed at the mix of people and the purposeful activity going on around them. The nuns made themselves comfortable on a weather-beaten wooden bench that stood against the railing.

In little more than half an hour the ox carts returned with the rest of the party, and sizeable hampers of food, which the Finches had prepared to satisfy the large appetites of the little people.

Mother Camille arrived with the second cartload of children and as she shooed her charges towards the platform, she found an African man at her elbow. A little surprised at his closeness, she turned enquiringly to him. "Daniel!" she gasped in surprise. "How are you? How is everything at the mission? Is everyone all right? I mean, except for poor Father Swelsen."

Her pleasure and relief at seeing him transformed the tense lines on her face and she gripped his arm as she looked searchingly at him.

"Yes, Mother," he smiled back at her. "We are all well."

He paused for a moment, unable to resist a little bit of drama with the astounding news that he had to impart to her. "Except for Father Swelsen, of course, who needs urgent medical attention."

The nun looked at him uncomprehendingly, unable to speak for a few moments.

Her voice was breathless when she finally spoke, her lips working oddly. "But Father Swelsen perished, didn't he?" she stammered.

Daniel's smile sliced his face in half, teeth gleaming and eyes shining in an otherwise weary face.

"No, Mother, he did not." And, there, outside the Mikalongwe train station, in the tropical heat amidst the bustle and noise, he told her what had happened; she put her head on his shoulder and wept with joy.

Finally, she wiped away her tears. "Let me see him please, Daniel. Where is he?"

"Come," he said, and led her to the priest; his guard stood around him in an isolated corner of the station platform.

She greeted the other mission men warmly and then turned to look at the priest. She stood immobile as she stared down at him. His head was black and blue and swollen to twice its size. There was a deep gash on his cheek around which the blood had turned to black, and his features were almost unrecognisable in the swollen pulpy mess that was his face. The priest appeared to be unconscious, oblivious to the hushed voices and the men of the escort, who waved palm fronds above him to keep away the predatory, buzzing flies.

The nun crossed herself and tore her gaze away. "Where will you take him?" she asked.

"There is a truck waiting for us in Blantyre and it will take him straight to the hospital. Tobias will come with me."

"God go with you," she said to the men, as a faint toot in the distance heralded the imminent arrival of the train. A cheer rippled along the platform.

There was a bustle as families began to call their children to them. Mother Camille returned to the other nuns and their charges. Under cover of the activity and the noise she was able to circulate to the other nuns and tell them that Father Swelsen was alive. The nuns were ecstatic, furtively wiping away tears of joy and trying to find out what had happened and where he was now.

Mother Camille briefly relayed to them what Daniel had told her, but warned them of the extent of his injuries. "His wounds are fearful and he needs our prayers as well as the medical attention that he will soon have."

There was a chorus of assent and hands reached for rosaries. However, there was no opportunity for the sisters to ask to see the priest, as a few minutes later the train came screeching into the station, belching clouds of sulphurous smoke. Armed guards from within leapt nimbly onto the platform and spread out to cover the entire platform, as well as the area immediately behind the stationmaster's office.

The first ones to embark were Father Swelsen and his bearers and all the other passengers stood aside to allow them passage. Once they were installed comfortably the rest of the passengers got on the train. It was all quickly accomplished and as soon as the engine drivers had stoked up with water and coal and the armed guard had climbed back on board, the train was on its way back to town.

Barring tree trunks across the rails, thought Mother Camille, as she glanced through the window at the retreating station, they would soon be out of danger. She decided to take this opportunity to tell the children that Father Swelsen had survived the attack, and it was all they needed to turn the day into a total success. Disbelief turned into joy, young voices rose in excited chatter and Berta's eyes filled with tears of joy as she sought out Elsa.

"He's alive! Father Swelsen's alive!" she called out to Elsa, running to her and hugging her tightly.

"I know!" replied Elsa, equally moved. "I know. Thank God."

Young spirits rose rapidly and it was a chattering, excited group that arrived at the station barely half an hour later. The first to disembark was Father Swelsen's cohort, and they were taken to a small box-body, a strange-looking vehicle made from a Ford with a boxed section welded onto the back. It disappeared in the direction of the hospital. The girls disembarked with the other passengers and stared wide-eyed at the motorised transport that awaited them.

Sister Magdalena, interested in all things mechanical, explained that the two trucks at the edge of the platform were part of the fleet that had been brought into the country from Southern Africa. They were needed for transportation of troops and equipment to Nyasaland's northern frontier, where all was poised in a state of readiness for a second German onslaught from German East Africa.

"But since there is now this problem with the uprising, some troops and equipment have been brought back here to the south," she concluded.

Adults and children were packed into the backs of the trucks and taken to the headquarters of the African Lakes Corporation. The company had been set up by the early Scottish missionaries to offer trading in goods to the natives, as an attractive and viable alternative to trading in people. Trade had flourished, especially in calico, one of the most desired commodities of all, and now the company had spacious premises in the town.

During the short journey Berta and her little friends stood at the back, just behind the cab, holding onto the rail and shrieking with delight as the wind whipped their faces. They waved gaily to the natives they passed and to the occasional motor car that passed them going in the opposite direction.

"This is exciting, isn't it?" shouted Berta into Mona's ear.

"Um," nodded Mona, with shining eyes.

On their arrival at the African Lakes complex, the group was taken to the rice warehouse, where they were asked to organise themselves as well as possible. The employee escorting them, a harassed-looking Indian gentleman, explained that about three hundred Europeans, Indians and the nuns' charges had come to Blantyre to seek protection from the rebels, and each group had been allocated one of the company's buildings, which were situated around a large square in their considerable premises on the outskirts of the town.

He finished off with an apologetic look on his face. "The rice warehouse is for you but I'm afraid that it's impossible for any sort of conventional bedding to be made available. You'll find that there are stacks of hessian sacks available and people are using those."

"Why is he staring at you?" hissed Berta, as she prodded Elsa's hip with her elbow.

"Quiet, pest!" hissed Elsa back. "Behave!"

As the man walked away with a smile in the older girls' direction, the nuns went into a cluster of murmuring voices. They pulled apart and called out.

"Come on, girls, let's see what we can find to sleep on."

A search by the nuns and the older girls revealed hundreds of hessian sacks waiting to be used to transport the rice; the children were all given a few sacks to shake out.

"Get the girls to shake them out hard," Mother Camille told the other nuns. "Goodness knows what could be nesting in there."

"At best cockroaches and at worst scorpions, I suspect," said Sister Jeanne with a grimace.

These remarks were overhead by the girls, who promptly dropped their sacks with squeals of horror.

"Take no notice," Sister Magdalena told them soothingly, handing them back their bags. "Sister Jeanne was only thinking about what might conceivably be in them, not what is likely!"

Their fears proved unfounded, however, and enough sacks to lie on and use for covering were soon in neat piles.

Sister Jeanne had a thought. "How about we lay down full bags of rice to act as mattresses and use the empty ones as sheets on top?"

"What a good idea!" said Mother. "They'll be quite hard to lie on, but the floor will undoubtedly be harder!"

The children agreed enthusiastically and everyone set to hauling bags of rice and laying them out in neat rows on the floor.

"I think I know why there aren't any insects in the bags," commented Sister Assumpta. "I'm certain that I can smell insecticide."

Some sniffing by the girls and the other nuns confirmed Sister Assumpta's diagnosis.

"Well, it's not surprising," commented one of the nuns. "If it weren't for that, insects would devour the entire crop."

"The good thing is," commented another, "that the insecticide will keep the mosquitoes away. I hear that many people are suffering badly from bites."

The final task was to find somewhere relatively secluded for the nuns to sleep. Berta and her friends, in the course of noisily exploring the warehouse and scaling piles of filled bags of rice, found a sheltered little alcove in a corner, surrounded by chest-high banks of full rice bags.

"Excellent!" applauded Mother Camille, when they showed it to her. "This will do for us very well. Thank you, girls."

Outside, the compound of the African Lakes Corporation, or Mandala as it was known, was buzzing with activity. Elsa and Berta, with a few of their friends and with Paulina reluctantly trailing behind, had gone exploring, and were able to return to the rice warehouse with specific details of who was there.

"The women and children from the estates are in the upper floor of the offices, the clearing house and the motor accessories portion," reported Elsa.

"And in part of the goods shed," added Berta.

"The Italians are in the packing room and the small store at that end of the square," broke in Paulina, pointing in the direction of the opposite end of the square. "The Indians are in the transit shed and the nursing staff are in the offices next to the dispensary."

Mother Camille turned in a quiet aside to the other nuns.

"The Indians feel threatened too. Rumour has it that Chilembwe intends to kill all non-African men and send the women and children back home. Only a few women will be permitted to remain, and those only as teachers." Their eyes flashed the question at one another: *What do they plan for us?*

"I wonder who's in the marquee in the square?" asked Elsa.

Berta promptly replied, "Oh, that's for the German residents and the prisoners of war."

"Oh," said Paulina weakly, visibly shrinking from the idea of prisoners of war running loose.

"Don't worry," said Berta reassuringly. "They are very nice. One of the prisoners, a German colonel, has been helping with all the arrangements."

"How do you know that?" Elsa asked disbelievingly.

"I heard some people talking," replied her little sister, smugly.

"You, my girl," warned Elsa darkly, "are going to get into trouble with your curiosity one day."

But Berta stuck out her tongue just the tiniest bit, so that no one else could see, and raced off with the other children, who were equally happy and excited and ran off to explore and make new friends

Mealtimes were surprisingly good. The farmers had brought some of their staff with them and their cooks were made welcome in local homes, where they prepared food in large quantities. Blantyre residents, who spent their nights in the safety of the compound but returned home during the day, visited the compound at lunchtime with large oven trays filled with basic but filling fare. Even Berta had had enough to eat at the end of each meal.

The Stanleys – long-time friends of the Deuss family – came from their quarters to find the Deuss children and ensure that they had sufficient to eat; the food that they brought was enough for the whole party. No one went hungry. Routine went out the window and the nuns' charges played all day to their hearts' content.

As dusk approached, Sister Magdalene suggested to Mother Camille that they calm down the children with a bit of singing, and all the nuns eagerly adopted the idea. The children in the vicinity were sent off to call the others and soon they were all outside the rice warehouse, sitting on hessian sacks in a semicircle on the ground.

Sister Therese, their music teacher, suggested that they sing the duet about the swallow and the butterfly, and there was enthusiastic agreement from the children. The nun separated them into two balanced groups and the girls' clear voices started, "*Je suis une brune hirondelle*". I am a brown swallow.

"*Je ne suis qu'un blanc papillon,*" joined in the second group. I am only a white butterfly.

Sweetly their lilting voices rose in the mellow dusk, first one group then the other responding with the plaintive melody. Then they all joined in the triumphant chorus.

"*Soyons unies, soyons amies, Rien n'est plus doux sur cette terre...*" Let's be friends, let's be united. Nothing on this earth is sweeter...

There was a second's pause after the last note had died away, and then there was loud applause. The girls turned in surprise to see that they had a large audience of people who had been attracted by the music.

"Sing it again. Please sing it again!" came the calls.

Sister Therese smiled, looked enquiringly at Mother, who gave her a nod, and started her little choir off again.

By then the early evening darkness had fallen and the lights from hundreds of lanterns lit the windows of the offices and warehouses in the compound, as the refugee families prepared to put their children to bed. As the last note whispered away into the twilight sky, it was clear that the very young children were struggling to stay awake. After hurried prayers they were put to bed, and a few hours later the older ones followed.

Although their mattresses of bags of rice were hard and their sheets of hessian were rough, in no time at all they were soundly asleep. The sisters followed soon after and retreated to their little shelter.

Berta and Elsa had wondered how the nuns could keep to their order's rules in this situation. The orders precluded them from eating or drinking in public or taking part in community activities in any way, although they were free to visit and undertake pastoral duties and in fact were encouraged to do so where a need had been identified.

In fact, the sisters had discussed the problem of privacy during the day with Mother Camille, commenting ruefully that they were in no position to follow the order's rules at the present. She had even joked with the girls about it.

"Sleeping behind a pile of bags of rice is the best we can hope for," she had sighed, giving the starched flaps of her wimple a tweak to get them back into shape. "They've become sadly limp," she joked.

55

The night passed quietly and for any who awoke there was the reassuring sound of the sentries' footsteps as they patrolled the perimeter.

***

The compound awakened early to the crisp, dew-filled air. Men had to get to work in their offices in town and breakfast for all had to be prepared. Servants bustled to and fro and young children cavorted around in their pyjamas, enjoying this newfound liberty. Normally they would be being washed and dressed for school, but ordinary life had been suspended.

The convent girls awoke early, pulled on their dresses and after a hurried look around for the nuns, who could be heard quietly chanting their morning prayer behind the rice bag barrier, ran out into the brilliant sunshine. The older girls followed more sedately; Elsa and Paulina perched with Mona on the veranda wall of the office block, from where they had a clear view of everything that was taking place in the compound.

"With any luck, Papa should be here by lunch," mused Elsa.

And, as if on cue, Berta tore up to them demanding, "Do you think Papa will be here today, Elsa?"

Elsa had calculated correctly. At midday, as they finished their lunch, there was the dear and familiar sound of a large and powerful motorbike roaring into the compound, closely followed by another.

"Papa!" shrieked three very excited young girls, wiping the crumbs from their mouths and racing to meet their father.

As Ludwig dismounted from his prized Norton motorbike, a rifle hanging from a holster on his back, a cannonball in the form of Berta greeted him. Following more decorously were Elsa, her face a huge smile, and Paulina, who was trying, unsuccessfully, to hide her delight. All three were enveloped in a hug and Berta noticed that her father's eyes were misty as he held them close.

"So, how are my girls?" he mumbled gruffly, his fine-featured face drawn into anxious lines.

"Oh fine, Papa," squealed Berta, holding him tightly.

"OK, I suppose," sniffed Paulina.

"You'll have to tell me all about it when we get home," replied Ludwig, looking eloquently at Elsa.

"When are we going home?" they asked in unison.

"We leave first thing tomorrow morning. The uprising seems to be over and the government forces are chasing the leader. I believe that he and a small remnant of his supporters are fleeing to the border of Portuguese East Africa, so I believe that it's safe for us to travel. I've brought Aleki with our other motorbike and sidecar, and I've asked Mr Stanley to lend us a motorcycle and sidecar, with driver, to get us back to Matope. We'll catch the paddle steamer home from there tomorrow evening. Now, why don't you go and do what you were doing before I came so that I can have a bite to eat and find the Stanleys. I also want to find the Finches to thank them for what they've done for us."

Berta was reluctant to go, but finally loosened her grip on him and went to play with the other children in the compound; Ludwig strode away with a final glance backward and a broad smile.

The day passed quickly; at dusk, as the night darkened and the stars shone with hard, white brilliance, the refugees in the compound gathered around the rice shed, asking for music. Nuns and girls were happy to oblige and sang enchantingly of French folklore and life in days gone by. A few other members had brought their guitars and joined in with Scottish and Italian renditions; it was a happy chattering group who finally dispersed and made their way to their various lodgings in the compound. Ludwig had found a place to sleep with the other men in a long shed on the northern side of the compound, and soon there was a calm velvety stillness, broken only by the sound of the sentries' steps and the low-voiced murmur of a few men who had stayed up to enjoy a nightcap together.

The following morning Ludwig and his family were ready to leave early, although Ludwig was a little apprehensive about travelling while the rebels were still on the loose. He was reassured by the volunteers, in whose opinion the revolution was over; farmers were returning to their farms and normal life was hesitantly picking up its old tempo.

"And don't forget, Ludwig," one told him, "that the rebels have returned the wives and families of the two murdered farmers to their friends. They had them completely at their mercy, yet not a finger was lifted against them. On the contrary, it is said that they were very kind to them."

Another followed up quietly. "Having said all that, be vigilant. There are the remnants of a failed uprising on the loose; their mood is not likely to be good."

Ludwig nodded grimly. Turning away, he and the girls bade the nuns an affectionate farewell.

"Thank you for everything you have done to save my girls' lives," he said, emotionally, to Mother Camille and the group of sisters. "I am forever in your debt."

After some hurried goodbyes to the Stanleys and to the new friends the girls had made, they were ready to go. Berta arrived a little late. "I've been saying goodbye to Gemma. She's sick," she said, as she clambered into

Ludwig's sidecar. Elsa was in Aleki's and Paulina was with the Storey driver. Her scowl was fierce.

"Why me?" she kept on asking her father. "Why couldn't I go with you or Aleki?"

"No reason, Paulina," said Ludwig tersely. "It had to be someone who went with the borrowed driver, and it just happened to be you."

She continued to whine and he stood there for a moment, glaring at her, his hand running through his fair hair in frustration. Then he cut short her continuing complaints.

"We've got no time for this," he muttered as he strode to his bike. With a roar the three motorbikes sprang to life and the cavalcade disappeared down the road in a cloud of dust, leaving the nuns and their few remaining charges waving in the middle of the road.

Ahead lay a long, arduous journey, made even more so this time by the small but real possibility that they might collide with the fleeing revolutionaries, who would now be tired, desperate and angry.

CHAPTER SEVEN

The little town of Fort Johnston slumbered in the midday heat and, in her large brick-built house, Victoria busied herself in preparation for the arrival of her husband and daughters. The telegram had been cryptic and Kahn, her husband's business partner and good friend, had called to read it to her.

"Arriving mid-day tomorrow with girls. All well. Ludwig."

She offered up a silent prayer. *Thank you, Father*. These past few days had been a nightmare since word had filtered through to the Fort about the uprising. At first, they had thought their daughters and all the convent girls safe. After all, Nguludi was some distance from Blantyre and Zomba, where the main events were taking place. Then had come the telegram telling them about the destruction of the mission and convent, but that the girls were safe and could be collected from the Mandala compound. From a distance, though, this news was not totally reassuring. Victoria was tearful, shaken out of her usual calm.

"They say the children are safe, but no one knows what Chilembwe's men are planning! Maybe they will attack the safe houses next."

Ludwig hid his fears, which were just as strong as his wife's. "No, Victoria. There has been time to organise the defences; all is well. You'll see."

And as he left for Blantyre on his motorbike, Aleki close behind, Victoria struggled for composure in front of the servants. All she could visualise was the long journey ahead of them, with no escort and rebels on the loose. At least they were visibly well armed, rifles across their backs and cartridge belts around their waists; she consoled herself with the thought that that should put off any wandering insurgents.

That night she didn't sleep at all and Mataya, her faithful shadow, hovered, anxious for her mistress and distressed that she was unable to help. Daylight seemed an eternity in coming but, when it did, Victoria felt the shadows retreating and optimism taking their place. The telegram finally dispersed the last of her fears and she set to energetically preparing the girls' rooms. Victoria was taller than the average Nyasaland African who is of Bantu origin and who, over the years has merged with the Chewa, Yao and Ngoni tribes, all of whom are slight in build. With a very upright carriage, she strode to and fro, giving orders in her deep voice to her small army of servants. Edisoni, the cook, and his assistant, Njoka, were given detailed instructions for the preparation of food.

"Don't forget that little Donna Berta is coming!" she reminded them. Indeed, everyone smiled indulgently at the healthy appetite of the youngest daughter who, although quite skinny, was capable of putting away impressive amounts of food.

Edisoni chuckled. "Don't worry, Mama. We'll have more than enough for her!"

With a smile, she turned her attention to the garden, which did not escape the welcoming preparations; Victoria took a great pride in their home and wanted her daughters to see it at its best. She called for the head gardener, Kampango, and walked around with him, giving instructions.

"Look, Kampango," she said, pointing to the space between the blooming rose bushes, "just look at those weeds. If you don't get rid of them soon, they'll be taller than the roses! In fact," turning around and taking in the whole of the front garden, "there are weeds everywhere. What have you been doing for the past week?"

Kampango scratched his neck in embarrassment and moved from foot to foot. "It's the rains, Mama, as soon as you weed a patch, within a few days…"

Victoria cut him short with a wave of her hand. "Rubbish! I don't want any excuses. Just get the job done."

"Yes, Mama," he said, his expression penitent, and he walked away with shoulders slumped, looking like a dejected ten-year-old.

Victoria turned away and then hovered for a moment, as she stood in the front garden and looked back at the house. It meant a great deal to her, this house. She and Ludwig had moved to Mangoche soon after their marriage, and together they had planned this graceful one-storey home which, although typical of its time, with its mellow red brick exterior, high ceilings inside and a corrugated roof, was lent an individual charm by its sprawling design. From the driveway a flight of red brick steps, flanked by ceramic pots of luxuriant shrubs, led up to the front veranda, which ran almost the width of the house. Sitting on the steps were two large brown dogs who watched their mistress intently, panting, with their red tongues rolling out of their mouths in the heat. How she loved her home, how proud of it she was and how grateful she felt to have all of this and a loving husband and children as well.

Her inspection of the garden over, Victoria walked slowly up the front steps back into the house and paused for a brief rest on one of the veranda chairs; it occurred to her that they needed some new reed mats. She favoured the ones with bright designs, reds and greens mainly, and considered them as essential to sitting and chatting as chairs. This was a bone of contention between her and her husband.

"Victoria, we have chairs, comfortable ones," he said to her more than once. "Why sit on mats?"

Her response was always the same: "Because, Ludwiki, this is what I am used to and this is how I am most comfortable. When I am chatting with family and friends, this is how I prefer to sit. With acquaintances or strangers I am happy to use the chairs."

And, shaking his head with a little laugh, Ludwig gave in. He seemed to Victoria to understand that he must respect her culture as she respected his.

The issue of shoes, however, was more difficult to deal with. Despite her privileged upbringing, shoes were not considered appropriate wear. Victoria felt no need of them. After all, she had Mataya, an ex-slave who had been given to her in her early teens by her father, and who did all her running around for her. Slaves and servants who did her bidding had surrounded her all her life, and a *machila* was at her disposal should she wish to leave the house. As she had said one day to Ludwig as they sat chatting and the subject came up, "Why should I wear shoes? The *mzungu* brought them here and they are welcome to them. They are also welcome to their clothes. I will wear mine. Next you will be telling me to wear *mzungu* clothes."

She had used the Chichewa term *mzungu*, white foreigners, and her usually calm face had clouded over, large shadowed eyes pensively looking at her husband.

Ludwig had smiled. "No, Victoria, I won't, because I like the clothes you wear."

Victoria and the women in her family favoured a style of dress worn by the more affluent African. This consisted of a long, ankle length dress with short or elbow length sleeves, in a plain and usually neutral colour. On top of the dress was worn a colourful sleeveless and shoulderless type of pinafore, which reached the knees and generally had a halter strap which went around the neck, or straps over the shoulders to keep it in place. Peeping below the hem of the skirt, starting at the ankle and traveling upwards, was a close fitting three-inch-long cluster of silver bangles.

She had snorted to hide her pleasure at the compliment.

"Humph!" and the matter was closed – for the moment.

Victoria hated these tensions and felt justified in feeling aggrieved. Why should the foreigners expect the native Africans to follow their every example? And which way should the children go?

In fact, the children swung easily between the two cultures. At school they wore shoes and socks, but when they were at home they felt free to kick them off and play barefoot.

"Girls!" Ludwig would call, "I wish you would put on your shoes when you leave the house. You've forgotten about the *matekenyas*, I think!"

And the girls would scurry to get their shoes. The *matekenya* was an insect that burrowed into the tip of the toe, just under the nail, where it laid a sack of eggs. It had to be left there, despite the pain it caused, until the grubs were almost ready to hatch. At that time it was easier to pick at the skin all around the sinister lump until the whole sack could be carefully lifted away. If the sack were damaged any grubs that escaped would burrow back under the toenail, leading to a much worse situation than the first. Berta had had the misfortune to be chosen as a host to the *matekenya* insect when she was seven years old and the entire family had never forgotten the incident.

For Victoria, the clash between the two cultures was not so simple to overcome. Why should she conform to European habits? Her father, Joao Roque, was a wealthy businessman from Portuguese East Africa. He was the son of a local African dignitary and when, at the age of fifteen, he had completed his missionary education, he had come to the attention of the Portuguese authorities as an exceptionally bright and able young man. So much so that they sponsored him to live in Portugal for three years, where he completed his education and learnt the craft of the goldsmith.

On his return home he worked hard and eventually amassed a small fortune. He had a large plantation at Sena, in Portuguese East Africa, where he grew, amongst other crops, cotton, tobacco, groundnuts and coffee for export and maize for local consumption. In fact, it was in the course of business that he had met Ludwig Deuss.

Ludwig was working to expand his import/export business at the time and heard of the heavy crop yields that Roque was producing. He had visited the plantation to meet the owner and, coincidentally, caught his first glimpse of Victoria. Her face softened as she remembered their first meeting and, with a tender smile, she got up from her chair and resumed her preparations for the arrival of her family.

CHAPTER EIGHT

It took Ludwig and his entourage two hours for what was normally an hour's ride, over difficult roads, to the native settlement at Matope. The heavy summer rain had caused deep furrows to be dug by each passing vehicle and the hot sunshine which always followed had hardened them into miniature canyons. With concentration and deft steering the little party arrived intact and the motorbikes were parked by the little jetty at the river bank. Most of the village seemed to have gathered there to await the arrival of the steamer; the younger children gathered shyly around the travellers, interested but utterly refusing to be drawn into any kind of conversation.

The paddle steamer arrived almost exactly on time, and the little family boarded after waving away the driver who had travelled up with them.

Since it was the rainy season, the level of the river was high and there were very few sandbanks to negotiate. And so they made good time, although they travelled against the strong current in the deep swirling water. At first the beauty of the reed-edged river and its environs went by unnoticed, as the girls sat on the deck with their father and told him about the events of the past week. They were anxious to see their mother again. As Berta confided to her father, she wouldn't feel completely safe until all the family were together again. He put his arm around her and held her close.

But time skilfully did its soothing work and it wasn't long before, unburdened of their immediate shock and fears, the sisters became aware of the familiar bustling and colourful vibrancy of the river's edges. Birds of every description and colour rose in clouds from the reeds as the steamer approached, and the girls cried out in delight as they recognised species that they had learnt about in school and from their father. Swallows, wagtails, starlings and thrushes formed a cloud as they rushed from danger, darkening the bright blue sky above them. Ludwig's suggestion that they draw any new birds that they saw was met with excited approval and many happy hours sped past as they observed, sketched and chatted excitedly.

In the quieter moments, Berta engaged her father in serious discussion. She liked school, apart from the fact that is that it took her away from home for so much of her life, but she still had unanswered questions about it; and what little she had heard of the Chilembwe philosophy had brought all her queries to the forefront of her mind again. Sitting on the deck, calmed by the swishing of the water as the steamer's bow cleaved through the resisting water, she looked rather worriedly at her father.

"I'm really glad to be going home. Why do we have to go to school at all?" she asked.

"Because there are many things that you need to learn if you are going to be happy in your life, and we can't teach you all of them at home," explained Papa.

"Well, what about the little school near the harbour?" she asked. "Irena goes there."

She was referring to a little African girl to whom she was close in age.

"Now, there's a good question," replied Papa, making himself comfortable for what promised to be one of Berta's convoluted conversations. He explained that there were different types of schooling for different children. The little indigenous children would go to the missionary school down the road, because it would be difficult for their parents to afford to send them further away. He, however, was able to send them to the convent in Nguludi, where they would learn very much more. They would also learn French, he had told her, a most useful language in the civilised world at the time.

He suddenly interrupted their conversation: "Look!" pointing to the river's edge. "Bush pigs!"

These were frequently to be seen, noses rooting busily amongst the reeds at the water's edge, their bristly, mud-stained ungainly forms making waves and crushing tender reeds. Intent on their foraging, they gave only cursory sideways glances to the wheeled giant ploughing through the water a short distance away.

Berta was momentarily diverted. "Ugh, how ugly!" she commented and her little nose wrinkled in disgust. But then they were past and she returned to their conversation. "Papa, why don't you speak German at home? Why do we speak in French and English?"

"Questions, questions, questions," he smiled, giving her a quick kiss on her forehead. "Well, you see, it's like this. Your grandfather and all our family moved to Switzerland from Germany about thirty-five years ago, when I was a small boy. We are Swiss now and, anyway, I don't think that German would be of much use to you. Far better to learn English, which is spoken in most parts of the world."

"Is Chisena spoken in many parts of the world?" Berta wondered. Chisena was the language the children spoke with A Mayi and all of her family.

Papa smiled and gently pulled her nose. "No, my darling," he said. "It is only spoken at Sena in Mozambique, where A Mayi comes from, and where grandfather Roque lives."

"Not much use, then," concluded Berta.

"But of course it is!" exclaimed her father. "You can speak to your mother, your grandparents, your aunts and uncle. Of course it's of use!"

And so it went on, with the little girl questioning and probing, trying to make sense of the major events that had taken place in her life. Meals were a welcome diversion, board games took up much of the rest of the time, and by the time the sun began its lazy descent in the western sky, the girls were all ready for bed in their narrow but comfortable bunk beds. The racing water against the sides of the steamer was a soothing lullaby and they all slept soundly and dreamlessly.

Night descends quickly in the tropics; as the sun coloured the river fiery orange with its setting glow, the frogs and crickets emerged and their full-throated cacophony was audible even as the steamer pounded by. As nightfall approached the craft became a quiet, dark shadow, with few lights on as it laboured up the river, its wake catching the light of the rising moon like a rippling, cascading bridal train.

Then there was an abrupt change. The engines were cut, the anchor weighed and the boat creaked to a halt. It was not safe to travel for much longer in the dead of night. Besides, the African passengers needed to cook their evening meal; as the boat slowed to a stop, a crescendo of voices and clattering utensils arose from the lower decks. Ludwig, leaning over the rail, watched with a smile as, with much laughter and jesting, the passengers were transported to the shore, where their cooking fires transformed the sinister darkness of the reed-lined bank to a brightly lit carnival scenario.

When, having eaten, the passengers were returned to the steamer, quietness descended, with only the sounds of the cicadas and the frogs breaking the utter stillness of the star-studded night.

The following day, in the late morning, strident blasts of the foghorn announced their imminent arrival at Fort Johnston, their home landing stage. With much threshing from the paddles and roars from the struggling engines, the little steamer edged to the jetty and, with a final triumphant blast, subsided against its edge.

The jetty was located at the eastern edge of the town, which sprawled along the banks of the Shire River, very wide at this point and home to the docks which handled the paddle steamer traffic to and from Lake Nyasa northwards, and the sea ports in Portuguese Africa. It was throbbing with colour and noise. Scores of locals had come to watch the entertainment, passengers were waiting to board and stevedores were standing beside crates and containers of all descriptions, which they were about to load. Ludwig and his men wheeled the motorcycles down the ramp and onto the jetty, threading their way through the good-natured, noisy crowd. The girls collected the very few bits and pieces that they had in the cabin and joined the men on the jetty. Ludwig decided who should ride with whom and, the scene at Blantyre still fresh in his mind, ensured that Paulina would be riding with him. With that hurdle overcome, and Paulina sitting smugly in the sidecar beside him, soon they were riding in a cloud of dust down the wide tree-lined avenue that was the main street of the port town of Fort Johnston.

Fort Johnston was a pretty little town, particularly now, when rainfall was plentiful and plants drank their fill. Towering jacaranda trees laden with blue bell-shaped flowers alternated with flamboyant trees, called thus because of their long hanging clusters of scarlet blossoms. They lined the edge of the main roads, strewing the sidewalk with the blossoms they scattered with each little breeze. In the brilliant sunshine and under cloudless blue skies, the colours were striking against the backdrop of the hard-packed earth road and, a short distance away, the lines of white, rickety shops, with their chaotic stocks spilling onto their verandas.

The Fort's wide, straight roads reflected its military origins; it was one of several that had been built as one of the measures by the British to curb the rampant slave trading that was taking place in central Africa, despite the official abolition of slavery. They were originally manned by Sikh and Zanzibari soldiers, who patrolled and fought on the slave routes until the trade in human cargo decreased or sought other, less policed routes; then the military function of the forts gave way to a thriving economic environment. Since Indian foremen and labourers had been imported during the late part of the last century to advise and work on the railway, which was slowly inching into hitherto inaccessible parts of the country, small shops were springing up like mushrooms all over the southern and central regions. The Indians had been quick to spot the market for tinned foodstuffs and household goods and, by dint of hard work and existing on next to nothing while they found their feet, were fast becoming indispensable to the population and economy of the outlying areas.

The girls beamed as they roared past Ludwig's business premises, proudly signposted as "Deuss and Kahn – Importers and Exporters". From the shady veranda Mr Mussa, the *capitao* or shop manager waved, a big smile creasing his plump, shining black face. He wore his usual garb, as did all the Muslim men, of long flowing white robes known as *nkhanjos*, and a fez perched precariously on the top of his head.

"Hello, Mr Mussa," shouted the girls.

Ludwig employed Muslim men in his shops all the way from Fort Johnston to Beira in Portuguese East Africa. He trained them up to become managers and, after a few years, gave them the funds to go and open up their own shops in outlying districts.

"You know, Ludwig," his close friend Alfred Stanley had commented recently, "if you carry on training and encouraging these men to spread out and start their own businesses, you are going to be responsible, single-handed, for the spread of Islam in Central Africa!"

Ludwig smiled. It was, he knew, a true word spoken in jest.

"I am glad to be of some positive influence," he had replied. "They are a good people and I have the utmost respect for them. It is little enough I do for them after the years of faithful service they have given me."

A block away and parallel to the main street was a similar, albeit much quieter road and here, on the corner and occupying an acre plot, was the Deuss residence.

From the road it seemed very quiet, none of its inhabitants visible. The property was surrounded by a brick wall interspersed with metal railings; an opening at the front led to a circular driveway which wound around a garden of palm trees, yuccas and sisal plants, interspersed with beds bursting with a riot of colour: cannas, zinnias, dahlias.

The girls' excitement mounted as they turned left into their drive. A short distance more along the circular drive and they were home. The procession drew up at the ornately bricked flight of steps at the front and by the time they had climbed out of the sidecars, Sondo and Tanteni, their two large dogs of indeterminate parentage, had come around the house and hurled themselves at their mistresses. They did so, first out of habit, then out of recognition, ecstatically jumping on them and trying to lick their faces.

"Down, Sondo. Down, Tanteni," ordered the girls, trying to pat the animals whilst disengaging themselves from their heavy caresses.

"There, girl. There, Sondo," they soothed as the dogs slowly calmed down.

Berta raced up the front steps calling for her mother, "Mayi! Mayi!" she called. Mother. When referring to her, they called her A Mayi, a respectful term for The Mother.

By now Mataya, A Mayi's shadow and faithful servant, had excitedly called her mistress who came down the front steps of the house, arms held out in welcome. The girls threw themselves into those dear and familiar arms, all talking at once, until at last their mother pleaded, "My children, let's go and sit down and then I can hear what you are trying to tell me!"

She spoke to them in the Chisena language and they responded in that language. They were equally at home with Chinyanja, the language of southern Nyasaland and, of course, they were fluent in both French and English.

On the cool veranda there were comfortable chairs with colourful, plump cushions and, in addition, the servants had laid out intricately patterned circular straw mats. Victoria sank gracefully onto one of the mats, tucking her legs to the side, and the girls sat around her to tell her about the trauma of the past few days. A warm, soft, fluffy presence slid in between them and they all stroked their gently purring cat, Mpaka, as they told their mother of the distressing events they had so recently experienced.

"Why aren't you sitting on the chairs, Victoria?" asked Ludwig, as he finally came up the stairs a half-hour later, having sent Aleki to the servants' quarters at the rear of the house for refreshment and rest before he went home.

Victoria glanced up, her attention diverted briefly from the children. She smiled. "Ludwiki, you know that I prefer to sit on the mats when I am chatting to the children." Her tone was gentle but there was a flicker of impatience in her eyes.

Ludwig paused and opened his mouth as if to say something further, but decided against it and walked to one of the chairs, where he stretched out comfortably. He turned then and smiled as he looked at his wife, her daughters around her, the four most important women in his life, happy together and wondering about how long it would take to rebuild the school, so that the girls could resume their education.

That evening, Ludwig announced that he would be able to go on the big game hunting trip that he had planned some time before. When the political uprising had erupted, he had wondered whether it would be safe to head for the bush, but it seemed that the government forces had taken control of the situation and that it was now only a matter of time before Chilembwe was apprehended and the incident assigned to the history books.

"One very good piece of news," he told his avidly listening family, "is that Chilembwe has sent the kidnapped wives and families of the murdered men back to their homes."

He told Victoria what he had learnt about the end of the uprising and continued thoughtfully: "You know, I can't help but have sympathy with the man. I can see what he wanted for his country. It is just so unfortunate that he chose violence as the way forward."

Victoria snorted: "And you think that anyone would have listened if he had gone the peaceful way? I can't imagine that!"

"You're probably right," agreed Ludwig, pensively.

"But," continued Victoria, "I cannot tell you how relieved I am about the families being reunited. I found the situation extremely distressing."

The family was sitting on the veranda at that quiet time of the day when stillness was descending on the little town. They had had supper and were feeling comfortably full. As a family they had a plentiful and healthy diet, most of it supplied by their own little farm. The pressure lamps hissed gently in the sitting room behind them, sending a warm pearly glow to where they sat, and the crickets took up their positions in the garden and shrilled their evensong. It was very warm. The heavy rains, which fell regularly at midday, had moistened the earth and brought a bit of cool, but this had long since vanished.

They spoke in low voices, relaxed in the intimacy of their evening gathering. Every now and then there would be a sharp slap as one of them squashed a mosquito that had alighted on a bare limb to drill for its evening meal.

"So," concluded Ludwig, "I shall be going hunting any day now."

"Hunting! Can we come, Papa?" pleaded Elsa and Berta without, it has to be said, much hope.

"Of course not, my dears," responded Papa, as he went to get his guns, brushes and cleaning oils. Returning, he sat busily oiling his guns, a shotgun and two rifles. The smell of gun oil assailed their nostrils.

"Uuum. I love that smell," said Berta, eyes closed as she sniffed appreciatively.

"Why not?" she asked after her brief distraction.

"Why not what?" asked her father.

"You know. Why can't we come with you?"

"It's too dangerous and it would be too exhausting for you – as I have told you before."

"But…" started Elsa, only to be silenced by a stern look from Ludwig.

He turned to Victoria and explained to her what it was the girls were asking. Paulina moved even closer to A Mayi and said, sanctimoniously, "I prefer to stay with A Mayi, Papa, and learn about cooking and things about the house."

She ignored the glares in her direction by her sisters.

"Where are you planning to go?" Victoria asked her husband.

The language had turned to Chisena.

"Into Mozambique," he replied. "I hear that the elephant are plentiful there at the moment and they are damaging the village gardens, in particular one rogue bull. If we don't do something there will be no food for the villagers in the winter."

"Elsa, Berta," admonished A Mayi, as she turned to the girls. "You know that it is not possible for the two of you to walk such long distances – imagine a week of walking from dawn to dusk – and it would be very difficult for Papa to have to watch out for you as well as to stalk and kill the game."

"Well," said Elsa, coming as close to a sulk as her pragmatic and even temperament allowed her. "I am sure that if Richard were here, he would be allowed to go."

Richard was the only son and the eldest in the family. He was at present finishing his education in South Africa.

"Of course he would," exclaimed Papa. "He's twenty-one years old, bigger than I am, and very fit. And he's a man."

"Wish I were a man," mumbled Elsa under her breath, but not low enough for Victoria's keen ears to miss it. She laughed.

"Silly girl!" she said. "You'd hate going hunting. Walking for hours every day, not having proper baths and washing in rivers where crocodiles could be lurking, checking in your camp beds to make sure that no spiders or snakes have crawled in…"

She was interrupted by two shrieks. The argument had been won. The girls had decided that to go on the hunting trip with their father was perhaps not such a good idea.

CHAPTER NINE

Two days later, early in the morning, the family was awakened by the sound of unusual activity in the big walled garden behind the house. Berta was the first of the children to throw on whatever clothes she could put her hands on and race out to see what was happening.

As she ran out into the back yard she breathed in the cool, crisp morning air, and then breathed in again as she felt its crystal freshness invigorate and freshen her. The dew, which lay abundant and sparkling on the grass, caught her eye and she walked heavily over it, imagining herself as some brooding giant, watching out for his prey as he prowled around, leaving his large footprints on the grass. She felt the magic of the early mornings in this part of Africa, the air fresh and cool, like a caress against the skin. The sky above her was still dark and then deep crimson where it fell to touch the earth. There it hovered to meet the sun as it slid over the hills on its journey upwards to full daylight. The raucous birdsong made her smile; every bird and fowl sang a boisterous ode to the coming of a new day.

The cocks were crowing, heads held high and chests puffed out as Berta greeted the house servants, who were already bustling about their morning duties. She spotted Ludwig crouching beside a large number of packages of all shapes and sizes, which lay on the ground in a chaotic fashion. On the left was a mound of camping equipment, which included everything from a stack of folded tents to little stoves, kitchen utensils, bags of rice and tins of corned beef.

She ran across to him. "Good morning, Papa!"

Ludwig turned to smile at her and greet her, but he was clearly absorbed in what he was doing, and she had to contain her questions. She walked away to find something else to do. She heard him address Aleki.

"There seems to be a lot of *katundu*, Aleki," said Ludwig, as he gestured to the baggage.

"Yes, *bwana*," acquiesced Aleki. "It is everything that you ordered."

A little distance away fifteen African men squatted, clad only in loin cloths and puffing away at little misshapen cigarettes. Half were slaves, taken away from their duties in the fields especially for the hunt. The other half had been employed specifically for the hunt. Two senior huntsmen and a gun bearer sat slightly apart. All talked amongst themselves desultorily while they awaited their orders.

Ludwig walked around checking off items against a list in his hand. He was dressed for the hunt, in beige cotton shorts and a matching short-sleeved jacket. Despite the heat he was wearing puttees and sturdy walking shoes. Beside him was Aleki, similarly clothed but wearing sandals.

"The drinks, Aleki. I don't see them," said Ludwig, pencil poised. The drinks were of crucial importance. The water in the rivers and streams was dangerous, likely to be infected by bilharzia, a water dwelling bacterium which burrowed through the skin and was able to cause serious damage to the urinary system and the liver if left untreated for a long time. At home, there were large earthenware filters into which boiled water was poured, thence to be filtered very slowly and become totally safe for consumption. In the bush, water would be boiled and then cooled, but it was always a good plan to have some soft drinks handy in case a circumstance arose where they found themselves far from drinkable water. Aleki lifted a pile of tent poles and unearthed six cases of lemonade, filtered water and soda water.

A grunt of satisfaction came from Ludwig and the inventory check continued: "Good!"

Elsa and Paulina now joined the group and walked around sedately inspecting the proceedings. Berta, by contrast, skipped around and asked endless questions. Ludwig, however, was not to be distracted, and she got such short responses from him that she gave up and wandered down the back yard to inspect the household animals. The older girls browsed cursorily before deciding to go back upstairs and get washed and properly dressed.

It was common for big houses to have very large back yards, or compounds as they were called, measuring from a hundred square yards or less to a half acre, depending on the size of the house, and enclosed by a six-foot brick wall. At the far end there would be a line of rooms, built against the wall, to house the servants, the slaves and their families. There would also be a communal cooking room and bath house. The area in between depended on the owner's lifestyle and interests. In the case of the Deuss family, it was a busy, warm place. At the back wall was a friendly teeming expanse of yard where the servants' babies, toddlers and young children played outside their homes. Running around amongst them were the chickens and any other animals that they chose to rear.

Toward the centre were the family chickens, turkeys and ducks, complete with a green smelly pond, geese, a couple of hand-reared goats (whose mother had died in childbirth) and a little deer brought in by native hunters who had killed the mother for meat and could make more out of selling the young. Paulina had a pronounced maternal streak and treated the deer and the goats as though they were babies, feeding them with a baby's bottle and generally nurturing them until the goats could return to the herd and the deer could be returned to the wild.

Against a side wall were the chicken coops, where the hens nested and slept at night, enclosed in a little yard fenced by chicken wire. This was next to useless because the chickens simply took a running jump at it and sailed over, amidst much squawking and noisy flapping of wings. Their wing feathers were routinely clipped, but the effect did not last for long.

Adjoining the kitchen was the dairy, which was of particular interest to Berta since, at times, she was allowed to help mould the butter. In this room the separator was kept to separate the cream from the milk; at the other side of the room was the churn where the butter was made. Beside it was a long table with wooden moulds into which the butter would be pressed and then turned out in the shape of bricks. It was then wrapped in greaseproof paper and either sold to the inhabitants of the town or kept for the family's use.

Close to the back veranda, in the shade of a large, heavily leaved mango tree, the two dogs were tethered and, just out of their reach, was a pole with a hut on top, to which was tethered the family's pet monkey, Jesse. Jesse was a capricious baboon who could be very affectionate at times. However, she had a penchant for human males and was an incorrigible flirt. When one of the men in the family approached, she would promptly bite the nearest female, usually Berta, who seemed permanently to have bite marks on her arms.

Berta now headed straight for the latest newcomer to the community. He was a chubby ten-month-old and was the first son of Njoka, the kitchen boy, whose job in the house was to assist the cook preparing the food. Njoka was at work in the house but Maria, his wife, was sitting on a mat in front of their room, propping up the baby in his first efforts to sit upright.

The older children of the other servants were playing with cars they had made out of bamboo pieces and wire. They smiled shyly and greeted Berta as she approached.

"*Moni, moni,*" she replied, waving and giving the timeless greeting.

"Oh, Maria, how the baby has grown!" she continued as she rushed toward the mother and child.

Maria was pleased.

"*Moni, Donna.*" She smiled, looking up as Berta approached; it was common to greet one's employers with this term, which meant 'madam'. She was a pretty girl, not much more than sixteen years of age, if that. Her skin was the colour of dark chocolate and gleamed with health and the help of a little Vaseline petroleum jelly, a favourite amongst the African girls.

Berta sat down beside them and held her arms out to the baby. "Come," she said to him in Chichewa. "*Bwera!*"

But he pressed his arms to his fat little chest and drew away from her, looking pleadingly at his mother. The girls laughed and Berta satisfied herself with giving him a little tickle on what she called his delicious, squidgy tummy, at which he laughed delightedly.

Just then, Berta heard a change in the sounds coming from the house. She turned to look and saw that the local District Collector, Carrain, had just entered the yard from the side gate. From snippets that she had heard she knew that there was a tension between this man and her father; she wondered why. What was it all about?

CHAPTER TEN

Ludwig was pleased with the way Aleki had collected the provisions that were needed for the forthcoming big game hunt. As the two men inched their way around the medley of baggage that they would be taking with them he thought that he could not have done better at assembling this himself. The itemised list was being ticked off steadily; the few items that were not already there had been ordered and would be collected or delivered in the course of the day.

Another thought occurred to him and he noted down that he needed Victoria to select one of her kitchen assistants to accompany them as cook, together with an assistant of his own.

Ludwig did not look up immediately when the door at the entrance of the back compound opened and shut noisily, but finished the note he was writing before glancing sideways. He tensed visibly when he perceived the man walking towards him to be Carrain, the District Collector, or D.C. as this branch of the foreign office was called. He was a strange-looking man. Dressed always in immaculate white shirt and shorts, he was slightly taller than average and wiry, with thin, bandy legs. He did not tan well and his sharp-featured face wore a permanent look of lobster-hued sun irritation. His walrus moustache did not help to alleviate the overall weasely impression that he gave.

As he approached Ludwig his face was set in familiar lines of disapproval. Ludwig, for his part, was always meticulously polite to him, although he did refer to him when discussing him with the family as "that hyena", a heavy insult in a land where the hyena epitomised all that was cowardly and devious.

"Morning," announced the D.C. in clipped, ultra-patriotic tones.

"Good morning," replied Ludwig, a questioning lilt in his voice, his pencil hovering above his list.

Carrain came straight to the point: "Going hunting again, are you?" he asked, in his nasal, high-pitched voice.

"Yes," agreed Ludwig, indicating with a wave of his hand the equipment that lay around them.

"Guns licensed and in order, then?" Carrain asked abruptly.

"Of course," replied Ludwig.

"Going far?"

"I'm not certain yet. It depends on a number of things."

"When do you plan to return?"

Ludwig put the list and the pencil into his breast pocket and turned to give his whole attention to his inquisitor.

"Is there a point to all these questions?" he asked, very quietly.

"I just like to know. I believe your pals are about to storm Karonga from their territory in Tanganyika."

"My pals?" Ludwig's voice was very quiet.

"The Germans," sneered Carrain.

"As you know very well, I am Swiss."

"German yesterday, Swiss today. What's the difference?"

Ludwig's face was stony with anger. He went and stood very close to Carrain. "I think you should go now."

"Don't you threaten me," spluttered the official, looking down into Ludwig's face, but backing off hastily. "I'm going, all right. But I'm watching you and don't you forget it."

And with that, he turned and left by the side gate.

Without a word, Ludwig strode up the back steps and onto the back veranda, where A Mayi was sitting and discussing with the cook what he should cook for lunch and supper. It was a large veranda and housed the food safe and cheese cupboard along the house wall, as well as the buckets, bowls and raffia moulds for the cheese making. In the centre was a low table on a large rush mat surrounded by four comfortable wooden armchairs with bright cushions. At the far end were doors leading to the kitchen and pantry. The whole was gauzed in against the flies and mosquitoes. At A Mayi's feet sat Mataya, her former slave, legs tucked up beneath her, ready to do her least bidding. Mataya knew that she was legally no longer a slave, but absolutely refused to leave her mistress.

"Ee," she would say emphatically. "And where would I go? Does the fish leave the water? Does the bird leave the sky? No! And I will not leave mama!" She used the affectionate term for a loved older acquaintance or better.

Ludwig sat down heavily in a chair, elbows resting on the arms of the chair, fingertips touching, his face scowling and staring at the floor.

A Mayi and Edisoni stopped their conversation and looked at him in surprise; then A Mayi dismissed the cook.

"Start the roast now and we'll talk about the rest later," she said, her eyes on her husband. At any rate, she would never have looked a servant in the eye; inferiors were never looked upon eye-to-eye unless from above, through hooded eyes.

Edisoni padded away, leaving a silence behind him. The silence lasted quite a while but A Mayi would never have considered breaking it. Her husband was clearly distressed and he would speak when he was ready.

Eventually he spoke: "Carrain was here," he said.

"Yes, I saw," responded A Mayi, quietly.

"He is getting worse. Today he almost accused me directly of being a spy."

"Eh-eh! A spy," she mused. "For whom?"

"The Germans. He cannot forget that our family was German in the last century, before we emigrated to Switzerland and adopted Swiss nationality."

"But Ludwiki, does it matter what he thinks? We know the truth, so his lies cannot hurt us." Victoria had the charming African inability to pronounce certain consonants, coupled with the necessity to end every possible name with 'i'.

Ludwig looked at his wife, her big brown eyes in a polished ebony face gazing at him earnestly. The love he felt for her was in his face as he stroked her cheek gently with his forefinger.

"Ah, my precious Victoria. Who knows what he can do? Who knows, indeed."

"Maybe," she responded anxiously, "we could get some *mankhwala* from the African doctor. This medicine will make him have loving thoughts towards you."

The tension broke. Ludwig laughed out loud. "Oh, I hope not," he chuckled. "I can't stand the man as he is normally. What on earth would I do if he decided to love me?"

Victoria laughed, happy that she had made her man feel better. She smiled up at him as he got up from his chair and started for the door.

"I'd better get back to work," he said. "Love me, indeed." And he chuckled all the way down the steps.

The deep unease that he felt, though, could not be dismissed so easily. The rank of D.C. was at the lowest point of the hierarchy, barring only the Assistant D.C., or the A.D.C. as he was known. The position had started off as simply a collector of taxes but, since 1905, the role had slowly developed and expanded to be the representative of the government amongst the people, mainly farmers. New recruits were now receiving training for the post and were altogether a different breed from the originals like Carrain. The problem, as Ludwig saw it, was that these men had the ear of officials up the line. And who knew, he mused, what this vitriolic little man could think up to prejudice authorities already involved in a war and anxious about the safety of its borders.

He returned to the back yard, where the bustle recommenced; packs were moved around, the inventory was completed and each of the bearers was assigned a load, usually about sixty pounds.

The bearers were told to report to the house at five o'clock the following morning and were then dismissed. Those who had been hired for the hunting trip went back to their homes, and the permanent staff dispersed to carry out their normal duties.

By now it was seven o'clock in the morning, late by African standards, so Ludwig had a quick cup of coffee and headed into town to the shop. The family sat down to a hearty breakfast of fruit and cereal, followed by scrambled eggs and tomatoes and toast. Fruit was always plentiful. Mangoes, avocado pears and bananas grew wild as well as being cultivated in the gardens. The milk was brought to the house by Moses, the livestock overseer, as soon as milking was completed, at about six o'clock in the morning. The fresh cream would follow later when it had been separated in the dairy.

In the cool of the morning, when most of the mosquitoes had retired, sated after a night's gorging, Victoria suggested to her daughters that they make their way to the little farm where Victoria would examine the neat rows of vegetables, choose some for the day's consumption and give orders to the gardeners for the digging, weeding and planting that should take place that day. Ludwig had decided some years previously to start the small farm out of town, where Victoria supervised an army of gardeners who supplied the family and their friends with fruit and vegetables all year round.

Edisoni called for the *machila* bearers and, as they drew up at the bottom of the steps off the back veranda, Victoria stepped in with much scolding of the hapless men who, it seemed, were not holding it properly. The girls wheeled out their bicycles and the little entourage started off.

The vegetable garden formed a corner of a large acreage of pasture where their hundred or so head of cattle grazed and where pig pens housed a score or more of pigs, also bred for the table. A herd of about fifty sheep and goats roamed the pastures alongside the cows; these supplied the family with milk and cheese as well as meat. Away from the animals at the opposite corner of the land were Ludwig's bee hives. He had started these as an experiment and had become very involved in them. Fresh honey from bees that fed on wild flowers had now become a staple part of their diet. The beeswax he exported.

At the far end of the area were the cattle kraals. These were securely built and fenced and kept the animals safe during the night. A little hut on the edge was for the night watchmen, who would keep the fires going all night and watch out for predators.

Beyond could be seen several acres of rows of trees; Victoria turned to Elsa, her arm pointing in their direction. "Do you notice how the coffee trees have grown? They're doing very well. Papa hopes that by next year they will have started producing coffee beans."

Elsa smiled and shook her head. "Isn't he amazing, Mayi? Always starting something new and always successful."

The day's orders having been given, the little group headed back for home, anxious to get back indoors before the sun was overhead and uncomfortably hot. They entered by the side gate and, as they walked up the back steps, Berta spotted movement in the dairy. In a trice, she was there in the hope that butter was being churned and if so, of being allowed to mould some of it. Yes, she was just in time.

The big metal churn was standing beside a table and from it dribbled the remains of the buttermilk which remained, after the cream had been turned around at speed by pushing the handle at the side of the churn. From the smooth cream that had been poured in the opening at the top there remained the solid mass of butter and the liquid that was let out through a hole in the bottom of the churn. The buttermilk would be fed to the dogs, the pigs and indeed, to anything that needed fattening up.

"May I please, Moses?" she asked him breathlessly, eyeing the lump of fresh butter he was holding between the two little paddles in his hands.

"Of course, little madam," he responded, smiling, and he handed over the mould and pusher.

Victoria popped her head around the door. "Moses, is it all right for Berta to interfere with your work? Are you in a hurry to do anything else?" She spoke in Chichewa, the native tongue of the man.

"Ah, no, A Mayi," he replied, smiling broadly. "The milking is done, the butter is made and the cows and goats are grazing. I have to mend the kraals and the fences, but it doesn't matter if I delay a few minutes."

"You heard, Berta," said A Mayi, lapsing into Chisena. "A few minutes, Moses said."

"Yes, Mayi," responded Berta, too busy to do more than glance up briefly.

When she was finished slapping the butter and forcing it into the mould she proudly took the wrapped pound of butter that she had formed to show A Mayi and her sisters. It was duly admired by A Mayi and Elsa, but a muttered comment from Paulina that it was "only a silly lump of butter" was unfortunately heard by an outraged Berta. A Mayi managed to nip the inevitable fight in the bud by suggesting that Berta put her butter in the kitchen fridge. Fortunately, she was happy to visit the kitchens, since she was hungry, and with a final glower at Paulina she ran off to find out what was being prepared for lunch.

The kitchens were an important feature of the house. In the nearer one, used for cleaner tasks, was a gleaming new Dover stove, which was fed by coal and had an art to gauging how much coal to put in to get the desired heat on the top burners and in the oven. One servant, the kitchen boy, was allocated to keep this clean and help Edisoni, the cook, with the food preparation and washing up. The back kitchen, which was used for messier jobs, had a series of Primus stoves on a table. They were used primarily for frying tasks, whose smell had to be kept out of the rest of the house, and there was a large stone sink for washing pots and pans. Another kitchen boy was responsible for the cleanliness of this kitchen. Leading from the front kitchen was a pantry where all manner of stocks of food and ingredients were kept. This was kept locked because staples like sugar and tea were apt to be consumed in quantities far greater than the sum of the inhabitants' consumption.

The butter having been safely put away, and Berta mollified by the news that lunch was roast duck, the rest of the day unwound at a gentle pace; the girls found much to do in their lively environment.

Elsa and Berta headed for book shelves in the sitting room: they loved reading and so there was always time for that too. For Paulina the favourite pastime was embroidery, and she was often to be found bent over a piece of work, always exquisitely done.

"Why do you take so much trouble over it?" challenged Berta one day, as Paulina undid a section of the embroidery for the third time.

"Because I want it to look beautiful and to be perfect," was the reply.

"But no one is going to see your mistake, Paulina. It's not noticeable."

"Yes, it is," was the retort. And she scowled. Paulina was good at scowling; her plain face would fall into discontented lines. She was very much a 'mummy's girl', always carrying a tale or two to A Mayi, who would hug her and try to talk her out of her complaint. Unlike the other two, who were pretty little girls, she was a plain child and her complaining nature did nothing to improve her looks.

That night Ludwig said his goodbyes to his family, giving each of his girls a hug and a kiss. As always and unless it made Victoria uncomfortable, he spoke to them in French or English.

"Don't wake up to see us off," he said. "We shall be leaving very early, before dawn."

"When will you be back, Papa?" asked Elsa, holding on to his hand.

"A week to ten days, no more," he promised.

Berta felt a frisson of foreboding and ran up to him, throwing her arms around him.

"Papa, please be careful," she cried. "I don't want you to die or get badly hurt by an elephant." She burrowed her head into his chest.

"Promise you'll come back to us!" her muffled voice said.

He held her close.

"Of course I promise, silly," he said, kissing the top of her head. "Off to bed with you now."

In a chorus of, "Goodnight Mayi, Goodnight Papa," the girls trooped to their bedrooms, where their little night lights had been lit and their mosquito nets let down and securely tucked in. They slid into their beds through the opening in the net, careful to shut it quickly behind them and tuck the ends in again. A mosquito or two in the net could mean a disturbed night's sleep, not to mention swelling from the bites and the possibility of contracting malaria.

The night sounds were familiar and soothing. Crickets in the garden chirped their moonlight serenade and the frogs in the pond croaked deep in their bellies, relieved to have some time to themselves without sharp beaks trying to lance them. Sondo and Tanteni barked at any passers-by who dared to come too close to the gates and the house servants' voices rose and fell as they squatted around their fire eating their evening meal, the day's work over.

The three girls were soon soundly asleep.

CHAPTER ELEVEN

Ludwig and his camp were ready to leave in the pitch pre-dawn darkness, while his family slumbered peacefully in the quiet house. Only Victoria heard him leaving; she drowsily wished him good hunting before subsiding once again into the softness of their bed.

He kissed her and stroked her cheek. *"Tsalani bwino,"* he whispered with a smile, amused at her efforts to open her eyes. Stay well.

"Jumo will take care of everything while I'm away, but ask Dietrich if you need help of any sort," he whispered.

She nodded sleepily.

He slipped downstairs to the back of the house, where Aleki and all the bearers waited. As he emerged from the house they rose and started to position their loads onto their heads.

Ludwig walked across to Aleki, who was helping one of the bearers to stabilise his load.

"Aleki, Good morning. Everyone here yet?"

"Yes, *bwana*. We are waiting for you."

Ludwig peered under the load Aleki was trying to secure.

"Is there a cushion under there, Aleki?" he asked. They carried a supply of round cushion head supports for the bearers which, in appearance, were like very large doughnuts made of rushes. They were put on the head first and on top of them went the loads, thus protecting the bearers' heads from discomfort from the loads that they were carrying.

"Sure, *bwana*," was the response. A few further adjustments and the bearer relaxed and straightened up with a smile.

Ludwig nodded and walked around the bearers, mentally ticking off items that they were carrying. Although he was wearing a linen jacket and matching shorts, safari gear, he shivered slightly in the early morning chill. He rammed his floppy felt hat onto this head and ran his fingers around the tops of his puttees to ensure that he had wound them around his legs securely, before running lightly back into the house and to the gun rack in the hall.

He swiftly took down two rifles, both Mausers, a .450 for the elephant and a .3030 for smaller game. Next, he reached out for a shotgun for wild fowl. He had oiled these carefully two nights before and, after a moment's thought, pulled open a drawer and extracted a pistol. Finally, he slipped a pair of binoculars around his neck and slung a cartridge belt around his waist. He bent and reached into a small cupboard under the rifle rack and took out several boxes of ammunition. It took minutes to fill his cartridge belt.

Arms full, he walked carefully back outside and down the steps. Kalulu, his gun bearer, immediately came forward and together they loaded the guns and ammunition into a sack-like receptacle that hung on the bearer's back, suspended from two broad straps which went around the wearer's arms. Two hunters who doubled as scouts and trackers, but also had provisions to carry, stood close by and watched with interest.

The hunting gear having been taken care of, Ludwig then looked around for his personal bearer, Chilombwe, who would stay close and carried a change of clothes, several bottles of filtered water and numerous packets of biscuits. Aleki was just completing the loading of his back sack.

Ludwig gave a final glance at the gathering. "OK, Aleki," he called softly. "Let's go."

Aleki stood to attention with a broad smile. "Yes, sir!" Then he turned to the long line of bearers, said a few words to them and stood aside as they filed past and out of the entrance to the back compound of the house.

From the information that he had received, Ludwig was fairly certain that they should be heading in a north-easterly direction into Mozambique and so, with Aleki at his side, he strode away to reach the front of the line and lead the way from there. He had hunted in these parts before and was confident of finding their target without any difficulty.

The first hint of dawn was faintly lighting the sky as the procession wound its way through the town. There were quite a lot of people about despite the early hour, mainly workers coming in from the villages to start work at six. This was normal in hot weather stations like Fort Johnston, where the summer heat made it impossible to work long hours. The day started at six, with breakfast at seven-thirty to eight, and all offices closed down at two o'clock in the afternoon.

Ludwig felt as though he was on holiday. Walking briskly away from the office in the early morning cool, looking forward to some hunting and not having to think about coming back to work for at least ten days, made him feel good, young and strong. This was the life!

Twenty minutes later the men turned off the main road and onto the much narrower track leading out into the bush.

Despite the recent and continuing rains the terrain never looked lush in this part of the country. It was rocky, sandy ground, quietly undulating and mainly populated by thorn trees, baobabs, palm and mango trees and many indigenous patches of shrub. Its beauty was in its clean sparse lines, broken here and there by little settlements where a jumble of thatched huts sought shelter under the luxuriant foliage of the mango trees. Always there would be a stream of sweet rippling water nearby, visible from afar because of the reeds and grasses that grew along its banks. Encircling the whole were the villagers' gardens, where they toiled in the heat to produce maize, cassava, potatoes, beans and groundnuts. In a good year, there would be enough to feed the family and leave a surplus with which to trade, but the last few years had been hard, drought alternating with heavy, continuous downpours, both of which annihilated the crops.

Things were looking good, thought Ludwig, as they passed village after village with healthy, thriving gardens around them. He thought he might offer to buy provisions if they came upon a particularly well-stocked garden. It would be easy money for the villagers, who would then not have to carry the produce to town for sale.

As the sun rose higher in the sky, breaks were called more often to relieve the perspiring bearers, and the party walked from stream to stream, where they could be sure of being able to drink their fill. Ludwig looked on enviously as the men drank greedily of the clear, sparkling water, squatting by the water's edge, hands cupping and lifting rapidly. They were used to it, he reflected. If he tried to do the same he would probably be incapacitated by bowel problems within two days, as had happened to so many unwary Europeans in the past. He sighed and signalled for his bearer to bring him his filtered water.

When the sun was fully overhead, and it became difficult to move with heavy loads in the heat, Ludwig and the scouts went ahead to look out for a suitable place with shade and access to water. They walked up a small hillock sprouting with new green pasture grass amongst the gnarled, dry stumps of yesteryear and, as they descended the other side saw, about a mile distant, a cluster of acacia and mango. Some twenty yards to the right was the tell-tale line of reeds and tall green grasses; a stream. Ludwig went back up the hillock and, catching the attention of the train approaching him, pointed to the spot they had discovered. An hour later, the entire party was in the comparative cool of the shaded area by the stream and Ludwig declared a stop for the day.

The bearers put down their loads thankfully and stretched. They were of average height, very slim and markedly sinewy. When necessary they could lope along under heavy weights for several hours without apparently tiring; until very recently the Nyasaland native men had provided the main means of transport for goods needed at the war front in Karonga, in the north. Motorised transport was very new indeed.

While camp was being set up under some acacia and mango trees and close to a stream, Ludwig, his gun bearer, Aleki and four bearers who doubled as scouts set off to bag some game for the pot. But first it was polite to visit the headman of the nearest village and explain their presence. The village was easy to spot, some half a mile away, and they set off towards it on a faint narrow track which indicated that they had animals, probably goats, and that this was their way to pasture.

As they approached they were spotted by a group of young children, who ran towards them, curious and excited. Ludwig's efforts to strike up a conversation with them were met with heads averted and shy glances out of the corners of their eyes, but they consented to give monosyllabic responses to the other men.

"Will you show us where your headman lives?" asked Aleki.

The response was a chorus of "*Inde, inde*", yes, yes, and they danced ahead, shrill excited voices filling the still, hot air.

As they approached the village a cluster of young mothers ran up and tugged their children away from the party. They were clearly very agitated, scolding the children and landing some telling smacks on their heads. Some of the younger ones started to wail loudly; others bit their lips and tried not to cry.

"What's wrong?" Ludwig asked Aleki in some bewilderment.

"Their mothers are afraid of the *chifuamba*, the slave traders. The children have been told not to speak to strangers outside the village and they are being scolded for talking to us."

Ludwig was in full sympathy with the women. "I see," he said. "The mothers are quite right and perhaps we should have thought of that before we started trying to befriend the little ones."

His thoughts flew to his little Berta and how she had only recently overcome her fear of Muslim men. She had always hidden under the dining room table when they came to the house, and no amount of embarrassed coaxing from Ludwig would get her out. Probably, he reflected, it had had something to do with the dreaded Arab slave traders, with their long white robes; he wished that he had talked it over with her rather than being irritated.

They had by now reached the village and awaiting them was a young man who, after cordially greeting them, asked them to follow him to where the headman was waiting. They went as bidden and were taken to where a dignified, elderly man stood awaiting them at the entrance to a thatched hut that was considerably larger than the other huts around it. Courteous greetings were exchanged and hands shaken, right hand outstretched with the left loosely gripping the wrist of the right; this was a traditional greeting, where each man showed that he was not hiding a weapon in either hand.

Mats were brought out by the headman's women and the party was invited to sit down. They all sat down and a soft and gentle conversation in Chichewa ensued, where first the weather was commented on, then its effects on the crops and then concern was expressed about the war, and the fact that so many young men had been called up was lamented upon.

Ludwig was patient because he knew that this was the way that things were done. It was impolite to get straight to business; one talked of generalities first or, if the parties were acquainted, news of their respective families was exchanged. But finally, Ludwig found an opening as the headman told of how the extreme weather in the past few years had caused crop failure.

"And now," commiserated Ludwig, "there is an elephant that is also causing damage to the crops."

The headman became animated: "Yes, I hear it is terrible," he said. "It is bad enough that the herd is feeding on the crops but one of the elephants, a young rogue elephant, is causing wanton damage. Many villages are in serious trouble food-wise because of it."

"This is why we are here." Finally, an opportunity to state the reason for their visit. "We have been asked by the villagers to come and shoot the elephant."

The headman nodded. "That is very good, very good. Can we help you in any way?"

But Ludwig was able to assure him that, much as the offer was appreciated, they had come equipped.

Troubled by the mothers' reaction to their befriending the children of the village, Ludwig cautiously broached the subject to the headman. "I noticed that the people of the village were afraid of us when we first arrived." He looked questioningly at the headman, who shook his head gently and looked down. When he looked up again his eyes were troubled.

"Yes," he responded. "Although things are much better now there is still a great fear of the slave traders. Every now and then we hear of raids, entire villages taken away, and we are reminded that it is not over. We still have to be careful."

Ludwig commiserated gently with the Africans whilst keeping to himself the reflection that being careful would be of little or no avail if the village was targeted by the slavers.

Little remained now but to find out the exact whereabouts of the last village that had been savaged by the elephants and to offer the headman some of whatever game they bagged while they were out. The directions seemed clear enough and were given by the headman with much reference to the local topography. Hence, they knew that they were to look for signs such as an extraordinarily large baobab tree, a hillock with palm trees at its base, and a river which fishermen trawled in their dugout canoes.

With many expressions of respect and friendship, Ludwig and his men departed. There was no sign of the children.

Although it was the wrong time of the day for antelope, there were prolific numbers of guinea fowl and partridge and within an hour the hunting party had shot enough for their needs and those of the village. They started back for the camp with the birds tied to poles carried by the bearers. On the way, they stopped off briefly at the village to present the numerous birds to the headman, much to the delight of the villagers. The children reappeared, able at last to be friendly now that it had been established that the hunting party was indeed what it had said it was. Finally, wilting in the heat, and with the children's goodbyes ringing in their ears, they made their way back to what was home for the night.

Ludwig's camp bed had been set up under a tree, with a mosquito net suspended from a branch; beside it was his folding canvas chair. The natives had brought their own rolls of bedding, comprising a bamboo mat and a blanket: these would be laid on the ground later. It was fortunate that, during this season in the lowlands, regular midday torrential downpours were over and, on the first day, all the rain that fell was a slight shower that had the effect of cooling the hot ground for a few moments of relief.

Two wood fires were going and the cook and his assistant set to plucking and cleaning the birds. These were stewed and eaten with *nsima*, the native's staple diet of maize meal. For Ludwig there were potatoes to go with the meat and, when the meal was ready, he sat apart from the others to eat. He would have enjoyed Aleki's company but knew that embarrassment would spoil the meal for his manager. It would have been the first time that he had eaten with a white man, let alone his boss.

After lunch everyone relaxed. There would be no more travelling that day and several of the party sloped off to explore the neighbourhood. Ludwig called Aleki across and suggested that they hunt antelope in the late afternoon.

"We'll find them more easily at dusk and at dawn," he suggested.

Aleki concurred: "But we need to start walking early tomorrow so, yes, it is better that we go shooting this evening."

That agreed, Ludwig took the opportunity to make notes in his journal and then settled down to read. At half past four the cook brought tea and biscuits and by five, the hunters were ready to go.

As Ludwig said to Aleki, there was so much game, and all the animals were so relatively tame, it seemed heartless to shoot them. But he consoled himself with the thought that it was purely for the pot and, once it was clear that there was enough for the following day, the lifeless animals were strung up on poles and the party tramped back to the camp.

The cook was waiting and, once the animals had been skinned and cleaned, they were roasted on the waiting spits and left to dry overnight over the dying coals.

As darkness fell, paraffin lamps were lit, but not for long. The camp became a hive of activity as the bearers piled the provisions in the centre of the encampment and laid mats close together on the ground all around. Finally, they lit wood fires around the perimeter to discourage mosquitoes, hyenas and lions, while Ludwig designed a rota for two-hour shifts of guard duty.

This done, everyone but the guards on duty settled down to sleep under the stars; Ludwig, secluded in his tent, felt sleep elude him. As he lay on his camp bed his thoughts returned to the villagers they had visited that day, and he felt the familiar anger and frustration that people should still live in fear of being snatched by the slave traders.

A man of intelligence and with a keen mind, Ludwig had followed the debate on slavery, although resident in a country that was by and large apathetic. When he first arrived in Portuguese East Africa he had seen at first hand the extraordinary and intolerable plight of the people captured by the Arab slavers during their raids into the interior. Powerless to intervene against the armed might and numbers of the traders, as the missionaries had found before him, he had written to his father in Switzerland of the horrors he had witnessed.

... although I have read David Livingstone's accounts, nothing could have prepared me for the nightmarish apparition of the masses of filthy, thin, terrified men, women and children, staring ahead with sightless eyes as they waited, dumb with misery and the loss of hope, to be bought or transported on the death traps that are the slaving vessels. They stand, sit or lie in their own waste, not even allowed the dignity of relieving themselves in the bushes. These poor, inoffensive creatures are kidnapped each year by Arab and African slavers, brought to Nkhota Nkhota on the west of the lake shore and shipped across the lake into Mozambique.

The problem is that the demand for human stock is insatiable in East Africa, India, the West Indies and America. On the other hand, the supply of human cargo in the interior of the continent is apparently inexhaustible and this contributes to the carelessness with which the human cargo is transported. The slavers are wasteful because their supply is plentiful.

After the legal abolition of slavery, and once the human traffic across the lake had decreased, albeit slowly, it took many years for slaves to finally realise that they were free; many preferred to stay with their previous owners, in which case food and housing was substituted by a wage. This was what had happened in Ludwig's case. A dilemma arose when the previous owners could not afford to employ all the freed slaves and the slaves refused to leave. The general solution was to allow them to remain under the old enslaved conditions until time had worked a solution.

It would, however, take time, a long time, before the evil atmosphere of slave trading days was wiped from the atmosphere. Business was still brisk in Portuguese East Africa and the East; entire villages in the more remote areas were still disappearing, as well as the incautious lone traveller. The girls, when they were out on their own, walked warily and the sight of an Arab in his distinctive white robes, however innocent, was enough to terrify them.

And today, he reflected soberly, he had seen for himself how this evil still tainted even the remotest, most peaceful of people.

He tossed and turned some more then focused his mind on his mission. He must get some sleep. There was another long day ahead of them tomorrow. There was an elephant to be hunted.

CHAPTER TWELVE

The family missed Ludwig and counted the days to his return, but A Mayi saw to it that there was no undue pining.

"Stop moping," she scolded, as they asked her for the hundredth time when they could expect him back. She sent the girls off to the town, where there was much to see and do. They had been able to spend such a little time at home in the years since starting school that these days were precious, despite the tragic events that had made them possible.

Every year the girls spent only four weeks at home. Since the journey took one week by *machila*, the only time it was possible to come home was the annual summer holiday in December and half of January. Of the six weeks, two were spent travelling, leaving them with only four weeks at home. This was hard, not only for the girls, but also for Victoria and Ludwig. And so it had become customary for the couple to travel to the convent in Nguludi from Fort Johnston three times a year, at Easter, in July and in October. Two weeks were spent on the road and the week in between was spent enjoying the hospitality of the nuns at the convent, whilst seeing the girls at every possible opportunity.

So it was that, until the uprising had been quelled completely and the priests' house rebuilt, the girls were able to rediscover their beloved home and spend time with the people who formed the most important part of their young lives.

Many mornings were spent with the animals at the house and then at the little farm just out of town. An early start was needed because, by midday, the heat would be uncomfortable; it was wisest to be back home by eleven o'clock. February was at the tail-end of the summer season, with the heavy midday rainfall starting to abate and giving way to spontaneous heavy showers. An unfortunate side effect to this rainfall was that in these lowlands there was a plethora of places ideally suited to mosquito breeding – hot, wet, humid spots where the larvae could grow and multiply unchecked. At least the heavy rain meant that the roads were less dusty, if only for a few hours after the deluge and, to Berta, the heavy sweet smell of the thirsty earth embracing the rain was magical.

After lunch it was customary to have an afternoon rest. Victoria dozed peacefully on one of the sofas in the sitting room while Paulina sat close by, usually embroidering. Elsa and Berta preferred to lie down in their bedrooms and indulge in their love of reading. The house was quiet during this period; even the chickens seemed to need a rest and the back compound gently slumbered in the afternoon heat. The servants took the opportunity to go into town, where they could gaze at the shop wares and meet friends at the market.

The girls too enjoyed walking into the town itself where most of the shops, predominantly owned by Indians, lined the wide main avenue. Each shop had a wide front veranda the width of the building. On these verandas were displayed various wares, bicycles and household goods usually, and any remaining space was rented out to aspiring entrepreneurs.

Perhaps their favourite shop, after their father's of course, was the African Lakes Corporation, Mandala as it was popularly known, whose veranda housed a tailor with his treadle sewing machine. He sat facing the road, apparently oblivious to Berta's staring at his legs working like pistons to keep up the speed of the machine. His hands flew hither and thither, pushing and pulling the fabrics while he stitched the pieces together. On a bench behind him was a pile of fabrics awaiting their turn. To his right was a large wicker basket into which he tossed the completed items. On his left was another similar basket containing the scraps of material remaining from each job. Sitting perched at the edge of the veranda, legs dangling over the edge, were friends and acquaintances who took time off from their work to come and have a chat and pass the time of day. Every now and then the shop assistants, having no customers, would come out and join the others, their conversation punctuated by sharp sounds as they automatically slapped at the roving mosquitoes searching for their next meal.

"Why is it called Mandala?" Berta had asked Ludwig one day as they strolled to his shop. "Surely that means glasses?"

"Yes, you're right, my girl, it does," he responded and explained to her how the name had stuck.

"The Africans were fascinated by the first manager's glasses and promptly gave him and the company a new name!"

"Have they given you a name, Papa?" she asked.

"No, I don't think so," he replied, his green eyes twinkling. "If they have, I'm not sure that I want to know it. It might not be very complimentary!"

Berta looked up at him. "Oh no, Papa," she said. "They could only find good things to think about you."

Ludwig smiled and gave her a quick hug.

Outside Ludwig's premises was a shoe repairer. He sat on a bench at a rickety wooden table. This was covered by pieces of leather of all shapes and sizes, and the tools of his trade. Berta had often wondered how he found enough shoes to repair. Not many of the Africans wore shoes. She had spoken to Ludwig about it.

"Well, there are quite a few of us who do wear shoes, you know."

"But surely not enough to keep him busy?"

"Well, on our own, no. But don't forget that the steamboat calls regularly on its way to and from the lake, and they always bring a lot of work for him to do. He also makes belts, and harnesses for oxen ploughing the fields."

The market was an exciting place for young people and every now and then the girls joined Bensoni, the head house boy, on his daily shopping trip there. The day after Ludwig's departure, Elsa and Berta decided to do just that, when Bensoni told his mistress that he needed to go the market for supplies.

"Can we go too, Mayi?" was the enthusiastic cry from Elsa and Berta. Paulina preferred to stay at home and do something useful with A Mayi, as she put it, and so it was only Elsa and Berta who made their way down the dusty, busy street with Bensoni.

Everyone who had anything that might conceivably find a buyer came to the market. Anyone who wanted anything came to the market. It was the perfect place for buyers to meet sellers and it was a hive of activity and colour. Within the designated area the natives spread their mats at any convenient spot, set out their wares on them and settled down comfortably to await the customers and chat with one another. Sellers of similar items tended to stay together, so that in one area could be found a dazzling array of beans and pulses. These were measured out in small, deep tin platefuls which were then tipped into the buyer's receptacle. The sellers tended to be women and they dressed colourfully for the occasion. Little puff-sleeved blouses in bright floral designs were topped by the *chirundu*.

The vegetable sellers had little pyramids of tomatoes, onions, green beans, marrow, aubergines, okra, onions and potatoes, and any other vegetables in season, displayed on their mats. The fruit displays were mouth-watering, as Berta never tired of commenting. There were piles of large mangoes, bananas, pineapples, avocado pears, oranges, tangerines, custard apples and pomegranates, depending on the season.

The girls always chose a banana and a tangerine to nibble while they walked around the market and Bensoni paid for them out of the housekeeping purse. A Mayi would have had a fit had she known. The young women in the family did not walk around in public, eating. And worse, who knew if the fruit was clean? It was because of this that the girls chose fruit with natural coverings.

Rice and ufa, the ground maize meal which was the staple diet of the natives, came in sacks and was again measured up for sale by the plateful. The buyers would bring their own receptacles, usually little wicker baskets into which the women would securely pack their purchases. They would then pack them into large wicker baskets and carry these on their heads to their homes. Cassava and sweet potatoes were much in demand, and many children could be seen with a white stick of boiled cassava in their hands, to ward off the hunger pangs until it was time to go home.

The meat stalls fascinated the girls. Carcasses of beef, pork, chicken and goat were hung up and cut to order. The offal and the head would go first, being the cheapest; you needed to be quite well off to buy from the body itself. Huge green flies buzzed around the meat in clouds and the butchers swiped at them, but nobody seemed to mind.

"Ugh!" shuddered Elsa, and they moved away, sending the flies buzzing away angrily.

The barber was always fun to watch. He set up his little shop under a shady acacia tree and was never without a customer. A crowd of potential and past customers and their friends sat around, encircling the barber and his present customer, passing comments on the haircut in progress, the state of the fishing at the moment, the hut tax that had to be paid each year and what were the best crops to grow for a quick return.

"Bensoni, have a haircut, please, so that I can watch?" called out Berta impishly.

Bensoni chuckled. *"Eh eh, donna w'angono, a-ee!"* No, little madam.

Berta loved the bead stalls. Here you could find beads of the deepest natural colours in all shapes and sizes. Quite often, the woman running the stall would be working with the beads; the most popular items seemed to be arm and leg bangles made from several layers of different coloured beads and worked into intricate designs.

This time, Berta squatted on her haunches by the women, cheeks in hands, big brown eyes alight with interest, and she asked in her gentle and charming way if they could show her how to do it.

"Please, *a Mama*," she entreated, using the vernacular to address the women.

"Eh eh," was the response from a particularly kindly soul. "Come, little madam, sit beside me and I will show you."

And with the patience that is so common amongst the African people when dealing with children, the woman took Berta through the steps.

"Do you want to try now?" she asked.

"Oh yes!" she said and eagerly took the dainty work.

But, alas, it was far more difficult than it appeared and, to her horror, she dropped several beads before handing it back, brick-red with embarrassment. The woman and all her friends at the surrounding stalls laughed merrily; this would be talked about for days and from now on, Berta would undoubtedly be treated as one of their own.

There were children everywhere. They were beautiful, with their round shiny faces and big black eyes. The only thing that marred them was the number that had distended abdomens, and Victoria had explained that these were caused in the main by tape worms and the shortages of food that came in the wake of intermittent drought. There was an ongoing government programme to treat the disease but it was difficult to convince the mothers of the need for action, hence the slowness with which results were becoming apparent.

Some of the children sat with their mothers, helping to display their wares and to serve customers. Others played boisterous games and chased one another amongst and under the stalls, shrieking with excitement. If they made a mess or caused one of the traders' meticulous displays to keel over, they would be caught quickly and rewarded with a sound cuff about the ears.

"Oh, poor little boy," sympathised Elsa as they watched a little scamp being hauled up and punished. He went off to find his mother, bawling at the top of his lungs.

"Do you think that his mother might get angry because someone has smacked him?" wondered Berta.

"I doubt it," said Elsa, smiling. "He'll probably get another slap from her just so that he doesn't get tempted to play around again."

"Elsa, why do the children wear such ugly clothes? Look, they are full of holes and, in fact, look at that little boy over there, the one with the khaki shorts. There are more holes than shirt."

Elsa thought a moment before replying: "Listen, Berta," she said. "There are some jobs that pay a lot more than others. That means that the people with the good jobs can afford to buy better things for their families. The ones with the jobs that don't pay very well, very often have to make do with what they can get."

"Yes, I can see that," responded Berta, "but why is it that you don't see Europeans or people like us wearing holey clothes?"

"Well, it just happens that they have the best jobs."

"Well I don't think that's fair," retorted Berta. "The good jobs should be shared by everyone."

"I agree," said Elsa. "The problem is that not everyone can actually do the better jobs. You have to be educated to do them."

"Well, that's easy to fix," said Berta, with the quiet satisfaction of having sorted out a serious problem. "We all have to make sure that everyone gets to be educated."

"Yes," said Elsa quietly. "Yes, that is the answer to the problem; how nice it would be if it were really that simple. Anyway, Berta, do remember that a lot of people who have got more money than they need help those who are in need. For example, have you ever seen Ntokosani, Maria's baby, in rags? Or any of the household children? And do you know that

94

Papa buys large bags of *ufa* for all the staff so that they don't have to buy any? And sugar. And tea. And cooking oil. And whenever we have to have new clothes the ones we've grown out of are given to our servants."

Berta was mollified. She had a strong sense of justice and was easily distressed at anything she thought to be unjust. She had an idea. "As soon as we get home I'm going to go through my clothes and toys and see what I can give away."

"Now, careful!" laughed Elsa. "Speak to A Mayi first!"

The noisiest section of the market was the livestock area. There were mostly chickens for sale but there was the occasional goat. The chickens had their legs securely tied together with palm fronds and were then left to lie on their sides on the dry earth. This restrictive position did not stop them from squawking at the tops of their voices each time they were touched by the buyers or disturbed in any way. The chicken vendors would also have little piles of fresh eggs as well as any other produce they had brought to market. On the very few occasions that Bensoni had had to buy eggs because the home ones were not laying well, he had learnt to treat them with caution when cooking with them, breaking each one into a separate dish before adding it to the mixture being prepared at the time. When chickens ran around all day, laying their eggs wherever it took their fancy, the eggs could be difficult to find. An egg laid craftily in a bushy shrub, under a pile of leaves, might not be detected for several days. When that egg was cracked open the smell would send anyone in the kitchen running for the door. At other times, the hens would become broody and lay their eggs in hidden places so as to hatch them. When they were found, collected and sold, there would be a sad little half-formed chick in the shell.

There were stalls of freshly-made biscuits and little cakes sent by the Indian women, but the girls were not allowed to have any of these. Bensoni would indulge them as far as fruit was concerned, but he would not allow them to eat food prepared by just anybody.

"No, madam," he said to Berta in response to her request, his good-natured face set in stern lines.

Berta whined as they passed by an appetising display and Elsa scolded her.

"Now stop pretending to be hungry," she snapped.

"But, I am – hungry I mean," she complained.

"Rubbish, Berta," came the response. "You had a huge breakfast and you've just had some fruit. You're just greedy and I can't imagine why you're so skinny."

"You're not. Skinny, I mean," said Berta, slyly eying her sister. She wondered if she dared tell her that she was plump. It wasn't true but it would annoy her anyway. She decided not to. It was now very hot and tempers were becoming short.

They took their leave of Bensoni and headed back home.

"I do hope Papa will be home soon," Berta confided to Elsa. "I miss him already."

"Um," said Elsa, her casual tone hiding her unease. Why, she thought, did her father have to go on these dangerous trips? There were government officials who were paid to do these jobs. Did he not realise how much his family worried about him, just waiting to see him walk unharmed through the front door?

CHAPTER THIRTEEN

"I miss Papa," announced Berta at breakfast, with her mouth full of toast and honey, a few days after her father's departure.

"Don't talk with your mouth full," scolded Paulina, adding: "We all miss him, anyway."

Their mother hastily intervened: "Paulina's right, Berta. I think we all miss your father, but he'll be back in a week."

Elsa smiled at her family. "Yes, we do miss him. But I must say that it's great to be at home, such a treat!"

And it was true. Happy afternoons and evenings were spent at home, where there always seemed to be something to do. The animal and vegetable farm was unfailingly interesting and Victoria and the girls often set out to be there before dusk, when the animals were being herded into the stalls. Victoria preferred to be carried by *machila*, the base of which was well cushioned to avoid injury to the passenger if tree stumps or large stones were crossed; these could cause painful collisions. The girls preferred to walk but, on the return journey, Berta was often tired and climbed in with her mother, face cushioned against her ample breasts, thumb firmly in her mouth.

As the sun prepared to slip behind the mountains in a blaze of crimson, pink and violet, the young cows and bulls were separated from their mothers, after having had a last suckle, and were put into mud and wattle sheds where they kept cool in the summer and warm in the winter. The fully grown animals were left outside in a fenced area, the kraal. Close by, the same routine was followed for the sheep and goats, whose shrill bleating drowned the gentle lowing of the cows. The *londas*, or night watchmen, then built up fires every thirty yards or so; these were fuelled by wood and dried cow dung. Their light not only gave comfort to the animals and the men during the night, but they also discouraged mosquitoes and tsetse flies. Most importantly, they kept the main predators – lions, leopards and hyenas – at bay.

The tsetse fly was still a major problem in this part of the world. Ludwig had explained to his daughters why it was that donkeys and horses could not be used for transporting people and goods in most of the country.

"They are particularly vulnerable to being bitten by the tsetse fly," he explained.

"So, how does that make them ill?" Berta wanted to know.

"The tsetse drops parasites called trypanosomes – now there's a long word you don't have to remember! – into the blood when it bites the animal. The animal is then likely to get the disease that we call sleeping sickness."

"But then you give them medicine and they get better?" was the hopeful response.

"No, sadly the animal always dies."

Infected animals became drowsier and drowsier until they finally died from starvation. There was no cure. There were also cases of human beings contracting the illness, but these were few and far between.

The bee hives were a strictly forbidden area and the girls were only permitted to visit them with Ludwig. Since they were all frightened of bees and hated being stung, they didn't need to be told this more than once and they kept well away.

The walk back home at dusk was a leisurely, peaceful affair as the lowing and bleating receded into the distance. The thick undergrowth by the side of the road housed colonies of bats and, as they walked past, there arose from it their distinctive, musky smell. This, together with the smell of wood smoke from many village fires, helped to paint the exotic picture of Africa at dusk. Despite the hour it was still very warm and the mosquitoes were out in full force. Slapping at them soon became a reflex action.

Berta, snug in the *machila* against A Mayi, listened drowsily as her mother, Elsa and Paulina talked about the animals and the garden.

"Mayi, I thought that there seemed to be fewer baby goats today," observed Elsa.

"Did you count them?" asked Paulina.

"No, I didn't but I thought last time we were here, a few days ago, that there was one with a black ear and a white one; but I couldn't spot it today."

"I'll speak to the *capitao* tomorrow," said A Mayi, thoughtfully making a mental note to talk to the supervisor. "He has told me that he is not happy with one of the shepherds that Papa employed last month. I think it is time that the *capitao* understood that the animals are his responsibility and that he is accountable for them."

Theft was an ongoing problem but with a strong *capitao* the problem should be contained. The other problem was with the milk. It was expected that the herdsmen would take enough for their and their families' personal needs, but there had been instances in the recent past when they had been found to be taking far more than their needs and selling the surplus.

"We'll come again tomorrow and try to find the kid that you couldn't see today, Elsa," said A Mayi finally as they neared home.

"Yes, Mayi. I hope that I was wrong and that it's there."

The family always looked forward to their evenings together. Living so close to the land, they were drawn into nature's gentle rhythm. Speech and thoughts slowed down as twilight turned to night, the natural world settled down to sleep and the stars came out to dazzle and bewitch with their sparkling beauty. As they sat together on the veranda, Papa would point out the constellations. He was a serious astronomer and had piles of charts in his study, on which he had identified and noted the positions of constellations in the southern hemisphere. Berta recalled once, when she was only five years old, all of them being woken up from sleep at midnight and taken outside by Papa to see a phenomenon which, he told them, no one would see again for seventy years. Once they had unglued their eyelids, they too were enraptured, even Paulina. What a sight! A spray of stars beyond counting spread out in the sky like a stately procession of glittering bejewelled beings. Halley's Comet! She treasured that name and wondered if she would be here to see it when it next came this close to earth, in seventy years, as Papa had said.

Bedtime was usually early, nine o'clock at the latest unless they had visitors, and so they had an hour or two together on the veranda or in the sitting room during the winter, when there could be a sharp coolness in the evening. They played games together and Papa taught them how to play card games. Berta was not a good loser and Paulina was even worse.

"I think you had a turn too many, Papa. That's why you were able to make up the threes and win the game," she grumbled.

"And, you Paulina, I am sure you took two cards instead of one. Look, you've got more in your hand than you should have," chimed in Berta.

"Girls, girls, stop this," scolded Papa, smiling. "It is the mark of a lady to be able to lose graciously."

"But..." they both broke in.

"No buts," said Papa, sternly, his smile fading. "Any more of this and you shan't join us until you can assure me that you can behave."

Papa had very strict ideas of how young people should behave. He came from a well-to-do background, cement factory owners in Bielefeld in Germany until the late 1800s, when his parents, lured by its wealth and stability, emigrated to Switzerland, where they subsequently took out Swiss nationality. Ludwig had definite expectations of his children's behaviour.

To fill in some of the time until their father's return, the girls made a point of visiting his premises, with the big sign "Deuss and Kahn" over the door and on the edge of the roof. Mr Mussa, the manager, was always delighted to see them.

"Hello, hello, pretty young ladies," he would greet them. "And what can I offer you to drink?"

"Oh, nothing, thank you," they replied shyly. "We've just come to have a look around."

"Of course," he beamed. "What would you like to see first?"

The store didn't contain much that was of interest to them. Half was devoted to camping and fishing gear; anything could be bought, from tents to fishing flies. The other half was a general store offering grocery items and fancy goods of all sorts. Ludwig had stores at intervals from Sena in Portuguese East Africa up to Fort Johnston in Nyasaland, and he had taken on Kahn, a fellow Swiss, when it became clear that he needed help in running his expanding empire. The stores were a relatively small part of his business, however, and his association with Kahn was restricted to the Fort Johnston section, under the umbrella of Ludwig Deuss and Co. Ltd.

Of fractionally more interest to Berta, because they provided opportunities for raucous games of hide and seek with her little friends, were large warehouses behind the stores which housed the goods from which most of Ludwig's income was derived, goods which he imported and exported to and from Nyasaland, Mozambique, Angola and Rhodesia, to Switzerland and Germany and vice versa. He dealt mainly in groundnuts, beeswax, cotton, millet, rice, tobacco, tea, sugar cane and tung oil, camping gear and provisions, including soft drinks, and had a transport route running between the three countries to Beira and Nacala in Mozambique, the nearest sea ports. From there the products were sent on cargo ships to Italy and thence by road or rail to Switzerland and Germany. Prior to the war breaking out, they had used the west coast of Africa, which was more convenient for transporting to and from northern Germany. Ludwig had prospered during the past twenty-five years and now owned considerable holdings in Blantyre, the country's capital. Public perception had it that he owned half of the city and that the other half was owned by a contemporary; the rumour was close to the truth.

The company's registered office was at Fort Johnston, with its head office in Hamburg, and Kahn's main function was to keep the accounts of the company and to maintain stock control. With such a variety and quantity of goods travelling back and forth a firm hand had to be kept on stock movements and payments for stock.

The girls' main interest, after the confectionery across the room, was the camping equipment. As their usual method of travel to school was by walking and camping, a journey of seven days, they enjoyed looking at all the latest camping equipment.

A gleaming pressure lamp caught Elsa's attention. "Ooh," she said, "this is beautiful! Does it give off much light?"

"Oh, yes, Miss Elsa," Mr Mussa assured her. "It's like the light of day. You'd be able read a book comfortably or even embroider with this light. Progress is a wonderful thing, isn't it?"

Berta's attention had been caught by a brass Primus stove. "Look at this stove. It's got two places to cook on! I like this," she declared, fingers busily investigating screws and knobs.

"Berta," said Paulina sharply. "Don't touch. You might break something."

Berta looked at her witheringly but knew that she was right.

"Oh, all right."

Suddenly, there was a commotion at the door and a small party of Europeans bustled in. At their head was a young woman, loud of voice and appearance, who came towards the counter with such force that the girls were forced to step backwards in order to avoid a collision. The young woman gave no indication that she had noticed their existence and, on reaching the counter, turned around and beckoned imperiously to a slightly older man.

"Now, I absolutely refuse to travel back to Cholo in the discomfort that we came in, my dear," she announced to him as he reached her, and she launched into a shrill catalogue of apparent disasters. The man, undoubtedly her husband, looked uncomfortable and glanced repeatedly at Mr Mussa with an apologetic smile, while he gently tried to stem the flow of words and get to the root of the problem which, it appeared, was that more comfortable camping equipment was required.

The couple had clearly been in the shop before because as they girls backed off towards the door, with covert grins at Mr Mussa, the suave gentleman was doing a good job of pacifying the woman, whom he addressed as Mrs Haze.

As they left the shop, Berta said, in an absolutely accurate imitation of Mrs Haze's accent and body language, "And now, we should go home for lunch, my dears."

The trio managed to hold back the laughter until they were well away; they finally exploded, holding their sides and wiping away their tears at the verge of the road, while passers-by stared and smiled with them. It was Elsa who was the first to pull herself together and whisper to her sisters.

"We're making a spectacle of ourselves! A Mayi would be furious!"

Chastened, but with eyes dancing merrily, they made their way home to lunch, not knowing that they had just tapped into a significant slice of the future. The days would come when Berta's memories of the shop and Mr Mussa, the packed shelves, the smells of leather, wood and paraffin, the cheerful chatter of customers and her father's name over the door would slip into her mind and a soft gurgle of laughter would once again rise in her throat and the strength would come to deal with that awful Mrs Haze, as Berta would come to refer to her!

CHAPTER FOURTEEN

Ludwig, Aleki, his two scouts and his gun-bearer trudged up the steep little hill, stunted dried bushes and grasses whipping at their legs. The heat was seasonally intense but there were generous clumps of thickets which, green foliaged after the rains, gave them shade as they passed. When they reached the top they were cooled by a light breeze; they paused under some acacia trees to look around and see what the new landscape brought them.

It was the fourth day of the hunt and they were well inside Portuguese East African territory. Relations between the peoples of the two countries were friendly and there was a steady migration from the Portuguese territories to Nyasaland, as men fled the compulsory, almost slave labour that was enforced upon them for six months of each year by the government.

The hunters were always greeted as friends at the villages they passed, but it was proving difficult to track down the herd of elephant. They were directed first here and then there by the villagers, who only had rumour to go by, and it was becoming clear that the herd was moving comparatively quickly and randomly. There was ample water available and the villagers' gardens were full of enticing vegetation. Add to that the fact that trees were covered in tender young shoots after the rains and it became clear that the herd was content to meander aimlessly, where their fancy took them. This made it difficult to anticipate their movements. But now it seemed that they had struck lucky. Looking down into the plain before them there was clear evidence that elephants had been visiting. Everywhere there were trees that had been knocked down, and branches had been stripped and left in tangled heaps.

Ludwig turned to his companions and pointed to the devastation. "Let's go and see from close. We might be able to gauge how far they have moved on."

The scouts nodded and the men walked rapidly down the side of the hill, bracing themselves against the possibility of sliding on the tiny stones that covered the dry ground. Once on level ground they made better speed, and a brisk walk of almost an hour brought them to the first of the felled trees. Scores of birds were picking at the worms and insects that had been exposed by the uprooting; their cheerful twitter seemed oddly at variance with the bleak destruction around them.

Lumpenga called out as he examined a tree. "*Bwana*, this is recent, maybe yesterday."

Ludwig walked across to him and the gun-bearer pulled away a piece of bark from a branch on the ground to expose the moist, cream colour inside. "One more day and this will be dry and white," he said. "Also," he continued, moving to big square balls of elephant droppings that littered the area, "these are very fresh."

"You're right, Lumpenga," said Ludwig, looking pensively around him. "We're close."

He thought for a moment and called the men to him. "We need to find out in which direction the herd has gone so, Davidi," as he turned to another of the scouts, "you stay here to guide the rest of the party. Aleki, Lumpenga, Chilombwe and I will move on in this direction. Follow us and we will double back to meet you."

The elephant trail was clear from here and shortly after the party came upon a village surrounded by fields, whose crops had been torn up and trampled into the ground. Felled trees lay everywhere.

"What unfortunate people," said Ludwig to Aleki, who strode beside him. They approached to find the entire village, including the small children, tidying up and trying to save whatever plants had not been destroyed or consumed.

A small deputation, led by a dignified man who was clearly the headman, came towards them. Greetings were exchanged soberly and Ludwig immediately offered his commiserations on the misfortune that had befallen the village.

The response was typically African. There was no sign of self-pity or distress and the headman replied with dignity and acceptance: "Yes, it is bad for us. But we will plant again quickly and trust that we will have enough food to last until the new crops are ready."

"How big is the herd?" asked Ludwig.

"The headman thought for a moment: "Maybe fourteen," he replied eventually.

"Fourteen!" exclaimed Chingongwe.

"Yes, but the main herd is not so much of a problem," the headman continued. "They take only what they want to eat and they prefer the shoots on the trees. No, there is just one rogue. He is like a mad thing, running around, making a big noise and destroying everything in his way." He shook his head. "He is mad."

Not wishing to delay the villagers any longer, Ludwig and his men politely took their leave, assuring the headman that their mission was to kill the troublesome rogue, and voicing the hope that they would be troubled no more.

The little party resumed the trail and as the sun rose high above them decided that it was time to start looking for a suitable spot to camp. On this fertile little plain there were many clumps of heavily foliaged trees that would give them the shade they needed; they chose one that had the tell-tale line of reeds and luxuriant grasses close by, which assured them of a water supply. They leaned the guns against one of the trees, gratefully unloaded their water supplies from their backs, and sat down on the ground to await the arrival of the rest of the party.

When the porters, with Davidi in the lead, finally wound their way towards them, there followed the usual bustling activity as each man set to with his appointed task. Soon the shaded areas under the trees were looking like home and the cooking pots were bubbling on the wood fires. Ludwig called the whole party to him and they left what they were doing to gather around him expectantly.

"We've caught up with the elephants at last," he told them, for the benefit of the porters who had missed the action during the day. He explained briefly what the present situation was.

Turning to the hunting team, he continued. "Tomorrow morning, at dawn, when the elephant have started feeding, we must be in place and ready to get the rogue."

Davidi spoke up: "*Bwana*, we need to go today when the sun is ready to go down, to see exactly where the herd is. We can then decide where we will hide tomorrow."

"Yes, indeed, Davidi. You are quite right. We will set off at five o'clock."

The men dispersed and stood or sat in small groups until the cook announced that food was ready, whereupon they fell upon their food like the energetic and well exercised men they were. Afterwards, most of them snoozed, while Ludwig read, made notes in his journal and oiled his guns.

Tea and biscuits were served at four-thirty and a few minutes before five found the hunting party ready to move and checking guns and ammunition. Since they would be close to the animals, Ludwig had his powerful rifle slung over his shoulder, loaded but with the safety catch on. They left with the cheerful calls of the porters in their ears, "*Pitani bwino!*" Go well.

They made good time over the flat terrain and it was simple to follow the path of the elephants; there was no mistaking the tender young trees torn out of the ground or the saplings that had collapsed from the weight of the passers-by. And, of course, the huge droppings that punctuated the strewn vegetation as a testimony to the amounts that had been eaten.

The increasing abundance of vegetation suggested that there was a river close by; a few palms soared up towards the sky between acacias and mango trees. It would have been difficult ground to cover had the elephants not trampled several pathways through it; they followed the tracks, bearing left towards a series of well wooded hillocks close by. Ludwig was thinking that, if the elephants were in the vicinity, that higher ground would be exactly what they needed, with a greater than 180 degree field of vision.

The scouts, Davidi and Lumpenga, were well ahead, intent on the ground before them and cutting a swathe from left to right with their keen vision. Suddenly, they stood upright and waved their hands aloft to get the rest of the party's attention. They put fingers urgently to their lips.

Ludwig, Aleki and Chingongwe stopped in their tracks and waited. In the stillness a faint sound reached their ears, a tearing, crashing sound and the splashing of much water.

They had almost walked into the herd which, it seemed, was at the river's edge about fifty yards away to the right, for their evening drink. *I should have realised that they were close*, thought Ludwig, *because there is no birdsong.*

He thought rapidly. To their left was a profusion of thickets and acacia trees reaching right up to the lower slopes of the first of the hillocks. There was plenty of cover there and it would be useful to observe the herd as it returned from the river, verify the numbers and see where they would go to bed down for the night. This tactic would give them a sound advantage when they returned in the morning for the shoot. The only disadvantage here would be the light, which would start failing within the next half hour.

After a hurried consultation with Aleki, who approved the scheme, Ludwig gesticulated to the scouts ahead to go to the left, towards a clump of thickets, and all the men moved forward. In moments they were concealed by the bush and moved further in, where Ludwig put his proposal to the scouts. They had barely had time to communicate when there was a trumpeting and the sound of bushes being uprooted and dry branches crackling with sharp, snapping sounds. The noise was coming from a small clearing, clearly visible, about fifty yards away.

Startled, the men dived for cover and approached the clearing cautiously. Ludwig signalled for Lumpenga to come close, unslung his rifle, checked that it was loaded and held it in front of him as he moved ahead, gesturing to the three remaining men to stay behind.

They crept forward over the churned-up ground and suddenly, they saw him.

He was a fine elephant, big and clearly well fed. As they watched, he tore up some shrubs and, holding them in his trunk, he trotted around the clearing, trumpeting, ears flapping, massive feet pounding the soft earth. This was not normal elephant behaviour; this young bull was clearly a rogue. He was what they had travelled for and Ludwig's immediate reaction was to take advantage of the situation that had fallen into his lap and shoot the elephant while he presented himself to them. Another point in their favour was that the rest of the herd was at the river's edge. It was not likely that they would get another such opportunity.

After a whispered consultation the men crept forward, inching their way towards the target, breathtakingly conscious of the risks they were taking with their lives in this unpremeditated, unexpected encounter. For those moments, nothing else existed for them, not the sounds of the other elephants, not the distant sounds of the birds, not the scratches to their faces, arms and legs as they hugged the cover of the thorny bushes. Nothing but the grey giant prancing in front of them.

When they were in rifle range Ludwig stood up calmly, put his rifle to his shoulder and waited. As the elephant turned in his direction, he took aim and shot twice. The bull died on his feet; he slowly crumpled to the ground with a thud which reverberated beneath their feet.

Ludwig reloaded quickly and moved forward to ensure that the animal was dead. At the sound of his feet stepping noisily on dry twigs, and with heart-stopping suddenness, there was an enraged squeal from a thicket about thirty yards to the right. Startled out of their wits, both men whirled around and saw every hunter's nightmare. What they had not noticed in their intent observation of the bull was that a young female with her calf had also stayed away from the river and had been completely concealed by the grey thickets, a mere forty yards or so away.

Ludwig hissed at Chilombwe to keep still in the hope that she would ignore them, but there was no chance. The shots had frightened and enraged her and she was standing, head straining backwards, ears pinned back, trunk wildly slicing the air. Then her myopic eyes located the hunters and as Ludwig saw her prepare to charge, he shouted to his bearer to run to safety, reasoning that when she gave chase only one of them was likely to survive. His mind raced on, weighing up, discarding, coolly weighing up the situation in the span of a moment. Unless he shot her first; then both would have a chance. He had to stop her. Lumpenga tried to argue that he would stay with him, but Ludwig shouted at him to go.

"Go Lumpenga! Go quickly!"

He braced himself to shoot as the cow came straight at him. When she was about twenty yards away, he fired. The bullet got her between the eyes but still she came on, a massive grey beast growing larger in his view by the second, shaking the earth beneath him. And then Ludwig did a very stupid thing. Before he was completely steady on his feet, he fired again. The kick from the gun hurled him several feet backwards, onto his side, and the butt of the rifle sliced his cheek open.

Winded, he tried to rise, but the elephant was almost on him. He felt the earth pounding under her as she approached and the excruciating pain as the edge of her massive foot glanced off his shoulder. He felt her trunk encircling him like a vice and then he was flying through the air, branches and thorns slashing and tearing him. He hit the ground and then there was only darkness.

CHAPTER FIFTEEN

"Why don't you visit the port?" A Mayi asked the girls on the Friday before their father's expected return. She could see that they were missing him and thought that this would be an enjoyable distraction.

"They've built new offices along the river bank and I think the paddle steamer is passing through today," she concluded.

The little port at Fort Johnston was a short distance from the shopping and residential areas of the town and had developed a colour and rhythm of its own; it was an important stage of the route going up and down river, to and from the lake. A Mayi's idea was leapt upon by the girls.

"Yes!" said Elsa, her face brightening. "I'd like that."

Berta agreed enthusiastically and even Paulina showed a flicker of interest. To see one of the paddle steamers coming in or going out was an event, colourful and stimulating, and preferably not to be missed.

All the traffic from the eastern coastal ports travelled from Beira and Chinde up the Zambezi River and then up the Shire River, before transferring to the road so as to circumvent the Shire cataracts. After a journey inland, they re-joined the Shire at Matope and went on uninterrupted to join Lake Nyasa.

The Fort was situated on the Shire, which was the outflow from the lake so that, having called at Fort Johnston, the boats went on to the lake, which was more like an inland sea, measuring three hundred and sixty-five miles long and fifty-two miles wide. Ludwig and the girls had spent many happy days sailing on the lake in one of his sailing boat fleet, drinking in the beauty of the lake's surrounds.

In the midst of the colour and movement Berta's eye was caught by a tall, white-clad Muslim nearby and she tensed. For all of her young life she had been warned about the Arab slave traders. From A Mayi she received cool, factual advice; but from Mataya and the servants in the home compound the advice was garnished with ghoulish details designed to make her quake with fear. She stared at the Muslim man, tense and ready for flight, but then she saw him turn around and address two small boys following him and she relaxed. He seemed harmless. She turned to her sisters as they watched the stevedores lifting crates on and off the boats. Their dark skins gleamed with sweat, and they chanted with a deep, heavyweight chant which rose to a crescendo when they needed to muster all their strength to lift and place the crates in their places.

Berta strolled past the Queen Victoria Memorial to the water's edge, where the dark green waters of the Shire swirled around the boats, the current rapid as it began its journey to the sea. The river was very wide at this point and thick belts of reeds lined the shores; fishermen sat amongst them, keeping a wary eye open for the pythons and crocodiles that favoured that location. The men patiently waited to make the catch that would ensure a tasty and nutritious meal that day and maybe the next. The sought-after tiger fish was plentiful and prized for its meaty, oily frame, with only the abundance of fine, fork shaped bones to mar its culinary delight.

Further back from the river, offices and warehouses had sprung up to deal with the growing volume of trade. Through the windows Berta could see clerks, usually British, with a few Asians, sitting at their desks, shuffling papers and perspiring freely.

She walked amongst children who played everywhere, eyes wide with wonder as the cargo went back and forth. Women who had come to get water paused, with their earthenware pots perched on their heads, to gaze at the passengers, who leaned on the rails and surveyed the busy scene and the town beyond. Everywhere, children and adults alike clutched cassava or sticks of sugar cane, chewing and sucking at the sweet fibrous centre.

Berta returned in a rush to Elsa and Paulina with what she thought was an exciting suggestion. "Can we go aboard the steamer?" she asked, bright eyed.

Paulina was appalled. "You can't do that," she said. "First of all you're not a passenger and secondly, you'll most likely not come off in time and wind up who knows where." She added, ghoulishly, "You might even be taken by the *chifwamba*." Slave traders.

Berta stuck her tongue out at her and turned to appeal to Elsa. At first Elsa thought it unwise, but on reflection and undeterred by Paulina, she finally agreed.

"We have to be quick though, Berta. They look as though they are about to finish loading the boat. We don't want to get stuck on board."

"Don't say I didn't warn you," was Paulina's parting shot to their disappearing backs.

They both edged their way up the narrow gangplank, pressing against the ropes to allow stevedores to get past them. Once up, they decided to walk around the deck and see whether they could get a glimpse of the interior. It was difficult to walk on the deck because the passengers were crowded around the rails and most of the remaining space was taken up by chickens, vegetables and all the other produce with which the Africans travelled. There was nothing much to see on that level, so they went up a narrow staircase, where they found the deck much clearer. From there they looked into an enclosed area which appeared to be a small dining room, with tables and chairs in the centre and comfortable looking padded seats around the walls.

This was clearly an area for the more expensive ticket holders.

They walked to the rear of the boat and saw beneath them the lower deck piled high with coils of sisal rope, beyond which were the huge circular paddles and, to the side, the chain which was attached to the lowered anchor. As they watched, the engines began to splutter and roar amidst clouds of smoke, the paddles started to move and the anchor began to inch up with an awful creaking din. The deck began to shudder beneath their feet. Just then there was a sharp blast of the foghorn.

"Oh my goodness," gasped Elsa. "It's leaving."

As one they raced for the stairs, flew down with feet barely touching the steps and ran for the gangplank, pushing the hapless passengers out of their way and murmuring repeated apologies. *Chonde! Chonde!* They were just in time. As they reached the gangplank two of the sailors were about to detach it.

"Please, stop!" shrieked Elsa. "We need to get off!"

The men shook their heads disapprovingly and stepped back. Wobbling precariously as they went down the ropy gangplank at speed, the two girls reached the quay, out of breath and not a little scared by the experience.

Paulina looked at them sanctimoniously. "I told you so," she said.

Elsa and Berta decided simultaneously but separately that they wouldn't tell anyone about their escapade, but they had reckoned without Paulina, who chose her moment to drop it into the conversation with maximum effect that very evening.

The evenings were the times when Victoria told them about her life as a child in Sena. Many happy evenings were spent on the veranda, where they talked in the semi darkness about the past and made plans for the future. Behind them, the hiss of the pressure lamp was just audible from the sitting room and outside, the *londas* talked desultorily while the dogs restlessly howled at shadows in the darkness.

"Elsa and Berta did something today that I fear is going to shock you, Mai," Paulina began.

Victoria looked at her, startled. "What on earth do you mean?"

Elsa broke in, "Oh, Paulina, you're being so silly!"

Paulina was not deterred. "I'm telling Mayi because I think it's important. You could have been seriously hurt and, at the very least, you behaved badly in front of many people who know our family and we will be shamed."

And she launched into the tale, with appropriate expressions of horror and graphic descriptions of dangerously swaying gangplanks, hooting foghorns and highly inconvenienced, swearing stevedores.

As she finished, all eyes turned towards Victoria, who was sitting very still as though frozen with shock. Her eyes were cast down and her hands folded in her lap. It seemed an eternity that she was immobile and silent.

Elsa was concerned. "Mayi, please don't be shocked…"

At last Victoria looked up and they saw that her eyes were brimming with tears, tears of laughter. A chuckle escaped from deep in her throat and her shoulders shook as it turned into a full-throated laugh. It was minutes before she could talk; finally, she wiped away her tears with her handkerchief and looked at her daughters.

"I wish I could have seen it," she said. "What panic! What confusion!"

Paulina was outraged. "But, Mayi…"

Victoria interrupted her. "It's all right, Paulina. I understand your kind and caring motives that led you to tell me but, really, this was nothing but a prank and," looking at Elsa and Berta, "I'm sure you two have learnt a lesson."

She started to chuckle again. "Those swaying gangplanks always feel really insecure; you must have looked so funny as you tried to come down quickly, no doubt slipping and sliding and hanging onto the rope for dear life."

And she went off into another peal of laughter until Elsa, Berta and finally, grudgingly, Paulina joined her.

When everyone had quietened down Berta demanded to know more about their grandfather's plantation. It had taken hold of her fertile and vivid imagination, which had given it an almost magical aura and her appetite for detail was insatiable.

"Your grandfather was always busy when I was growing up, you know," she said to the girls seated around her. "The plantation was huge and then he bought the island in the middle of the river, which made him even busier because there were more crops to be grown." And she explained that there was the added advantage that the silt left behind after the annual flooding gave a very heavy yield. The girls had been on occasional visits and were familiar with both the plantation and the island which was, they had been told, at a point in the river between two and three miles in width.

"But, Mayi," said Elsa, "Grandfather, has got lots of slaves to help him."

Victoria agreed. "Yes, but they do need supervising every minute of the day. Most of them have no initiative at all!"

Berta broke in: "Does Grandfather treat his slaves well, Mayi?"

Victoria smiled. "Yes, of course. He knows that you can only get good work out of them if you feed and rest them well."

Visiting their grandparents was a huge treat for them and the next visit was scheduled for December, which gave them a few months of pleasurable anticipation.

And so the days passed, full of interest and as busy or as lazy as they wanted them to be. When seven days went by and Papa was not back, the family was disappointed but not alarmed.

"Well, let's be sensible," rationalised A Mayi. "It would take two days to reach Mozambique, another two to return and that would only leave three days to find the rogue bull elephant. We are expecting too much."

When twelve days had passed and there was still no sign of Ludwig everyone started to feel apprehensive. A Mayi did her best to disguise her anxiety and launched instead on a massive house cleaning and clearance. There were servants everywhere, no one could find anything anywhere, and it was impossible to sit down without being cleared around. Paulina joined in with the cleaning but Elsa and Berta, after a morning at it, decided to leave the house and go for a long walk.

On their return they saw from a distance what appeared to be a small crowd at their house. Puzzled, they quickened their pace. As they drew near, Paulina spotted them, detached herself from the group and ran towards them. Her face was blotchy and her eyes swollen from crying.

"What is it, Paulina?" cried Elsa, alarmed.

Unable to speak, Paulina reached them and threw herself into Elsa's arms. She started to sob.

Now very anxious, Elsa held her close, patted her back and asked again, "Paulina, you must tell me what is wrong."

Berta stood close, staring at Pauline with unbearable anxiety, her eyes huge in her face, which had turned very pale, the freckles on the bridge of her nose standing out sharply.

Paulina drew back and looked into Elsa's face. She struggled to speak. Finally, she said, "Elsa, Papa is dead."

***

Elsa and Bertha stood as if turned to stone. Then, Elsa gave a low, anguished moan. "No! How?"

Without waiting for a reply, she gently moved Paulina aside and started to walk towards the house, but she could not contain herself and broke into a run. She reached the drive of the house with tears streaming down her face and blindly pushed through the small crowd. Behind her ran Berta, who was still deathly pale and resolutely refusing to believe the meaning of the words that she had just heard.

They ran up the drive, up the flight of steps, across the veranda and into the sitting room where A Mayi was sitting on the sofa, their neighbours Dietrich and his wife Ada sitting close to her. The room was silent, all the faces drawn with anxiety. A Mayi was sitting, her hands crossed in her lap, staring sightlessly through the doorway.

Elsa and Berta hurtled through and flung themselves on their knees in front of her, their faces on her lap, their hands reaching for hers. Elsa began to sob. Berta's face was still frozen and pale, her eyes enormous as she turned and looked searchingly into A Mayi's.

A Mayi fondled them gently. "There, now," she crooned. "It's going to be all right. We must be brave for Papa."

Elsa continued to sob quietly, her body shuddering as she tried to contain herself. "But, Papa's dead," she managed to say brokenly.

Victoria's hands jerked away from their heads. Life came back into her face. "What? What did you say?" she asked.

"Papa," whispered Elsa, as she raised her head to look at her mother. "He's dead."

"Who told you that?" asked Victoria, visibly shaken.

"Paulina," replied Elsa "Why, Mayi, what is it?"

"No, no, my child. He is not dead. He is very ill. He was attacked by an elephant. That is all we know at the moment." She looked up towards the doorway.

"Paulina must have misunderstood the bearer who ran home to tell us what had happened. Where is she? We must find her and tell her the truth."

Distraught, she started to rise, but Kahn forestalled her. "I'll find her, Victoria," he said to her gently. "You stay here with the girls. When they bring Ludwig home you must be here where they can find you."

He strode to the door and ran down the steps.

Inside there was subdued rejoicing. Elsa's tears, now tears of joy, were running even more freely and Berta had joined in. "He's alive, he's alive," they kept whispering to one another.

Somehow, the misunderstanding had acted as a catalyst and had roused everyone from the dumb hopelessness that they had sunk into when hearing of Ludwig's accident. To be sure, it was very serious and there was no certainty that he would survive, but now they were able to focus on the hope that was blossoming in their hearts. They had been reminded that he was alive, he was still with them; they could hope now for his life to continue.

At last Elsa was able to ask, "Mayi, tell me. What exactly has happened to Papa?"

"I only know what I have already told you. The bearers are carrying him home and Lumpenga ran ahead to tell us that Papa had been injured.

They're coming through the bush, so we can't take a truck or a cart to meet them. We just have to wait here. Lumpenga has gone back to the outskirts of the town where the road ends and the track they followed begins and as soon as he sees them, he will alert us. Mr Kahn has a truck ready so that as soon as they are sighted, he will go to pick him up and take him straight to the hospital."

The question in the family's mind now was whether to go and wait at the beginning of the track or wait patiently at the house. It was difficult almost to the point of being impossible to just sit patiently and wait. The agony of not knowing how Ludwig was, threatened to consume them. Shortly, however, Kahn returned with Paulina in tow. Her face was transformed at the news that her father was in fact alive and she threw herself at A Mayi, holding her tight.

"Silly girl," smiled her mother, "what a mistake to make! You'll be the death of us yet!"

"Sorry," came the muffled response from somewhere in the region of A Mayi's ample bosom. "I thought Lumpenga said that he was dead."

"No, no. He said that Papa was very ill and looked as though he were dead. But he isn't and soon they will bring him home and the doctor and the sisters at the mission will fix him up."

She lifted Paulina's blotchy face up. "Now, listen, we are going to think and pray with hope, not fear. That goes for all of us. Now, girls, ask everyone what they would like to drink and let's get some little cakes and nuts to feed everyone."

The girls leapt up to do her bidding and soon each of the assembled sympathisers had a cool drink and sticky honey cake beside them. The distraction had the effect of dragging their minds from the unbearable tension of the moment, albeit briefly, and allowing optimism to grow once again in their hearts.

The next few hours limped by, with the tension returning to engulf them in misery. The brief respite and the renewed hope had lifted them, but now it plunged them back into the darkness. Victoria and her friends preserved a brave front and kept up a series of activities designed to distract and busy the girls. *Capitao* was mysteriously unable to complete the butter making, the chickens needed feeding three times and eggs needed to be collected from the most unlikely places in the compound. Three mothers in the compound suddenly needed to go to the market for essentials and the five children had to be tended. Edisoni found that his assistant cook was making a mess of shelling the peas and needed help; and Mr Kahn would be deeply grateful for some aid in checking the cartons of goods that had arrived at the port that morning. Elsa and Paulina weren't fooled but understood the benefits of keeping busy; they were grateful for the clumsy but kindly attempts to keep them occupied.

Then suddenly it was over.

CHAPTER SIXTEEN

Afternoon was giving way to dusk when there was a flurry at the front door and Lumpenga stood there. He was breathless and streaming with sweat. The whites of his eyes gleamed in his contorted face.

"They're arriving," he almost shouted. "They're about ten minutes away."

Everything was dropped. Kahn raced to the truck with A Mayi and the girls close behind. Victoria got into the front and Lumpenga and the girls leapt into the open back. A few more seconds and they were speeding down the road.

It was not far to the end of the main street, which was in fact the road leading into and out of the port. As the hard-packed smooth surface gave way to gravel there was a footpath on the right leading up into the hills and thence to Mozambique. Kahn stopped in a spray of gravel and dust, turned the truck to face the way in which they had come and parked very close to the edge of the road at the point where the track began. They all piled out of the vehicle and looked up the path, shading their eyes against the glow of the setting sun. Yes, there they were. A splash of colour on the path amidst the trees and rocky outcrops was making its jerky progress towards them. As it approached, they could see that it was a group of men carrying a litter on which there appeared to be a body.

The girls started to run towards the cortege calling, "Papa, papa, we're here!"

They finally reached the group and pushed aside some of the bearers to get close to their father, but then they stood frozen, speechless with shock. This couldn't be Papa, surely. This gaunt skeleton with only skin covering the bones of his face, which was a ghastly grey colour, was a stranger. And the blood. His upper half was caked in blood, darkened to black; flies buzzed around trying to alight on him. And what was more bizarre was that a piece of hollow reed was protruding from his mouth through lips that were bloodless, cracked and stained with old, dried blood.

The bearers gently pushed them aside as they stood staring, paralysed. The cortege silently moved on past them and on towards the road. The initial horror dissolved and lent them wings. They raced after the bearers and past them.

"Mayi, Mayi!" Paulina and Berta ran to Victoria, threw their arms around her and clung to her, tears silently coursing down their faces, unable to speak, able only to sob brokenly. Elsa followed behind but she saw the anguish in her mother's eyes and knew that she had to be strong for her. She could not afford to show her horror or her breaking heart.

Where she found the strength to deal with the next few hours, Victoria never knew. The broken body of her husband was carried tenderly onto the truck and Kahn carefully drove the short distance to the hospital. There the litter was lowered gently and put onto a stretcher; the nuns and doctors hurried to help carry him into the building. There, he was taken away from them to the small, simple operating theatre.

"No, A Mayi," whispered one of the nursing nuns, Cecilia, as Victoria tried to go after him.

She held Victoria close as the other nuns rushed the stretcher away, "You must let us do what we can for him now."

For the first time, Victoria's iron control cracked and tears coursed down her cheeks.

"Sister, remember he has a heart condition. And remember how much we need and love him." She put her head on Sister Cecilia's shoulder and wept. The nun held her and stroked her gently. Then she led her to one of the two small wards, made her sit down and gave her a glass of water.

"Victoria," she said, "I would like to suggest that you send for some clothes and stay here with us for the moment. This ward is free."

Victoria accepted gratefully, with a smile and a nod. She was still beyond speech.

Soon, however, the moment of weakness had passed and Victoria was once again able to face the situation stoically and return to her children, who needed her badly at this moment.

After a few minutes, when Victoria had managed to reassure the girls as much as possible, and had told them of her plan to remain at the hospital, Kahn took her aside to the other end of the veranda and suggested that he take the girls home until there was further news. He also suggested that Ada spend the few nights with them until Ludwig was out of danger. Victoria accepted that this was the best course of action. She asked Elsa to pack a small suitcase for her and tried to reassure her little family. "Now, you must try not to worry," she urged them. "See, this is the best place he could possibly be at this moment. The doctors and nurses are looking after him and he will get the best care possible."

Elsa looked worriedly at her. "Will you be all right on your own? Should one of us stay with you?"

"No, no, thank you, my child. How boring it would be for you. Just waiting until Papa has been patched up would drive you mad. No, you get yourselves home and make sure that everything is ready for when Papa gets home. I shall only stay here for a short while, until Papa is well on the mend."

She told them that Ada would be staying with them until her return. Berta brightened.

"Oh good," she confided. "She plays Rummy really well, so that will help us forget for a while that you're not there!"

"Good girl," applauded Victoria, who was amused despite herself. "Remember to feed the chickens, won't you? Don't forget Jesse's afternoon play and she does like a banana after her play." She smiled at Paulina and Elsa above Berta's head.

"I leave everything in your hands, my children. May God bless us and keep us until we all meet again."

With that blessing, she kissed each one, said goodbye to Kahn and returned to the ward.

Feeling desolate, the children squeezed into the cab of the truck with Kahn, while Lumpenga and the other bearers climbed into the back. Everyone was subdued. The bearers were deeply attached to Ludwig, to whom they felt they owed almost everything they had. There was silence as the truck started up and bumped along the road to the centre of the town in a cloud of dust.

The next three weeks were a nightmare for the family, and in particular Victoria.

As the doctors explained to Victoria after the first three-hour operation, they had found that in some ways Ludwig's injuries appeared worse than they were. His shoulder and upper arm were crushed and despite their best efforts he would never have full use of them again. He was concussed and had four broken ribs. His right leg was broken and he was covered in cuts, abrasions and contusions. There were several deep cuts in his scalp and this accounted for much of the profuse bleeding.

"The good thing," explained the doctor, "is that there is no internal bleeding that we can detect at this stage. Also, your husband is very fit. The problem is that it has taken a week to carry him back here and the fact that he's still alive is due entirely to the devotion of his bearers."

Lumpenga had told A Mayi that since Ludwig had been unconscious from the time of the accident, the bearers had kept him alive by planting a hollow bamboo in his mouth and pouring water down him virtually day and night as they carried him. However, the injuries had suppurated in the meantime and there was now serious infection to be dealt with.

In the beginning Ludwig appeared to be recovering well, although he was still not lucid by the end of the first week, but there was a sudden downturn on the twelfth day, when a secondary infection developed and he hovered on the brink between life and death for three days. There was now concern that he was no longer physically capable of fighting these new onslaughts and it seemed to Victoria, looking on in anguish, that it was the doctors' and nurses' dedication alone that kept him alive. She was also constantly by his side, talking to him, bathing him with cool water and stroking his head. She looked at the point of exhaustion, but no argument would persuade her to get some rest.

"I feel that at my touch, my soul holds fast to his soul and keeps him with us," she explained.

She realised, however, that it would be of no help to anyone if she prostrated herself with exhaustion, so she asked that Mataya be allowed to come and sleep on her mat on the floor in the ward. Victoria would then get a little sleep whenever possible, since she could rely on Mataya to awaken her if Ludwig made any movement. Mataya was delighted; she knew no life away from her beloved Victoria.

One of the doctors, Hans Freijl, had a quiet chat with her. He spoke comfortably in the Chichewa dialect. "Mayi," he said gently, "Ludwig has a problem with his heart, has he not?"

"Yes," she replied. "That is one of the reasons that he came to Africa in the first place. When he completed his education the family in Switzerland thought that a visit to Portuguese East Africa, where his uncle was already settled, would be beneficial. And it has been so. The weaknesses with which he arrived seem to have been shaken off and he works long and hard with no adverse effect. In fact, he seems to get stronger with each passing year."

The doctor looked at her thoughtfully, hands pushed into the pockets of his white overall. "I won't hide from you," he said, "that his heart is finding it very difficult to cope at the moment. We are doing everything possible, as I am sure you know."

Victoria hesitated for a moment and then made the decision to voice her thoughts. "Doctor," she started hesitantly, "I am very grateful to you all for what you have done. I don't believe that Ludwiki would be alive today if it hadn't been for you. And I also know that he needs you until he recovers. But, I feel I must tell you what is in my heart."

The young doctor looked at her curiously. "Of course, tell me please."

"In our part of the world," she said hesitantly, "we still believe in our own herbal medicines, the *mankhwala*. We have used them since time before our knowledge and we know that in many cases they do indeed cure." She paused and looked up at him uncertainly.

"I agree," he said, admirably hiding his personal misgivings. "Do please tell me what is on your mind, Mayi."

"There is one in particular," she continued, "which is known to make the heart and all the body strong in times of great trouble. I would like to invite our doctor and ask him what he thinks. I think that together you will get a good result."

"Can I think about it and let you know later on today?" asked Hans.

"Of course, doctor," acquiesced Victoria, "but I think that we must hurry."

Hans discussed the matter with the other doctor, Eric, and the nuns shortly after. They were startled and uneasy at the suggestion.

"But there might be danger for Mr Deuss if the medicine does not agree with him," suggested one of the nuns anxiously. "For all we know, there might be ingredients which we would consider to be poison."

"I agree," responded Hans, "but these remedies are given regularly to African patients and Victoria is very confident of this man's abilities. I gather they have used him before."

They finally made the decision that it would do no harm to try the native medicines. As Eric put it, "Ludwig is in a bad way. He doesn't seem to have the reserves to fight much longer. The medication is working very slowly. We have nothing to lose."

Accordingly, Victoria was told to call the native doctor. A message was sent to Edisoni, who quickly dispatched one of the servants to the nearby village where the medicine man resided.

He found him sitting outside his hut in an open-sided shelter. A roof of rushes rested on ten poles on four sides. Around him were many little earthenware bowls, some shallow and some deeper, shaped as gourds. In the centre was a small log fire on which a brew was gurgling in a deep pot. He wore very little, just a swatch of cloth arranged around his lower body, and the only other distinguishing feature was his hair, which was worn longer than most and hennaed to a light reddish brown. His whole attitude was one of calmness and stillness.

He bade the messenger sit down and listened carefully to what he had to say. He then asked him a number of searching questions, after which it did not take him long to gather up his instruments and herbs, put them in a rush basket and start the walk to the hospital. His lithe, muscular body rapidly ate up the miles; before long he reached the hospital, where he was greeted courteously and taken to Ludwig.

Victoria waited anxiously outside as the examination and diagnosis took place. Two of the nuns waited with her, one of them Cecilia, and their interest in what she knew of the medicine man helped to distract her until the healer reappeared. The three women looked at him wordlessly.

"A Mayi," he started, bowing respectfully. "*Bwana* Ludwiki is indeed a sick man. But do not worry. I have here some *mankhwala* which will soon make him better."

He handed her some pieces of bark wrapped in a banana leaf.

"I questioned the bearer before coming," he continued, "and I thought that I would need this. And indeed I do. You must boil one piece of bark in a cup of water for five minutes and leave to stand until it gets cold. Then give it to your husband. You must do this every two hours. At the same time, you must boil these herbs in a big pot of water. This water must be used to wash his wounds. I shall come again in two days' time."

Another bow and he was gone.

Victoria and the nuns hurried back inside with the bark and, while Victoria recommenced her vigil at Ludwig's bedside, the nuns prepared the medicine. Soon Sister Cecilia was back with a noxious smelling liquid.

"It smells awful," she told Victoria in a whisper. "I hope we can get this down him."

They raised his head and spoonful by spoonful they managed in painfully slow stages to get the comatose Ludwig to swallow the potion. A positive development was that, during the process, he began to stir and make small noises in his throat. As Sister Cecilia commented in a low voice, they had never thought of giving him something so awful that it would rouse him. Despite herself Victoria gave a little giggle, her first for many days.

Within hours there seemed to be an improvement and by next morning Ludwig was lucid for the first time since he had come home. Through half-open bloodshot eyes he looked slowly around the room, his eyes finally alighting on his wife, who sat in a chair close to his bed. Her fingers fondled the beads of a rosary and she stared unseeingly out of a window.

"Victoria, where am I?" he asked.

She started and turned to look at her husband, disbelief and joy transforming her weary, sad face. She reached out and took his hand, which lay on the counterpane. She lifted it to her cheek and then kissed it, murmuring through her tears of relief, "Ludwiki, Ludwiki... thanks be to God..."

Ludwig smiled weakly at her and asked again, "Where am I? I don't remember coming here."

"You're in hospital," she told him, her face a picture of happiness as she stood up stroked his head.

"What... I remember now. The elephant charged us..." He began to show signs of agitation.

"Yes, my husband, everything is all right. Sleep now."

He frowned with the effort of speaking. "The bearers... are they... all right?"

"Yes," soothed Victoria. "There is nothing to worry about."

"Victoria," he said, gripping her hand, "I must speak to... Kahn. Call him."

"Yes, I shall," she replied. His eyes closed and he went limp again.

121

In a state of excitement, Victoria immediately went to tell the nurse on duty that Ludwig had finally regained consciousness. She was delighted and came to see Ludwig and check his blood pressure. She was able to assure Victoria that things were looking good.

The doctor was called and, after a quick examination of his patient, shook his head wonderingly. "The improvement is remarkable." He smiled at Victoria as he got up to leave. "It could be coincidence," he said in a low voice to Sister Cecilia on his way out, "but I think something here bears further investigation. Keep a close eye on the patient, please."

Now Victoria's priority was to do as her husband had asked and call Dietrich Kahn.

When she explained to the nurse what Ludwig had asked, she lost no time in sending a message to the priest's house asking if they could spare a messenger. Within a very short time the messenger was there, looking smart in his beige shirt and shorts, and ready to go. Victoria gave him two messages, one for Kahn and one for the girls. They must be told immediately about their father. She anxiously watched the messenger as he left the veranda, got on his bicycle and departed. Reassured, she returned to the ward to resume her vigil by Ludwig's bedside.

Within the hour Kahn had arrived, looking extremely worried. He hurried inside and walked to the ward, which he entered with a questioning, anxious look at Victoria and the nurse; they were at that moment giving Ludwig his potion, which he was now well enough to resist.

"No, no, Dietrich," smiled Victoria, as she accurately read his apprehensions. "It is good news this time. Ludwig is much better and wants to speak to you."

Kahn smiled with relief. "That's good. I'll wait outside while you finish what you're doing," he said as he headed back out through the door.

Now that Ludwig was returning to consciousness he was making his will felt, and it was becoming increasingly difficult to get the unpleasant tasting potion down him. The nurses persisted, however, because it was clear that it had supplied the extra boost he had needed.

Half an hour later the nurse came to call Kahn where he sat on the veranda wall, looking out at the gardens. She beckoned to him to come and he followed her.

"Don't stay more than five minutes, please," she said in a low voice. "He is only just regaining consciousness and can't communicate for more than a few minutes at a time."

He nodded his understanding and went to stand quietly beside the bed. Victoria motioned to him to draw up a chair from the next bed and he did so, setting it close to Ludwig's head before sitting down. His shock at the sight of his friend's emaciated, skeletal face was clear in his open-mouthed stare.

When ten minutes had passed with no movement from Ludwig, Victoria leaned close to him and told him that Kahn had come to see him as requested. Ludwig stirred and struggled to open his eyes. Once he had located Kahn he became fraught as he tried to say too much and failed.

"Hey, Ludwig," interrupted Kahn, smiling down at him. "You have re-joined us; I am very happy to see you! Calm down and take your time. I am in no hurry and will wait here until you have told me what you want to say. Now relax. I'm not going anywhere."

Ludwig looked up at him gratefully and closed his eyes again.

An hour passed and still Ludwig did not stir.

"How are the children, Dietrich?" asked Victoria in a whisper.

"Fine as they can be," he answered quietly. "Of course they are terribly anxious about their father, but Ada is doing everything she can to distract them. By the way, we have them at our house overnight and they seem to enjoy our evenings together. The day time is easier to cope with as there is so much for them to do. They can't wait to come and see you both."

"And I can't wait to see them. In fact, I have sent a message to them that their father has regained consciousness. But I have told them that they can only see him tomorrow. I am sure you will agree," Victoria said with a glance at Ludwig's haggard appearance, "that it is best that they do not see Ludwiki until tomorrow, when he should be a bit stronger."

She paused a moment. "But, I've just had a thought. The girls could come each morning now that Ludwiki is better and I could sit with them for a while on the veranda. I think it would do us all a lot of good."

Kahn heartily concurred, smiling as he looked at her. "You seem like a different person, Victoria. You look like a young girl again."

"Thank you, Dietrich," she responded, her eyes twinkling. "A young girl indeed! Oh, and Dietrich, please would you take that little bag to the house for me? I've got a bit of washing that needs to be done. Elsa can bring me fresh clothes when they come to visit tomorrow."

"I'll see to it," he assured her.

"Everyone in town is asking about him," he said presently, "and a message came up on one of the transport trucks from Khalid Laxmi and Alfred Stanley in Blantyre. They want to know if there is anything they can do to help. They are going to come up and see him when we let them know that he is able to receive visitors."

"How good they are," said Victoria. "Such a long journey and no doubt they will come by motorbike. But for the moment and for some time yet he will not be able to receive visitors. Please thank them for us."

"Carrain was also asking," he commented, with a dry look at her.

"I wonder what he wants. I'd rather he stayed away," she observed.

"Victoria," Kahn said, changing the subject, "I took the liberty of sending Richard a telegram when Ludwig was first brought back. He was in such a bad state I felt that his son would never forgive us if we did not give him the opportunity to travel up and see his father. You had too much to cope with at the time and I didn't want to burden you further so I just went ahead and did it. He should be here any day now."

He looked at her uncertainly. To his relief her face broke out into a delighted smile.

"Richard! Here! Oh, praise God. How wonderful!"

Tears of joy trickled down her cheeks. In her weakened emotional state tears were always close to the surface. Richard was their firstborn, a fine, strapping young man, and it was a year since they had last seen him. One of the few drawbacks to living in this African paradise was the fact that educational facilities were limited. They had been very fortunate with the girls but there were no such facilities for boys. So Richard had been sent to a good and expensive school in Cape Town, where it was generally perceived that the negative attitude of the white settlers to the black Africans and people of mixed race would not be so pronounced.

"Thank you, Dietrich," she said mistily.

Some more time passed and Kahn wondered whether he should go away and come back on the morrow, but Victoria respectfully suggested that since he had promised Ludwig to be there when he awoke, it would be best if he did just that. Maybe he would like to take a stroll around the garden or have a coffee with the nurses? Kahn decided that that was a good idea and it was on his return to the bedside that Ludwig started to stir and finally opened his eyes.

For the first time his gaze was clear as his eyes travelled around the room. He saw Victoria sitting on his left. His cracked lips stretched painfully in a small smile.

"*Moni*, A Mayi" he whispered. He had greeted her formally in jest and she reciprocated with a delighted smile.

"*Ndithu*, A *Bambo*," she responded, equally formally. Indeed, sir.

His thin hand reached out, found hers and held it tightly. They looked at each other emotionally.

"How long have I been here?" he asked.

"Ten days," she responded. He closed his eyes.

"Mon Dieu!" he whispered.

Victoria came closer. "Dietrich is here to see you, as you asked."

Ludwig's eyes flew open again and he swivelled his neck cautiously to his right. "Ah, Kahn," he breathed. "I'm so glad you have come."

"Of course, old friend. How could I not!"

124

"Listen," said Ludwig, starting to look anxious again, "I don't know the extent of my injuries and whether I shall survive this. I must know that Victoria and the children will be financially secure if I don't recover."

Kahn started to make soothing noises.

"No, no, Kahn," said the sick man, irritably. "I know that things don't look too good and it is better to face up to that."

He paused for breath and continued more slowly: "I have a great deal of property in Blantyre. If I die I want Victoria to inherit most of it, as well as the Fort Johnston and Portuguese properties, and my present will provides for that. However, I want to exclude four properties, which I need you to arrange to go into the children's names right away."

Slowly but lucidly he gave detailed instructions to his friend and partner and when he had finished, he lay back onto his pillow once more, his face white and his lips encircled with blue. He slipped into semi-consciousness once again while Victoria clung to his hand. She smiled tremulously at Kahn.

"You don't need to wait," she said. "Please just ask the nurse to come."

Kahn rose, gave Victoria a reassuring smile and a wave and left, taking with him Victoria's bag of washing. Elsa, she knew, would see to it and get some fresh clothes to her almost immediately.

***

Meanwhile, at the house, something had happened which had helped immeasurably to lift up the girls' spirits. Some villagers from Portuguese East Africa had turned up at the house with a baby elephant. They had travelled a considerable distance and said that it was the calf of the elephant which had trampled *Bwana* Deuss.

At first the girls were too stunned to take it in but once they realised that it was indeed so, and that this was their latest pet, their joy knew no bounds. The villagers were well rewarded with items of clothing, food and some money and departed in high spirits, while the girls set themselves to thinking through how they were going to cope with their baby elephant.

The entire compound was interested in the new addition to the family's menagerie. The little children from the far end came forward, hiding shyly behind their mothers' *chirundus*, only their faces and huge eyes showing. The dogs sniffed around warily and leapt back nervously each time the calf moved one of its large feet. The monkey, Jesse, chattered angrily, annoyed that someone else was the centre of attention.

First the calf had to be tethered and amidst advice from all the staff and their families who had gathered around, and with the help of Njoka, a rope was tied around its left hind leg and then attached to the trunk of the mango tree.

The discussion about what to call him, for it was indeed a male, raged long and hard and by some miracle, Jacko was the name that was finally hit on that all three girls liked.

The animal was thin after its long walk, its skin hanging loosely on its small frame and it was clearly pining for its mother as it looked anxiously to and fro, its little trunk reaching out to and testing every person in its vicinity. The girls stroked its head gently.

"I think it's hungry," suggested Elsa, as the little trunk travelled upwards and nuzzled them. There was general agreement on this but what to give it? The servants' wives suggested maize but no one could see any teeth when they gingerly approached Jacko's mouth.

"Bread?" suggested Berta.

"Silly," said Paulina scornfully. "Can't you see it's just a baby?"

Berta was too happy to take offence at Paulina's tone. "Milk!" she said brightly. "*Nkaka*," she explained to the wives, who chorused their approval of this.

"Milk?" It was Paulina again. "In a cup, I suppose?" she added, sarcastically.

"Berta," chipped in Elsa, hastily to avert the argument that seemed imminent. "Could you run and ask Mr Mussa if he could let us have some baby teats. I'll find an old lemonade bottle. Paulina, you ask Edisoni to let us have whatever milk there is left."

They scattered and met in the front kitchen fifteen minutes later with bottle and teats. Edisoni had a word of warning however as he handed over the milk.

"Madam," he cautioned Elsa, "you will have to mix the milk with a little bit of water until the elephant gets used to it. Otherwise he could get a very bad tummy and die."

"Oh, yes, Edisoni. Thanks."

Edisoni was quite right, they had lost many little orphaned animals through giving them too rich a mixture; his advice was timely.

The first feed was a marathon event.

To begin with, Jacko kept trying to grasp the bottle in his trunk but between the three sisters, they eventually managed to keep his writhing trunk out of the way and put the teat into his mouth. He tried to suck but nothing much seemed to happen until Paulina had an idea.

"The hole in the teat is too small! It's made for human babies!"

A frantic dash to the kitchen followed and a sizeable hole was cut into the teat. Success followed. Jacko sucked and gurgled to his heart's content, to the satisfaction of his besotted spectators.

126

Paulina then had the idea of cutting up some bread and soaking it with milk to see whether Jacko could be enticed to eat something solid. She raced back to the kitchen, prepared the food and brought it back in a little tin bowl. The girls laid it cautiously on the ground in front of Jacko.

"Bet you he overturns it," said Elsa.

The other two nervously agreed and watched as a snaking trunk cautiously lowered itself to the proffered bowl, daintily tested its contents with its sensitive tip and then picked up a piece. Back went Jacko's head and into his mouth went the milky bread. Everyone held their breath but they need not have worried. Jacko was clearly delighted with this new taste and the bowl was very quickly emptied.

Jacko was soundly congratulated and hugged, kissed and stroked. As long as he would eat there was not likely to be a problem in raising him. The native onlookers smiled broadly, laughing and clapping their hands softly to show their pleasure.

"Well done, little madam, *donna wangono,*" they chorused, before dispersing to get on with their chores.

"Can't wait to tell A Mayi," smiled Berta. "She'll be so pleased. And Papa, when he wakes up."

She spoke blithely, but Elsa's face sobered. She alone was aware of the extent of their Papa's injuries and her young heart ached with the anxiety of waiting to hear whether he would live or not.

At just that moment the mission messenger arrived, slipping in through the side entrance to the back of the house. He approached the girls and addressed himself to Elsa, after first bowing respectfully. "*Moni, mama,*" he began.

She smiled at him questioningly: "*Moni.*"

He explained that he was bringing a message from the hospital and Elsa felt a sickening shock. She could only look at him wordlessly, fearing the worst.

When he told her that her father had regained consciousness she could only smile, weak with relief and happiness.

"What? What?" clamoured Paulina and Berta, who had not understood the message. When Elsa told them, they danced around in excitement, clapping their hands. Even Paulina shed her morose style and hopped from one foot to the other in excitement.

And so it was that when Kahn arrived a little while later he found the family bright-eyed and bursting with news. Papa had regained consciousness and they had an elephant!

First, though, they wanted to know about Papa and how he seemed. They listened raptly as Kahn told them that he had had a good discussion with their father and that he was much better. He was then able to tell them that all three of them would be able to visit their parents on the morrow. At this momentous news even Paulina executed a little dance of joy. It was almost too good to be true; the black cloud seemed to be lifting from their lives.

Fortified then with the best news that they could have hoped to receive, nothing would do but that Kahn should be taken to the back of the house to see Jacko and hear all the details of his coming to their home. He managed to elicit the main pieces of information from the torrent of words that assailed him and commented thoughtfully that it would be interesting to hear from Ludwig what exactly had happened on that fateful day.

"There's more to it than meets the eye," he confided to them. "Your father would never have hunted a female with a calf. Clearly, a female has been shot and killed and I wonder how it all came about. We shall just have to be patient until your father can tell us the story."

With that he took his leave, after leaving the bag of laundry and asking Elsa to pack a few things for her mother.

"What time do you think we can go and visit A Mayi and Papa?" she asked him.

"About ten o'clock in the morning should be fine," he guessed. "By then he'll have been cleaned up and seen by the doctor. Yes, I'm sure that'll be fine."

They waved him off at the front and he reminded them that he and Ada would be expecting them as usual at about six that evening. They chorused their thanks.

It seemed an eternity before it was time to set off to the hospital next morning. The two younger girls had slept soundly, but Elsa had slept fitfully, dreading just a little to see what awaited them at the hospital. Her father's ravaged appearance was imprinted on her mind and, try as she might, she could not erase it. She glanced across at her sisters, both soundly asleep, and wished for the optimism of youth. At sixteen, at this moment of crisis and without her parents, she felt old.

Leaving the Kahns, after a good breakfast, the girls went past their house to feed Jacko and collect A Mayi's clothes. The baby elephant seemed to be very content and was lying on his stomach on the ground in the shade of the mango tree. The dogs also lay on their stomachs a few feet away from him, ears cocked, and watched him with interest. The monkey squatted near her pole and also watched the elephant whilst picking at her fleas, whether real or imaginary it was not possible to tell, since searching and picking at her pelt seemed more of a habit than a necessary occupation.

As the girls appeared all the animals started to vie for their attention, but eventually they were able to approach Jacko, who seemed to recognise them, his trunk curling around them in some excitement. He was soon fed and Elsa was able to pack A Mayi's clothes before the three set off for the hospital.

A Mayi was waiting for them, having been alerted by one of the native women who sat outside sunning themselves and their children while they awaited their turn to see the doctor at the clinic behind the hospital.

When they saw her figure on the veranda they all broke into a run. They reached her, Bertha in the lead, and threw their arms about her as though they would never let her go. These two weeks without her had been an eternity to them.

"Careful," she chided, struggling to keep her balance. She tried to look stern as behove a woman of her stature and age in public, but a smile flitted over her mouth as she held the girls tightly to her.

Elsa broke away first. "You look thin, Mayi," she said, with a worried frown.

"Ah well," replied her mother. "It has been difficult, but I believe that the worst is over now."

"Can we see Papa now?" asked Berta, emerging from her mother's embrace.

"Yes, let's go. But remember, girls, that he's still very weak. So don't ask questions and keep as quiet as you can."

Three heads nodded willing assent and the trio trooped behind A Mayi into the ward.

Ludwig was lying in the bed with his head propped up slightly on two pillows. He was still waxen and emaciated but there was one big difference. His eyes were wide open, looking at his family quizzically. He smiled.

His girls walked forward quickly and quietly and gently kissed him on his forehead.

"Papa, you're back," whispered Elsa, and they sat beside the bed, clasping his hands and smiling at him through their tears. "You're back."

CHAPTER SEVENTEEN

The next two weeks went by in a flurry of happiness.

The girls visited Ludwig each morning for a few minutes, always careful not to tax him. He was better some days than others; they learnt to withdraw quietly on the days when his weakness lent him eyes that were slow to focus and his breathing was distressed. A Mayi was able to reassure them that, despite his apparent weakness, his progress was steady and it was just a question of time before he fully recovered.

At last the day arrived when the nuns told the family that their father was well enough to have them around for the whole day on the following day, with the proviso that he be allowed to rest for an hour in the morning and an hour in the afternoon.

The girls arrived in some excitement, armed with books and drawing equipment, and spent the first two hours in happy conversation with their parents. As Ludwig's eyelids began to droop and his head fell to one side, they quietly slipped off their chairs and left their mother crocheting peacefully beside him. When they had walked no further than twenty yards, Paulina had a change of mind, turned back to the veranda, got her embroidery out of her bag and settled down to work beside her parents.

Elsa tried to coax her back. "Come, Paulina, let's explore!"

Paulina shook her head, put a finger to her lips with a frown and pointed at Ludwig. Elsa took the hint and turned away; there certainly was no point in waking up the patient.

She turned to Berta, "I'm going to have a look at the gardens in the front of the hospital," she said. "Are you coming?"

But Berta had other plans and set off for the hospital building with a wave and a smile for her sister.

"Behave, Berta," called Elsa. "Remember that there are sick people in the hospital who shouldn't be disturbed."

The Mission hospital was at the end of town opposite to the port. The Catholic nuns and priests had built up, over the years, a complex of school, day clinic, hospital and church. It was set in a few acres of ground which had been tastefully landscaped. Elsa headed for the front of the main buildings, where she wandered along stretches of green grass interspersed with borders of brilliantly coloured flowers. Dotted all over were indigenous trees and shrubs, palm trees mostly, but also mango and poinsettia, whose big, scarlet flowers drew a splash of colour across the green canvas around them. The well children of the native patients played, squealing while running around the trees and shrubs, and Elsa laughed as the gardeners shouted at them irately to keep out of the garden. Bordering the flower beds and standing alone in their own circular beds were hibiscus, oleander and azalea shrubs, whose vibrant colours vied with the others, creating a happy dancing symphony of hues. Elsa thought that she would like to create something like this at their home but doubted that there would be sufficient space. Their garden was crowded enough with the beds of flowers that A Mayi had cultivated over the years.

At the rear and to the side was the large vegetable and fruit garden, which supplied the nuns and their little community with their fresh produce. A Mayi and the nun in charge, Sister Alex, had known each other for some time and both would pass on to the other any seeds or seedlings that she knew the other would welcome.

The hospital was very small and catered mainly to outpatients, who came from many miles away and waited on the cool verandas, sometimes for hours, for their turn to be treated. In case they needed to remain overnight before walking back home, they came prepared with their sleeping mats, which were spread on the verandas for them to sleep. Others who had to be admitted into the hospital were put into wards. The nuns fed all of these with *nsima*, together with a relish of tomatoes and onions stewed with any of the vegetables in season, and beans or dried fish. It was a noisy, cheerful atmosphere with the well children running around and playing, whilst the sick nestled on their mother's laps as they sat on the floor of the veranda. Berta strolled around, ever curious, and came back to her parents, highly amused with something to report.

"Guess what?" she said as she tore up to A Mayi, who was sitting by Ludwig's chair.

"What?" both parents replied in unison, laughing at their synchronised response.

"In the ward where the sick people are, they have loads and loads of visitors and when I asked them if they went home at night, some of them said 'no' and I asked them where they slept."

She broke off to chuckle. "They said they slept in the ward," a pause here for maximum effect, "underneath the beds!" And she went off into fits of giggles.

However, A Mayi was in no mood to laugh. "Berta, do you mean to tell me that you've gone into the ward and actually spoken to the patients?"

Berta stopped giggling, her eyes wary now. "Yes, well, sort of. I just peeped in to see what it was like and sort of got talking…"

When she left her parents a few minutes later her face was flushed, and a passing nurse heard only a muttered "… didn't do any harm so I don't see why …"

131

Berta loved the church and would often slip into its cool interior to sit; she did so now to soothe her bruised feelings and to reflect a while. She was endlessly fascinated by the different textures of the building materials around her, the colours and the smells. The church was brick built in a traditional style complete with Gothic windows with stone sill, and it was surprisingly attractive given its location in a far-flung corner of the country and the perennial shortage of money experienced by the missionaries. Inside, its pews, which stretched halfway down the nave, were lovingly crafted by volunteers from *Mulombwa*, a hard and heavy wood, and the vaulted ceilings and the windows let in the light whilst keeping in the cool. Behind the pews and up to the back door there was a wide open space where the natives would spread their cloths and mats and sit down for the service. They particularly enjoyed the singing, which they did with gusto, not always strictly in tune, and at full volume; it could be heard from a considerable distance away.

A Mayi and the girls attended mass there every Sunday. Not only the townspeople attended but throngs of people from the villages made their way in groups, dressed in their best clothes and laughing and chattering. Sunday mass was a much-looked-forward-to social and religious event of the week. Years later the smell of wax on wood mingled with the smell of sweet peas and roses would always remind Berta of the lovely, cool and peaceful church at Fort Johnston.

Now that Berta had been reassured that her beloved Papa was going to get better, her natural curiosity, which so often had led her into scrapes, led her further afield than she had previously been. Leaving the church she spotted the little native children at the day clinic at the rear of the hospital building. She felt such pity for their sad little faces, often tear streaked and with flies clinging to their eyelashes, despite their mothers' constantly swatting hands.

There were always many mothers awaiting their turn with the doctor, each sitting on the square of material which was normally used to anchor the baby to their backs. With infinite patience they fondled their children, rocking them gently and singing to them in the knowledge that in due time they would be attended to. No one ever complained, even though they may well have waited for hours. Berta wanted so much to help, but she knew from the times when mothers brought their sick babies to Victoria at the house for her to treat them, getting close to them warranted a scolding from her mother.

"Berta, come back here," she would complain. "We have no idea what diseases the children have. You cannot just go up to them and try to play. I know you mean well; maybe when you are older you might be in a position to do something for them."

So now, Berta looked on briefly from a safe distance and then retreated, satisfying herself with playing with the well siblings who were cavorting around the garden, dodging the irate gardeners, and happily chewing at the cassava tubers or sugar cane sticks which their mothers had brought for the day's nourishment.

The nuns were aware of the distances travelled by the villagers and had a small cooking area adjoining the clinic, where the mission helpers, aided by relatives of the patients, would brew up a large earthenware pot of *nsima*. Each family unit would be given two bowls, the larger one with the *nsima* and the other one with the relish. Having washed their hands, each member, using their right hand, would take a piece of the *nsima* approximately the size of a thumb, roll it with the same hand until it was smooth and shapely and then dip it into the relish. This part was then bitten off and the rest of the piece disposed of in the same way. Then, some more *nsima* was taken. The girls had often watched their servants eating their meal and had pleaded with A Mayi many a time to have some of the same. She would look like a thunder cloud.

"No!" she would say emphatically. "*Nsima* is for villagers, not us!"

The girls therefore contented themselves with occasional acts of disobedience, slipping out of the house as night fell, with guilty glances around and a delicious shiver at the thought that a lion just might be lurking around the corner, or a snake be lying like a shadow on the ground. They moved quickly, slipping into the safety of the circle of women diners in the home compound, squatting amongst them around the wood fire and awaiting their turn to take, mould and dip the cornmeal into the day's relish. It was a community experience to be one of the group, the firelight flickering in their faces, the delicious smell of wood smoke wafting around them, as they faced one another in the glowing circle in the darkness. The men spoke in low tones and then only when their hunger had been appeased; the women sat several yards away eating from separate pots, while the dogs skulked outside the circle of light, hoping for any remains.

The forbidden fruit made their hearts beat faster, made them feel adventurous but actually, they were not too keen on the taste and, after one such stolen moment, were content not to have any more for months. It was many years later that Victoria told her daughters that she and their father had been aware of these escapades.

"We always knew something was up from your expressions of innocence, and from the darkened back veranda we'd watch you furtively slip out and join the servants' wives around the fire. Then we'd have to make a quick dash for the front veranda when we saw you returning."

She chuckled. "What you didn't realise was that your clothes and hair were reeking of wood smoke, which totally gave the game away; your father and I could barely look at each other otherwise we'd have burst out laughing!"

She sighed. "We laughed a lot during those days, didn't we?" she finished off wistfully.

Now that the girls stayed at the hospital for long periods during the day, Victoria was able to summon her *machila* and spend some time each day at home, secure in the knowledge that Ludwig had his family at hand. Soon she recovered her strength, mental and physical, and her deep voice was heard once again ordering and berating as she went around her home like a whirlwind.

The happy day arrived when she could return home in the evenings to sleep, and the girls were able to leave the Kahns and reinstall themselves at their home. Things were returning to normal.

The one thing that all the family were anxious to hear was Ludwig's account of his accident. The bearers had not been questioned because he had been in such a serious state that the story of how it had happened had been irrelevant. Now that he was on the road to recovery, interest was rekindled in the event. How had such an experienced big game hunter allowed himself to be trampled by an elephant? Patience, counselled Victoria. Papa would tell the story in his own time.

It was after two weeks of convalescence that Ludwig was able to sit on the veranda in a comfortable armchair for a couple of hours in the morning and early evening. At the start he tired easily and would drift off to sleep for most of the time, but gradually his energy levels expanded until he was able to sit for two hours, fully awake and alert.

"My goodness, it's good to be alive," he confided to Elsa, who was sitting beside him one morning on the shady veranda, while Berta played hopscotch close by. He breathed in the warm, scented air. "It's funny how you don't think about how precious life is until you almost lose it! Just listen to those birds. And it is a real tonic to hear the children squealing as they play." He turned to face Elsa and smiled fondly at her. "And how fortunate I am to have my four girls looking after me so well."

"We can't wait to get you home, Papa," she replied, smiling back at him. "We miss you terribly. Evenings just aren't the same without you."

"Oh yes," he teased. "You just want to thrash me at Rummy, don't you? Speaking of which, are Paulina and Berta better losers yet?"

He chuckled as Elsa raised an eyebrow expressively at him. No further comment was needed.

A few days later, as father, mother and three daughters sat on the veranda engrossed in a game of Rummy, Paulina noticed out of the corner of her eye that someone, a man, was striding briskly up the drive to the hospital.

"I wonder who that is," she mused absentmindedly, as she frowned over her hand of cards.

"Who?" asked the others, equally engrossed.

"Him," she said, proudly putting down three Jacks. "Coming up the drive. Three Jacks!"

They all glanced up, went still for a moment then, as recognition dawned, Paulina and Berta raced down the drive. Elsa followed more sedately, with only her very rapid footsteps betraying her excitement.

"Richard!" they all shrieked as they threw their arms around him. Victoria and Ludwig smiled their welcome from the veranda and Richard tried to reach them, whilst disentangling himself from his sisters' enthusiastic embraces.

They were all proud of him. He was slightly above average height, well-built and with the lithe grace of the born athlete. His finely chiselled features in his naturally brown face, darkened even further by the sun, showed the signs of strain, but he smiled at his parents with deep affection. When he reached them, he hugged and kissed his mother and then turned to his father.

"Dad," he said, as he reached for him and gently held him close. "We're going to have to fatten you up. Mayi, have you not been feeding him?" he joked, to mask his emotion as he furtively dabbed moist eyes.

"You look quite thin, too," grumbled A Mayi. "Don't they feed you at school?"

"Well, it's been a long journey," he said, and filled them in on the details of his trip.

It was a long and tedious journey, he told them. From Fort Johnston there was a road and then steamboat journey to Chinde in Portuguese East Africa. Then there were several days by train to Cape Town in South Africa.

"In the middle of summer it's even more tiring than usual," he concluded.

"And how is college going, son?" asked Ludwig.

Richard's expression darkened.

"What can I say, Dad?" he asked, spreading out his hands. "College is fine and we should be getting our last term's results soon. I feel confident that I've passed and passed well. We're kept very busy and I'm enjoying the work. As for the rest, you know how it is…"

Ludwig nodded soberly. It had been difficult to send Richard to the southern part of their continent, where racial discrimination had become ugly and a way of life. But there had been no other option. There was no other country in Africa that had the educational facilities for children of mixed race that South Africa had. It was just a question of bearing the indignities that were imposed at every opportunity, concentrating on the reason for being there and getting it done as quickly as possible so as to return home.

"What really gets to me, Dad," said Richard finally, clasping and unclasping his hands as he spoke, "is how those damn whites who don't have a fraction of what we have are yet considered far above us socially simply because of their colour. Which, by the way, often goes with thick lips and frizzy blond hair."

He laughed grimly.

"You'd have to search hard to find an Afrikaner who has not a drop of black blood in him. It's enough to drive one to drink."

He paused and, with a visible effort, smiled.

"Anyway, we all know that sad old story and the reason I am here today is to rejoice. And rejoice is what I am going to do! Come here, Berta, and let's have a hug." And, before she could escape he had lunged for her, caught her and subjected her to some fierce tickling. Berta squealed with delight whilst pleading to be let go. This was a two-edged sword and she finally made her escape, breathless, rumpled and very happy to have her brother back home, whilst hoping that there wouldn't be any more tickling.

The nuns had come out to investigate the commotion and were duly introduced to Richard, whose charm won them over immediately. They sat and chatted for a while then rose to leave. Sister Cecilia wondered whether anyone would like something to drink and Berta was the promptest to reply, "Yes, please, Sister!"

"I'll go and get something," smiled the nun, upon which Berta leapt to her feet with an offer to help.

"Thank you. That would be nice, Berta," and they went off towards the kitchen, Berta in full flow. A Mayi smiled helplessly.

"I can't seem to teach her to be, er, quieter, more restrained…"

Richard laughed. "I'm pleased about that. She's our very special ray of sunshine."

"I couldn't agree more," said Ludwig. "When she enters a room, she lights it up."

A bustle from the doorway and the nun and Berta returned with two trays of cold drinks and biscuits.

"This lemonade is made from the lemons in the orchard," said Sister Cecilia, "and cook bakes the biscuits."

The family thanked her warmly and settled down to the simple treat, while Richard regaled them with stories of his antics at college. Their laughter rang through the building, making one of the nuns comment that it was good to hear them laugh again.

Finally, Ludwig's drawn face reminded them that he needed his rest and he was wheeled back to the ward.

The next few days followed this pattern of visits to the hospital and quiet evenings at home. Richard was always the centre of attention but the girls didn't mind; he was their hero too. Only one thing marred Victoria's joy at having her son with them for a few days, and that was his new habit of drinking several beers each evening. She remarked on it quietly on one occasion and saw the flash of irritation in Richard's eyes as he answered jovially enough, "Oh, come, Mayi. I'm a big boy now!" She had to concede that this was so, but since it was not customary in the family to have more than one or, at most, two drinks when there wasn't company, she felt that this was a worrying development.

Victoria quickly changed the subject and they talked of more general subjects like the war, its effects on all of them, and developments in their little world of Fort Johnston.

Drinking or not, she thought, how wonderful it was to have Richard home.

CHAPTER EIGHTEEN

On his second day home, after the girls had told their father about Jacko, their new elephant, Richard tentatively asked his father about the accident.

"If you don't want to talk about it," he added, "that's perfectly fine with us."

However, Ludwig seemed more than ready to talk about it and the family drew close as he told them about the ill-fated hunting trip. He spoke pensively of the last evening, blaming himself for having allowed the situation to develop.

"We should have just gone back to camp and come back rested the following morning. We would have been able to pick the location for the final scene and done the job neatly without having to kill the female too. I had seconds to come to a decision, a decision that would affect lives and, at that moment, it seemed the only thing to do."

"It was a terrifying experience," he concluded, the memory bringing out beads of sweat on his brow.

"It was bad enough believing that I was facing death, but the knowledge that my carelessness might lead to the deaths of some members of the team led to seconds of excruciating remorse such as I have never experienced. I know now what they mean when they say that one's heart breaks…"

The family were appalled as his narrative drew to an end and there was silence for a minute. Then Victoria broke the spell.

"Praise God you survived, Ludwiki," she said, in a practical tone of voice. "Next time you tell me that you are going hunting I will have a lot to say about it. Hunting. Pah!"

The family were of course full of questions about the trip and it was a very chastened Elsa who finally admitted, "What a good thing you didn't take us with you, Papa."

Despite Ludwig's slow recuperation, it was a happy time for the family, who made the most of having Ludwig and Richard at their disposal.

All too soon it was time for Richard to return to his studies. The family was sad to see him go. His effervescent and dynamic personality lit up every room that he entered and his presence was the best possible antidote to a tendency for the family to slip back into anxiety on days when Ludwig was unwell. Although all the family would miss Richard, Ludwig would probably feel it the most. Father and son got on well together and shared similar interests. It was refreshing for Ludwig to be able to talk with him about the business, hunting and fishing, politics, sport, the war and a host of other subjects. He hugged him tightly when he came to the hospital to say goodbye.

"Take care of yourself, my son," he said. "I am so glad you were able to come and see me. It has been a real tonic for me."

Richard hugged him back. "You take care of yourself, Dad," he said, a catch in his voice. "When I come again in December I want to find you out and about. Maybe we can go big game hunting together?"

They both burst out laughing at the look on Victoria's face. The tension of the parting diffused and when Richard left, giving a final wave before turning onto the main road, it was to a smiling Ludwig, and a slightly weepy Victoria. Ludwig took Victoria's hand and squeezed it.

"We'll see him again soon, Victoria. I'm sure of it."

During the next two weeks many of Ludwig's friends, acquaintances and business colleagues came to visit him. He was respected as an astute businessman and had a reputation for being honest; he was therefore generally liked.

Dharap and Stanley, his business friends and rivals, travelled up from Blantyre to spend a day with him and Victoria put them up for the night before seeing them off back home on their motorbikes. Ludwig had a strong affection and respect for Dharap in particular and he greeted the visitors with delight: they spent a day on the hospital veranda catching up on their news, leaving Ludwig exhausted but happy.

Sister gave him a little scold as he helped him back into his bed.

"You've tired yourself, Mr Deuss. You really shouldn't!"

A grin lit up his weary face.

"Oh, but I so enjoyed their company, Sister. I've known Dharap since he started up in business many years ago and taught him just about everything I know."

He paused. "Do you know, I can honestly say that I love him almost as a son. He's a fine man."

Back at their home, Berta was agog with excitement at having the opportunity to quiz the men about the latest news in transport.

"Where is your car, Mr Stanley?" she wanted to know.

"Oh, I couldn't come in that," he laughed.

"Why not?"

"Because the roads are little more than paths suitable for ox carts and where they're making roads for transport to the front most of them are not yet passable. No, the motorbike is still best!" And he laughed and ruffled Berta's springy hair.

The girls enjoyed having the men to stay. They had all the latest news from the capital as well as the gossip and A Mayi, Elsa and Paulina listened eagerly, their eyes shining in the light of the hurricane lamps as they chatted on the veranda after dinner. Berta sat with her chin cupped in her hands and tried not to show that she was bored and sleepy. Her drooping eyelids let her down, though, and she was hustled off to bed, protesting under her breath.

There was a steady stream of local visitors to the hospital until Sister Cecilia took it on herself to regulate the number and timing of visits. Much as Ludwig enjoyed seeing everyone again, he did find it tiring after a while and was grateful for her intervention.

Kahn had some disturbing news on one of his frequent visits. "Carrain keeps asking after you," he said casually one day.

Ludwig snorted. "I can't think why," he replied with a frown.

Kahn chose his words carefully. "He asks a lot of questions."

"Like what?"

"Oh, like why were you in Portuguese East Africa? Or indeed, were you there at all; did you just say that that was where you were?"

Ludwig stiffened. "What the hell is he getting at," he said quietly.

Khan shrugged and continued: "And, he said again that he can't understand a European man of your standing marrying an African woman. I told him that that was none of anyone's business but your own."

Ludwig reddened in anger. "What is wrong with him?" he fumed in frustration. "He said that to me once and I gave him hell. I consider myself extremely lucky to be married to Victoria. Does he think for a moment that I would prefer to have some pale whining white wife with an equally pale and whining, miserable stick of a son? Can't he see beyond a person's colour? Can't he see a person's value? And anyway, Victoria's background is infinitely better than his will ever be. My God, he makes me so angry…"

"Look, perhaps I shouldn't have mentioned it," broke in Kahn. "It's just that he worries me and I think that you should be on your guard."

Ludwig nodded, calming down with an effort. "Thank you, Dietrich" he said, with an attempt at a smile. "I would much rather know what is going on, even though I blow my top! I apologise for the remarks I just made about white wives; you know I don't mean it! Fortunately, I can't imagine that there is anything this man can do to harm us."

He shifted his position in his chair and grimaced. "I'll just have to learn to put up with his nonsense."

PART TWO

CHAPTER NINETEEN

Two months after leaving hospital Ludwig's recovery was complete. All he had left to show for the nearly fatal hunting accident was a thin, livid scar from the bottom of his left ear down to just below the left corner of his mouth and a weakness in his right arm and shoulder, which also caused him a considerable amount of pain.

"It will improve with time if you treat it gently," the doctor said, as he gave him a final check before discharging him.

It wasn't long before he was back at work and once again travelling to and from Portuguese territory, buying local commodities for export and receiving imports for passing on to customers. The breathlessness and weakness that he had suffered in Switzerland as a young man did not resurface (as the doctor had warned they might) and the only legacy of the accident was a stiffened shoulder and a slightly chastened attitude towards African animals and the wild. He had taken for granted his superior marksmanship and hunting ability and had been left with a profound reminder of the unpredictability, strength and cunning of his prey. He would not make that mistake again.

Meanwhile, news had reached the Fort that the Chilembwe uprising had totally and finally been put down. The leader had not received the local support that he had banked on and had fled with a small band to Portuguese East Africa. Before he could reach there, however, there was a skirmish with government forces and he was killed. Not long after, Ludwig received a notification from the sisters at the convent to say that the devastation of the convent and church buildings had been so extensive, it was unlikely that rebuilding could be completed before January in the following year.

Berta was very excited at the news but, in fact, the girls were torn between disappointment at not returning to school and delight at spending more time at home. They enjoyed school, but their long stay at home was a unique event for them and they had forged new and stronger bonds with their parents. When they first came home, the daily routines of their family had been unfamiliar to them, given their long absences, and for the first time they had become part of the busy daily activities of their parents and each had to some extent evolved a niche for herself.

Berta now helped with the separation of the cream from the milk and the churning and shaping of the butter. She also helped Ludwig with his cheese making and his bees, and derived much pleasure from participating in the processes involved in preserving the cheeses and labelling the jars of honey. The pantry was looking charming with three young girls to sort, label, stack and arrange the produce to its best advantage. Berta had also had time to renew her early friendship with Mataya's daughter, Irena, who became her devoted shadow during those wonderful summer days, when it seemed that nothing could take away the magic of the little family's being together.

Elsa had proved very useful with Ludwig's business paperwork and with organising the many-faceted home activities. Paulina had taken over the supervision of the feeding and care of the animals.

Victoria was delighted with these developments; it was the first time that her daughters had shown any inclination for any sort of household tasks. It was natural that they should feel this way, she confided to Mataya, as previous visits had been so very short. There had simply been no time to settle in. No sooner had they found their feet than it was time to start preparing for the return journey. It was also a pleasant break for her to have some help in the daily organisation of so many servants.

Jacko the elephant continued to thrive. His appetite had grown by leaps and bounds and the gardeners now had an additional brief – to bring enough greens each day for Jacko. It seemed that he would eat or drink anything; Paulina grumbled sometimes that it was a full-time job giving him enough to keep munching. The hanging skin had disappeared and he was now a sturdy and slightly potbellied little elephant.

The calf had become very fond of the children, who spent much of the day playing with him. He was perfect for the English games taught to them by Sister Adelaide, like "Oranges and Lemons"; the three and Irena would chant the rhyme as they ducked and ran under his tummy; they had no trouble improvising with the bit about "chop off their heads". They also rode him and fears about his trampling things in the compound disappeared when they realised how extremely sensitive the soles of his feet were. Even small objects were hovered over and then daintily bypassed.

"I don't know how long we'll be able to keep him here," mused Ludwig one day, as he sat on the veranda with Victoria, watching the girls playing with Jacko. "He's growing very fast."

Victoria was not sentimental about animals, although she had developed some affection for the menagerie in the compound.

"Fortunately, we have a lot of space at the farm," she replied. "We will need to build a strong enclosure for him, though."

"I would like to take him back to the wild," confided Ludwig. "It would be by far the most sensible and the kindest thing to do."

Victoria was dubious. "Will the elephant herds accept him? Will he even know their language?"

"You're right, of course," said Ludwig. "I've been planning to speak to one of the government game rangers for advice. It'll be a very tricky business."

"I wonder how the girls would take it," Victoria said. "They're very fond of him."

"Yes, I know. But they are sensible and I think they'll be the first to realise that he'll soon be too big to handle."

That evening after dinner Ludwig broached the subject, and Elsa and Paulina immediately saw the logic of Ludwig's thinking. Berta, however, needed convincing; but when the size of a fully-grown elephant was graphically described to her, with Ludwig pacing the veranda to show length and using arms outstretched upwards to show height, even she reluctantly conceded that it was the only course of action.

"But we've still got a little time to enjoy him, haven't we?" she asked, her sunny, optimistic nature immediately locating the bright side of the affair.

Ludwig moved on to the news that it would be a minimum of ten months before the school reopened and said that the situation was causing him concern.

"Maybe most people wouldn't agree with me," he explained to the girls, "but I believe that women should get the best education possible if they are to live fulfilled lives, with some degree of independence and dignity. Just think. The alternative could be the fate of being shackled to an unsuitable man for life." He looked earnestly at his daughters.

"You probably find it hard to believe now, but the problem is that many men are capable of bringing unhappiness to their wives. And, if the women have no education and no private income, there is no escape for them. Your Aunt Elsa is a university graduate in Physics, and although she is unlikely to ever need to find a job, she has the means to do so if she wishes."

He discussed the matter with his wife later, as they sat companionably on the veranda in the approaching dusk, while the girls played Rummy noisily nearby.

As Victoria had had no formal education she wisely listened without comment to his thoughts, knowing that in speaking his thoughts aloud he would surely reach a solution. And she was right. A few days later he announced to her that he would take over the girls' education for the interim period, but he suggested that she plan a two-month-long trip in October and November with the family, to visit her parents at Sena in Portuguese East Africa. Victoria was delighted. It was two years since her parents had travelled up to visit them and, because of the distance involved, it was rare that they could manage a family trip during the school holidays.

"In the meantime," explained Ludwig, "I'll send off to the bookshop in Blantyre for some books; until they arrive we can all work with the encyclopaedias that I have." He laughed.

"There should be enough in them to keep the girls on their toes!"

When the news was broken to them the girls were thrilled. Elsa's eyes widened in excitement. "Oh, Papa!" she exclaimed. "Could you also teach me some astronomy?"

"My pleasure," he grinned, "on condition that you work hard on the maths!"

Elsa's face fell. Maths was not her strong point but, she felt sure that with Papa teaching her, it would probably make a lot more sense. When she said as much, looking at her father anxiously, he smiled at her to allay her apprehensions and told her that he had no doubt how well she would cope.

Paulina could not see a bright side to any of it. She didn't care for any academic work and was much happier doing her household chores, caring for the animals and embroidering. She didn't feel that her father would be quite as tolerant as the sisters at the convent had been and she sat, glum and quiet, contemplating an immediate future that seemed to promise an unpleasant use of brain power.

"Why so glum?" Ludwig's voice broke in on her thoughts.

"Oh, nothing," was the colourless reply.

"Come on, Kitten, out with it!" said her father playfully.

"Well," she said, choosing her words carefully, "I'm not all that good at anything and I expect you'll get cross with me quite a lot."

"Come over here," smiled Ludwig, putting his arm around her as she came up to him. "Stop worrying. It's going to be fine. We're going to enjoy our lessons together, I know it."

Mollified, she sat down close beside him. Maybe it wasn't going to be that bad, after all.

Berta was totally ecstatic. To be at home with Papa and A Mayi and have school as well was simply heaven on earth, and she told the family so many times during that first evening.

"Berta, if you say that once more I shall throw something at you," complained Paulina eventually.

"Oh, sorry," Berta replied, instantly contrite. "You see, it's just that it's perfect being here…"

A cushion hit her and she yelped.

"I warned you," muttered Paulina darkly then, seconds later, yelped too as the cushion was returned with force.

A Mayi sternly intervened: "You should be ashamed of yourselves, both of you," she scolded. "Any more of this and you can both go straight to bed." Peace was restored.

A Mayi sighed. *When would these two start to get on together,* she wondered; *this constant bickering was getting her down.*

Ludwig, however, had just had a thought that he felt sure the girls would enjoy.

"Girls, you know that I've started drawing maps to show the routes that I take to visit my factories and stores."

"Yes, Papa."

"How about if we start a large map, so large in fact that it'll take up half of the study wall; together, we can chart the routes and devise some emblems to show where each of the properties is."

The girls thought for a moment and then Elsa's face lit up. "That could be good fun, Papa," she said. "Could we draw, colour and cut out factories and stores from pieces of card and pin them onto the map, do you think?"

"And colour in the rivers and hills and mountains!" Paulina was enthusiastic.

Berta wasn't far behind. "I'd like to find out which plants grow where, and colour them in as well."

Elsa went a step further. "You know, Papa, you might even find when you look at the detailed map that there are better routes than the ones you normally take."

Ludwig was delighted with the girls' response and they planned the first steps on the spot. "Tomorrow," said Ludwig, "I'll have the basic map up and you can start adding your thoughts to it."

Nothing else was talked about until bedtime.

CHAPTER TWENTY

Ludwig was away from home more than he liked during the next few months. His factories stretched in a line from Chinde in Portuguese East Africa through Nyasaland to West Africa via Quelimane, Tete, Chiromo and Luangwe to Chicoa. They worked at almost full capacity, preparing and packing goods for export, and needed frequent visits. There was also the steamer company he owned together with its lighters, or barges as they were called, which were used to load and offload the steamer. These had to be supervised and maintained. Add to that the countrywide chain of stores, and the agencies Ludwig held for the German East African Line at Chinde and for the Aberdeen Line at Quelimane, and it was apparent to one and all that only one with his indefatigable energy could have hoped to control such a thriving and diverse business empire.

He was quite excited to find that Elsa enjoyed coming to work with him and was proving to be a valuable asset. It was difficult to find sufficient capable staff to recruit. So many men were at war. One hundred and twenty-five thousand had been recruited as carriers of food and supplies to the soldiers at the northern and eastern fronts during the period, whilst nineteen thousand were already recruited in the Nyasaland army of the King's African Rifles. Add to that at least twenty thousand who were migrant labourers in Southern Rhodesia and South Africa and it could be seen that of an adult male population of about two hundred thousand, not many remained for peacetime occupations.

"There are times when I sympathise with Chilembwe's views," grumbled Ludwig to Kahn one day, as they worked in the warehouse and discussed their struggle to find enough men to load their latest consignment onto the steamer. He was referring to a letter to the Nyasaland Times that the revolutionary, Chilembwe, had written a few months before the uprising, where he complained that a significant proportion of the adult native population were now involved in a war effort that had very little to do with them or their needs.

"These unfortunate people," he muttered, "having to leave their homes and families to fight another man's war."

"True," grunted Kahn as he finished counting bales of groundouts. "No need to decapitate a few whites to make your point, though!"

They became aware that there was someone hovering at the open door.

"Yes?" called out Ludwig, unable to see who it was against the bright sunlight.

"Good morning, sir," came a voice; a young man walked hesitantly toward them.

"Ah," said Ludwig, recognising Majid, the eighteen-year-old son of a neighbouring trader. "Good morning. What can I do for you?"

The young man was clearly ill at ease, his fingers nervously clenching and unclenching.

"Excuse me, sir," he said deferentially. "I thought that Elsa might be here."

Ludwig's eyes narrowed and his smile thinned. "No, she isn't. Is there anything we can help you with?"

"Oh, no. No, thank you, sir. I was just passing by and thought..." he stumbled in embarrassment. "I thought... oh, yes, I thought I would check up on the delivery date of the calico that my father ordered. In fact," and his face brightened with inspiration, "of course you can help me. Can you tell me please, sir, when the calico is expected?"

Ludwig fixed a level and almost hostile gaze on the boy. "Now, Majid, I had this discussion with your father just two days ago. How come he wants the same information again?"

Majid flushed. "Oh, I didn't realise that he had already asked you. I am so sorry to disturb you, sir. Good day."

The last was said as he beat a hasty retreat out of the warehouse.

Ludwig turned to find Kahn chuckling silently. "Kahn, this is not funny," he spluttered. "Do you think that young idiot has designs on my daughter?"

"Ludwig, it is actually very funny. You have started the cycle of 'No one is good enough for my daughter' and if you had any feathers, they would be very ruffled indeed. Face up to it! None of the girls is going to be your little girl for ever."

Ludwig, however, refused to accept Kahn's point of view, pointing out that he was not and never had been in the least possessive of his daughters; when the right man came along, he would be able to see this clearly and without prejudice. Kahn merely smiled and started counting another pile of bales.

When Elsa came in a little while later she joined in with the stocktaking, and the job was completed in a short while.

"Thanks, my girl," smiled Ludwig. He handed her a pile of well-thumbed pieces of paper. "When you come in tomorrow can you file these together with the others and then I'll show you how to cost every item so that we have a total stock figure."

"Of course, Papa." She took the papers, smiling, and found an empty space on Ludwig's desk to deposit them.

Ludwig rubbed his hands with the satisfaction of an unpleasant job completed. "Now, I don't know about you but I'm hungry. I expect lunch must be ready."

"I imagine so, Papa, and yes, I am hungry."

They bade goodbye to Kahn and walked the short distance to the house companionably.

Ludwig appeared to be in jovial mood as the family sat down to lunch. "Oh, by the way," he said suddenly to Elsa. "Young Majid called, asking if you were there."

Elsa looked up, startled, then quickly looked down at her plate again. Her voice was cool when she spoke. "Oh, yes? I wonder what he wanted."

"He didn't seem clear about that. I wondered if you had any idea."

Before anyone could speak, Berta chimed in: "Oh, he's always hanging around Elsa. And he looks at her with big cow eyes. I find these lovey-dovey things so annoying!"

"Berta!" gasped Elsa. "You're talking rubbish, as usual. Don't talk about things you know nothing about."

Berta looked stricken; not for the world would she do anything to offend her beloved Elsa. Clearly she had now said the wrong thing.

"Oh, I'm so sorry, Elsa," she pleaded. "I didn't mean to upset anyone or say the wrong thing. It's just that…"

Elsa cut in icily: "Enough, Berta! Don't say another word." She got up quickly from the table, asked to be excused and ran from the room. Her footsteps could be heard running down the hallway and into her bedroom. Then the door slammed.

There was silence at the table. Ludwig's face was thunderous, and he completed the meal without another word.

When he and Victoria went upstairs for their afternoon snooze he tried to clarify his feelings to her. He lay beside her on the bed, hands behind his head, staring at the blue sky outside the window.

"She's too young to be having a relationship, no matter how innocent, with a young man. For that matter he's too young by far as well. He's got no business chasing a respectable young girl. He's still wet behind the ears, has achieved nothing on his own, he's still a babe." He paused, searching for the right words.

"And I don't want her to marry an Indian."

Victoria looked at him with a quizzical expression in her eyes and a faint smile on her lips, and dug a playful finger into his side.

"The white man is colour blind," she teased.

He turned to face her. "All right. All right," he muttered. "I know what you're thinking. You, her mother, are black, so why should I object to an Indian? Well, it's completely different. Your father's an educated man and your family is one of considerable substance. There's a lot that I can relate to in your culture, even though mine is from several thousands of miles away. Our children are well educated and are being brought up well in every sense of the word. I don't want to throw away what we have achieved. How do you think Elsa, an independently minded, accomplished young woman, would fit in with a man whose father until recently was a labourer on the railways? How do you think she would fit in with the Indian custom of being completely controlled by her mother-in-law? It doesn't bear thinking about. And, let me tell you that I would feel this way about any man, black, white, yellow or somewhere in between, who didn't match up to our situation."

"Ludwiki, why are you saying all this, when all that has happened is that Majid tried to speak to her today?"

"Aha!" he snorted. "That's how all these things start. An innocent little chat, then an innocent little hug, then an innocent little kiss and then and then and then to God only knows where!"

There was a silence. Then Victoria spoke in her deep, soothing voice: "Why don't you speak to Elsa? Tell her what you have just told me. She is a good girl and I know that she will listen to what you have to say. You can't leave matters like this. After, I shall speak to her also. I think she will be able to talk about it more easily with me."

Ludwig turned on his side to face her and gently stroked her cheek. "You are such a good woman, Victoria," he said quietly.

She smiled at him, pleased, and inched closer to him. She kissed the tips of her fingers and ran them lingeringly up and down his lips. "And you are a good and kind man," she whispered.

Her fingers travelled down to his neck, down his chest and lingered on his abdomen. Ludwig reached for her and made gentle yet exciting love to this woman of his who, after so many years, still held the power to rouse him at a touch, who excited him just at the sight of his fair skinned hand against her silky black skin. This woman; his woman.

Later, he hugged her once more, kissed her on her nose and settled down to snooze for the little that remained of the lunchtime break.

That evening, he and Elsa had a chat which ended with his daughter in tears for her abrupt behaviour at leaving the table. She then went to find her mother and threw herself into Victoria's arms. Tears were shed on both sides and Victoria took the opportunity to broach the taboo subject of sex to Elsa and explain its relationship to love and marriage.

"Your father and I are simply trying to protect you and to help you to stay chaste until you find someone with whom you want to share your life. We don't want to see you hurt, my child," she explained.

The crisis seemed to be over – at least for the moment, as both parents wisely realised.

***

Elsa wished that her father had not made such a fuss about her friendship with Majid. Her feelings towards him were ambivalent; and far more important to her was that she was beginning to think that she had found her niche in life. She enjoyed business.

Who would have thought that working in a dusty office adjoining an even dustier warehouse, adjacent to a shop filled with such unfeminine gear as camp beds, kerosene lamps and cooking stoves could be so interesting!

It was the mechanics of it all that interested her so. At first glance it all seemed so simple: get the stock in, sell it and make a profit. But it was actually far from simple. The stock had to be brought in from Europe and there would be months to wait after placing the order as the goods came on cargo ships that stopped at numerous ports around the western and southern coasts of Africa, before travelling north and docking at Chinde or Beira in Portuguese East Africa. And then, from the coast there was a long way to travel to the interior, partly by road and partly by paddle steamer.

And then you had to be sure that you were ordering the right things. Papa travelled the length of the country and into Portuguese East Africa, or P.E.A. as it was commonly called, to get the orders, and then you had to assess the local consumption and order for that. Add to that the probable consumption during the transport interval and you had the amounts to order. And after all of that, much of it was still a best guess. And, if the order was short of something, there would be a four-month wait before you could get the item in.

When the large packing cases arrived at the jetty, they were loaded onto oxcarts and trundled slowly down the main street to the warehouse. Elsa found this the most exciting bit. The wooden packing cases were opened up and then the items were taken out, one by one, pristine and smelling of new canvas, varnished wood and whatever else the goods were composed of. They were counted and checked against the delivery note and then each item was costed. Mr Kahn had shown her how to do this on a percentage basis and she had been surprised at how easy she found this to do, when at school she was so weak at maths.

When all this was done, Papa would decide how many of each item should be displayed in the shop and she would arrange them tastefully on the shelves that ran around all four walls. She often called Berta to help her with this; she was imaginative and bold and her ideas were often useful.

Mr Mussa sometimes invited her to help serve customers, and she watched him closely as he helped the people who came in to find what they wanted. Some tried to knock down the price and she thought that she would never be able to respond to it the way he did, with so much charm and a rueful admission that he simply couldn't lower the price.

"We make so little profit as it is," he would confide sadly to the customer.

Running through the excitement of this newly found occupation was the Majid situation, which intruded irritatingly. Majid, whom she had known since they were both little children, suddenly seemed so different. Their easy camaraderie seemed to have disappeared and when he appeared out of the blue, as he so often did, she found herself tongue tied and feeling the hot blood rushing to her cheeks when he spoke to her. She had to force herself to walk erect as she normally did, because her eyes seemed to be drawn to her feet; it was agonising to have to look at him.

It was quite funny, really, the way he would almost always happen to be going the same way when she and her sisters ventured out for a walk. Unfortunately, Berta was beginning to notice and was beginning to ask awkward questions.

On one occasion she had asked Elsa whether Majid was her young man. Elsa had been startled and had taken her aside.

"Please, Berta, please don't say things like that. Don't even think about them. We are not allowed to have boyfriends and Papa would be very angry if he heard you say it. I might even get into a lot of trouble. Promise me you won't say another word?"

"Of course not, Elsa," responded the younger girl. She threw her arms around her sister impulsively. "After Papa and A Mayi, I love you more than anyone in the world!"

And the two girls had hugged.

No, Elsa reflected, she would never deliberately upset Papa and A Mayi. She understood that a girl cheapened herself if she had relationships with men before marriage; she would not embarrass her parents by going down that road. Not that she had any intention of doing so: Majid wasn't that attractive! Was he?

CHAPTER TWENTY-ONE

Ludwig was in his element. His health was almost completely restored, business was good and, best of all, he had his girls at home with him. There was just one sinister cloud on his blue horizon, and it erupted into a crashing thunderstorm with an unexpectedness that took him completely by surprise.

It was towards the end of Ludwig's recuperation, when he had started giving the girls their lessons. It was a cool and pleasant morning and he and Berta were sitting on the front veranda with books of French grammar in front of them.

It was difficult to concentrate. The flowers in the garden were in bloom; orange, scarlet, yellow and purple blooms jostled for space in the crowded beds. The trees threw their dappled and cooling shade on to the green lawn, where birds of all descriptions pattered about, darting from one place to another as they pecked at the ground for juicy titbits. Ludwig interrupted the lesson for a moment to point out to Berta the wagtails, comical figures as their large tails swayed up and down like fans with each step that they took. Suddenly, a large grey dove descended, sending all the small birds scattering in a crescendo of outrage. Berta laughed aloud in delight, her French verb conjugations forgotten for the moment.

Just then there was the sound of footsteps approaching on the drive, and a few moments later the District Collector came into sight, dressed as always in gleaming white shirt and shorts and pith helmet astride his head. Ludwig rose to his feet as Carrain ascended the steps and greeted him cordially.

"Good morning," he said.

"Morning," Carrain replied, with a cursory look at Bertha. "I wondered if we might speak in private?"

"Of course," replied Ludwig. He turned to Berta. "I'll leave you to your verbs," he said, ruffling her hair, "won't be long."

He led the way into his study, which opened out on to the veranda, sat at his desk and gestured to Carrain to sit opposite and waited for him to speak.

"I believe you have a young elephant," Carrain began in his usual pompous manner.

Ludwig nodded. "Yes. It's no secret."

"I wonder whether you are aware that the Crown has the right of confiscation of any animals from the wild."

154

"Actually, no," responded Ludwig. "But why would the Crown concern itself with an elephant calf legitimately obtained?"

"It is not ours to reason why," came the stuffy response. "The law is simply there to be obeyed."

Berta could tell from her father's next words that he was becoming angry. "So what exactly are you trying to tell me?"

"I'm simply stating the law to you. I am communicating with my superiors in London to ask what, if anything, should be done about the calf and I shall report back to you in due course."

Ludwig cut in, "I plan to return the calf to the wild when I am certain that it can fend for itself."

"I will thank you to do nothing of the sort," retorted Carrain. "The elephant is Crown property and I shall tell you in good time what is to be done with it."

Ludwig nodded and struggled to control the anger he felt at this new turn of events.

Carrain's eyes roamed around the study as he spoke and alighted on a row of magazines tidily stored on one of the bookshelves. He went closer and pulled one out.

"The British Bee Journal," he read out. "You have them sent out?"

"Yes, I do," replied Ludwig. "I'm a regular contributor in fact and because of it, have correspondence with bee keepers all over the world, who write to me for advice."

Carrain didn't comment, but replaced the magazine and continued to probe the contents of the study. Ludwig bit back his irritation at the man's bad manners and waited for him to take his leave.

"What are they?" Carrain asked, looking at the shelves of books and papers behind Ludwig's desk.

"What?" asked Ludwig.

"Those rolls of parchment."

"The ones on the left are maps that I am drawing of the areas where my shops are located."

Carrain looked at him speculatively. "Why are you doing that?"

Ludwig shrugged. "There are no accurate maps available and I enjoy doing it."

Carrain paused. "Umm. And the ones on the right?"

"Astronomy is one of my hobbies. Those are charts of the constellations."

"I'd like to see one."

"I didn't know that you were a fellow astronomer."

"I'm not. I would just like to see them."

Ludwig rose from his chair, picked up an armful of the charts, brought them back to the desk and laid them in a pile in the centre of the desk. That done, he sat down again, rested his elbows on the arms of his chair, joined the fingers of both hands and waited.

Carrain looked nonplussed, hesitated for a moment and then reached out for one of the charts. He unrolled it, held it open with both hands and peered intently at the mass of meticulously entered data. A long silence followed.

Eventually, Ludwig spoke: "I won't explain the mathematical projections that are dotted all over the page. You don't strike me as the sort of person who is comfortable with them. Fortunately, to someone who knows what he is looking at, the major constellations are easily recognisable – even when the map is being held upside down."

Carrain started and loosed the chart which recoiled and snapped shut. A hot red flush rose from his neck towards his face, and when he eventually spoke it was between clenched teeth: "You're an arrogant bastard," he hissed. "You think that you are a law unto yourself. You've made yourself some money and think you can do what you like."

"Excuse me," interrupted Ludwig evenly. "I have always had money. I was born into it, but I have never felt that it put me above the law."

Carrain flipped an impatient hand. "You come to British territory, marry a native woman – have you no decency, man? We whites should be sticking together. And, coincidentally, you just happen to be around when the Germans are attacking the northern part of the country."

Ludwig interrupted him, his face white with rage. "Quiet!" he shouted. He got up and circled the desk to face the British official, who hastily rose from his chair and backed a few steps towards the door. When Ludwig next spoke his voice was icy.

"When you came today I made the effort to forget your past actions towards us and be civil. But that was a waste of time. You are one of the breed of Englishman who has come out here from nothing in your home country, nothing at all. And suddenly, for the first time in your life, you have an area of supposedly inferior people as your subjects. Power at last. And you're too much of an idiot to handle it. Get out of my house, you scum. And if you ever try to come near me or my family again, you'd better bring some of your soldiers because, I swear, I'll whip you to within an inch of your life."

Ludwig stepped back and gestured to the door. Carrain seemed unable to move.

"Get out!" Ludwig roared.

The official suddenly found his legs and bolted for the door. When he reached it, he half turned and hurled a stammering threat over his shoulder. "I'm going to get you, Deuss. Just wait and see."

Out on the veranda, Berta was standing, staring at the study door, clearly distressed about the altercation. She hastily stepped back to avoid a collision and, with her father, watched as Carrain scuttled down the drive and away to safety. Berta turned to her father. "Papa," she said, her face pale and her eyes wide with shock. "What was he saying to you? What did he mean?"

Ludwig put his arm around her and squeezed her gently. Then he turned her around to face him. "Listen, my darling," he said gently. "The man is mad. Take no notice of anything he said. And don't worry, he won't dare come near us again." He hugged her again.

"Now, I need a few minutes of quiet so I want you to get back to your books. I'll be with you shortly and you had better know those three verbs!"

He ruffled her hair, turned on his heel, went back into his study and quietly closed the door.

Ludwig did not mention the incident to Victoria – no need to distress her – but he did on that same evening recount the whole incident to Kahn, to whom he confided his anxieties as they worked at the shop.

"I know I shouldn't have lost my temper," he said as he sat at his desk, absently arranging and rearranging his pens. "But the bastard's continual harassment, his insolence and this last openly expressed disdain of my marriage made me lose control."

"I don't blame you, Ludi," consoled his friend. "But I shouldn't worry too much. All our business transactions are completely above board, we have no skeletons in our cupboards. I don't honestly see what he can do to you. He's only a minor official. Think of it. In the hierarchy of the Colonial Office he is second from the bottom!"

"I know, I know. That's what I keep telling myself. But don't forget that he has the ear of the people further up the hierarchy."

"I have such a sense of foreboding," he concluded unhappily. "I really need to get over it."

He paused and reached a rapid decision.

"Kahn, before I leave to drop the family off at Sena I need to discuss an important legal transaction I would like to enter into with you."

And, sitting at each side of the desk, the two spoke in quiet voices for a considerable time. When Ludwig finally left to go home he seemed to have shed a burden, and it was with a lighter step that he ran up his front steps to spend his evening with his family.

In the ensuing week he had a series of meetings with Kahn and then exchanged letters with his lawyer in Blantyre. Finally, a registered envelope of documents arrived for him. These were signed and witnessed by the two friends and returned to the lawyer. The final shadows had been chased from Ludwig's mind; if anything should happen to him, his family would be taken care of.

CHAPTER TWENTY-TWO

The months flew by in the placid riverside town and it seemed to Berta that she had hardly had time to enjoy her day before it was gone and another was on the horizon.

She had become proficient at making butter bricks and had even managed the skill of making butter curls for the table. Ludwig had also allowed her to insert the copper skewers into the sheep's milk cheese that would very soon be a fair imitation of the famous Roquefort variety. She learnt how to store some of the cheeses in brine and to dry others to make a creditable version of Parmesan. Of the bees she was still wary and was content to watch her father at work while she followed at a short distance, safely ensconced in a top-to-toe contraption made of mosquito gauze.

Ludwig had put a basic map that he had drawn of the country up on the wall; it also included Portuguese East Africa and stretched beyond the Nyasaland borders into the north-west. This had challenged the girls' capabilities; Paulina had made and cut out outlines of tiny factories, houses and shops from card, while Elsa was involved in plotting the actual routes taken by their father. He helped them with this, and also to plot mountains, rivers and other topographical features, while Berta went through their encyclopaedias for names of plants and trees.

"Would you help me draw and cut out some plants and trees, Paulina?" she asked. Paulina happily accepted and Ludwig was asked to order map pins so that they could enter the details of their coloured cut-outs.

"It's wonderful how the girls have taken to charting my routes on the map," he said to Victoria. "They've already got me rethinking how I go about things."

Victoria smiled. "Do you know, Ludwiki, I've never seen my country looking like that. It's so interesting; now I see why it takes so long to get to Sena. Who could have known that we have so many rivers? And that our local rivers feed into the far away Zambezi, which is the only river that I knew as a child! Although people did say during the floods that water was coming from other rivers in the hills. Now I know which ones!"

Ludwig nodded at her and smiled. "It is interesting, isn't it? And the nicest thing about it all is the way it has the girls working well together for long stretches at a time. I'm trying to think of what else they can add to it to keep it going!"

They laughed companionably.

Berta spent a lot of time playing with Irena and Jacko, and many evenings were spent sitting close to her mother, hearing about her childhood in Sena, on her father's plantations.

With May came the winter and a welcome relief from the heat of summer; by June it was chilly enough in the evenings to wear a cardigan and sometimes light the log fire in the sitting room, which Ludwig had insisted on installing but which the family rarely used. Best of all was the dramatic decrease in the number of mosquitoes and the cessation of the heavy summer rains. During the winter there would be, at most, a short-lived foggy drizzle early in the morning.

At this time and because of the cooler weather, Ludwig took the girls with him on one of his small fleet of sailing boats, which he kept on the lake to deliver and collect goods from the lake shore traders. The trip took about ten days and covered almost three-quarters of the lake's length of three hundred and fifty miles. Between stops they skimmed the deep blue waves, sails billowing above them and the sunlight glittering on the crests of the waves. At each stop there was the inevitable crowd of people flocking from their villages into the port town to see the big boat come in, free itself of its load and then immediately take on another.

Going on to the lake was a prized treat for Berta and her sisters. From north to south it was breathtakingly beautiful and its shores varied endlessly. Miles of long, white, unspoiled beaches gave way to dense green foliage that grew almost to the water's edge. At other points formations of huge boulders tumbled like little hills from inland to the lake's edge, where they overhung the water and provided shelter for thousands of varieties of fish. The boat would come in close to shore at these points and the girls would lie on their stomachs on the narrow deck, peering into the crystal clear water, to spot the brilliantly coloured fish of the cichlid family.

Many villages hugged the shore at points where there was a supply of fresh water and the bamboo racks where they dried their fish gave off a distinctive smell, which could be detected from a considerable distance.

"Oh, Papa, what a smell!" the girls would complain, hands fanning their noses.

The villagers' dugout canoes lined the beaches, ready for the next fishing trip, and provided a fun park for their children, who played endless games in and around them. As the name implied, the canoes were made from huge trunks of trees, generally the *Mkuyu* tree, whose insides has been whittled out to form the interior of the boat. There was an art to their making; they were almost impossible to capsize. Although prone to swaying wildly from side to side when being boarded or when a passenger moved, they always righted themselves immediately.

"Papa, can we swim?" was always Berta's question as they docked.

And Ludwig allowed them to. As he said to his *capitao*, as they leaned on the rail monitoring the proceedings, there wouldn't be any crocodiles in the vicinity with the noise and the activity. The calm looking, deserted parts of the shore, with clumps of reeds adorning the shore line and, incidentally providing cover for the lurking crocodiles, were the ones to be wary of.

At home, Victoria opened up a few more acres at the little farm to plant maize and beans for drying. With so many men away at war, Ludwig feared that food might become scarce and it was essential that they have at least enough to feed the family, their servants and their slaves. In the event there was no crisis. The women in the villages were perfectly able to continue their planting and harvesting with their sons and daughters, in the absence of their husbands, and the crop yields were heavy during the period of the war. Women traditionally worked in the fields, primarily looking after the groundnut crop, while the men tended the corn and cotton, although all took part in the harvesting. The women, however, also looked after the fowl, animals, home and the children, so the absence of their husbands was no great hardship. And, as Mataya commented rather caustically to A Mayi, they probably found it a great relief not to have to put up with their husbands drinking *kachasu*, the potent palm wine, each night and the probable arrival of a new baby each year.

The remark reminded Victoria that there was a mystery attached to Mataya's union ten years before to another slave, Chimombo. The two had known each other since they had been children on Roque's plantation, but became separated when Mataya, who had been given to Victoria as her personal servant on her reaching puberty, left the plantation with Victoria on her marriage to Ludwig. A few years later on a visit to Sena with her mistress, Mataya and Chimombo had met again and had fallen in love. Their union had been sanctioned by Roque and when Victoria and Ludwig, with Richard and Elsa, left to return home they had waved goodbye to little Mataya, her slight bandy-legged form standing rather forlornly next to Chimombo at the side of the driveway. Because of her prior close relationship with Victoria, she was not sent out into the fields to work, but was given a job in the Roque home as a housemaid.

Three years passed before Victoria, with Ludwig, Richard, little Elsa and the latest arrivals, Paulina and baby Berta, visited her parents again. As they approached the house, Victoria had hardly righted herself from stepping off the *machila* before Mataya hurtled towards her and fell at her feet, tears of joy flowing down her face, her arms around Victoria's legs.

"Careful, Mataya," scolded Victoria, laughing. "You're going to knock me off my feet!"

"I have missed you, Mama," she repeated again and again. She finally dried her tears, picked up the two older girls and instantly took charge of them.

Her surprise news was that she had a baby girl of her own, little Irena. Victoria insisted on seeing her almost immediately, and it was a truly joyful occasion when Mataya brought her from the servants' quarters, where one of the wives cared for her while Mataya was at work.

Both Victoria and Mataya revelled in being together again and, at the end of the visit, Victoria asked her father if she could take Mataya and the baby back home with them. Roque was very amenable, but was concerned about Chimombo.

"Do you want to take him, too?" he had asked.

But Victoria and Mataya had talked this through and Mataya was insistent that she wanted to come without Chimombo. It was her opinion that he wouldn't want to come anyway.

"What! And miss out on all the girls on the plantation and the palm wine?" she said drily. "He's a bad one, Mama."

More than this she refused to say. Something very painful to Mataya must have happened in that relationship, Victoria thought but, as she caught the mischievous look that accompanied the caustic comment about Chimombo's apparent interest in women and wine, she was reassured that whatever hurt had been inflicted, the pain seemed to have disappeared.

So it was that when Ludwig and his family set out on their return journey home, Mataya walked, singing, beside Victoria's *machila*, little Irena securely fixed to her back.

The baby grew into a sturdy toddler, and then a pretty little girl, who went to the mission school down the road. Until Berta left for boarding school at the age of seven, she and Irena were inseparable. The sight of the two little girls, one black and shining, the other with a skin like smooth milk chocolate, similarly dressed, running around the compound was a familiar one. Mataya never mentioned Chimombo again and, as far as Victoria knew, had no contact with him on their visits to Sena.

Soon it was September and time to start preparing for the journey to Sena. The excitement aroused by the preparations rose to fever pitch, with only one sober note; when Khan dropped by the house to deliver some of the goods that Ludwig was taking to the family in Sena.

"You're quite certain that it's safe to go, Ludi?" he asked.

Ludwig paused in his sorting of the equipment that had just arrived. "Of course. Why ever not?"

"You know how hypocritical the Portuguese government is being at the moment, saying that slavery must stop and on the other hand actively encouraging it. It makes the situation down there lawless, to say the least," responded Kahn, with a worried frown.

Ludwig nodded. "Yes, I agree. But we shall be travelling on a conventional route with large numbers of other people and once we arrive at Roque's place we shall have his protection. I'm going to make quite certain that the family never leaves his property – it's big enough! – and they will always be surrounded by Roque's men wherever they go on the plantation."

"Yes," responded Kahn, uncertainly. "I'm sure you've got it all organised – as usual!"

The packing continued. Normally, this would have been an enormous exercise, since the traveller would take the customary gifts of produce of all sorts from his garden, live fowl and indeed, anything he had that would appeal to the hosts. This case was slightly different, since the Roques had vast quantities of every sort of crop and animal. All that would be taken from the home would be a selection of Ludwig's cheeses and many jars of honey, for which grandmother Roque had a special fondness. From his shop, Ludwig prepared a sizeable quantity of tents, torches, paraffin stoves and lamps, and any other items that he imagined his in-laws would find useful. He also took large quantities of brightly coloured materials, from calico to finer embroidered silks for the ladies of the house. The girls took with them doyleys and tablecloths that they had embroidered, and Berta proudly packed away a colourful doyley threaded with beads, a present for her grandmother. For her grandfather, she had managed to find a little brightly coloured tin with a hinged lid in one of the Indian shops; just the thing for his snuff.

Slowly the pile of cartons on the back veranda grew, in direct proportion to the excitement of the family, as they counted down the days to their departure. The trip would be quite tiring, involving as it did the first two-day step by steamer on the rugged and crocodile-infested Shire River to the small settlement of Matope, which nestled on the river banks. There they would disembark and the long procession of slaves and other bearers would wind its careful way along the dusty track to Blantyre, the bustling main town. The slaves carried the family's baggage and camping equipment for the three-day journey. The other bearers carried the *machilas*. From Blantyre they would catch the recently completed train connection to Chinde in Portuguese East Africa. Once the family had been installed on the train, the bearers would return to Fort Johnston. From Chinde it was a short final stage on foot to Sena.

These were precious days, the kind of days of which memories are made, memories that would be rekindled in years to come, to be relived and tenderly put away again before being awakened again and again to bring light and joy to dark days.

163

CHAPTER TWENTY-THREE

The day of their departure dawned bright and cheerful and the house was a hub of activity from the early hours, as preparations began to board the ferry at midday. Squatting on their haunches on the dewy ground outside the back veranda, chatting to one another, the bearers waited for their loads. They wore beige tunic tops and matching shorts and they smelled of a type of carbolic soap. The natives were particular about personal cleanliness and habitually bathed themselves carefully each morning, leaving a final film of soap, whose smell they liked, on their skins. They were eating freshly boiled sticks of cassava which Edisoni and Njoka had prepared for them, and by his side each had a steaming cup of tea with milk. Each cup would have three to four teaspoonfuls of sugar in it; they liked it sweet.

Ludwig busied himself with ensuring that the gifts they were taking were securely packed in wicker baskets. He would be staying at Sena for two weeks and then returning home. Beside him was his trusted *capitao*, Aleki and another supervisor, Jumo, who were travelling with the family. Aleki would remain with them for the two months of their stay and ensure their safe return home. When the baskets were full they were topped with hessian cloth, which Aleki sewed securely to the thick rim of the basket using a large curved needle and twine.

In addition to the luggage and the gifts, camping equipment and food for the entire party had to be carried for the thirty-six-mile leg of the journey between being dropped off by the steamer at Matope and getting to Blantyre, and the railway station, by road. *Machilas* were packed for the same purpose, as were the carrier's sleeping mats and sparse personal belongings. Finally, it was decided, in response to the girls' pleas, to take their bicycles so that they could ride part of the way. Ludwig's Norton motorbike which, as his family teased him, seemed to have become an extension of his body, was ridden to the ferry together with another, a B.S.A., for Aleki, and then stored with the other goods.

Victoria's voice could be heard instructing the servants who were remaining behind how to manage the household and menagerie while she was away. Mataya trotted behind her, only taking a few minutes off to get Irena ready. It was taken for granted that Mataya would never leave A Mayi's side and Irena would naturally be with her mother.

The animals in the compound had sensed that something unusual was going on. The dogs walked restlessly up and down, jumping onto the girls and barking loudly at anybody passing by the drive. The monkey chattered incessantly, baring her teeth and leaping onto anyone who came into her range, dogs included. The ducks, geese and chickens seemed to be noisier than usual, squawking loudly and jumping into the pond with boisterous splashes. The babies in the compound became uneasy and started to wail and their mothers called angrily to the over-excited toddlers to calm down. Berta too, felt tense, although excited at the prospect of the holiday ahead.

The girls finished their packing early and came downstairs to see what they could do to help. Elsa and Pauline followed in A Mayi's turbulent trail and Berta ran out to give her father a hand. By midmorning they were ready to move, just as the steamer's arrival at the jetty was announced with a sustained blaring of its foghorn.

An excited buzz arose amongst the small crowd, which had been joined by Kahn, who had come to bid the travellers goodbye. The bearers stood up in anticipation and Aleki organised the loads that each would carry on his head. First they put onto their heads the doughnut-shaped ring of sisal which would act as a cushion against the hardness of the load and then they topped this with the hessian container. A bit of juggling and wiggling and balance was achieved. This was accompanied by much laughter and grunting. Soon the twenty-two bearers were organised into a long line and, with Aleki at their head, walked swiftly towards the jetty, chanting one of their songs, whose rhythm gave them poise and strength.

Finally, A Mayi, after a last look in every room of the house in case something had been left behind, climbed into her *garetta*, a one-wheel bush chair, resembling a rounded sedan chair, covered by a canvas canopy and mounted on a wheel with stout wooden poles on either side. This was then pulled and pushed by two servants, one in front and one behind. Ludwig led the way on his motorbike and the girls followed behind on their bicycles. In high spirits, the little procession made its way to the jetty and, pushing their way through the milling crowd of uniformed men, climbed aboard the river steamer, the girls' chatter and laughter floating on the gentle breeze.

Once aboard, A Mayi, Paulina and Berta went to explore and settle themselves in, while Ludwig and Elsa stood at the railing and watched the unusual activity on the jetty below.

"Are these more soldiers setting out for the north, Papa?" asked Elsa.

Ludwig nodded, his eyes scanning the scene below. "Yes, more South African troops are being deployed and our own Kings African Rifles as well, to deal with the continued German threat."

Elsa turned to look at her father. "Do you not feel any loyalty towards the Germans, Papa?"

Ludwig snorted. "Why should I? We're not German, thank goodness, and I wish Lettow-Vorbeck, their Commander, would just admit defeat and go away! This stupid little war is costing so many lives, it's tragic."

"The poor soldiers…" said Elsa, with a sigh. "And worse still for their families, who are going to have to try and live without their husbands and fathers."

Ludwig stared ahead. "If only that was the whole story; unfortunately, it's much worse. Quite apart from the soldiers there are the porters and carriers, the *tenga-tenga* as they are called, who have to carry supplies to the troops, including food and ammunition, sometimes walking two hundred miles to do it." He turned to Elsa. "Can you imagine that? And apparently, they are frequently overloaded, so there is a high mortality rate."

Elsa was horrified. "But, Papa, that's awful. And so unjust."

"Don't I know it? They've even got them building roads and cutting and transporting firewood. From what I hear, we're probably talking many tens of thousands of men in total. Who knows what the real number is?"

Ludwig suddenly stopped. "Look, Elsa, under that huge acacia tree," he said, pointing. "I've just noticed that army trucks are parked there and it looks as though they're putting the wounded into the trucks and, I imagine, taking them to the hospital. They must have been brought by this steamer on its way southward."

Elsa's hand went to her mouth and her eyes filled with tears. Ludwig glanced at her, then abruptly changed his tone and put his arm around her, to give her a quick hug.

"Don't worry, my dear, they'll be well looked after and safely out of harm's way. Anyway, my girl, we're off on our holiday! There's absolutely nothing we can do about what's happening in the war, so let's go and find the others and do a bit of exploring of our own."

Elsa fished for her handkerchief in her pocket and surreptitiously dabbed at her eyes as they went down the narrow staircase and had a quick look at their cabins, which were very small; but the summer heat had not yet begun and so they were tolerable. Back up on deck they found the rest of the family, the children in a high state of excitement. They hung over the deck rails on the narrow decks and watched the loading of the cargo, while A Mayi sat on one of the deck chairs on the foredeck under a canopy, Mataya and Irena on a mat at her feet.

Ludwig signalled to A Mayi that he was going downstairs and she waved and nodded back. She was perfectly content here, where she could feel the refreshing river breeze, while Ludwig was down below checking that all the stores had been loaded and that all twenty-four carriers were on board.

Quite apart from the soldiers and the *tenga-tenga*, the entire dock area was crowded with interested onlookers, who watched and commented on the proceedings. Children dashed hither and thither but some stood quietly, in wide-eyed contemplation of the preparations for a journey which they could not imagine, even in their wildest dreams. Dockers, struggling with heavy loads, shouted and swore at the children who got underfoot, and boxed the ears of any who did not get out of the way in time. Babies on their mothers' backs yelled anxiously as they were jostled by the excited throng; enterprising families went through the crowd with large aluminium trays of roast groundnuts, baked bananas and sticks of boiled cassava, fare for hungry travellers. Steamboat day was a holiday.

Three short blasts from the foghorn warned that departure was imminent. Minutes later there was a quiet shuddering underfoot and the steamer edged out from the jetty. The tiny engines gathered power and belched volumes of smoke before the little river steamer, with a burst of energy and a fanfare of foghorn blasts, left Fort Johnston and set her course southward, away from the lake from where the Shire flowed. The noise startled the wildlife and what had been calm banks shrouded in blue-green reeds burst into teeming life as birds arose and reached for the sky.

The journey took them along the luxuriant banks of the Shire, where the tops of African huts could be seen at frequent intervals amongst the vibrant foliage. This was in contrast to the lake shore, where slavery had ravaged the population and in doing so had ravaged the land. Planting crops was not possible when villages were subjected to raid after raid and energy had to be spent trying to be at the ready at every moment to resist capture.

Here, abundant growths of papyrus lined the banks and at this time of the year thousands of circular bird's nests adorned the tips of the reeds and swayed in the breeze. At intervals, massive trees with thick dark green foliage rose from the river banks, their roots half in and half out of the water, like giant fingers grasping the earth for a hold.

"Paulina, look!" called Berta excitedly to her sister. As Paulina approached the rail, Berta grasped her arm and pointed excitedly to the tree roots. Her voice turned ghoulish. "Crocodiles don't like to eat their prey as soon as they kill it, so they hide the rotting corpses under the roots, which are below water level. Who or what do you think could be in there now?"

Paulina shook Berta's hand off with a shudder. "Be quiet," she said. "You talk rubbish sometimes."

"No, I don't. Papa told me so and you can ask him if you like."

But Paulina knew that it was true and both girls uneasily eyed the crocodiles, which could be seen sunning themselves on the little sandy beaches that edged the water, where there were no reeds. As the steamer approached, they lifted their massive heads and crawled, their rear ends and lethal tails swaying, into the river.

Every now and then Ludwig would call out to them, "Come girls, quickly!" and another breath-taking scene would unfold before their eyes.

Large open plains stretched into the distance, with little vegetation apart from small shrubs and stunted trees. Silhouetted against the misty blue hills in the distance, were large herds of buffalo, often with some zebra or deer standing a prudent distance away. They were able to observe the large glossy beasts and make a quick sketch before the thick banks of reeds brought the curtain down on the view.

Another stretch of sandy bank opened up the vista again and in the middle distance could be seen varieties of buck and impala.

"Oh, Papa," Berta called, "just look at how gracefully they run and leap!" She had a sudden thought. "D'you know, this is what it must have been like in the Garden of Eden!"

Ludwig grinned: "Yes, probably, but without us making such a noise; and if there were all these crocodiles, hopefully they had fewer teeth!"

Berta shivered in delight. "Oh, Papa, don't!"

Progress was swift unless shallow waters were encountered, for the rains had not yet begun and the river level was at its shallowest. Here, the expertise of the captain came into play as the river was gently negotiated and, with many a scraping of the keel, the river boat slid once again into deep water. Ready on deck for emergencies when the captain's skill was not sufficient, were a supply of long, thick bamboo poles and, should the vessel be grounded the crew, amid much singing, pushing and grunting, would lift her into deeper waters.

Ludwig spent his time between chatting with the captain on the bridge, pointing out flora and fauna to the girls and sitting with Victoria. Meals were basic and were served in a tiny 'first-class' dining room adjoining the saloon, an equally tiny lounge area. Arrangements had been made for *nsima* and bean stew to be served to Aleki and the carriers on the lowest deck. Most of the African passengers, however, waited for the steamer to make its nocturnal stop, when they would prepare a meal on the banks of the river.

In the hour before dawn, the bustle below decks started and the journey resumed, and it was midmorning when the vessel slowed down in the middle of the river at Matope, their destination, where the water was deepest. Engines straining and puffing smoke noisily, the craft edged slowly alongside the small jetty and the chaotic disembarkation of the excited passengers, their baggage and their animals began. While the crew noisily unloaded the cargo, Ludwig called his family to the top deck to see the view.

"Bring your paints!" he added.

The girls rushed up, with A Mayi close behind, and stared entranced at the view that met their eyes. But it was the foreground that was most fantastic. The docking steamer had alerted the birds and flocks of them frenetically swept across the sky, their species too numerous to identify. Crocodiles and storks shared the shallows and the sandy banks on the opposite shore while hippos gambolled close to the steamer, some closer to the shore and in full view, others with just their mammoth heads showing.

Pencils raced over paper and tongues chattered in the excitement of the moment until Ludwig recalled them to their situation and suggested that they disembark. Reluctantly, the girls left the deck and packed their paper and colours. A half-hour later the entire party was on the river bank and preparations were being made to move on to the second stage of their marathon journey.

CHAPTER TWENTY-FOUR

The journey to Blantyre, the commercial centre, was accomplished in three days, without any mishaps. Victoria was carried in her *machila*, with frequent breaks for her and her carriers. The girls rode their bikes until they became tired and then they, too, were carried by *machila*. Ludwig rode his motorbike up and down the line and frequently branched off to bag some game for the next meal.

Finally, they were on the outskirts of Blantyre; tents were pitched on a grassy hillside thick with silver-barked eucalyptus trees, while Ludwig set off on his motorcycle to see his friend Stanley, to let him know that they had arrived.

When he returned two hours later it was with Stanley in his new car, a black model T Ford, roaring behind him. Berta was the first to run and greet them. She threw herself into Ludwig's arms.

"Oh Papa, look at that car," she whispered. "Can I sit in it? Please?"

Cars were a rarity outside the main towns and in fact motorised transport had only become fairly common in the last year, since German forces had attacked the northernmost frontier and attempted to penetrate southwards in September of 1914. It was becoming impossible to recruit enough bearers to carry essential supplies to the front; so trucks had been imported from South Africa and roads opened up to the north, to get troops and supplies to the vulnerable front before another attack could be launched by the Germans.

While Berta and Elsa examined the car and coveted its shiny metal sophistication, it was arranged that the family should go to the Stanleys' home, where they would spend the night before catching the train at Limbe, Blantyre's sister town, six miles distant. Aleki, with Jumo and the carriers, would remain on the outskirts of the town and, on the following day, he would ensure that the carriers marched to the station in time for the goods to be loaded, before the train's departure at midmorning.

Ludwig called Aleki and Jumo aside and they squatted on their haunches underneath a sweet-smelling eucalyptus tree. He turned first to Aleki. "Aleki, please make sure that you are all at the station by six o'clock tomorrow morning."

Aleki nodded his assent and Ludwig turned to the junior supervisor: "Aleki will leave the B.S.A. motorbike with you, Jumo," he said. "Please make sure that you buy enough food for yourself and the carriers for the journey back home."

Jumo tried to hide his delight. Motorcycles were expensive and were generally owned only by the well off. To have the machine in his care for the journey home was a treat beyond imagination.

"And," added Ludwig, accurately interpreting his expression, "remember that if there is so much as a scratch on it when I return your life will not be worth living."

They talked briefly and then Ludwig reached into his pocket and passed Jumo a pouch containing money, to cover the expenses until home was reached. Then, rising, he re-joined the party still congregated around the car and they drove into town, with Ludwig following behind on his Norton.

After an early night the family was up at the crack of dawn and ready to move on, but not before Stanley had drawn Ludwig aside with words of caution. "You know what you're doing, I'm sure, Ludwig, but you are sure of your safety on this trip, are you?"

Ludwig looked at his friend in startled surprise. "What do you mean? Not thinking of the slavers, I hope. I had this discussion with Kahn before we left!"

Stanley looked serious. "News from that part of the world is that the slave traders are still very active; there have been numerous reports of abductions."

Ludwig chuckled. "Yes, I'm sure, but we shall be on my father-in-law's land, with hundreds of his people around; I shall take good care that the girls are never in any kind of remotely dangerous situation."

He put his hand on his friend's shoulder. "Thanks for the concern, Stanley. Much appreciated."

A Mayi walked up to them, a question in her eyes. "Anything wrong?"

"No, no!" replied Ludwig hurriedly, with a warning glance at Stanley. "We were just coming."

The three returned to the main group, who were clustered around the car in the drive and, with thanks to Mrs Stanley for her hospitality, they departed in the car, with Mr Stanley at the wheel. Natives on the side of the road stopped to gaze in awe as the speeding piece of metal went past, easily outstripping the cyclists and bullying the motorcyclists into clinging to the side of the road to let them overtake.

They shook their heads in wonder. How this modern piece of machinery ate the miles was marvellous indeed!

***

They arrived at Limbe train station in good time, to find the carriers already there and waiting for them. Whilst Ludwig bought the tickets the family and retainers waited on the platform, an exuberant hub of activity. Natives, loaded with luggage and bound for Chinde, on the Indian Ocean, or for stations before, milled around the platform. Wicker baskets packed with fruit, vegetables, pulses and eggs surrounded them. In little wire containers were live chickens and, although they protested vociferously, they were much more fortunate than the others, whose legs were bound and who were either left to lie on the ground or hang upside-down from their owners' hands. Excited children ran everywhere, their pretty round faces aglow, teeth sparkling white against dark skins. And, as if all that weren't enough for a mother to think about, there was the inevitable baby on the back. The babies generally slept soundly in their mobile cradles but with the mayhem around them at this moment, most of them were looking around them in wide-eyed interest.

The Asian stationmaster, Mr Singh, strode up and down the platform directing events, herding the passengers and attracting attention with shrill blasts of the whistle he wore around his neck. His face was ruddy and sweating in the summer heat and dark patches spread under the armpits of his khaki uniform. Meanwhile, the engine driver and his assistants started to work up some steam for the engines. The hissing filled the air and slowly the chug, chug, chug began.

More shrill blasts and the passengers began to fill the three central third-class carriages, which were Spartan in the extreme. Slatted benches set as close together as possible constituted the only seating, and shelves for luggage ran the length of the carriages, just below ceiling level. In the front of the train was one carriage optimistically marked "First Class" and at the rear was the baggage compartment. The second carriage was the dining car.

"Come, A Mayi, come, girls!" called Ludwig, and ushered them into the first-class carriage. Here, they had two sleeping compartments and the seats were upholstered in a dark green canvas fabric. As Bertha found when she sat down, they were quite comfortable. Two long seats facing each other ran along the width of the compartment. A door on one side opened out into the corridor; on the other side were two large windows. In between the windows and set into a wide polished wood panel was a tiny wash hand basin. Up high and close to the ceiling were racks for the luggage. As Berta soon discovered, the backrests of the seats could be lifted up and attached to heavy hooks in the ceiling, thus forming an upper bunk bed. Ludwig and Victoria installed themselves into the one compartment while the girls took over the second. The three were enchanted with their introduction to steam locomotive travel, and leaned out of the open windows to watch as Ludwig and Bensoni loaded the motorcycles and side cars into the baggage compartment. Ludwig returned to sit with the girls and Bensoni; Mataya and Irena turned into one of the general carriages to try and secure a space in the noise and bustle. They too had a hamper from the Stanleys, and each carried a roll of luggage which contained their sleeping mats, soap, towel and comb.

"Got everything?" asked Ludwig with a smile.

'Everything' constituted a hamper which the Stanleys' cook had prepared for them and a small wicker basket from which the welcome clink of bottles could be heard. Aleki had put them in the passageway leading to the carriage and the girls nodded, hungry already, despite having had a big breakfast before leaving town.

But they were too excited to eat just yet and leaned out of the carriage windows as the train tooted, the stationmaster whistled and the engine finally came fully to life with a strong chug, chug, chug.

"Keep your heads in, girls," called Ludwig from his seat. "You'll be black with soot by the time we get there!"

"Please, Papa?" They looked at him imploringly.

"Oh, all right," he grinned. "But keep your heads in until we are clear of the station or you'll have them knocked off!"

They drew back in, sat down and watched in fascination as they drew out of the busy station yard and headed for the open country, the wheels turning faster and faster until it seemed to Berta that they were going at a great speed.

The journey was from the relative highlands of the Limbe area to the lowlands of the Zambezi valley; the land sloped gently and continuously towards the ocean. The train sped through luxuriant woodland and gave a wide berth to the Murchison cataracts, which spewed crystal water and foam into the sparkling sunlight. On and on it chugged busily, over open plains and across rivers, stopping frequently to pick up and disgorge passengers and to replenish the engine's water supply.

On the few uphill sections the engine struggled and slowed to a crawl. The passengers didn't mind at all and took the opportunity to hop off the train, have a walk and then hop on again. Anywhere that there was a village in the vicinity, women lined the tracks selling fruit, vegetables, little wooden carvings and other fancy goods, and the engine driver was not averse to stopping so that the passengers could shop.

"Oh, Papa!" called Berta as she spotted some bananas. "I'm really hungry. Can I have a banana?"

Her father shook his head at her disbelievingly. "Hungry already?" he asked. "Don't forget we've got hampers from the Stanleys."

But, he finally gave in to the pleading eyes of his daughters and nimbly leapt off the train, bought a selection of fruit and climbed back up just as the train started to move forward laboriously.

Her hunger satisfied, Berta gazed out at the endless vistas. It felt to her that wherever you looked you could see forever. She drank in the beauty of the vistas unfolding before her and wondered whether any other place in the world could be so beautiful. It was the rainy season and the vegetation was luxuriant. It seemed that every shade of green had been splashed across the foreground of a vibrant canvas, becoming more muted as it faded in the distance, until it was claimed by the violet hues of the distant hills. The carriages rocked from side to side and the engine sounded reasonably quiet when they were on the plains. But when they forged between two hills the echoing sounds crashed into their ears.

Berta leaned out of the window for most of the time, only coming back in to ask Elsa whether her face was black yet. It was not long before Elsa could truthfully tell her that it was indeed black. At this gratifying news, Berta relaxed and her thoughts turned to food again.

The Stanleys' cook had done them proud and the family tucked into chicken and tomato sandwiches followed by fruit cake, but not before Ludwig had made up a package for Aleki and taken it to him, in the crowded compartment behind them. He was concerned that the servants' hamper might be sparser than theirs. Several bottles of homemade lemonade quenched their thirst in the increasing heat of the day.

The afternoon was spent playing games and dozing. Elsa tried to sketch the vast patchwork of colours outside the wide windows, but the movement of the train made it impossible.

Then the train suddenly screeched to a halt and heads popped out of all the windows to see what was the matter. Word spread fast. There was a herd of elephant crossing the line.

"Can I go and see, Papa?" came the call from three young throats.

"No, you may not," was the grim reply. "You will stay right where you are. If we watch carefully we will see them disappear into the bush."

And, true enough, about fifteen minutes later they saw a small herd of elephant ambling peacefully away from the tracks into the scrub at the side.

The train did not, however, immediately start again. The engine driver went to both sides of the train, bellowing, "Lavatory stop! Lavatory stop! Men to the left, women to the right! Watch out for snakes and such like!"

"Papa, what is going on?" the girls wanted to know.

Ludwig was highly amused. "There are no lavatories on the train except for the two in first class, so when someone needs to go, he tells the engine driver, who stops the train for everyone to go," he told them.

Berta was quick off the mark. "I need cabinet, Papa," she said. I need the lavatory.

"You minx," he said. "And no, you are not going out into the bushes. You will use the lavatory at the end of the corridor, but you have to wait for the train to start before you do."

Berta knew that it was no use arguing so she subsided.

The train came back to life, hissing and spitting, and the journey continued. Teatime brought lemonade and homemade ginger biscuits, but by early evening the children were hungry again and Ludwig soon announced that it was time to head for the dining car for supper. In expectant excitement the girls followed their mother and Ludwig into the dining car, where they had to have two tables, since each only held four. Victoria sat with Elsa and Paulina, whilst Ludwig had his meal with his youngest daughter. The fare was stark but the adventure more than made up for it. The first course was a watery vegetable soup, the second fried *chambo*, the country's delectable indigenous fish and the third sliced bananas covered with watery custard that had formed a skin on the top. As she polished off the last morsel Berta gave her opinion loudly; this was the best ever meal that she had ever had in her whole life, ever. Pauline, at the adjoining table, rolled her eyes heavenward, but forbore, at a frown from A Mayi, to voice the comment that trembled on her lips.

Dark night had fallen by this time and when the family returned to their compartments it was to find in some excitement that the upper berths had been opened up and the beds made. Fresh towels hung by the wash basin. After a bout of experimental bouncing on the lower and upper bunks the children were disappointed to find that they were unable to make out anything through the windows. There were no towns or cities with twinkling lights to entertain them. Africa slept.

They drew the blinds and climbed sleepily into their bunks. Soon the family too was asleep.

The passengers were awakened just after dawn by the steel screeching of the train drawing into a station. The by now familiar sounds of water being pumped into the engine reservoir and the stationmaster trotting up and down the station to the accompaniment of newly awoken babies crying, mothers calling and chickens squawking, assailed their ears. Up shot the blinds and three eager faces pressed against the glass and surveyed the busy scene, made all the more romantic by the rosy dawn glow with which it was enveloped.

"You should see yourself, Berta," said Paulina with a sigh. "You look a mess."

Berta scrambled down and went to look in the mirror above the wash basin. She was delighted to see that it was true. Her face was still blotchy with soot and her reddish auburn hair stood up in stiff spokes. Satisfied, she returned to the window. Paulina sighed again.

A knock at the door and a call, "It's Papa!" sent Berta racing across the compartment to let her father in.

'It's time to get ready, my dears," he said. "We get off at the next station." He looked hard at Berta. "But, unless you can clean yourself up in precisely two minutes, Miss, you can stay on the train to Portuguese East Africa." She was ready in one.

CHAPTER TWENTY-FIVE

An hour later and it was time to disembark. The train drew into the station with a great deal of hissing and snorting before it ground slowly to a halt in front of the little station building, which was a picture framed by flowering pink, red and white oleander shrubs. The family disembarked and Ludwig and Bensoni hurried to get the motorcycles out of the baggage compartment while the engine drivers tooted impatiently, eager to be on their way. Grandfather Roque, a dapper, upright man, awaited them at the station with what seemed to Berta to be at least thirty slaves, ready to carry them and their baggage to the plantation.

It was a happy and leisurely walk, Ludwig and his father-in-law riding part of the way together on the motorbike before Roque switched to a *machila* from where he could talk to his daughter. The girls rode their bicycles until they became tired, when they also were borne in *machilas*. Mataya, with Irena close behind, trotted up and down the line of slaves, talking happily and asking about her family. Much news was exchanged on all sides as the procession wound its way slowly through heavily cultivated fields, much of it sugar cane, as far as the eye could see.

Amongst the new companies that had been set up by the French and the British in recent years was the Sena Sugar Company, of which Ludwig's brother, Paul, was a Senior Manager. Ludwig had originally planned to join the company but soon saw what exciting opportunities awaited anyone who had the energy and the drive and, instead, started up his own agency business.

The leisurely pace continued until their destination came into view, a thousand acres set on the higher ground leading up to the hills which encircled Sena. A short while later and the homestead could be seen in the distance. The sun was setting in a sky brushed with violent red strokes and dusk was creeping in at the edges as they arrived at the plantation house, where *Mayi* Roque was waiting for them on the front veranda.

Pressure lamps blazed on the veranda and in the living room beyond, silhouetting Victoria and her mother as they bowed to each other, hands clasped in front, before embracing warmly. Ludwig greeted her similarly but the girls raced up the steps and hugged and kissed her, laughing with delight. They loved their grandmother. She was a small, slim woman who carried herself very erect. Like all African women of her class she was wont to look stern, but a twinkle in her eye often belied the straight line of her firm mouth; and when she smiled she seemed to bring the sunshine closer. She tried to listen to them all at once, her loving eyes travelling from one to the other, but she finally shook her head, turned to Victoria and ruefully said, "I can't make them out. Can you?"

Everyone laughed and just at that moment Victoria's two sisters, Anania and Francesca, arrived. The aunts were favourites with their nieces, to whom they were known as Tia Anania and Tia Francesca, *Tia* being the Portuguese term for aunt. Slim, with very straight backs like their parents, the aunts came into the room holding out their arms to their nieces. More affectionate greetings were exchanged and Victoria turned back to her father to ask, "Where is Louis?"

Louis was Roque's only son and the eldest of his children. He had trained him as a goldsmith, to take over the business to which he no longer had time to devote.

"It's so disappointing," the older man replied, "but he is on a trip to Beira to buy gold and collect orders for his jewellery. He's going to try and get back before you leave so we'll just have to wait and see."

Greetings over, it was decided that everyone should go upstairs and get cleaned up for dinner before they all settled down for a good chat. The long journey had taken its toll, however, because shortly after dinner the yawning youngsters bade their family goodnight and trailed wearily upstairs to bed.

The first week of the holiday was spent revisiting the familiar areas of the plantation, Elsa and Berta often accompanying Ludwig and Roque. The sprawling, brick-built house was cosy and cool with its large, airy verandas to front and back. In the Portuguese tradition, meticulous attention had been paid to the cultivation of lawns, trees and shrubs around the house and, from the beginning of the drive, it presented a pretty picture of hibiscus, oleander, azalea and poinsettia bushes against a backdrop of the deep green foliage of acacia trees. At the rear of the house and about half a mile away the travellers came to several acres of vegetables, peas, green beans, cabbage, carrots, onions and lettuce. Another several acres were devoted to citrus trees.

Ludwig looked around with interest and then turned to Roque with a puzzled query. "What do you do with it all?" he asked, with a sweeping movement of his hand, indicating the expanse of flourishing vegetation.

"Things have changed since you were last here," he replied. "Concessions have been granted to the British and French to enter this territory and open up plantations. Companies have followed the Sena Sugar Estates and have opened up previously virgin land and planted vast sugar estates, with European managers to oversee them. The managers bring their families and, as a result, there is now a market for fresh vegetables and fruit. It has been good for us and also for the country."

Roque went on to explain that in the lowlands, which could be flooded for up to five months of the year, he was harvesting large rice crops and the rest of the land was devoted to export crops. The Zambezi River formed one of the boundaries of his plantation and he had used the river water for an ingenious network of irrigation channels for the crops in the dry season.

"It all looks very efficient; of course, you will remember my groundnut requirements?"

"Yes, of course. That is planted each year as a matter of course."

"Speaking of my requirements, could you spread the word that I am here, Roque, and that I will buy as much beeswax as they are offering."

Ludwig was a big exporter of beeswax, amongst other commodities.

"Any quantity, Roque, the more the better," he said. "I can sell any amount to the consumers in Europe."

In the distance were the slave quarters, about a mile away, but the house slaves lived in a compound about one hundred yards from the house. Slaves who went to private homes were the most fortunate, since it was customary for them eventually to become members of the wider family circle. They lived, coupled and had children under the auspices of the family who had bought them and, in many cases, knew of no other life.

"Still using mainly slave labour?" Ludwig asked, as he squinted into the distance.

"Of course," was the matter of fact reply.

"It should have stopped a long time ago; when is it going to end?" Ludwig wanted to know.

"No sign of that yet," replied Roque with a shake of his head. "Especially now with these big new companies. It's much easier for them to use slaves than to try and recruit the locals, who often offer resistance. Forced labour is the norm. It's legally required for six months of the year for each and every man."

Ludwig shook his head in disgust and they moved on.

Meanwhile, Victoria had suggested to Mataya that she go and stay with her mother, who was one of the laundry maids. The mother's and daughter's reunion had been ecstatic and Mataya spent much of the day with her mother, but at night she preferred to set her sleeping mat on the back veranda, where she was close to her mistress.

"We're not here for long," said Victoria, "so I think you should spend as much time as possible with her."

But Mataya was adamant: "At night we'll all be sleeping," she explained, "so I may as well stay with you. But I'll definitely make sure that Irena spends more time with her. A grandmother is special and I want Irena to remember her fondly after we've gone back home."

Since Irena accompanied Berta much of the time, Berta was not pleased to hear that Mataya was insisting that Irena spend more time with her grandmother. She ran to find her mother.

"Can Irena stay to play with me, please?" pleaded Berta.

"Think, Berta!" counselled her mother. "She has family of her own to see here, family that she has never met and will not see again for a long time." Then she added, to Berta's crestfallen face, "But I'm sure there will be opportunities to play with you as well."

Slaves and *machilas* had been allocated to the family and Roque insisted that the girls be carried wherever they went. When Elsa and Berta complained to A Mayi that they would prefer to walk, their mother asked them to be patient.

"It would upset your grandfather to see you walking in the dust like a slave or a labourer. Try to humour him, please." She paused. "However, if you are some distance from the house and want to examine something which can't be done from the *machila*, then I am sure no one will mind." There was no mistaking the twinkle in her eye.

"Thank you, Mayi," whispered Elsa, and the girls ran off.

But Victoria called them back. Her expression was sober as she spoke: "Elsa, do not ever go out of sight of the slaves. The *chifuamba* are still seen from time to time and although I don't imagine that they would dare come onto your grandfather's property, one never knows. And, as always, keep away from reeds or plants that are taller than you are. Anything could be lurking in there."

"Oh, Mayi, I know," she laughed. "You've told me a hundred times! I promise, I will be careful."

Victoria's concern was well founded. Although the Portuguese government had outlawed slavery some forty years previously, they had, in reality, actively aided the trade and allowed trading outposts along their eastern shores which were also embarkation points for the east, the Americas and the West Indies. In addition, the slave trade benefited them; with each batch of slaves that arrived from the interior the Portuguese and mixed-race settlers had first pick of the consignments. Bowing to pressure from the British and the French, the Portuguese had finally put an end to this overt activity, but the legacy was an underground network of Arab slave traders who continued to operate for the thriving eastern markets.

But these thoughts were far from the girls' minds as they paddled in the river in the brilliant sunshine of their seventh day with their grandparents. The river had always been their favourite haunt on the mainland. At this point, it was about two miles across and the other side could not be seen. It was shallow at its banks but soon became deep and flowed swiftly and silently on its way to the sea. In the centre of the river were a few islands, their banks thick with luscious green reeds. One, the largest, was owned by Roque. On it he had two hundred or more acres of grain and groundnuts and, after these were harvested and the floods had been and gone, he would plant rice in the fertile silt as the second crop of the year. The girls loved the island. The second month of their holiday would be spent there.

Berta and Paulina hitched their skirts up to their voluminous bloomers and played in the clear water. Elsa was more decorous and simply held up her skirt to avoid being splashed.

Crocodiles were a constant menace and every year a number of infants would be snatched from their mothers' arms as they bathed them in the shallows. And when cattle came to the river's edge to drink young calves would disappear in a storm of threshing foam. The girls knew, however, to avoid the reed banks which were some thirty yards distant and to sound the alarm if a solitary gnarled apparent tree trunk came floating slowly by. This was the predators' favourite disguise. The slaves, too, kept a wary eye open and squatted close to the water's edge, chatting as they cast their glances up and down the river banks. Their life would not be worth much if any of the girls was hurt.

The bank was busy at this point. Young mothers with babies on their backs had come to collect water in their earthenware gourds while the toddlers played in the sand. They also brought their washing daily and the clothes were lathered with carbolic soap and slapped against large slabs of rock at the water's edge until they were clean. The Africans had a song for every activity and as they rhythmically pounded their clothes their sweet, clear voices rose into the fragrant morning air. Invariably the songs would include a snide comment about one of the mothers and the melody would dissolve into merry laughter.

When the washing was done, the young women would go home to the village, water and washing balanced on their heads, babies strapped to their backs. Toddlers walked alongside. There was work to be done in their gardens with the rains no more than a month away; there were hungry men to feed.

Suddenly, the boisterous chatter of the slaves stopped. They faced upstream and started to mutter in some agitation. The young mothers' song died and the girls followed the slaves' gaze upriver and froze in horror. A huge dugout canoe was approaching in the distance, the current carrying it rapidly down the swirling depths of the current. Elsa froze when she made out two figures on board. In their pristine white robes and white turbans they were unmistakably Arabs. Surrounding them were about half a dozen men, clearly their local acolytes, and at the back of them stood a man in European clothes. He was dressed in the usual garb of the settler, khaki short-sleeved jacket with matching shorts, and on his head he wore a wide-brimmed khaki felt hat which shadowed his face. All carried guns. Slave traders.

This was the sort of scene that nightmares were made of.

With a little scream, one of the mothers hoisted her baby more securely onto her back, grabbed her toddler by the hand and ran away from the bank. This was the signal for everyone to follow suit and there was pandemonium as the mothers collected their children and the slaves thrust the girls into the *machilas*, lifted the poles to their shoulders and ran for safety. At the same time there was a roar of excitement carried down the wind from the canoe and it turned sharply to head for the shore. They had been seen. Berta longed to get out of the *machila* and run but they had left their sandals on the river bank and she knew that her feet were too tender to run on the path which, although smooth, had sharp little pebbles embedded in it.

Her heart pounding, she glanced back and saw that there appeared to be an argument taking place in the canoe, which by now had run aground in the shallows. The natives were standing on the bank, as was the man dressed in the European clothes. There was in fact a violent argument going on; the European was shouting and waving his arms, in one of which he held a rifle. More they did not see as they turned a bend, and Berta was astonished to find that all the others who had been at the river bank had vanished into thin air. Not even a rustling of the tips of the sugar cane plants that stretched as far as the eye could see on the left gave a hint that someone might be sheltering in them.

A further fifty pounding yards on the slaves, breathless and perspiring in rivulets, turned into a dense thicket of reeds, pushed onwards for about twenty yards and then bundled the girls out of the *machilas* and gestured to them to lie flat and still on the ground. One sped back to the path where they had made their entry and hastily pushed any reeds that had been spread apart back into their positions. He crawled backwards swiftly, covering their tracks with a bunch of dried reeds as he went, and then lay down beside the others. Quiet descended and nothing but the absence of bird song and the unnatural stillness betrayed the drama that was being enacted.

Berta lay still, her cheek against the rough, reed-strewn ground. Her heart pounded and she could scarcely breathe. A few feet away she could see one of the bearer's feet and she was horrified to see that his ankles and calves were slashed and bleeding from their headlong flight into the razor-sharp reeds. Stinging pains along her arms and cheeks warned her that she had probably suffered the same fate. Just beyond she could just see Elsa's scratched and bleeding face, also pressed into the ground, her eyes warning her not to utter a sound, a reassuring little smile playing on her lips. Of

Paulina she could only see an out-flung arm, scratched in a thousand places, and a few drops of blood inching downwards.

Suddenly, she remembered the pythons. *Oh, God,* she prayed, *please keep the pythons away.* She knew that they nested in the river banks amongst the reeds. *Please, God, don't let there be a nest close by.*

She was distracted by the sound of soft footfalls on the road. They paused, it seemed to her, exactly where they had left the road. There was a low murmur of voices. More footsteps joined them, but this time it was the sound of sandals. Some more murmuring and they all moved on. A man's voice rose and carried clearly to where the girls were hidden. He spoke in Portuguese and the girls struggled to understand what he was saying.

"Just give it up," he said. "I am certain that the three girls are Roque's grandchildren. It is well known that he has been expecting them for weeks. It would be madness to tamper with his family or his slaves. He is tough and ruthless and I certainly don't want to tangle with him."

"I want to make sure that they are his," said another voice, with a strange guttural intonation. "If they are not Roque's we have found a little treasure. They are pretty; those fair skins would fetch good prices in Saudi."

The European man broke in, "This is not a hunting trip. I said that I would show you the territory and I want nothing to do with anything else. I am not my father, Abdul. I think differently about these things."

The voices faded as they moved on, still arguing heatedly. Silence descended once again and the bearers lifted their heads cautiously, signalling to the girls that the slavers would be returning and that they must stay still. Berta lay, her cheek on the bed of dry reeds, the sweat of terror pouring down her face. A drop of sweat seared its way into her eye and she bit back the cry of pain, not daring to raise an arm to wipe it away.

Then suddenly a child wailed. The faint receding murmur of voices was cut short and in the utter stillness, the child wailed again. There were excited shouts and the sound of feet pounding and plants crackling and swishing. Then a woman screamed and there was a crescendo of sound, a woman crying, begging for mercy, men shouting, a baby wailing. Berta felt that she was going to vomit and burrowed her face in the fallen reeds on which she lay. She noticed, as though in a dream, that her hands were shaking like leaves.

The sounds came closer, the woman's loudly crying and pleading, the panic-stricken screams of her child, the rough voices of her captors. She called out again and again.

"A-ee, a-ee. Please sirs, leave us. Let us go. A-ee!"

There was the sound of a slap cracking through the air.

"Shut up!" was the brutal order shouted at her, "or I'll kill your child."

The woman's voice stopped instantly and only her quiet sobbing could be heard, mixed in with her broken voice attempting to calm her baby.

As the party drew closer they heard the men jeering at the woman. They heard her stumble and the blows that rained on her. They heard her whimper and the angry shouts at her to keep quiet. They heard the threats when the child wailed again.

Berta felt anger overcoming her fear. Hysteria fogged her mind. She could not let this woman be taken. She had to go to her. She had to help.

As though reading her thoughts, Elsa and one of the bearers turned their heads slowly towards her, their fingers to their lips. In Elsa's eyes blazed the message, *No! Stay quiet!* A cautious hand reached out and held Berta's ankle gently but firmly. *No!*

Other footsteps came pounding up and voices were raised, some in jubilation, others urging caution.

The man they had assumed to be European was speaking urgently, yards away from where they lay, transfixed with fear. "Let her go, Abdul," he was saying quietly. "You cannot hunt here. This will lead to trouble. Let her go, man."

There were a few murmurs of assent, others raised in argument, and the voices moved on, gradually fading away towards the banks of the Zambezi where they had beached. Quiet fell again and Paulina moved. Instantly, one of the carriers jerked around to her urgently, motioning her with his finger to his lips to keep quiet.

Another eternity passed and suddenly soft footfalls went past again. A trap had been set. The slave traders had left some of the men to follow behind in case someone came out of hiding too soon, and Paulina had almost done just that.

No one moved for a long time.

Eventually, one of the bearers got to his feet and motioned to the rest to stay where they were. He stealthily crept back towards the road and they saw him disappear in the direction of the river bank. They had almost given him up when he came back and motioned to them all to come out of hiding.

"They're gone," he said quietly.

Elsa looked at him intently, a question in her eyes. He nodded.

"All of them," he said.

Once back on the road, the girls stepped into their *machilas*. They were badly shaken, very afraid and dazed. The shock of almost being caught was overshadowed by the horror of the woman's – and her baby's – abduction. Paulina and Berta sobbed quietly.

"Come on, little madams," said one of the carriers in the Chisena language with a reassuring smile. "Let's go home."

With that, the six bearers broke into a trot homeward.

CHAPTER TWENTY-SIX

Over the next few days the atmosphere at the Roque home was subdued.

Ludwig had his own demons to fight. "How?" he kept asking himself. "How could I have been so foolish, so unaware of the real dangers? How could I not have taken Kahn's and Stanley's concerns to heart?" He had almost lost his girls, his precious daughters.

The near abduction of the girls had deeply shocked the entire family. As Roque said to the adults in the evening after the girls had gone to bed, he was aware that some slavery continued but, by unspoken agreement, each of the planters' homes, families and workers were sacrosanct. Any raiding was understood to take place further in the interior and the majority of that was done by the Africans themselves for sale to the Arabs. Yet, even for these sporadic raids, their days were numbered. Western powers were now openly critical of Portugal's support of the inhuman trade in the area. Slavery on a mass scale had had its day. Roque put the event into perspective.

"It was one of those completely unexpected, freak incidents. The girls were on our property where the river constitutes the boundary and it was just unfortunate that an Arab slaver was on the river that day – in broad daylight. The chances of that set of circumstances combining were very small," he finished.

Ludwig decided to be more forthright than usual on the subject, which he generally avoided since it was a sensitive issue.

"The fact remains," he said, "that the whole situation is intolerable. When I first arrived in Portuguese East Africa I saw at first hand the extraordinary plight of the people captured by the Arab and African slavers during their raids into the interior." He paused, looking down and shaking his head.

"There seems no end to the cruelty of the slavers. Do you know that once they capture their victims in the interior they force them to carry loads of ivory to the ports to save their transportation costs? And if a mother can't carry both the ivory and her young child, then she is forced to abandon her child which is left to die?"

The women were staring at him, wide-eyed.

"No, surely not!" expostulated Victoria. "Surely it pays them to look after the people so that they will get better prices for them?"

Ludwig shook his head. "No, that's the extraordinary part. The demand for slaves is huge in places like East Africa, India, the West Indies, America and so on, but the supply of victims in the interior is also huge.

So, the slavers are quite careless; but then, the Arabs in particular are known to be a cruel race."

Victoria turned to her father. "Pai, why is this allowed to continue?"

Before he could answer, Ludwig replied: "The British outlawed it in 1807, but the Portuguese government says one thing and does another. It tells the international community that it is against slavery but, in reality, does nothing whatsoever to stop it. On the contrary, it encourages its own form of slavery; Portuguese land owners are always the first buyers when new lots of slaves are brought from the interior."

Roque interrupted mildly, but his expression had become quite grim: "I see what you are saying, Ludwig, but I think you forget that most of these victims, as you call them, are savages themselves. We have shown many times that they are incapable of making the smallest decisions for themselves and that, if you allow them to be so, they too are brutal to one another."

Ludwig held out his hands. "But of course they are unable to make decisions for themselves," he protested. "They have been in captivity for so long they have lost the ability. As for brutality, is that a reason to enslave them and their families, often under truly brutal conditions, for all time?"

"But think," countered Roque. "The conditions that many of them live under, when they are slaves, are very much better than those they lived under in their villages in the interior. Riddled with disease, constantly fighting tribal wars, being decimated by wild animals. It is not a good life."

"Maybe not," replied an exasperated Ludwig. "But that does not justify enslaving them and treating them as they do. They are human beings just as much as we are."

There was a silence and Ludwig made a strong effort to bridle his passion; the last thing he wanted was to fall out with his father-in-law, for whom he had a strong respect. And, anyway, it would solve nothing. There was absolutely nothing that he could do about the situation; it was the way things were.

"Anyway," he finally said, in a more neutral voice, "I have told Aleki that the girls are not to go anywhere without him from now on. I have also given him a rifle to keep on him at all times."

He paused, his face showing his concern.

"Do you know who the woman was that was taken?" he asked.

"I believe that she came from a village on the higher ground, where she lived with her husband and three children."

"Oh, the poor woman," broke in Victoria, her face still drawn with shock. "How terrible for her and her family. Thank God for our slaves;

without their prompt action we would surely have lost our children." Her lips quivered and her eyes were bright with unshed tears.

Ludwig put his hand on hers. "It's over now. They're safe," he consoled her. "But, unfortunately, we can do nothing for that poor woman and her child."

Turning to his father-in-law he said, "I shan't be going back as planned, but shall wait to take the family home. Another thing; I would like to reward the slaves involved," he added.

Roque waved the suggestion away. "I have already done so," he said. "I gave them money and their freedom."

Ludwig nodded, satisfied.

"But," continued Roque, "they have refused to go. They were born here, you know, so they are second generation slaves. They are part of our family. You understand that they were saving themselves as much as the girls, of course. Their fate if they had been caught would have been terrible, as it is for all the slaves who are sent away on the slave ships. They will most likely remain on the estate, as all the others have done who could have left by now if they had so wished. At least they now have the money to build themselves and their families a nice hut, buy some new clothes and, who knows, maybe a bicycle!"

The girls had not ventured from the house since the incident. They were nervous and Paulina and Berta had woken up a few times during the night, screaming. As Victoria said to Ludwig, they had been traumatised and needed time to heal. "What's made it worse," she sighed, "is that it's happened so soon after the terrifying events of the Chilembwe uprising."

The two aunts had been invaluable. As two spinsters with time on their hands they had been more than happy to devote their days to the girls. All the cuts had been bathed with antiseptic and then iodine had been dabbed on.

"Ouch!" yelled Berta. "That hurts!"

For of course it did. The children were well used to the sting of Iodine and dreaded the arrival of the little dark bottle.

Tia Francesca, her dark strong-featured face full of energy and fun, teased the girls until they were able to smile a little when remembering the incident.

"I don't know why you were worried," she said to them with mock seriousness. "When they got a good look at you they would have dropped you and run away crying!"

Tia Anania was the quiet, gentle one. She was fairer than Tia Francesca, with a fine featured face, and she was more likely to take one of them on her lap and stroke her hair when they felt vulnerable.

"Why aren't you married, Tia?" asked Berta one day as she sat on Tia Anania's lap, thumb in her mouth. It was rare to see Berta sucking her thumb and it showed how unsettled she still felt.

Tia thought a moment and finally said with a wistful smile, "Well, as you know, Grandfather loves us all very much and, well, he just never seems to have met anyone whom he thinks is good enough to marry me."

"Or me!" broke in Tia Francesca with her wide smile, as she looked up from the tray cloth that she was crocheting.

Berta digested this information before replying: "Well, I think he's right," she pronounced, to everyone's amusement.

As he observed his daughters closely, Ludwig decided that they needed to be given an opening to discuss their fears and their worries. Perhaps, he reflected, if he could set the traumatic event into some sort of perspective, they would be able to deal with it more easily. They had dipped into the subject of slavery at various times in the past but never in any depth. Now, he judged, was the time.

Accordingly, two mornings later, he suggested to them that they have morning tea in the garden, sitting under a huge avocado pear tree, on the side of the house that had been paved for that purpose. It was a favourite spot to sit on a hot day, cooled by the shade and surrounded by beds of brilliant flowers. Several cane chairs painted a dark green were set in a circle around a cane table, also green.

"A lovely idea, Papa," enthused Elsa. "I'll call for cold drinks, tea and biscuits," and she hurried off to the kitchen, while Ludwig, Paulina and Berta made their way to the side of the house and made themselves comfortable on the chairs.

Presently, Elsa returned with one of the house servants, who carried cold drinks and biscuits on a tray. Another followed shortly with the tea. Elsa served and the group settled down to desultory chatting, mainly about the forthcoming trip to Roque's island. As they talked, Ludwig was casting around for a way to bring the conversation around to the issue of slavery, when Berta did the trick for him.

"Papa," she suddenly said. "Will we be safe on the island?"

"Safe? Safe from what, Berta?"

"You know," she replied, anxious eyes on his face, "the chifuamba."

He smiled reassuringly at her. "Of course! You know, girls, what you experienced was something very unusual, and something that is dying out."

"You mean that people are not being taken as slaves anymore?" This was Elsa.

"As a general rule, no, they are not. You see, it is actually a crime that is punishable by law and what we see here is simply what is left of a long battle that anti-slavery protesters have been fighting to get rid of slavery for good."

Elsa spoke quietly: "Papa, at school we are taught that slavery is evil and illegal and then we come out of school and find that it's happening anyway. I don't know what to think any longer."

And Ludwig led them into a discussion of the beginnings of the slave trade, by the Arabs from the east and the Africans from the south, who formed a deadly alliance that was to lead to the enslavement of many millions of hapless Africans.

"The tragedy is that this evil became accepted as a way of life, not only here but in many parts of the world and somehow, people became blind to its immorality and cruelty.

"Many came to regard slaves as barely human and were concerned with only two things. First, how to get more work out of them and second, to wonder whether the owners could be held responsible if a slave died of physical abuse or neglect. Imagine, girls!"

Ludwig could see from the expressions on the girls' faces that this was strong stuff for youngsters of their ages, but the attempt to capture his daughters had awakened a simmering unease in his mind and brought it to a rippling boil. His children had to know the truth, however ugly it might be.

Berta slipped out of her chair and climbed into her father's, pressed close against him. "So why do we still have slaves?" she asked.

"Good question, my dear," he replied, smiling down at her. "You see, when slavery was first made illegal, there had been no way of controlling the trade. Vast numbers of men would have been needed to just make a dent in the abduction of such large numbers. Secondly, many of the slaves did not want freedom."

Paulina broke in, "How can that be, Papa? How could they not want to be free?"

Ludwig thought a moment. "Well, take a look at our own slaves. They are still with us because they don't want to go. It's costing me a lot of money to employ them but I can't tell them to go. Most of them don't even know where they came from. It is probable that entire families have been wiped out, so they would have nothing to return to even if they knew where to go. They have no education and very basic skills in the work place. Most have no initiative whatsoever because all of their remembered lives they have had no voice. They have been told how to do everything, down to the tiniest details of their lives, so that they find it very difficult to make the smallest decisions. It will take at least a generation of care, support and education for them and their children to repair the damage that slavery has done to them."

"Did all the slaves want to stay with their old owners?" was Berta's next question.

"Oh, no!" Ludwig was emphatic. "Many owners had been cruel and from these the slaves left whether or not they had anywhere to sleep or anything to eat. Those owners found themselves with serious problems when their workers disappeared." He smiled grimly.

Ludwig in fact had relatively few slaves, bought, as he said, out of compassion. All of them had subsequently refused to leave him, and these were deployed in the vegetable gardens and livestock duties. On hunting trips, however, they came into their own. They were expert trackers and water seekers and he relied on them for the success of the hunting party. For their part, going on these trips was the highlight of their existence. They were free in the wild for a time and doing something at which they excelled.

"The day of the slave is over, at least in Nyasaland," finished Ludwig. "As the years go past and they become more secure in their new world, they are becoming more courageous and more and more are making the break from their previous owners and going to the District Commissioner's office to be declared free men."

But Ludwig wasn't finished: "Girls, there's one thing I want you to remember me for and that is that no slave ever died or was badly treated while in my care. This is something I am proud of. I also want you to know that we owe a lot to the slaves. With them, colonists all over the world have been able to expand their businesses very much faster than they would have been able to do had they been forced to pay for their labour. And look at Mataya. She has been devoted to A Mayi ever since she was given to her on her thirteenth birthday. She would never leave us."

Father and daughters talked around the subject for a while longer. Although, for the children, slavery had been a fact of life, sanitised no doubt by the fact that slaves were treated well in their environment, the abduction of the African woman and her child had savagely rewritten their perceptions. They were able now to perceive the practice in its full horror.

"I'm glad we had this talk, Papa," said Elsa eventually. "The whole subject is more horrible than I had realised; but at least I know now that people are fighting against it and that one day, soon I hope, it will be over."

"And," said Paulina, "at least we know now that people like the ones who tried to capture us are not normal. They are like thieves or murderers. And we just have to stay out of their way."

"Quite correct, my dears," smiled Ludwig. Their responses were all he could hope for in such a difficult, as yet unresolved state of affairs.

A few days passed before the girls' father and grandfather suggested that they all take a motorbike ride to the part of the estate where the livestock were kept. The girls had kept to the safety of the house for days and the family felt that it was time for them to face the outdoors. Although doubtful at first, the idea finally began to appeal to them and the five of them crammed themselves into the sidecars, with Berta sitting pillion behind her father.

It turned out to have been a very good idea. In the brilliant sunlight, with the cool breeze streaming past their faces, the horrors of that day began to shrink in their minds. By the time they returned home, their cheeks were flushed, their eyes were shining and their faces were wreathed in smiles.

They went around to the back of the house where they left the motorbikes and walked up the back steps into the house, chattering happily and calling out for their mother.

Her answering call came from the front veranda and they made their way towards her, Berta running helter-skelter in front of the others. They reached the veranda and stopped in confusion, when they found that their grandmother and Victoria were apparently entertaining visitors. Sitting beside Victoria was a woman of mixed race and opposite was a young man who resembled her sufficiently to be her son. Roque strode forward and greeted the visitors, whom he introduced to Ludwig as neighbouring plantation owners, Senhora Maria Mendoza and her son, Rafael.

Rafael Mendoza rose gracefully to his feet and shook hands politely, his gaze lingering on Elsa, who looked down in embarrassment. He was a fine-looking man, taller than average with a strong build, wavy black hair and striking dark eyes.

"I am pleased to meet you," he said, smiling down at them.

At his words the girls froze and they stared at him, faces paling and their eyes widening with shock. Ludwig looked at them with a puzzled frown. He spoke sharply to breach the awkward silence. "Girls, ask your grandmother if you can help her with anything."

Good manners took over; Elsa asked her grandmother for instructions and the three made their way to the kitchen to supervise the bringing of tea and cakes.

Once in the kitchen, Elsa closed the door behind them and looked at her two sisters. "It's him, isn't it?" she said.

Paulina and Berta nodded dumbly. His voice had given him away. His was the voice that had spoken to the Arab slavers.

CHAPTER TWENTY-SEVEN

Elsa walked to the kitchen window, shivering, her arms wrapped around her body. Her mind screamed in terror, horror, disgust; all the emotions that she had felt when that poor woman was being dragged away. She seemed to hear, indeed feel, the thud of the blows, the baby's terrified screams, its mother's broken, shuddering sobs. She closed her eyes and put her fists over her ears, clenched her teeth so that she would not scream, tried to find air to breathe into her aching lungs.

Paulina looked at her and went swiftly to her side, and the cook who had been putting some water on to boil looked round in concern.

"What is it, Elsa?" Paulina whispered. She put her hand on Elsa's arm and felt her body shaking. Alarmed, she gripped Elsa's shoulders. "Elsa, tell me, please. What is it?"

Through chattering teeth, Elsa managed to get out a few words. "I'm remembering that woman and her baby…"

Berta moved to her and she and Paulina held her close until they felt the shaking subside. The cook approached. "Shall I call A Mayi, little madam?"

Pauline looked at him gratefully. "No, it's all right," she said quietly, "but can you help Berta make her a cup of tea with lots of sugar in it?" And she led Elsa to the chair by the window, soothing her, calming her and then making her drink the hot, sweet tea. Both girls knelt and sat back on their heels at Elsa's feet, looking up at her, holding her hands, stroking her arms.

Finally, Elsa's breathing slowed down, her body slumped and she felt the relief of quiet tears streaming down her cheeks. She smiled shakily down at her sisters and clasped their hands in hers.

"Thank you" she said. "I don't know what came over me, but I'm afraid I'm in no state to go back in there. Can you manage without me? I'll do what I can in the kitchen, but I just cannot look at that man again."

She stood up, and then swayed, clutching the chair for support.

"What's the matter with me?" she muttered. "I'm always the strong one and just look at me!"

Paulina looked at her anxiously. "I was just thinking that. Would you like me to call A Mayi?"

Elsa smiled. "No, thank you, Paulina. I'm already feeling much better. I think that I must have been denying the shock of that dreadful day and now, seeing that man and remembering it all, it hit me badly." She paused.

"I shall always feel wretched about what we saw and heard that day, but I hope I've got the worst of the shock out of my system."

Steadier now on her feet, she set about instructing the cook as to what he should take out to the guests.

"Off you go now, you two!" she said to her sisters. "Cookie will be out with the tray in a few minutes and you can have a good look at that ghastly man in the meantime!"

The two younger girls, once they had recovered from both the shock of seeing Rafael and then watching their sister collapse, were happy, even anxious to return to the veranda, to get a better look at this man who had been involved in the traumatic events of the previous week.

They paused at the door and Berta said in a dramatic whisper, "If you feel ill again, just tell Cookie to call us, all right?"

Elsa smiled and nodded.

Half an hour later, Elsa heard the veranda chairs being scraped back and the murmur of voices saying goodbye. When she was sure that the visitors had left she emerged, still not quite steady on her feet and, her face grave, she went to sit by her father.

"Papa," she started.

Ludwig interrupted her. "Are you all right, Elsa? You look strange. What's wrong?"

"No, it's nothing, Papa. I just wanted to say how sorry I am that I was so ill-mannered when we came out to see the guests."

Ludwig looked at her questioningly. "What happened, Elsa? I was quite shocked that you of all people should behave like that."

"Papa, you remember that we told you that there was a Portuguese man with the Arabs on the river that day."

"Yes?"

"Well, that was him. It was Rafael Mendoza."

The revelation was followed by an appalled silence.

"Are you absolutely sure?" asked Ludwig, quietly.

"Oh, yes, absolutely," chorused his daughters.

"I'll never forget that voice," said Paulina with a shudder.

Ludwig looked questioningly at his father-in-law.

"I am totally astonished," Roque told the gathering, and he went on to tell them about Rafael's father, who had been the offspring of a Portuguese military man and a local girl. At the time, the potentially rich Portuguese territory was in a shambles. The raiding Kisawa and Landeen tribes considered the Portuguese a conquered race and regularly plundered the small forts they set up. They even exacted tribute from the inhabitants, who included powerless militia. The mixed race people, although officially regarded as whites, tended to side with these warlike tribes, which made it

193

difficult to formulate secret plans for defence. In order to give these people, and they were many, who belonged neither to the European nor the African races, a sense of identity, and to give them a reason to resist the marauding tribes, the Portuguese authorities gave them vast tracts of land, *prazos*, to do with what they wished. It was hoped that they would start producing crops and raising livestock, which would develop the colony and improve its economic prospects, whilst giving them reason to repel the invaders.

"Well, it didn't work with Rafael's father who, by all accounts, was a brutally savage man, who not only exploited his slaves mercilessly but kept any free villagers on his land in a constant state of terror, by selling them off whenever he had need of guns, ammunition or alcohol."

Roque paused a moment to recollect. "The man died young from his excesses, leaving a widow and small son, Rafael. However, I have always considered Rafael to be a fine young man; he transformed the plantation which he had inherited from his father, and which had been virtually derelict, into a prosperous, flourishing enterprise."

"It seems as though I might have been mistaken," he finished thoughtfully. "But, what do we do now?"

The subject was discussed in low tones, as dusk fell and the glorious flame-coloured canvas of the sky announced the coming of nightfall. Dusk had fallen when it was finally decided that nothing would be said or done. As Ludwig said, "Despite his unsavoury connections, Rafael did at least decline to be part of the exercise and strongly advised the Arabs against their intended action. I do not think that we have anything to fear from him, particularly now that he has met the girls." He paused. "I didn't much like the way he was eyeing Elsa," he muttered in an aside to Victoria, but remembering Kahn's poking fun at him, he refrained from saying anything further.

Ludwig was left with the uncomfortable feeling that he had been catapulted into a situation over which he had little control. Everything seemed to have changed. Roque's plantations had always seemed homely and secure, a good place to be to relax, wind down and enjoy the different culture. Now, he thought, he was going to have to keep his wits about him at all times. He sighed.

CHAPTER TWENTY-EIGHT

As the days sped by, life resumed its rhythm, tensions faded and the family began once again to enjoy the idyllic life on the plantation. The sun shone benignly on the people and the crops; activities began to prepare hundreds of acres for planting after the first rains. It was also time to go across to the island, because the grain and groundnut crops there would be ready for harvesting.

On the surface Elsa appeared as happy and carefree as her younger sisters, but she was struggling with mixed emotions that were too confused to share with anyone, even if she had wanted to.

Any young woman could not fail to be affected by Rafael's brooding good looks and his smiling charm. The problem was that the contrast between these attributes, and what she knew of his background and his connections with the slave traders, was quite frightening. How could one mind and one body house such disparate attributes? At times she felt that he wasn't to blame for the sins of his father and his inherited connection with the slavers; at others, the thought of him, particularly when they had heard his voice on that fateful day, made her feel physically ill.

And, yes, she had noticed the warmth in his eyes when he looked at her. On a physical level she had felt herself responding; then she had heard his voice and attraction was replaced by revulsion.

Rafael had visited a few times since the day they had met on the veranda and it became increasingly clear that he had a special admiration for Elsa. She was, however, always cool in her manner towards him.

"Mayi, I can't stand him near me," she confided to her mother, as they sat on the front veranda having a cold drink. "I know he's good looking and charming, but each time he speaks my stomach feels as though there's a knot in it."

"I'm not surprised," replied Victoria. "It will be a long time before you can hear that voice and forget where you first heard it!"

Matters came to a head one day when Rafael found Elsa apparently alone in the garden in front of the house. It was another cloudless day, not yet too hot, and the birds' chattering in the trees was the only sound in the otherwise tranquil, colour-filled garden. She and Paulina had been pruning roses, as Ludwig had shown them to do, and Paulina had gone to the back of the house to find another pair of gardening scissors. Berta had climbed a nearby jacaranda tree and, encircled by its heavy foliage, was lying on a cushion in a fork in the branches, reading a book.

Elsa was just rising from cutting a low branch on the rose bush when Rafael walked briskly across the grass towards her, pushing his felt hat on to the back of his head as he did so. His look was strained but his eyes shone at the sight of her.

"Good morning, Elsa," he said. He did not wait for her response to his greeting but stopped and stood opposite her. He spoke rapidly. "It's fortunate that I found you here, because I wanted to speak to you."

He took off his hat and stood for a moment playing with the fold around the crown. He seemed to be struggling to find the words to say, and when he spoke the words came out in a rush. "I'm sure that you have noticed that I have special feelings for you. I think that you are a lovely girl. I think that you are charming and intelligent and, in fact, I just wanted to tell you…"

He broke off in confusion as she stared at him with, as Berta later put it, a look of horror, a bit like she was staring a cobra in the face.

"I've taken you by surprise," he said. "I'm so sorry. I should have realised."

He put out a hand, as if to gently touch her arm and she shook him off agitatedly, unable to speak.

"Elsa, you barely know me and I hope that you will at least give some thought to what I have said. I want to marry you and, although the idea will seem strange to you now, I hope that you will start in time to think about me in a favourable light. I know that I'm rushing things, but you do live a considerable distance away and I don't know when I shall see you again…"

At last Elsa found her tongue: "I couldn't," she stammered. "Not now, not ever. Please go away."

That voice, she was thinking. It brings it all back. *Just go away.*

Rafael was confused: "What's wrong?" he asked with a puzzled frown between his handsome dark eyes. "I can't be that bad, surely, can I?"

Elsa's tongue deserted her again and Rafael took it as a sign that she was softening towards him. He reached out and gently pulled her to him, folding her in his arms and gently pressing his lips to hers. Shock immobilised her as his hands lightly caressed her back and his lips played sensuously against hers, coaxing them to open.

For a brief moment Elsa stood motionless, paralysed by the wave of desire that swept through her, making her unable to prevent her lips moving against his in response. Her hand rose to caress his neck and bring his head closer to hers. Rafael's grip tightened and, with a start, Elsa's sanity returned and she raised her hands to push him away. Anger and self-loathing flooded her, and gave her the strength to push him so hard he almost fell over and when he tried to speak, she raised her hand menacingly.

"One word and I shall slap your face, you disgusting, loathsome creature," she said through clenched teeth.

Totally confused, Rafael looked at her, raising his arms in defeat; at that point Berta, from her ringside seat, pushed the concealing foliage aside and said, "We recognised your voice, you see. We hate you."

He whirled around, startled. "What...?"

He searched the leafy branches in the direction of her voice and, when she obligingly parted the foliage further to get a better view, he stared at her in surprise.

"I had no idea you were there," he started. "What are you talking about?"

Ignoring Elsa's frantically shaking, head Berta replied: "You were with the Arab slavers. We recognised your voice."

It was Rafael's turn to be bereft of speech. Finally, he turned to Elsa. "Look," he said urgently. "I can explain."

Elsa started to turn away. "No, it's all right. I don't want to know."

"Please let me explain. My father had some strange friends, some dangerous friends, and if my mother and I are to be left in peace I have to at least keep up the appearance of friendship with them."

But Elsa was in no mood to listen. His presence so close to her was bringing back memories of the terrifying encounter with the slavers. Despite being in surroundings she knew to be safe, with her family and the servants a mere call away, her heart began to pound in her ears and she felt as though she were choking. She felt herself swaying.

Rafael's solicitous voice was in her ear. "Elsa, are you all right?" His hand gripped her arm, firmly yet gently.

"I think I'm going to be sick," she managed to gasp, before pulling her arm away and almost running towards the house.

At that moment Paulina came around the corner and Berta slid down from the tree; both raced after Elsa, leaving Rafael standing alone, his brow furrowed and a look of chagrin and frustration on his face.

"I'll come tomorrow to see how you are," he called after Elsa, before jamming his hat back onto his head and striding down the drive. From the safety of the veranda, Elsa watched him mount his motorbike and roar away from the house. With a sigh of relief she collapsed into one of the chairs, where her father found her a moment later, when he came out to investigate whose motorbike he had heard taking off.

"Papa," she said as she reached out to grab one of her father's hands. "Please don't ever let me be alone with Rafael. Please!"

Following this incident, Rafael called at the house the following day to speak to Ludwig, but both emerged from this discussion with stony faces and heightened colour; Ludwig explained to Elsa that the young man had stated his intention to continue to press his suit.

"I tried to explain to him how you felt and that you were unlikely to ever forget the company he was in the first time you became aware of his existence, but he simply refused to accept it," reported Ludwig to his anxious daughter.

"Does he at least realise how wrong it is to continue enslaving helpless people?" she asked.

Ludwig shook his head. "I'm afraid not. The way he sees it, although he is sticking to the anti-slavery laws, he sees little wrong with the trade. You see, what you have to understand is that he considers slaves to be a commodity."

Elsa grimaced in distaste. "And the woman and baby who were taken. Did you think to ask him about them and whether he could do anything about having them returned home?"

"Yes, I did. But I'm afraid he shrugged the matter off, saying that the Arabs had taken her and there was nothing anyone could do to get her back."

"Awful man!" cried Elsa passionately. "How I hate him!"

"Well, you have to see his point of view as well," cautioned Ludwig. "This is how he has been brought up; he has never known anything different. And he made me feel very guilty when he pointed out, very ironically I might add, that the slave trade would never have reached such gargantuan proportions had the eastern states, the Americans, the French, the British and the colonial West Indians not provided such a rapacious market."

Ludwig paused a moment, eyes staring sightlessly at the beauty of the turbulent cascading colours of the garden at the veranda's edge.

"He considered me hypocritical for taking the high moral ground and, do you know, my love, he's right. It was so easy to simply accept things as they were, to actually look on them as normal..." he said pensively. "I don't suppose there was much I could have done to change anything; I just wish I hadn't accepted the situation so easily."

He smiled wryly at his daughter. "And there I was, one of the members of the Congo Reform Association in England, fighting for the legal rights of the Congo Africans and failing to recognise and deal with the reality of the situation on my own doorstep."

He roused himself to deal with the matter of the moment and smiled at Elsa.

"But don't worry," Ludwig assured his nervous daughter. "I'm sure that he's decent enough not to do anything to upset or frighten you. Pity he has this background. He could have been a splendid young man in different circumstances."

"You're too kind, Papa," was Elsa's final comment. "Upbringing or not, anyone who could have watched that woman and baby being taken and not try to stop it must have a stone where most people have a heart."

No more was said on the subject, but it was a relief to everyone when plans started to be made for their imminent departure to the island.

CHAPTER TWENTY-NINE

At last the day the girls had looked forward to dawned bright and sunny. At five in the morning, Berta could already feel signs of the heat that would leave them all limp and enervated within a few hours.

"Can I go to the river and see the canoes being brought up from the mooring at the vegetable gardens, Papa?" she asked for the third time.

"No, and please stop pestering me, Berta. This is going to be a very busy day and I need you to keep quiet while we organise everything."

She hopped from foot to foot, itching to get going, to climb into the huge canoes that she had only seen moored so far, and jump from side to side so that the trunk of the Mikuyu tree from which they were made would make a hollow sound and roll as though it would capsize, which she had been told it wouldn't. Definitely wouldn't. She had asked about this most particularly the first time she had climbed into one of the canoes, and it had leaned perilously from side to side with each movement she made. If Papa hurried, he could take her and Irena to the main river landing stage about a hundred yards from the house and they could see the canoes being poled upstream. So exciting!

She raced off to find Elsa and Paulina, to find out if they would like to come as well but, having seen all of this activity in the past, they were content to stay at home and read. *Boring*, thought Berta, and raced back to where she could see Ludwig working with the men.

Hurry, Papa, hurry, she silently begged.

And they just made it. As they reached the landing stage, four monster canoes were being poled upstream, looking to Berta as majestic as any ancient Egyptian craft in her encyclopaedia. She looked around, thrilled by the carnival atmosphere in the bright sunshine and, with all the home slaves gathered to see the fun, the atmosphere was noisy and cheerful.

The canoes glided to a stop and were tethered at the river's edge, their bows gently scraping the sand in the shallows. With each movement inside them, they swayed like huge bloated eels, the booming that Berta had expected as they bumped into each other, echoing across the water. Four experienced slaves waited at the front and rear of each canoe, with long rigid bamboo poles at the ready to propel and guide the canoes to their destination.

The move would take a few days, and Ludwig had agreed that Berta and Irena could come with him to the landing stage each morning to see the canoes off.

After the arrival of the canoes, Berta didn't find the first day particularly exciting. Fifty slaves and some sacks of ground corn were poled across to the island, which was about a quarter of a mile downstream. Their task was to clean up the house and the slave compound, and Berta and Irena waved to them until they were out of sight.

On the following day the remaining food supplies, large quantities of gardening implements and drums of paraffin, were taken across, together with any furniture that was needed in addition to the fully furnished house on the island. Berta enjoyed this day more, as one of the men carrying food supplies fell into the water and there was huge excitement as he and the food were rescued intact.

The third day was livestock day and goats, chickens, pigs and cows with calves, who would supply milk, were loaded into the canoes. There was noisy chaos at the water's edge as the rebellious animals churned up the sand, furiously resisting the move into the canoes and drenching everyone in the vicinity.

"Just like Noah," commented Berta, gleefully.

There was mocking laughter and cheering from the onlookers when it seemed that nothing much was being achieved, despite the deafening noise and frantic activity, with wet sand flying in all directions. The audience lining the river bank shouted instructions, which was often contradictory, to the struggling herdsmen who hurled back their frustrations in colourful language. But finally, the battle was over, all the livestock had their legs bound and were carried on to lie submissively at last on the floors of the dugouts.

At last, it was the day for the family to cross. Slim armchairs made for the purpose, with plump comfortable cushions on them, were loaded into the dugouts. The width of the boats was such that two armchairs fitted two abreast comfortably. The largest canoe was for the family and had four slaves at each end. All the remaining slaves who would be needed for the month's sojourn would travel in the remaining three canoes.

Berta was enchanted by the holiday atmosphere at the busy stage. Children danced around excitedly and there was much laughter, behind coyly held hands, from the spectators, as the adults negotiated their way onto the canoes. First, at the water's edge, two servants linked hands, forming a seat between them, on which the ladies sat gingerly. They then walked through the shallows to the canoes and lifted the ladies into them. Then came the part that caused the watching crowds most to laugh, the normally dignified ladies making their way to the armchairs, with each step causing the craft to tilt dramatically, first to one side and then to the other, the passengers lurching in a drunken fashion whilst clutching the sides. Elsa, Paulina, Berta and Irena were taken across by the servants, piggy back, and the two younger girls jumped into the canoe nimbly, soon finding little spaces to sit in, but Elsa had a cautionary word as she went past them.

"Take care, little sister," she said as she squeezed past. "Don't move unless you have to and are told to. The river is deep and if you fall overboard there isn't much chance that we'll get to you before the crocodiles do!"

For once, Berta was quiet, staring in shock at her sister. "She won't move," whispered Elsa to Paulina. "Mission accomplished."

Finally, the canoes set off, the family in the lead, and made their stately way across the river, the farm workers in the following three canoes singing and clapping their hands to the rhythm of the thrusting of the long poles. In, push, lift, rest, in, push, lift, rest, they went as they glided over the deeply swirling waters. The polers negotiated both sandbanks and stretches of deep and rapid current with equal dexterity; docking at the island jetty was achieved smoothly.

There was only one slight hitch when Tia Francesca, in her haste to get out of the gently rocking canoe, mistimed her step and wound up with one foot in the canoe and the other on the river bank. With each movement of the canoe, it inched away from the jetty, leaving Tia Fancesca squealing as her legs were stretched further and further apart. With much shouting and argument, and with Tia Anania frantically clutching her sister's leg from within the boat, and Ludwig grasping her around the waist with both arms on the jetty, the craft was slowly brought back to land and she was able to step onto the shore, pulling down her skirt and struggling to regain her dignity.

Berta found this extremely amusing, although Tia did not, and her chortling was finally silenced by stern frowns from both her parents and a dig in the ribs from Paulina.

The island was beautiful and to the girls the visit was a treat beyond description; visits were brief and infrequent. The island was oval shaped and was hedged by luxuriant banks of waving papyrus reeds, except where sandy shores gleamed, white and inviting. Close to the river's edge the terrain was low-lying, although on a slight incline, but in the centre there arose a hillock, on top of which perched the house.

A wide path from the jetty wound its way up through hundreds of acres of groundnuts and grain, mainly wheat, sorghum, millet and corn, now golden and awaiting harvesting. A large acreage was also devoted to several varieties of beans, which would be eaten young and green if the family were in residence, but otherwise would be allowed to dry, when they would be shelled, dried and put into storage. Closer to the house and on the slopes to its rear were the vegetable gardens, full of choice vegetables grown especially in anticipation of this visit.

The procession wound its way up to the house, the women in *machilas* while the men and girls rode bicycles. Mataya trotted as always beside Victoria's *machila*, Irena with her – but darting off to chat with Berta at intervals. There was animated discussion as the Roque family brought the Deuss family up to date with crop information. After years of dealing together, Roque and Ludwig were comfortable with each other's requirements; Ludwig knew that his export requirements would be met, unless of course there was a weather crisis which could not have been predicted.

The house, which was a smaller version of the one on the mainland, was aired and gleaming and lunch was ready to be served when they reached it. The view from the front and back verandas was panoramic and swept through a three hundred and sixty degree view of the river and all the surrounding area beyond it. In the foreground was the river itself, its other bank framed in the distance by sandy beaches and dark green swamps. The burgeoning crops in the middle distance beyond the river were several shades of green, interspersed with the gold of the maturing grain and, in the far distance, the colours faded into the violet haze of the distant hills behind Sena. The river at this point was over two miles in width and both shores could only be seen from the vantage point of the house on the hill.

The month flew by. Everyone on the island helped with the harvesting, which had to be completed before the onset of the summer rains. From morning to dusk the workers gathered the grain in large baskets that hung from their backs. As each bag filled it was emptied and the contents stuffed into hessian bags, ready for transportation back to the home plantation.

One morning Berta pleaded to be allowed to help, and was finally given a basket by one of the overseers, which she proudly strapped to her back.

"Is that all right for you, little madam?" came the anxious question.

"Oh, yes. Of course it is. I am strong, you know," came the confident reply. Enthusiastically she stood side by side with the harvesters, trying in vain to match their speed as their fingers flew over the plants, expertly plucking selected leaves and tossing them over their shoulders into their baskets.

Slowly she fell behind until she was a solitary little figure, pith helmet on her head and with a big, almost empty basket on her back, the butt of the many good-natured, teasing comments that the harvesters made over their shoulders.

The sun beat down relentlessly and, in a grove of trees, a team of cooks made sure that there was water and food available for every worker on the island. Every two hours part of the workforce would take a break and queue up for water. Cassava and sweet potatoes for energy replacement bubbled away in large cauldrons set on wood fires and twice a day the workers ate their fill of *nsima*, with a savoury side dish of beans.

Before an hour had gone by, Berta had crept into the grove, put her basket down and drunk water thirstily. Then, she quietly slipped away to join A Mayi and the other women at home.

She found A Mayi sitting with grandmother Roque, companionably chatting in the cooling breeze.

"Home already?" asked A Mayi with a smile, as her youngest daughter walked slowly up to the steps onto the veranda.

"Um, yes," she replied, only her red, perspiring face and drooping shoulders betraying her exhaustion. "I thought you might need me here."

Her mother and grandmother glanced knowingly at each other in some amusement and then A Mayi turned to her daughter and smiled.

"Come, sit next to me," she said gently. "I'm sure that I'll have something for you to do a little later." Berta sank down gratefully by her side.

By dusk everyone from the humblest harvester to the overseers was exhausted, and soon after their last meal, when the sun had gone down and the full moon lit the dark night, almost everyone was asleep. Only Ludwig and Roque sat in the gauzed veranda where, relatively safe from mosquitoes, they could nurse their aching muscles and talk quietly until they too walked slowly to bed.

Deep replenishing sleep was needed, since the pace would pick up again each morning; just after dawn the large dugouts would be on their way, laden with the previous day's harvest, to the mainland, where it was processed in the large barns and packed for sale or for export, once sufficient had been stored for the family's needs.

The next day, this gentle rhythm was shattered quite suddenly, when in the midst of the harvesting activity a crisis occurred that pushed the crops right into the background.

CHAPTER THIRTY

The family was having breakfast, prior to the men leaving for the fields, when one of the overseers came to the house and demanded to see Roque. When told to wait until the family had breakfasted, he raised his voice and told the house servant that the matter was urgent. The ensuing altercation brought Roque to the front of the house. In some irritation he called out, "What's the matter, Joaquim?"

It turned out that one of the slaves was very ill. When asked what appeared to be the problem, Joaquim became very agitated and described how the previous day the man had seemed to have a fever, with a rash all over his body, and he had told him to stay home. This morning, however, he was very much worse and the rash had turned into pus-filled blisters.

"It looks like that bad disease, *senhor*," he said worriedly.

Roque swore quietly under his breath and turned to Ludwig, who had followed him out and was looking at him questioningly.

"Some years ago we had an outbreak of smallpox," he explained. "We lost quite a few slaves until I was shown how to prevent it spreading. I need to go quickly."

"I'll come with you," said Ludwig, immediately. His father-in-law looked at him uncertainly.

"Why take the risk? You'd better stay here."

Ludwig brushed his protests aside. "I'll be with you in five minutes."

When he reappeared he was fully dressed and had put on his pith helmet. Roque meanwhile had collected a wicker basket with two bottles of brandy and other odds and ends in it. Ludwig looked at the brandy and raised a questioning eyebrow.

"Sterilisation," said Roque tersely.

Joaquim picked up the basket and the three of them ran down the veranda steps. Just then Berta came flying out of the house, her helmet at the ready. When Ludwig saw her he told her sternly to stay where she was and not to go anywhere near the slaves until he and her grandfather considered that the situation was under control.

"Oh, Papa," she started, but he cut her short.

"Do as you are told, Berta. The situation could be very dangerous. Stay with A Mayi until we get back." And with that he raced after the other two men.

Berta hesitated. She was intensely curious but she was also an obedient child. She didn't like to deceive her parents but, on the other hand, something very interesting seemed to be going on. And, she reasoned, if she knew what was going on, she could come back and report to her mother. She abruptly came to a decision and, with pounding heart and guilty looks around her, slipped down the veranda steps and swiftly followed the men.

She reached them as they stood outside the slaves' housing quarters and she slipped behind a large empty paraffin drum. Her grandfather was giving rapid instructions to Joaquim and two other overseers and she saw them hurry to where the farm hands had started working in the fields. As she peered to try and see more clearly, they all removed their baskets from their shoulders, left them on the ground and filed to the compound, where they were organised into a long line.

As she watched, her father and grandfather put bands of a thin fabric across their noses and mouths and tied the material behind their heads. They then lifted a bottle which she recognised as brandy out of a basket on the ground at their feet and splashed their hands with the liquid before walking into the sleeping quarters. Shortly after they emerged followed by four slaves, also masked, carrying a man on a litter. The party walked towards a large avocado tree and set the sick man down in its shade. From where she crouched she saw her grandfather bend over and start to gently pick at the blisters on the sick man's body with what appeared to be a small penknife. He then gestured to Joaquim, who brought the first of the line of workers to him. Roque handed him a wad of cotton wool soaked in brandy, with which he rubbed the upper part of the slave's arm. To Berta's horror her grandfather brought up the penknife with which he had picked at the pus-filled blister and, with its point made three sharp jabs on the man's arm. Another of the overseers covered the pricks with a small plaster. The man moved on and the next came up. In the same manner the pus on the knife was injected into his arm. The next one followed.

Berta turned away and ran home, appalled at what she had seen. She burst into the house and ran to her mother, who was still at the cleared breakfast table with Elsa and Paulina. She stood close by her while she breathlessly described to her what she had seen.

Victoria was angry, and gave Berta the most serious scolding that she had had in her young life.

"Your father told you that you were on no account to go to the compound and yet you went. I would never have believed it of you. Almost half the people who get this disease die, and yet you went there. You have been very foolish and I am very angry with you. Now, I want you to go to your bedroom and think about your behaviour. Don't come back until you are ready to apologise."

Berta understood at last how foolish she had been and how deadly this smallpox virus was. Much chastened, she walked slowly to her room, where she lay quietly on her bed and wondered how her father was going to react when he heard the story. Then she thought about the recovery statistic and felt her stomach cramp in fear as she realised what her chances of survival were if she contracted it. *And I didn't even have any gauze over my mouth*, she thought miserably.

She waited in dread, her stomach feeling as though it was tied in a tight knot. Eventually she heard the two men's weary footsteps coming up the front steps and sat up to await her father's entrance. A considerable time passed and still he did not come. The suspense was unbearable. Finally, she heard him coming slowly up the stairs. He opened the bedroom door and stood in the doorway.

"Fortunately for you, I am exhausted and have a lot more on my mind than the bad behaviour of a silly little girl," he said. "All I will say is that I can see that you have been indulged and that things are going to change. I am deeply disappointed in you."

At this, Berta burst into tears, and would have gone into his arms had he not gently motioned her away.

"Stay away, Berta," he said tiredly. "I need to have a long hot bath before I go near anyone after this day's work."

As he left the room Berta threw herself on her bed and cried herself to sleep. She had learnt a hard lesson that day and it was the first step to a growing self-awareness and a new sense of responsibility.

The smallpox crisis caused a serious upheaval that year. The vaccination that Roque had administered had undoubtedly saved many lives; in the end, seven lives were lost, a much smaller number than would have been the case otherwise. Harvesting was delayed as even those workers who survived suffered a day or two of fever after the vaccination, so that it was fully a week before the original rhythm and speed of work returned.

Ludwig and Roque started to be concerned about the threat of imminent flooding. When the river was at its height it was impassable: they could be stranded on the island. Any day now the summer rains would begin in the highlands, the waters would cascade into the Shire and then the Zambezi rivers, and by the time it reached Sena, it would be deep and dangerous. It would overflow its banks for miles and its waters would be treacherous, with branches and whole trees uprooted in its relentless flow.

There was no way around it: the exodus from the island would have to take place before the flooding had reached this stage. The flooding was an annual event and provided the area with the rich silt that would give them the second crop of the year, but preparations had to respect the danger inherent in the massively increased volume and strength of the river's waters.

The problem was that so much work remained to be done, whilst the coming of the rains was imminent. All of the huge acreage that would soon be submerged by the floods had to be completely harvested and then cleared of all the redundant plants. These were piled high into bonfires and set ablaze as the fields were cleared. It was a race against time; the work continued and the overseers made frequent trips to the river to look for the tell-tale signs that flooding had begun.

Ludwig and his father-in-law discussed the situation and told their women that they should return to the mainland immediately. The men would remain and follow when all the preparations had been completed.

Grandmother Roque and Victoria were outraged. What? And leave the men on their own? Not likely! The men, exhausted, shrugged their shoulders and gave in.

Each day, from dawn to sunset, every able-bodied person on the island toiled in the sweltering heat, uprooting, plucking and cutting, while others packed and transported the produce to the mainland. Finally, it was done. The final grain and root crops were harvested and despatched to the mainland, and preparations began to ship people and livestock back.

Suddenly, amidst the feverish activity one afternoon, a cry went up as distant thunderous clouds darkened the northern horizon. At the sight, everyone was galvanised into action. People flew around, picking, pushing and carrying, while animals were herded to the water's edge and their legs tied. The remaining produce was piled at the jetty and what was left of the food and stores followed suit. The men, their overseers and the workers worked without pause, each following the plan of action allocated to him. Barely had the last of the produce and workers been shipped across when the call that everyone had been awaiting came.

"It's started!" called Joaquim as he raced up the hill to the house. "The river has started to turn muddy and is already starting to rise."

The family prepared to descend to the jetty. Grandmother Roque and her family had been ready to leave for some time. The house had been cleaned and was now locked up; everything that needed to be taken to the mainland was waiting on the jetty or had already been taken across.

Berta, meanwhile, was watching the rising river with fascination. Its smooth green flow was now turning brown and torn bushes and branches were floating on its previously immaculate surface. She stuck a small bamboo pole into the mud at the water's edge and marked the water level on it with her little red penknife. Fifteen minutes later she returned to find that her mark had been submerged and she excitedly made another to record the new level. She ran off to call her father, who came to inspect her stick. What he saw perturbed him and he returned to speak seriously to Joaquim.

"The water is rising fast," he told him. "We need to get away immediately."

The last of the produce and the workers left almost immediately, and an hour later everyone was aboard the canoe carrying the family. A final check was made to ensure that no one had been left behind, and the huge heavily-laden canoe began its difficult journey back home.

Although the distance was not great the return journey, probably just over two miles, was against the current – and a powerful current it was, swollen now with the flood waters from the hills. Although there were now four polers each end of the canoe, streaming with sweat, muscles bunched excruciatingly, it seemed as though they were barely inching upstream. Their goal was to reach the opposite bank, where the polers would disembark and pull the canoe upstream, with the help of several stout ropes which lay coiled in the bottom of the boat.

The tension in the boat rose as, with each minute's passing, the river seemed to swell even further. Mixed in with the leaves and branches there were now whole shrubs swirling in the current, bumping and scraping against the sides of the canoe.

Small islands began to appear, floating gracefully down the river. Ludwig explained to the girls that as the water level rose and the pull of the river became more powerful, small plants were torn away from the banks of the river. These bumped into other similar plants, their roots and foliage quickly intertwined and they began to form pretty islands of exotic water plants. The islands were alive with birds of all shapes and sizes that greedily poked and prodded their surfaces for prey that had become exposed when the plants were torn from their sheltered banks.

Frequently, a snake swept past, its head up as it battled against the current that had caught it up and prevented its returning to the safety of the shore. The women shrieked and prepared to hit it with anything handy should it try to slither into the boat. A little drowned piglet flowed silently past, the first of many drowned animals that they would see, and the polers chanted deep in their throats as they battled to keep the craft from being pulled downstream to the treacherous flats where the river met the sea.

Suddenly, Ludwig shouted, "Look!"

They followed his pointing finger and spotted a small island floating past with two long-legged birds perched precariously in the centre, wings fluttering outwards as they strove to keep their balance.

"They're going for a ride!" shouted Berta.

"Probably looking for some poor fish," laughed Ludwig, as they disappeared downstream.

A few minutes later, they spotted what appeared to be the same birds flying overhead back upstream. They watched them alight on another island and sail past them once again, heads held disdainfully high. Moments later one dived into the river and surfaced with a small fish in its beak.

"You were right, Papa!" called Berta, and settled down to be entertained some more by the river inhabitants.

After a long gruelling haul, three hours of muscle-tearing effort, the canoe beached and the polers leapt out, half of them hanging on to the canoe so that it didn't slip downstream, while the remainder quickly passed the ropes through holes fashioned for the purpose in the front. Two of the men then returned to the canoe and steered it while the eight pulled it upriver from the bank, holding the ropes over their shoulders. Their chant was now lighter, as they stepped more briskly on the riverbank and made their way home.

"Mayi, can I go with the men on the shore?" asked Berta, to whom it all seemed quite exciting.

The reply came from her father, "No, you may not. You'd just get underfoot."

A few days ago Berta would have started wheedling. She opened her mouth and then quickly closed it. She was learning.

After a half hour or so there was the welcome sound of other workers from the plantation coming towards them. Willing hands took over the ropes and for the remainder of the distance the two teams took it in turn to haul the heavily laden canoe upstream.

The final leg was difficult for everyone. The bearers were tired and the excitement and tension had taken their toll on everyone. Finally, the little landing stage was reached and strong hands reached out to help the passengers disembark. The weary female members climbed gratefully into *garrettas* and *machilas* for the final short stage home and the men followed on foot.

It was with a sense of relief that the party finally walked up the steps of the house. It had been great on the island, Berta reflected as she cuddled up to her mother before crawling into bed, but it was also good to be back home.

It was not long before the entire family were sound asleep, with only the sound of the crickets and the frogs to disturb the utter stillness of the night.

CHAPTER THIRTY-ONE

When the family awoke the following morning it was to see a transformed landscape. The floods had reached their climax and from about a mile away, along the southern perimeter of Roque's plantation, the Zambezi had disappeared into a huge lake, several miles long, which stretched into the middle distance. The original course of the river could be traced by the huts on stilts that were precariously teetering above the swirling waters and the tiny figures of the inhabitants could be seen going about their business in their little dugout canoes.

"Now you see why I chose the land on the slope leading up to the hills," said Roque, as the family stood on the veranda, trying to locate landmarks. "That and to avoid the mosquitoes in the swampy areas, where it's very unhealthy. Down there where you can see a small forest of acacias is where my boundary is. That will remain flooded for at least four days but, after that, the water will drain away and we shall plant in the silt."

He pointed to the east and the west. "Now, most of that land, and it isn't mine, will be under water for up to five months, so the plantation owners will have to work on what is above water until it clears. The villagers go up onto the hillside when the floods start and they will stay there until their land is usable again."

The girls stayed away from the flooded areas, since they were warned that they could be dangerous. Ludwig remembered one experience that he had had when he had gone exploring the flooded areas near the Sena Sugar Estates on his arrival from Switzerland.

"It all looked very calm," he reminisced, "but there was a serious undercurrent that we had to fight against. Worse, it was impossible to see what was happening below the surface because of the muddied water, and we were colliding with broken tree stumps and all manner of submerged vegetation. On several occasions I felt that we would have capsized had the dugouts been less stable."

"The hippos are an added danger," commented Roque. "What makes it worse is that they are in a very bad mood at the disruption to their lives and nothing would entertain them more than to overturn a canoe or two!"

Fortunately, there was enough to see and do at the plantation for the temporary curtailment of their activities not to have much effect on the sisters. The word had got around that *Bwana* Deuss was in the market for beeswax, and each day saw a long line of natives waiting to sell their wax to him. It had come as a welcome surprise to them when they had first discovered that they could sell a by-product which they had previously thrown away. Honey was highly prized by the local Africans and all the hives in the forest were promptly claimed by whoever discovered them.

Elsa and Berta watched interestedly as Ludwig, Aleki and other workers from the plantation weighed the wax, paid for it and packed it for transportation home, where it would be prepared for shipment to Europe. Pauline stayed at home working on her embroidery.

At midmorning on the third day after their return from the island, they had a pleasant surprise when their Uncle Paul roared up to the house on his motorbike. They greeted him enthusiastically and led him to the veranda, where the whole family sat to catch up on their news over coffee.

Paul had the same blond colouring as his brother Ludwig, but where Ludwig was slim and very tanned from his active life both indoors and out, Paul was showing the slight plumpness of the man the greater part of whose work was carried out from behind a desk. The brothers were very close and when Ludwig, the eldest, and supposedly the frail child in the family, had been sent by his father to Portuguese East Africa to join the Sena Sugar Company, it was on the understanding that his health would improve and that his uncle, the general manager at the time, would look after him. As it turned out, Ludwig had been very successful and Paul had subsequently come out to Africa to join the sugar company and, within a few years, was also working with his brother.

After catching up with their news, the brothers took off on their motorbikes for a ride around the plantation; when they returned it was mid-afternoon.

"I need to be going," said Paul, as he ruffled Berta's hair. "I don't fancy riding back in the dark. You'd be amazed at the things that I saw slithering, running and creeping across the road on my way here. The entire animal and insect populations seem to be on the move away from the flood water!"

"True," agreed Ludwig, "and by dusk the larger things will be about hunting the smaller ones. You need to be on your way."

There were affectionate farewells and, with a final wave, Paul was roaring on his way in a trail of dust.

"Well," commented Roque, "you've seen everyone now except Louis. He would have liked to have been here, but it can't be helped."

In the few days remaining, Rafael visited twice. The family cordially received him but, in deference to Elsa's wishes, they made certain that he was never alone with her. Berta in particular delighted in her role of match wrecker. When Rafael found Elsa on her own in the garden on his first visit he had barely had time to greet her before her little sister was standing firmly at her side, staring up at him unblinkingly. On the second occasion it was Paulina who came to the rescue, with an alertness quite foreign to her usual ambling demeanour. Rafael had shaken his head ruefully.

"Oh, Elsa," he said with a dry little smile. "What can I do to convince you that I am not evil? I really do care very much for you, and I know that I could make you happy."

Paulina snorted and Elsa shivered involuntarily with distaste, but Berta, for a reason known only to herself, collapsed into giggles, tears beginning to roll down her cheeks. It gave Elsa the excuse to turn away and scold her for her bad manners until finally, while refusing to meet Rafael's eyes, she turned away and made her escape, a still helplessly giggling Berta in tow.

"I can't help feeling a little sorry for the wretched man," Ludwig told Victoria with a wry smile, when Berta's bad behaviour had been reported to him. "He is so clearly besotted and she equally clearly loathes the sight of him. And then Berta causes embarrassment all around. Ah well, thank goodness we're leaving shortly."

There was one final job to be done.

On his marriage to Victoria, Ludwig had been mortified to be presented with a plantation as the dowry. It had come complete with a residential compound and a small army of slaves.

"No, Roque, no!" he had protested, hands held up in front of him.

The two men had argued for several days, before Roque informed Ludwig in icy tones that his refusal would cause serious embarrassment to his family.

Ludwig was mystified. "But why? And how?"

Roque explained it thus to his prospective son-in-law.

"If you do not accept Victoria's dowry it will mean that Victoria comes to you as a beggar to be your wife. It means that she has no value, that she waits for you to have some rice to put in her mouth."

Ludwig sighed in defeat. He knew better than to try and override custom and, as graciously as he felt able at the time, he thanked his father-in-law for his generous gift, and asked that he may make one stipulation. Roque considered what Ludwig had to say and finally agreed.

"So be it," he said.

He needed now to visit the plantation, which was overseen by Roque in his absence and, since he anticipated that the visit would take two days, he and his father-in-law left on their motorbikes early one morning, so as to be back on the evening of the second day.

On the evening of their return, after they had bathed and had dinner, the family congregated on the veranda as was their custom, to hear the news from the plantation.

"It's doing well," commented Ludwig. "Thanks to you, Roque, the crops are plentiful and appear healthy. I have to say, though, that I was shocked to hear about the neighbour."

It seemed that the neighbouring plantation was owned by a man of mixed race named Matekenya, who was known for his brutality to his slaves.

"I was told," said Ludwig, "that in his younger days he had been known to force his slaves to jump into the river when he thought that the crocodiles were hungry."

There were gasps of horror from the women.

"*Mon Dieu,*" whispered Elsa, while Berta was quiet for once from shock.

Ludwig continued: "I met some of his slaves working in his fields next to our boundary and when I asked them where their houses were they were petrified. 'They are not ours,' they said. 'Everything we have belongs to our master. You must not say that they are ours.' Our foreman tells me that whenever the landlord has financial problems he simply sells some of his people."

"What a terrible life they must lead," sympathised Victoria. "Is there nothing that can be done?"

Both men shook their heads. "Slaves have no rights. They are barely considered human."

Ludwig continued thoughtfully: "Such a crime against humanity. What it must be to own nothing, not even your very self. And to have to spend your life protecting your only asset, yourself."

Roque grinned. "You are indeed an unusual man, Deuss. There are not many around here who think as you do."

"Well they should! Slaves are human beings and deserve to be treated as such. When is this terrible thing going to end, for heaven's sake!"

"When you in Europe, the Americas and Asia – and we here – stop asking for them."

Ludwig, shaking his head in frustration, was effectively silenced.

Early next morning, Berta was awoken by the sounds of shouting and people running. Startled, she tumbled out of bed and made for the window, rubbing her eyes and pulling her nightdress down where it had ridden up over her bottom. She tugged the curtain aside and peered out. There was a rustle and a shove and Elsa joined her, sleepy-eyed but alert.

"What's going on?" she asked.

Berta surveyed the busy scene below her. "I don't know," she replied.

There appeared to be a dozen or more workers from the fields in the compound at the back of the house, milling around their grandfather; the house servants had collected and were standing in groups in the background, listening and observing intently. Roque was firing questions at the field workers and they all appeared to be trying to answer him at the same time, and in some excitement, until he finally raised his hands in frustration, shouted angrily and pointed at one of the men. The rest subsided and Roque listened intently to what the man was saying.

His response was rapid. He called for his motorbike, jumped onto it, started it and drove off, with the farm workers trotting behind him. They were soon left behind as he roared off down the track towards the fields.

The girls, now joined by Paulina, pulled on their dressing gowns and went downstairs to find out what the fuss had been about. They found their parents and grandmother sitting on the veranda at the back of the house having breakfast, boiled sliced sweet potatoes and baked plantains with honey.

In response to their questions, Victoria explained that the field workers had come to report that four male slaves appeared to have run away. They had been missed in the fields at the start of the day, and when their sleeping quarters were searched it was found that they had taken their meagre belongings and disappeared.

Elsa looked anxious. "So what's going to happen now?" she asked.

Ludwig broke in, "A search has been started. More than that we don't know." He sounded grim and abruptly changed the subject. "Get yourselves dressed, girls," he said, with an attempt at cheerfulness, "and come down for breakfast."

"Would you like some lamb chops and chorizo?" asked their grandmother as they turned away.

"No, thank you," they chorused, "too early!"

The runaway slaves were the main topic of conversation during the day; Roque only came home briefly at lunchtime to eat and have a short rest before leaving again to join the search.

"The fools!" he said to the family. "They want their freedom. For what? To go back to their miserable villages where they live like savages?" He snorted in derision.

"They'll be lucky if they are not recaptured by one of the neighbouring plantations.   And then they'll realise how lucky they are to have been bought by me. And I paid well for them. They looked in good shape, so I thought they would be a good investment. And now it looks as though I am going to lose them. Ungrateful fools!"

"You can't blame them for wanting their freedom, Roque," interrupted Ludwig mildly. "They are human."

"Barely!" came the acid response. "If they had an ounce of courage or intelligence they wouldn't be where they are today."

"But think," urged Ludwig. "They have spent all their lives running and hiding from people who would enslave them if they could catch them. They have not been able to plant crops or build sturdy homes. All their energy, their intelligence, has been focused on staying free as long as possible."

Ludwig sighed and turned back to his lunch, but Roque seemed to want to prolong the discussion, despite his evident hurry to get back to the chase.

"You still don't understand these people, Deuss," he argued. "You think that they are like you and me but they are not! Most of them are lazy, disloyal and incapable of doing any work unsupervised."

He paused, a piece of succulent stewed chicken on the end of his fork.

"There is a saying going around. If you free three slaves today, two of them will have sold the third by tomorrow." He laughed merrily. "I like that! I heard that from some travellers from the interior and, do you know, it just about sums up these savages."

Berta interrupted with a worried frown. "Grandfather, what will happen if you find these slaves?"

He looked across the table at her with a smile. "We bring them back home, of course."

"Will they stay?" asked Elsa.

"Oh, yes," he replied. "I'll have to punish them to make sure of that, though!"

The worried frowns intensified.

"How will you punish them? What will you do to them?"

Roque started to rise from the table; he smiled at his granddaughters as he said, "Oh, I'll think of something. It's nothing for you to worry yourselves about."

He turned to the adults at the table. "I have one more plantation to visit so I shall be home at dusk, with the missing men following, I hope." He turned to Ludwig. "Want to come with me?"

"No, thanks," was the dry reply.

"See you later, then."

And with that he was out of the door and moments later his motorbike could be heard roaring off down the drive.

The girls started to question their mother about the slaves' likely fate if they were caught, but she would not be drawn except to say that they would probably be flogged, but not too severely because they were needed to work in the fields.

"Your grandfather will need an example to be made of them and, no, I don't like it any more than you do. So let's say no more on the subject."

And that appeared to be that, except for that evening at bedtime, when Berta cuddled up to her father as the family chatted, and confided to him that she couldn't quite understand her grandfather.

"He is so kind and good to all of us and then suddenly he's not really kind anymore." She searched for words. "Sometimes, like this morning, I think it's not Grandfather anymore and that I am looking at a stranger."

Ludwig put his arm around her and hugged her. "Yes, I know," he said. "We have to try not to judge him, though. He has a job to do and sometimes we may not agree with how he does it. But, and this is most important, we can decide that we will do things differently in our own lives. It is our lives and our actions that we must pay attention to."

Berta thought about this gravely, and finally nodded before resting her head on her father's chest.

The final days of the holiday passed peacefully, and a few days later the family was at the railway station waiting for the train's arrival. Mayi Roque had made one of her rare excursions from her home and with her husband and daughters bade fond and tearful farewells to the family they saw so infrequently.

The train pulled into the station punctually and the customary mayhem ensued, as passengers and baggage disembarked and their replacements embarked. There was a final whistle blast from the station master and the idling engine chugged back into life. The girls and their parents squeezed into the carriage windows and waved as they moved away. They continued waving until the train rounded a bend and the little group on the platform was lost to sight.

CHAPTER THIRTY-TWO

After four days of jolting travel on road, rail and river in the December heat and dust, the river paddle steamer groaned and wallowed its way to sidle against the jetty at Fort Johnston. There were the usual crowds of interested townsfolk, children tearing around and calling to one another excitedly, hawkers selling food and the now accustomed sight of soldiers and trucks heading for the lake on their way to the north of the country, and the firing line.

The girls were excited to be back home and there was much to see and exclaim about. Most importantly, there was a letter from the Reverend Mother to say that the new school was nearing completion and that the January term would commence at the usual time in mid-January.

Berta had mixed feelings about returning to school. It would be a year that she had been at home and this had become her way of life. She enjoyed her unorthodox lessons with her father and was fully immersed in helping her mother about the house and at the farm. It was going to be a wrench to leave them all again, she confided to Elsa. Elsa was more pragmatic and was looking forward to seeing Mona and their other friends again, but Paulina was working herself up into a depression at the thought of leaving A Mayi, her father and the animals. She spent more time than ever with the animals, crooning to them and generally making a bigger fuss than ever of them.

"Oh, Paulina," said Berta, disgustedly. "You don't have to make such a fuss. I feel just as you do, but I'm not going around howling like a hyena."

Paulina was outraged at this deepest of insults and it was only Berta's swifter feet that got her to her mother before Paulina carried out her threat to scratch out her eyes.

A Mayi sighed wearily as both tried to tell their side of the story first. This, as she confided to Ludwig, was the only downside of having the girls at home. Paulina and Berta seemed to live on separate levels most of the time. "But," she added, "the rest of the time they are really good friends."

A week after they had returned home there was an incident that drew heavy clouds across their horizon of contentment.

It was a hot summer's morning and A Mayi and the three girls were sitting on the veranda having a cup of tea. It had been a busy morning. A Mayi had decided that she needed to go to the farm to see how some new seedlings were coming on, and they had all gone together, A Mayi in her *garreta* and the girls on their bicycles. They returned before the heat of the day became too intense and settled onto the veranda, where they could be sure of catching any breeze that might be flitting around.

Suddenly, they heard Ludwig's steps hastily coming up the steps at the front of the house and making his way inside, calling as he did so, "Victoria! Victoria! Where are you?"

"Here," chorused the girls and he came towards them.

It was clear that he was agitated and upset, and for a moment or two seemed lost for words. Then he spoke hurriedly to the little group.

"Listen, girls, I have some news that you are not going to like. Mr Carrain came to see me at my office; it seems that we have no right to keep Jacko, and that he must now be sent to a zoo in England."

There was an appalled silence while Ludwig explained the situation to A Mayi. The rest of the conversation was in the Chisena language.

"But Papa!" It was Berta who spoke first. "Aren't we going to set him free into the wild, so that he can find his family and go to live with them?"

"No, I'm afraid not. I have tried to get Mr Carrain to agree to it, but he refuses to listen. I'm afraid that he is on his way now to pick him up."

As the tears began to trickle down their cheeks he moved to the girls and put his arms around them.

"I'm so terribly sorry," he said. Berta glanced up through her tears and saw that his face was white and drawn. She had never seen him like this before.

"I'm so sorry," he said again. "I cannot stop this thing happening and I want you to be very brave."

As he spoke, there was the sound of an oxcart drawing up at the side entrance.

Carrain came through the gate, strutting with self-importance. He glanced at the group on the veranda and then beckoned to the ten or so natives that he had brought with him, calling out to Ludwig, "Untie her, please."

Paulina's stoicism deserted her and she ran down to put her arms around Jacko, sobbing as she did so. "No! No! Please don't. Please don't take him."

Berta followed and she too cradled Jacko, stroking his wrinkled forehead, the tears pouring down her face.

Elsa walked up to Carrain, her face seemingly carved of stone. "Mr Carrain," she said. "I am asking you to leave our elephant. He knows us and loves us; and we love him. When he is a little older we'll put him back into the wild where he belongs. Please don't take him from us."

For an instant, something flickered in his eyes, but it was quickly repressed. His voice was gruff as he said shortly, "I'm sorry girls. He has to go."

With that, he beckoned to the natives, who untied Jacko and started to walk him to the oxcart. He was uncertain and at first refused to move, looking at the girls and waving his trunk. But the men broke a branch off the avocado tree and whipped his haunches until he moved and went out of the gate, out of their lives.

Berta tried to follow, but Ludwig sped down the steps and cradled them all in his arms, holding them fast. "Let him go. He'll be happy at the zoo," he kept repeating. "Let him go."

As if to lend emphasis to his words, the paddle steamer's horn sounded, the paddle steamer that would be taking Jacko away from them.

Ludwig later told Victoria that he had never been so angry in his life.

"My heart was torn in two," he told her, his eyes moist with tears. "If it would have achieved anything I would have killed that man at that moment. Whatever he has against me, he is less than human to have taken it out on my girls."

The yard seemed emptier without Jacko, and there was always something to remind them of him. Elsa reminisced sadly how he had loved them playing 'oranges and lemons' under his tummy, when his ears would flap and he would trumpet with excitement. Paulina spoke of Jacko's huge appetite and how he would do a dainty little dance of happiness when she, Paulina, approached him with armfuls of succulent greens. Berta spoke, her voice breaking, of how she would miss their rides around the compound, where he trod so daintily amongst the poultry and children. Even the monkey glanced frequently at where Jacko had been tethered, and jabbered while she scratched her sides with a long arm.

This was the first bereavement of their young lives, for so they felt it to be. Only Ludwig's constantly reiterating to them that Jacko would be happy where he was going made the situation bearable during those first dark days.

"My instinct was right," he said wretchedly to Victoria. "My sense of foreboding was correct. This little man, this nobody, has indeed been given destructive power over people's lives."

Time passed, life returned to normal and the children once again became engrossed in their busy lifestyles. A surprise early Christmas package arrived from Grandmother Deuss and there was huge excitement as Ludwig slowly and carefully opened it up.

"Oh, hurry, Papa!" begged Elsa.

"Hurry!" squeaked Berta.

Ludwig paused, a twinkle in his eye. "Oh dear, am I really going slowly? I don't want to tear the paper, you see." And he continued to open the layers of wrapping with exaggerated care. The girls could contain themselves no longer and playfully tussled with their father, grabbed the parcel and ran to the opposite end of the veranda, where it was ripped open in seconds.

"Ooh!" they gasped. Their Swiss grandmother had sent them beautiful sets of clothes, gathered skirts, creamy blouses with lace ruffles and velvet waistcoats. Shiny patent shoes and white stockings completed the ensembles. They raced upstairs to try them on and came down again to pose and strut across the veranda.

Victoria and Ludwig looked on, smiling, their pride in their pretty daughters showing in their eyes.

"You'll have to write and thank your grandmother," Ludwig said.

As the return to school drew near, Victoria decided that her daughters needed new clothes to take back to school with them. Although they wore uniform at school they wore casual clothes at weekends, and Paulina and Berta were growing at such a rate that it was for them a necessity to get something new that fitted. The clothes that Grandmother Deuss had sent them were beautiful, but were suitable only for special occasions.

Although Ludwig stocked calicos in his stores, Victoria and the girls visited the Indian shops for the fabrics she had in mind. They had beautiful cloths, silks and chiffons mainly, in stunning, vibrant colours; but they also stocked cottons in pretty designs. It was to the latter that she headed. After much discussion they chose some simple but pretty designs on cream and beige backgrounds. Berta was utterly bored by the process and became more fractious by the minute. After the first half-hour she didn't like anything that she was shown, and whined to be allowed to go to her father's shop where she said that she would wait for them.

"Well, Berta," scolded her mother, "you can certainly go to your father, but don't you dare complain later that you don't like what I chose for you."

Berta was off; when the ladies met again, an hour or so later, she groaned when she was told that they now had to go to the Asian tailor on Mandala's veranda. But first Ludwig insisted on breaking off from working on his order book to discuss styles. He had very definite ideas of what the women in his family in Switzerland wore, and made clear sketches for Victoria to show the tailor. He also had magazines sent out to him regularly and made a point of scrutinising any fashion pictures.

"Nothing but the best for my girls," he joked, giving Berta, who was nearest to him, a quick hug.

It was approaching midday by this time and the heat was intense, so Victoria decided that the visit to the tailor could wait until the morrow.

"Come on, girls," she said to her wilting daughters. "It's time to get home out of the sun."

Early the following morning, the quartet approached the tailor and a detailed discussion of their needs followed. As well as dresses the girls needed bloomers. These voluminous knickers reached to just above the knee and were considered essential wear for girls with any sense of modesty. It went without saying that new school uniforms were needed, but this was a simple task for the tailor. Victoria simply brought the girls' old school uniforms and ordered copies in the new sizes.

Their school uniform was attractive. Made of white cotton, it was a long-sleeved dress reaching to the ankles. It had a fitted bodice and soft open pleats in the skirt. The neckline boasted a mandarin collar and the whole buttoned at the back of the neck.

Measurements were taken and the tailor asked to come to the house for a dress fitting session in four days' time. He knew of course that they would not follow the local practice of having their new clothes fitted on the shop veranda, in view of the inevitable crowd of spectators, who would openly stare in fascination.

"Yes, of course, *bambo*," replied Victoria.

In two weeks the dresses were ready and shoes, underwear and other necessities were neatly packed into the girls' trunks.

Christmas was a quiet event and was distinguished mainly by the church services. Villagers came from many miles away and the church was packed to the rafters for every service. The liturgical responses and the Christmas hymns were sung with great gusto and often out of tune. This, coupled with the waves of sound from excited and fretful children, made quite a din. Berta fidgeted through the entire service. She clung to Victoria's arm.

"When can we go home?" she whispered, after the first ten minutes.

"Shh," came the reply. "We've only just arrived." A few minutes passed.

"Is it time to go home yet? I'm getting a headache."

"Stop it! Read your book."

"I've read it lots of times. Is mass nearly finished now?"

A Mayi frowned ominously at her and she subsided, grumbling quietly.

Everyone greeted the end of mass joyously and they thronged out into the brilliant summer sunshine. The parishioners milled around, greeting each other, the nuns and the priests. It was a colourful scene. The native women wore their best clothes, brightly-coloured blouses with little puffed sleeves on their upper body and a long length of material in the same pattern wound around them. A similar strip of material was wound around their heads in the shape of a square-topped turban. Their faces shone and their teeth gleamed as they celebrated the important Christian feast. Expatriate, Asian and mixed-race women wore either hats or lace shawls over their heads, black for the adult women and white for the young. Dress design was modest, with arms completely covered and skirts well below the knee.

After mass there was the short walk home, where there was a celebratory lunch. Ludwig gave out the presents, which this year were books, colouring pencils and watercolour sets for the girls. Victoria presented them with beautifully wrought gold bracelets from their grandfather Roque.

Berta was to remember in later years that it had been a quiet, happy day. She had felt totally loved, a happy child completely secure in her environment.

CHAPTER THIRTY-THREE

Once Christmas was over preparations to return to school started in earnest, and it seemed to the girls that in no time at all they were ready to make the week-long journey. The day of departure dawned bright and sunny, with no hint of the rains that would certainly overtake them by midday. The slaves carrying the luggage and camping equipment had lined up in the back yard, as dawn prised open the black sky and doves awakened in the acacia trees. They crooned gently as the household awoke and stirred itself for departure. The girls, eyes swollen with sleep, made their final checks and Ludwig closed and strapped shut their sturdy trunks.

There were many tearful goodbyes. The workers at the farm and the animals had been bidden tender farewells on the previous day and all the home staff, their families and especially the little children, were greeted fondly. Tears were shed when the last of the animals had been cuddled, and particularly when Jacko was remembered.

Worst of all was saying goodbye to their mother. Having their mother close had been a memorable time for the girls; Berta felt the pain in her heart threaten to overcome her as she held her close, the tears streaming down her cheeks. A Mayi's voice was gruff with emotion as she reminded her youngest daughter that it would not be long before she and their father would be travelling to Nguludi for Easter.

"Be good until then, my little monkey," she whispered, holding her youngest daughter close, her eyes bright with unshed tears.

Ludwig stepped in to dissipate the tension and get the procession onto the road.

"Come, girls," he said. "We really need to get going."

As if to reinforce what he was saying, the brazen hoot of the paddle steamer split the air, a timely catalyst for the breaking off of personal emotions which forced everyone to hurry and move out. Ludwig turned to Victoria. Public displays of affection were completely out of the question and they stood facing each other, Victoria looking forlorn.

"I'll be back in twelve to fourteen days," he told her. She gripped his arm.

"Be careful, Ludwiki, it is the season for the snakes; they will be everywhere."

He smiled down at her. "Yes, I know. And the lions. And the hippos, because they will leave the river to search for food after dusk. Oh yes! And the huge, black spiders that crawl up the mosquito nets during the night. Brrrrrr. I'm almost afraid to go!"

"You laugh at me," said his wife, a reluctant smile tugging at her mouth. "But it's all true. Please be very, very careful!"

"Of course I will, Victoria. I have our precious treasure to guard, and I won't forget it for a moment."

"*Tsalani bwino*," he smiled at her as he moved off.

"*Pitane bwino*," she smiled back through tear-filled eyes.

The girls refused *machilas* and rode instead on their bicycles ahead of the long procession of bearers. Just before they disappeared from sight they turned back for one last wave. A Mayi stood at the gate, upright and stern, with Mataya and Julia beside her. She waved, and all the staff behind her solemnly waved goodbye.

The magical holiday was over.

The first two days were spent on the river paddle steamer; the first pangs of homesickness were soothed by the leisurely, albeit noisy passage down the river, as paddles and engines spluttered and belched their winding way. The floods had only recently receded and the rather tattered and soiled appearance of the reeds and papyrus bore witness to the strong muddy waters that had greedily overrun the river banks and claimed, for a short time, some of the surrounding land. In the aftermath villagers were busy everywhere: planting corn, groundnuts, sugar cane, cassava and cotton. Some of the men could be seen repairing their circular storage huts, which were perched high up on stilts. Here, the surplus harvest would be stored for consumption during the year, until the next planting. Little children, wearing only ragged shorts, over which their tummies protruded roundly, left their parents in the fields and ran to the water's edge to wave and shout as the steamer splashed by. The girls waved back gaily and Berta leaned far out over the railings.

"Get back in," said Elsa, her anxiety making her voice sharp.

Berta glanced at her, her body leaning far out and her feet six inches off the deck.

"Why?" she asked cheekily. As she spoke her pith helmet tumbled off her head, fell to the river below and bounced merrily in the wake of frothing water. As she leaned out further to observe her hat's progress, with cries of dismay, she overbalanced and hung precariously for a moment.

Suddenly afraid, aware of the danger that she was in, she tried to lean back but found she couldn't.

She screamed, "Elsa! Help! Help!"

Elsa rushed over, gripped her arms and pulled her back. Berta leant against her, shaking. The shock had left her speechless, but Elsa, who was equally shaken, shook her hard, shouting at her in a fury of anxiety and relief.

"If I hadn't been able to reach you, you would have fallen out, you silly, silly girl."

"I know, I know. I'm sorry!"

Finally, they both burst into tears and Elsa hugged her little sister closely.

"If you don't learn to listen," she scolded her, "I am going to ask Papa not to allow you on to the deck. You're a pest!"

Berta tearfully promised all kinds of reform and, on that note, was sent to the cabin to wash her face, and lie down until she had had time to reflect on her behaviour.

With Berta in a chastened mood, the rest of the journey went smoothly, and the party disembarked at Matope, from where they would cut across country to the convent. Normally, Matope was a sleepy little town, but now that the road was being extended from Blantyre to Fort Johnston, to enable the troops and equipment to be driven up to the embattled northern borders, the area was a churned-up mass of craters of reddish-brown earth, and men with all sorts of digging implements.

"What a mess," said Ludwig, as he surveyed the scene. "I had hoped that we would be able to use the new road." He turned to Elsa. "I'll go and have a word with the supervisor and decide which way we should go to Nguludi."

On his return, he had a discussion with Aleki and then walked across to the girls.

"The new road isn't useable," he told them. "We'll take our normal route across country and leave this chaos behind us."

Had they been able to take the new direct route, he explained to them, the journey would have taken no more than three days, but going across country would take the usual seven days, with hills and ravines to be skirted and, at this time of year, the inevitable downpour at midday. As they well knew, when the first few drops fell, the line would falter, spread out like scurrying ants and search for a route that would give the most shelter under the thick foliage of the trees. The girls would unfurl the umbrellas their father had brought them from the agency, but no one else took much notice of the rain. In this heat, they would be dry within minutes of its stopping anyway.

A short while later, the carriers had hoisted their loads onto their backs, Elsa and Paulina were lifted up onto their *machilas* and the straggly line was making its way to the ancient path that would take them to their destination. Ludwig travelled on his motorbike, in the lead, with Berta riding pillion and clutching him tightly around the waist. Aleki brought up the rear.

It was a bumpy ride at times but for much of the journey they followed well-worn, narrow paths used by the natives for probably hundreds of years. The soil was compacted until it was inches lower than the surrounding terrain and Ludwig had often commented to the girls what an extraordinary network of paths existed in Africa. Every village, every tribe, was connected; if one just carried on travelling east or west on these paths they would surely reach an ocean.

They hadn't gone far when Berta leaned forward to shout into her father's ear. "Can I ride my bicycle now, Papa?"

Ludwig held up his arm to alert the rest of the line and stopped. Berta slid off the pillion and stood beside him.

"Now?" he said.

"Yes please, Papa. These paths are really good for riding on." Her voice took on a wheedling tone. "Please?"

Ludwig smiled as he looked at her. It was their custom that if the condition of the path permitted, the girls rode their bicycles; otherwise they were carried in *machilas*.

"All right," he said, "but remember, no holding up the line. The minute you slow down, you get carried on a *machila*."

"Yes, Papa, and thank you," she said, smiling happily as she ran towards the bearer who was carrying her bicycle. She took it from him with a quick word of thanks, "*Zikomo*", and took her place in the line behind her father.

There was a call from Elsa: "Papa, I'd like to ride, too."

"Of course," he called back, "but do hurry or we'll never get going."

Elsa dismounted from the *machila* and, ignoring Paulina's muttered comment of, "You must be mad," quickly retrieved her bicycle from one of the carriers and joined the line between Ludwig and Berta. Soon they had left the noisy, pounding activity of the new road that was being forged out of the bush behind them. The harsh sounds muted and then disappeared and Berta became aware of the silence of the woods through which they were passing. Then she noticed rustling of leaves in a tall tree to their right and, peering into the dense green foliage, spotted three baboons, their cheeky brown faces framed by leaves as they stared at the passing cavalcade.

"Elsa, look," she shouted. "To your right, monkeys in the tree!" Then louder, "Papa, look! Monkeys in the tree!"

Without turning round, Ludwig called back. "Watch where you're going!"

Recalled to where she was, Berta just managed to stop herself from colliding with Elsa in front, and to restore her balance on dangerously wobbling wheels.

"Oops," she said.

Elsa, who had turned round to see what was going on, laughed. "Oops, indeed. If you had got me knocked off my bicycle you'd have been saying more than 'oops'!"

Their laughter rang out through the trees and, as if in response, scores of birds fluttered out of the protective foliage and flew in circles over the line, swooping high and low before returning to the trees.

"The birds look as though they're investigating us, don't they?" called out Elsa.

"Indeed," called back Ludwig. "This is their home and we are the visitors." A little further on he called out, "I think it's time we stopped for a bite to eat; I'll go ahead and find somewhere suitable. Don't leave this path, Elsa."

He stopped his motorbike with arm held up high and called out to Aleki to come to the front and lead the line until his return. Then, with a revving up of his engine, the motorbike leapt into action, as though relieved to be allowed to speed up a little and he was soon out of sight, vanishing into a tunnel of every shade of green from palest aqua to deepest emerald, from shapes and sizes of leaves beyond counting.

The line continued to move on slowly, always following the path and watching out for occasional deviations. Where there was a large stone in the way, the path moved either to the right or to the left before re-joining the original path. A fallen tree caused more of a detour, as it would be left where it fell; its green wood would cause too much smoke in the hut fires. Before it could dry out, the dampwood termites would have made a feast of it, so the path remained impassable and the new twist in the road aged until it looked as though it had always been there.

Every now and then the powerful roar of Ludwig's motorbike would announce his return to the line to check that all was in order. Then, with a smile and a wave, he turned back to the front and was soon lost to sight, although the sound remained for a while, growing fainter until it faded away completely.

The line meandered on, with the motorbike and bicycles struggling to match the slow pace of the walkers; the girls often dismounted when they saw something interesting, or when they came to a little stream which they would have to cross. An uphill stretch also meant a tiring struggle and Berta was just beginning to complain about tiredness and hunger when they rounded a bend and found Ludwig sitting sideways on his saddle, arms akimbo as he smiled at them.

"Well, that took you long enough," he said. "I'm starving."

He pointed to a large clearing a small distance from the path, shaded by large mango trees and with the sound of a little stream just beyond. "What do you think?"

"Perfect!" said the girls in unison, and they watched as the line of carriers filed into the space and, with obvious relief, took off their loads and sank to the ground, before heading off to the stream where they could be heard splashing and, from the sound of laughter, splashing one another.

While Ludwig and the girls explored the area, the cooks prepared lunch, western style for the family and native style for the bearers. From now on, Ludwig, accompanied by Aleki, would hunt for the day's food and most times they would return with a clutch of hares or a small deer. What they did not eat, Ludwig gave to the first villagers that they met as they continued their journey. If he had no luck they would eat tinned food which had been brought along for exactly that contingency.

That first afternoon they made good time after the short break for lunch and, by late afternoon, Ludwig's searching eyes and frequent departure from the track to reconnoitre the surrounding area had located the ideal spot to camp, a grassy patch by a river, though not so close as to arouse the curiosity of a hippo out for his evening meal.

By dusk the entire party was tired and ready to go down for the night, but there was much to do.

The bearers rapidly put up the family's tents under the watchful eye of Aleki and, branching outwards from them and forming a wide circle, they put their packs of bedding on the ground: they would go to sleep looking up at the stars. In the centre of the circle were two large cooking fires.

It was a busy scene, each of the bearers busily carrying out allotted tasks while the cooks and their assistants made their preparations to feed the small army. Each bearer stacked his load at the head of his sleeping mat, thus forming a barrier against possible nocturnal theft and, more importantly, nocturnal animal visitors. A few gaps were left in the circle where fires would be lit and maintained all night, not only to discourage animals but to keep mosquitoes and other insects to a minimum.

On the first night, after supper, Berta was the first to seek her bed in the tent that she shared with her two sisters. She looked forward to going to bed because the camp beds were comfortable, made of stout canvas strung on poles and with soft downy sleeping bags on them.

The hustle and bustle of the camp slowly quietened down until finally there was no sound but the crickets making their grating sawing sounds in the bushes, and the frogs grunting hoarsely in their throats in the damp reeds at the water's edge. The soft footfalls of the two *londas*, as they paced the perimeter of the camp in shifts, were merely whispers broken occasionally by a cough. The fires in the centre were also kept going as a deterrent against any lions and leopards prowling about in their nightly search for food. These precautions had to be taken, since the smell of cooking meat in the still night air would draw them like a magnet.

Dawn awoke Berta and in the dim, rosy light she looked across at Elsa, who lay peacefully asleep. Berta often wondered how it was that her older sisters could sleep so much. From her first moment of wakefulness, her mind churned with exciting possibilities for the day, most of which, she knew, would be vetoed by either her father or sisters. But enough remained to keep her upbeat and expectant. She yawned widely and noisily and looked across at her sleeping sisters. No reaction. Next she coughed. Paulina stirred and half turned towards her little sister. "Stop it, Berta," she said drowsily. "Go back to sleep."

Finally, after what seemed like an eternity, the camp was up, breakfast was over and preparations began for the day's march.

The next few days followed the same pattern, varying only in the terrain. The thickly wooded hills gave way to savannah grasslands of seemingly vast distances, punctuated here and there by thorn trees and baobab trees, with ribbons of bright green to trace the course of a river or stream. At this time of year, with the plentiful rainfall, streams would appear for a short time, giving life to plants and animals before subsiding as the rainless winter drew near. With the clear views into the distance, game could be spotted in their hundreds, many of the buck family, buffalo, the occasional glimpse of a lion, a family of elephants almost hidden by the trees and saplings by which they stood and fed and, of course, the monkeys of every shape and size, who would draw near to chatter and point before scampering away.

On the fifth night, Berta fell asleep as soon as her head hit the pillow, but she was awakened from a deep, dreamless sleep a few hours later by a deep-throated grunting sound close to her head. She rocketed into wakefulness and, eyes wide in the darkness, her breath in her throat, she struggled to locate what had awakened her. The sound came again and her head shot around to stare at the tent wall, inches away from her face. It was then that she saw the shadow on the tent, the shadow of a lion.

She screamed, "*Nkhango*! *Nkhango*!" struggled out of the sleeping bag and leapt onto Elsa's bed, shivering with fright.

The call of "Lion!" awakened the entire party in seconds. The watchmen took up the call and men wearing only their loincloths stumbled up from their mats to grasp a smouldering branch from the nearest fire and prance around looking for the intruder. Ludwig tore out of his tent dressed only in his underwear, his rifle cocked and at the ready.

Startled, the lion, which was now standing at the opening to the girls' tent, let out a deafening roar and faced his attackers, who were racing around like headless chickens, brandishing their smoking branches and shouting at the top of their lungs. Another defiant roar and he turned and loped for the gap between the tents. Ludwig tried to get a shot at him, but there were too many people milling around and, within seconds, the tawny beast had disappeared into the darkness beyond the encampment.

Ludwig raced to the girls' tent and hurried in. "Are you all right?" he asked tersely.

Berta flung herself into his arms, crying with fear. "He grunted right next to my head, Papa" she told him, choking on her sobs. "I was so afraid."

He held her close until she had calmed down and then went outside, where he called the watchmen and Aleki to him.

"What were you doing?" he demanded of the watchmen. "How could a lion get into camp without your seeing it?"

The sheepish and mumbled replies confirmed his suspicions.

"You were asleep," he spat at them in disgust. "Do you realise that you owe your lives to the fact that Berta heard him before he found you? As you very well know, a hungry lion doesn't roar; he only grunts so that he doesn't alert his prey. You would have heard nothing until he pounced on you. And then it would have been too late."

He turned to Aleki. "Don't let these men do sentry duty together again. Put each of them with a man who can be trusted."

Aleki went to do as he was bid; his voice haranguing the culprits could be heard above the other sounds as the camp reorganised itself for the rest of the night.

It was a good hour before everyone had quietened down and returned to their sleeping positions. A new sentry shift had been selected and the fires stoked up.

"I don't imagine that the lion will return," Ludwig said to his *capitao* in a low voice, "but tell the watchmen to keep the fires burning brightly just in case."

The sounds of men giving orders and settling down to sleep slowly died away and silence reigned once more, to be broken a few hours later by the dawn chorus, as the flocks of birds awakened and circled the forest, raucously searching for food for their young.

"How much longer before we get to school?" was Berta's first question to Elsa as she sat up in her bed. "I really don't like camping anymore!"

CHAPTER THIRTY-FOUR

The final days of the walk passed swiftly. The procession wound through valleys which were now green and luxuriant after the heavy summer rains. Little streams that would only survive until the end of the rains, gurgled merrily as they skipped over boulders, and covered once again the dry beds that had thirsted for their arrival. Schools of baboons chattered high above as they swung from tree to tree, following the meandering line of travellers; bush buck bolted on dainty legs to a safe distance to observe their passage. Monkeys were shyer creatures, content to hide in the trees and push the foliage aside to take a look out every now and then.

Snakes were always a hazard. They were not predatory creatures as far as humans were concerned, but when stepped on inadvertently would strike to defend themselves. The puff adder in particular belied its innocent and comparatively small size by packing a lethal venom which few survived. The passage was relatively safe, however, as the sound of the approaching procession was enough to send creatures large and small scurrying to safety.

Berta faced the final night on the road with trepidation; she moved her camp bed right next to Elsa's.

"Your bed is closest to the opening, so if a lion comes in it'll eat you first," Paulina informed her.

Berta was struck speechless, her eyes wide in her pale face and the freckles over her nose standing out in sharp relief.

"Stop it, Paulina," snapped Elsa, her normal equanimity fraying. She turned to Berta. "You'll be fine. The new watchmen will be on duty, the fires will be bigger and we'll all be quite safe."

And, indeed, it was a very quiet night. The sound of hyenas cackling over their prey and the occasional hoot of an owl were the only sounds that disturbed the deep calm.

As dawn broke, cups of scalding tea were brought to the family's tents, and breakfast followed soon after.

Within an hour the camp had been dismantled and packed and the party was on its winding way. The girls were in *machilas*; they had tired of the seemingly endless walking. As the procession wound its way up the last foothills the sun shone on the newly luscious vegetation that surrounded them; the birds rose in droves and wheeled over the treetops as they approached. Sensing their journey's end, the carriers broke into a rhythmic, improvised chant. They sang the tale of the journey and the visit of the lion and Berta smiled in delight as she heard her name.

232

The little madam Berta heard a noise, sang the leader.
Chorus: *Oh yes, oh yes.*
What is it? She said. What is it?
What is it? What is it?
I hear a noise, a bad noise.
Yes, it's true. Yes, it's true.
It's a lion. Oh, mama it's a lion.
It's a lion, a bad lion.

"This song will be sung for some time around their fires at night," Ludwig told Berta with a smile. "They won't forget you in a hurry!"

A final bend and they were looking down at the convent. Shock silenced them for a few moments. The bearers put down their loads and crowded around them as they all surveyed the pitiful scene below them.

"Oh, Papa, look!" the girls cried in unison, pointing at the desolation below them. The priest's house and the convent were nothing but charred rubble. Only the church, built of stone and still under construction at the time of the rebellion, was untouched.

"They even burnt the chicken pens," called out Pauline. "I hope that they let the birds out first."

"What a good thing we took the dogs with us," reflected Elsa. "They probably would have let them burn to death with the buildings."

The girls were subdued as they stood looking down at what had been their second home. Memories of those violent days had faded with time, but now they returned in full force.

"Poor Alicia," whispered Berta, her eyes filling with tears.

Ludwig put his arms around her and held her tightly.

"I know, my darling," he whispered against her hair. "I know. Sometimes terrible things happen in life and we can't understand why they happened. We just have to wait for the pain to go away and live the rest of our lives as best we can."

A final quick hug and he changed the subject.

"Now, let's see if we can spot the new school."

The little party gazed down at the groups of new buildings which had risen some fifty yards from the original ones. One seemed as though it might be the new school. The shape was similar to the old one and its new corrugated iron roof shone brightly in the sun. Numerous buildings around it looked as though they might be the kitchens and the storerooms and a large area to the one side had been levelled and planted with grass; trees had been planted around the perimeter. Those would be the playing fields, suggested Ludwig; he pointed out some mud huts with thatched roofs a short distance from the church. Could they be the priests' temporary accommodation, he wondered. At the mention of the priests, Berta looked stricken.

"Father Swelsen," she cried. "Is he all right, do you think?"

"I don't know, my darling," said Ludwig quietly, hugging her again. "We shall just have to find out." He turned to the bearers, raised his arm and pointed to their destination.

"*Tiyeni!*" he called out. Loads were raised once again and the final part of their journey began. Two hours later they were winding their way around the charred areas of the old site to the front of the new building. As they approached, Mother Camille and the sisters, who had been alerted by the gardeners to the arrival of strangers, opened the front door and stood at the head of the veranda steps to give them a smiling welcome.

It was a joyful reunion, all the more so after the fear and tension that had surrounded their last meeting, before Ludwig had taken his family back home. The nuns unbent sufficiently to hug the girls; normally they were not encouraged to show physical displays of affection. Berta felt a thrill of awe as the starched wimple brushed her cheek. She had never touched any part of that mysterious bundle of skirts, voluminous sleeves and starched headdress which was the nuns' habit. The allure held the girls endlessly. How many skirts were there? Did they have any hair under the wimple? Oh, thrill of thrills one day when Sister Jeanne unknowingly left a wisp of dark hair showing above her left ear. They had hair! Or at least, Sister Jeanne did.

Most of the other girls had already arrived and soon the Deuss family had been taken back into the fold. While Ludwig supervised the unloading of the baggage, the girls took their cases of clothes to their dormitories for, naturally, no man would be permitted to enter that virginal stronghold. Several jars of honey and a selection of cheeses were given to the grateful nuns. Aleki and the bearers were taken off to the servants' quarters, where they would be fed and housed for the night, although there was as yet very limited accommodation.

The girls had re-joined their father. He was sitting on the veranda enjoying a cup of coffee and chatting with the nuns when suddenly there was a voice, familiar yet strangely different, from around the corner. All heads turned as a man came around the corner, walking heavily with the aid of a stout cane. He was bent almost double at the waist and beneath a thatch of white hair his scarred face beamed at them.

"Aha, Berta," he called. "Want to see if I can catch you?"

There was a moment of horrified recognition and then the girls rose and ran to him.

"Father Swelsen!" they called. They circled him, all talking at the same time and his eyes went from one to the other, responding to one, turning to the other until he held up his hand.

"Now, one at a time, please!"

They quietened a little, Berta still dancing with excitement, and stepped back a pace.

"Oh, sorry, Father," responded Elsa, her shining eyes belying her words, "but what a wonderful surprise to see you!"

"It's so good to see you again, Father," laughed Berta, her smile threatening to split her face in two, "and no, you never could catch me so you won't now either!"

And, together, talking more quietly now, they made their way to the group on the veranda.

Ludwig rose and warmly clasped the priest's hand. He too was shaken at the change in his appearance. The glossy dark hair and beard were white and there was a livid scar down the length of his face. His stooping body bore witness to the terrible beating that he had taken.

The nuns brought a chair for him and the company settled down again. The girls sat on the edge of the veranda, quiet and still. It was unacceptable that they should join in the conversation or that they should fidget; they accepted these restraints, rather than going to play with their friends. They knew that they wouldn't be seeing their father for some time, and each moment with him was precious.

In response to Ludwig's gentle questioning about the night of the insurrection, the priest asked Mother Camille, with a whimsical smile, whether she would mind hearing the story of the burning of the mission one more time.

"Of course not," she smiled, "but I think these young ladies should go and unpack and join us later."

She gave the men a warning look and they understood that she did not want the girls' memories of that day to be refreshed. Though bitterly disappointed at being sent away, not even Paulina dared to sulk in front of the Reverend Mother. The trio obediently went off, only their rigid backs giving a hint of their outrage at being parted from their father.

Father Swelsen began his narrative by telling them how he had not expected the mob to intend any harm.

"I knew many of them; Chilembwe's church was only a few miles away and the people from the two parishes mingled freely. Also, we have employed many of them at various times in the gardens and in the building of the new church. I advised the nuns and the girls to leave because the Bishop instructed me to do so, but a strange mix-up occurred with regard to my staying. Apparently, Bishop Auneau sent me a message urging me to leave as well, but I understood the opposite. At any rate, I preferred to stay."

He shrugged his shoulders and continued telling his audience how he had found Alicia and how he and the gardeners had hurried to the priests' house, where he found a four-man escort from the bishop to get him to safety. With them he hoped to get Alicia to safety.

His listeners gave him their rapt attention, even though they had heard the details before. Hearing it straight from Swelsen gave it an added poignancy and, as he spoke, thoughtfully and slowly, it was clear that the events were still vivid to him, that he was still struggling to come to terms with the tragedy.

"With hindsight," he said, "I believe the mob must have been hiding in the bushes when I got home. I remember thinking what a strangely silent night it was, no sounds of dogs, or frogs or cicadas, just silence."

The priest stopped and absentmindedly chewed his lip.

"I've discussed this with my staff when we have been trying to put together the events of that night; we think that they must have been there for some time –they appeared so suddenly and quietly. By a miracle they arrived too late to see the departure of the nuns and the girls.

"I tried to address the mob from the veranda. I recognised a few of them as they drew close; I tried to talk to them but they shouted me down. They were wild eyed and agitated and seemed almost drunk; they seemed not to recognise me."

Again Father Swelsen paused; it was clear that the events of that night were still a painful memory. Slowly and succinctly he told his story and, at the end, he clasped both hands around the head of his cane and briefly dropped his forehead onto them. When he raised his head, the sadness in his eyes spoke to his listeners of the pain in his heart.

He murmured, "We found her remains under the bed, you know, Alicia's." His voice broke. "Her little bead bracelet was charred but recognisable. I have asked myself again and again whether I could have acted differently to save her life; my sole comfort is that I did what I thought best at the time and God would certainly ask no more of me than that."

There was a silence while the listeners tried to come to grips with what they had heard; and then Mother Camille turned to the priest, saying gently, "You are right, of course; you could have done no more. We are truly grateful that you survived, Father, and we hope that eventually we will all be able to put those dark days well and truly into the past."

Suddenly, the lunch bell rang, loud and harsh, startling the little group into a return to the present. Footsteps approached and the three girls, with Elsa in the lead, returned to the veranda to tell their father that they would be going in to lunch and to ask Mother Camille when they could see him again.

"Don't worry," Mother teased. "He isn't going to run away! You can see him again later this afternoon."

Reassured, the girls, together with the nuns who were on lunch duty, left hurriedly, to join the other girls in prayer before the meal started.

"Would you like to come and stay with us, Mr Deuss?" asked Swelsen. "We are living in mud huts, but they are comfortable, cool in the summer and warm in the colder weather."

Ludwig turned to the Mother superior. "If you don't mind, Mother," he said, "I would enjoy seeing and hearing about the present state of the renovations from Father Swelsen."

"Of course I don't mind," smiled Mother. "But I must insist that you both stay to lunch and come back for supper." She turned to Ludwig. "We have insisted on cooking the priests' food here," she explained. "There isn't very much that you can cook on a log fire!"

"Women are always the same," grumbled the priest. "Fuss, fuss, fuss."

Mother Camille rolled her eyes heavenward.

The girls spent the rest of the day preparing for the start of term and catching up on their friends' news. At five o'clock in the evening they all trooped up to the church in a neat crocodile formation for the service of Benediction. Berta looked around for her father and finally spotted him sitting next to Father Anthony. Ludwig was not a Catholic but, in deference to A Mayi, who was, had agreed to his children being brought up in that religion, and accompanied them to church on feast days.

After supper, as dusk drew a soft cloak over the activities of the day, the girls were allowed to stay up and spend some time with their father. They walked around the convent grounds with him, inspecting the damage and listening as he told them what was likely to be happening to the area in the near future.

"The Dutch headquarters of the Marist Priests are collecting money to rebuild the priests' house at the moment," he told them. "They expect to have enough by 1918. And I am sure that more money will be forthcoming to finish off the convent nicely."

"It's fine," said Elsa. "It's nice that it's all new inside."

"Yes," agreed Berta. "And I like the smell of paint."

"You're mad," said Paulina. "You also like the taste of burnt matches. You're strange, you know."

Ludwig hastily intervened. "I suppose we all have our peculiar habits," he laughed. "If it isn't burnt matches it's tobacco and if it's not tobacco it's something else."

Pauline started to make a rejoinder but he turned around swiftly to her and frowned lightly. She subsided.

The bell for evening prayer rang and the little group turned to head back to the convent, Berta complaining bitterly that they should have to return so early. As they approached the common room, Ludwig kissed each of them goodnight, saw them in and turned away for the brief walk to the hut that he was sharing with Father Swelsen that night.

The children slept soundly in the first conventional beds they had slept in for a week. At six o'clock the next morning a nun, walking up and down the dormitory with the tinkling bell in her hand, roused them to a beautiful clear day. Through the windows the sky was a clear, cloudless blue and the birdsong seemed to chivvy them as they tumbled out of bed and got washed and dressed.

Before the girls could go to breakfast, they were called by Mother Camille to say goodbye to their father; he was at the front of the building organising the last of the carriers. His hair shone like corn amongst the dark heads around him in the bright morning sunshine and he turned as he heard his daughters run towards him. Mother Camille followed more sedately.

"Well, girls," he smiled. "Good morning to you."

They spoke for a few minutes and Ludwig, who hated saying goodbye to them as much as they did to him, cheerfully brought the conversation to a close.

"I'd best be getting on," he said briskly. "We need to make as much headway as we can before the midday downpour hits us."

He kissed and hugged each of his daughters, speaking tender words to them as he saw the tears glistening on their lashes and running down Berta's cheeks. She clutched his arm, pulling it towards her and looking up intently into his eyes. "Papa, please don't go. I feel frightened."

"Oh, my darling," he said, drawing her close, "don't forget that it's almost Easter and A Mayi and I will be down to see you then." Over her head, he looked at Elsa, who came and put her arm around her little sister's shoulders, pulling her gently away from their father as he turned away.

She bent to whisper: "Don't cry, darling. You'll upset Papa and I know you don't want to do that."

Berta raised a tear-stained face. "Maybe we won't see Papa again," she said, with a sob in her voice.

"No, no, darling! Don't think that. He'll be back with A Mayi before you know it!"

Ludwig said his goodbyes and thanks to Mother Camille and then walked briskly to his motorbike, where he was joined by Aleki on his; together they led the procession down the bumpy rough-hewn road, still bordered untidily with building materials. Just before they turned the bend away from the convent Ludwig, his hair glinting golden in the sun and his eyes screwed up against the glare, turned around and waved to his girls. They waved back and blew kisses as he rode out of sight.

They would never forget that moment, the moment he rode out of their lives.

PART THREE

CHAPTER THIRTY-FIVE

A letter from Ludwig Deuss to Elsa Deuss

10th December, 1916

My dearest daughter Elsa,

How are you? It is very difficult for me to imagine the pain that you must all be going through. I know that my own pain sometimes threatens to drown me. You see? I'm being very open with you. You are now a young woman and what a privilege I feel it is, that I can open up to you.

I am writing to you because you are the strong one and the eldest with Richard away. Now that things have quietened down a bit, I would like you to know what happened. Later, when they are older and better able to cope with it, I would like you to show this letter to Paulina and Berta. Knowing the facts will also enable you to be even more of a comfort to your mother, my beloved wife, Victoria.

Forgive me if this takes a little while, dearest Elsa. I need to put down all the details of the events that took place in the hope that this will clear some of the fog from my mind.

So, let's start at the beginning.

As soon as war broke out the Nyasaland authorities started to pay me very close attention and to question me about my 'allegiance' to Germany. I told them that I was a Swiss national, as they well knew, and that I had no personal feelings for Germany. I had very good customers there and that was that. I had set up my head office in Hamburg several years before because German firms were my biggest customers for beeswax and groundnuts. So I thought it sensible to send these directly to Germany and they were distributed by the German office. At that time, about fifteen years ago, there was not the least suggestion that a war, far less a world war, would occur in the foreseeable future.

Anyway, shortly after I took you back to school in January, Carrain instructed me to move my office to my shop at Mponda. I gathered that the reason for that was so that I would not see the British troop movements on their way up north to Karonga. As if I cared!

Two months after I took the three of you back to school at Nguludi, Richard surprised us with a visit. It was so good to see him and he made the house seem a little less lonely after you had all left.

Two weeks into his visit, we were startled one morning to be woken up at five by the sound of many footsteps coming up onto the front veranda. Then there was loud knocking on the front door.

We heard Edisoni go to the door; there was an exchange of words, after which he came and knocked on our bedroom door. When I called to him to enter he did so and told me that Carrain was downstairs with six local policemen. I told him to ask them to be seated on the veranda and to offer them some tea.

Richard had also been woken up by the noise and came to our bedroom to find out what was going on. I told him that we didn't know and asked him to dress quickly and come downstairs with me; it seemed certain that the news, whatever it was, wasn't good if Carrain was involved. I asked your mother to stay in the bedroom, since I knew how he felt about her.

We were dressed within ten minutes and went to find the men standing on the veranda. The young policemen, the askaris, *appeared to be very ill at ease and all but one refused to meet my eye, even though I was well acquainted with them and their families. I knew then that there was trouble ahead.*

Carrain walked straight up to me and told me that Richard and I were under arrest, prior to being interned.

You can imagine my shock.

I asked him on what grounds.

"On suspicion of passing information to the German Army in East Africa," he replied. "In addition, I have a court order authorising the internment of all people of Germanic origin." He showed it to me.

"But you know that that is ridiculous," I said to him, trying to keep my temper in check. "I am a Swiss citizen and have been one since I was three years old."

I was not unduly perturbed at this point. Carrain had tried to make life difficult for us on so many occasions that it seemed that this was just his latest effort.

Richard came forward aggressively at that point and I put my arm out to hold him back. I tried to send him a message with my eyes; I knew that we would play into Carrain's hands if we resisted.

"What evidence do you have of the allegation of spying?" I asked.

He ignored my question and produced a search warrant.

"I would like to search your study. Unlock it, please."

"It's never locked," I replied. "Feel free to search all you want."

He lost no time in going into the study and came out shortly holding my astronomical charts and the big map that you girls and I had been drawing of the routes to all my factories and stores.

"You will both be taken to Limbe and interned in the detention camp, where the German prisoners of war are kept," he said. *"A committee of senior administrative officers will look into the evidence that we have gathered."*

"This has nothing to do with Richard," I protested. *"He lives in South Africa and is only here for two or three weeks of each year."*

"We have evidence that he has been your accessory," came the reply.

I cannot describe to you how I felt in those moments. The conversation that we were having was so fantastic and so unrelated to our reality that my mind seemed to have turned to cotton wool. I could not grasp the implications of the accusation. There were no words in my vocabulary that matched theirs.

At the same time, I was angry. But I was determined not to let Carrain see that, finally, he was getting to me.

"Will you come quietly or are we going to have to handcuff you?" he asked, civil and relaxed for once.

Richard broke in. "Don't be a fool," he said to him. *Then he turned to me. "We'll need to pack a few things,"* he said curtly.

"How long will we be away?" I asked.

At that moment, Kahn rushed up the drive, looking anxious and dishevelled. He looked around.

"What's up?" he asked. *"Aleki just called to tell me that something was afoot."*

I told him what was happening and he turned to Carrain. "Mr Carrain, what on earth is all this about?"

"I would advise you not to become involved, Kahn," he replied with a pomposity that made me want to slap his face. *"The status of all foreign nationals, especially Germans, is under review at the moment."*

"Are you threatening me?" asked Kahn, very gently and mildly.

"No, just clarifying the position," he replied smugly.

"In that case please continue to clarify. First of all, is this an arrest?"

"Yes, it is and since it has nothing whatsoever to do with you, I shall answer no further questions."

I was beginning to get anxious that Kahn should not become involved lest he suffer the same fate, so I called him to me. "I'll just get some clothes," I said to the room at large before turning away, gripping Kahn by the elbow and saying to him quietly, *"Please telegraph my lawyer in Blantyre immediately and tell him that I am being taken to the detention centre outside Limbe and that he should contact me there. Could you please also go and get Ada so that she is with Victoria when I leave."*

I let go his arm, called Richard to follow me, and went to our bedroom, where I found A Mayi sitting on the bed, looking desperately worried. She looked at me wordlessly and I told her quickly what had happened.

I'll never forget the way she sat there, eyes huge, waiting to hear from me what was going on. I told her as quickly as I could and I tried to comfort her, telling her that she mustn't worry because I should be back in no time. When I finished, she sat quietly, staring at me, and then she said, in a voice that was dead, so dead that it sent shockwaves shooting through my mind, "I'm never going to see you again."

I was appalled. I sat down beside her and held her and told her that there was no chance of that.

"My lawyers will be onto it," I told her, "and before you know it, I'll be back here."

"I know I shall never see you again, Ludwiki," she said, and the look on her face as she said it haunts me to this day.

Richard knocked on the door and told me that I had better hurry. As I rose to pack he came in, portmanteau in hand, to sit with A Mayi and console her and try to assure her that we would soon be back.

It was very hard to leave her in that state. I called for Mataya to stay with her and then gave her one last hug before leaving the room and going to the front with Richard. I was still certain that the affair would come to nothing and was more angry for the hurt and worry that was being caused to my family than anything else. The idea that my charts could be used as evidence of any wrongdoing was laughable.

We left the house, without handcuffs, and walked to the police station, where a convoy of military trucks from the north had stopped on its way to Blantyre. The arrest had clearly been planned to coincide with this; Richard and I, and one native policeman, were immediately installed in the cabs of two of the trucks and the convoy set off.

I remember little of the journey. The new road was bumpy and the cab seats uncomfortable, but those were the least of my worries. My mind buzzed around in circles. What was going on?

In four hours we drew up outside the detention centre and Richard and I were taken through the guarded gates and installed in a small, bare room with two beds and little else in it. By evening we had met several of the other internees, as well as the German prisoners of war captured at Karonga. Do you remember that time after the uprising, when I came to Limbe to collect you and you pointed out the large tent in the middle of the Mandala compound where the German prisoners of war were housed? Who would ever have dreamed that I would be one of them in just over a year's time? Life is full of surprises, isn't it?

Anyway, to cut the story short, the next two weeks were a nightmare. Government officials interviewed us separately on many occasions and my confidence began to disappear. Nothing I said had any effect. My lawyer seemed to be helpless and told me that all he could do was to ensure that proper procedures were followed, which he did. He repeatedly asked me if the charges were true and I repeatedly told him that they were not. He spoke to several of the officials involved but to no avail. He told me that reading between the lines, they were inordinately worried about the possibility of an attack by the German army, after their first one had failed at Karonga. It seemed that reinforcements were expected from the south and, until they arrived, they felt vulnerable.

When we were told that I would be deported and my properties confiscated – I owned half of Blantyre you know, my dear! – but that Richard would be allowed to remain, my lawyer put in an appeal and we waited for the response.

Those days took ten years off my life.

We waited and waited. We walked endlessly around the perimeter of the fence. I tried to join in the sporting activities with the other internees and prisoners, but my heart felt as though it was dying inside me. Richard was wonderful, always close to me, always ready with a word of encouragement.

In the evenings we sat outside and Richard borrowed a guitar and played and sang to us. He sang Gounod's Ave Maria so beautifully – I don't need to tell you how beautifully he sings! – and to me it will always be the sound to which my heart was slowly breaking. Yes, Holy Mother, I thought, pray for us; pray for us, for we need your strength.

Three days later I was informed that my appeal had been refused and that we would begin the journey to Europe on the following day.

"What about my family?" I asked. "I need to ensure that they have an income."

The official was sympathetic and told me that before I left he would help me make an official application to pay an income out of the proceeds of my confiscated property and goods. We completed that a few hours later and I was told that it was unlikely that any more than 18 pounds a year for each of you girls and 12 pounds a year for A Mayi would be permitted. After all they have taken from me, that is all they are prepared to consider paying you out of it!

My lawyer said that he could appeal for more time so that I could see you all again but I refused. I wanted more than anything in the world to see you all for one last time, but at what cost! I could not put you all through that.

So, in my last hug to Richard was all the pain and love and longing that I felt for all of you. We wept in each other's arms and he kept saying, "You'll be back, Dad. I just know it. You'll be back."

And then it was over and I was in the back of a truck with the other internees, on our way to the railway station in Limbe.

Four weeks later I arrived in Switzerland. The family were all at the station to meet me. It was good to see them again but, without you, nothing seems like home.

Your aunts Edda and Paulina are fussing over me terribly. They say that I look ill and thin! Tell me, dear Elsa, wasn't I always careful not to let my weight get too high? How strange to be told constantly that I must eat more!

Your grandparents have aged a lot since I left. They seem to enjoy their very expensive nursing home where, I am told, the pretty young nurses keep my father on his toes. Imagine, at his age!

My health is not too good and my old problems with my heart seem to have resurfaced, but I am doing my best to get back into good shape. So please don't worry. We have excellent physicians here.

Now, about your financial situation. When I was in hospital after my hunting accident I put four good properties in Blantyre into your names, so you each have a valuable investment. Also, when I started to become aware of Carrain's implacability I came to an arrangement with Kahn. Under this agreement, in the event of my being unable to care for you, I made over my share of the business to him, in Nyasaland, Angola and Portuguese East Africa, and he undertook to support you all in every way until Berta reaches the age of twenty-one. Each one of you will receive a lump sum at that age, that is, when you reach your majority. It was the only way that I could safeguard your interests. So even if the British government pays you very little you are well cared for.

Grandfather Roque would have been only too happy to have you with them at Sena but what about your schooling? Elsa, you are such a wonderful family. You are such good people, and have had the best education I could buy you. You must not lose this. Soon you will be finishing school and I want you to keep in close touch with me so that we can plan your future together. Had I, in my wildest dreams, imagined that this could have happened, I would have transferred all the Blantyre properties into your names. However, you will be very well off with the present arrangement.

You may wonder why I am not considering bringing you all here to Switzerland. I have thought of that longingly, but I know that I would never be able to give to you, and particularly A Mayi, what you have out there in beautiful Africa. You children would make the adjustment in time, I am sure, but I do not believe that A Mayi would ever be happy and I could never take you away from her. And, in any case, it would mean giving up the hope that keeps me alive; that one day I may be able to return to you and our home.

I have been in touch with the British Embassy but, at the moment, they are unwilling to even consider my request that my deportation order be rescinded. This is probably the wrong time for me to be making these moves. May the war end soon and things return to normal so that I can start trying again.

That is my incentive to get my good health back – so that I can come back to you!

Look after your mother. My heart is with her and I cannot bear to contemplate what she is going through at this time. I was happy to hear from Kahn that your grandparents and aunts are staying with her at the moment. I am hoping that Tia Francesca and Tia Anania can stay with her on a permanent basis – until I return, of course.

I am writing a separate letter to Paulina and Berta. Take care of them for me. Don't let this tragedy take away from my little Berta her joyous nature and her bright, shining eyes that gave joy to my life. Keep an eye on her health too, please. She used to be such a delicate little thing – too skinny by far! And make Paulina a better loser at cards!

And you, my dear child. Talk to Richard, to the sisters, to anyone, when you are feeling sad. You must share your sorrow. You have always been so firm and self-contained that I worry about you. It is good to speak of your pain, so don't keep it to yourself. Thank you for always being a daughter that a man could be proud of. Have you any idea how much I love you?

Write soon and let me know how you all are and have a very blest and happy Christmas.

Your grandparents and your aunts send their love.

Your loving father always,
Ludwig Deuss

CHAPTER THIRTY-SIX

A Letter from Victoria Deuss to Ludwig Deuss

5th April, 1917

Dear Papa,
A Mayi has asked me to write this letter to you for her.
More from me at the end!
Elsa

My dear husband Ludwiki,
How are you? I think about you all the time and hope that you are well. I am always afraid that your old heart problems will start again. But, of course, you must have very good doctors where you are so I shall try not to worry.

We are very sad that you have had to leave us. But I must not complain about that. Your situation is very much worse than mine. I have the children and our home but you are going back to your old home as a visitor. How painful this must be for you. So much pain, here, there, everywhere. May God protect us.

I thought I would go mad when you left but people have been so kind! Mother Camille sent the girls home immediately so that I could tell them what had happened. Oh, Ludwiki, how sad their hearts are. Elsa, always so strong and sensible, has helped me to stand again on my feet. She now looks after the money for the house and Kahn does it when she is away at school. She is also helping at the agency; Kahn is finding it difficult without you and it is not easy for him to find a responsible employee.

Paulina does not say much; she just sits quietly and stares at the garden. I am trying to make her start a new piece of embroidery and the nuns at the hospital, who have called to see us, are going to lend her some magazines with designs in them. I hope that this will turn her thoughts away from you a little.

Berta, little Berta, walks around quietly now. Remember how she used to skip and run all the time! She has collected all the little things you left behind, your little torch, your penknife, your key ring with the elephant on it and your silver brush and comb set and taken them to her room; she says they make her feel that you are still around.

I must be strong! So many people are helping. My parents and my sisters take it in turns to come and stay with us and I am learning slowly how to live without you.

But not for long! I am sure that, as you said, this misunderstanding will be cleared up and you will be permitted to return home.

We all send you our love and greetings to all your family. They must be so happy to have you back home!

I wait for your letter.

All my love,

Your loving wife, Victoria

P.S. Papa, as you can imagine, A Mayi is having real problems adjusting, but she is being wonderfully brave and struggling to cope with her new situation. Sometimes we worry about her; she has lost weight and is very quiet, but she always pretends to be fine when we are around!

We all just need that date! The date you are coming home!

With fondest love,

Your ever loving daughter,

Elsa

Letter from Ludwig Deuss to Paulina and Berta Deuss

10th December, 1916

My dearest daughters Paulina and Berta,

How are you? I hope that you are well and still enjoying school.

Did you receive the little parcel I sent you for your birthday? It will probably take a while to get there.

How are the mathematics lessons, Paulina? And are you managing to stay out of trouble, Berta?

I miss you a great deal and wish that I could see you again. But we must be patient.

Your grandparents are very well but are getting quite old now. Fortunately, they live in a beautiful nursing home and are very well cared for. All of your aunts would have been more than happy to care for them in their old age, but it seems that they had planned all this from a long time ago and it is what they want.

Your aunts Paulina and Edda are well too and are always asking me questions about you all. I am so glad that I took that family photograph at

Sena on our last visit. They think that you look very smart in your school uniforms! What a pity, Berta, that you got one of your giggling fits. Your mouth looks quite peculiar, as though you are about to explode! Which you were, of course. Little monkey!

How are the sisters? Please give them and Father Swelsen my kindest regards.

I hope you are still enjoying your nature rambles. I am really looking forward to seeing your notebooks with your beautiful drawings. Paulina, your writing is always so beautiful. Yours is too, Berta, when you are not in too much of a hurry. Anyway, your paintings of the plants and birds make up for it!

Paulina, do make sure that Berta eats well. And, both of you, promise not to argue so much. It upsets A Mayi and it doesn't make you feel good either.

I shall write to you regularly and I hope you will do the same.

I shall be thinking of you on Christmas day in the bright sunshine and summer heat. I shall of course be shivering in my very big overcoat! You are not to giggle at the African ladies singing out of tune in church and you, Berta must not keep asking A Mayi if it is time to go home! I am sure that a very big and delicious lunch will be prepared for you and that you will be happy with your presents.

Your grandparents and your aunts send you their love.

Never forget how much I love you. I kiss you, my dear daughters.

Your ever loving father,
Ludwig Deuss

CHAPTER THIRTY-SEVEN

Letter from Ludwig Deuss to Dietrich Kahn

15th December, 1916

Dear Dietrich,

Thank you for your letter of October 12th, which I received today.

I am happy to hear that you and Ada are in good health. Also that the rains came on time and that planting has started.

Thank you both for keeping such a close eye on Victoria. You can have no idea how it grieves me that she still mourns for me as I do for her. You are right when you say that it was to be expected; we married when she was very young and we were seldom apart after that. I think that it would have been better had I died. Then my family could have mourned once and for all and then moved on with the good memories.

Communicating with the British Embassy here in Zurich is proving to be useless and I am beginning to accept that probably nothing can be done until the end of this damned war. I still find it difficult to absorb the catastrophe to our lives that it has brought. And we thought that we were neutral!

Yes, I think that it is a good idea that you start putting money aside for Richard and the girls for their needs when they finish their studies. Damn Carrain for his part in convincing the authorities that our agreement to sell my half of the business to you is void. I am only relieved that until now they have not managed to get authority from the Portuguese to annexe my interests in that country, so you will have the income from that for Victoria and the family.

I believe that the government are advertising for my debtors and creditors to submit their final claims and, from what I have been able to find out from my contacts, the final figure they hope to realise from my deportation is in the region of GBP50,000. A life's work gone, just like that! Fortunately, my father has been able to claim GBP20,000 over and above that as a loan plus interest which he supposedly made to me. They say that they will pay it because there can be no doubt that he, my father, is a Swiss national. No wonder they accused me of spying. Once my Swiss nationality was proved, there was no better way for them to get their hands on my assets. I suppose I should consider myself lucky that I wasn't shot! Dharap tells me that he has heard on the grapevine that there is quiet satisfaction in upper government circles because, since I left, the African

Lakes Corporation is operating much more profitably in the European markets. That would suggest that they have taken over my European customers. There they are with their Christian masks on, stopping at nothing to increase their market share. I look forward to the end of the war when I shall expose their dirty dealings.

Richard will soon have finished his education and it would be good to give him the capital to start off his own business. Civil engineers will make a good living from all the roads and bridges that are being opened up to the north for the transportation of troops and supplies.

I was amused at your account of how Carrain reacted to the news that my prime properties in Blantyre were in the names of Victoria and the children, and therefore out of the government's reach. How I thank God that I followed my intuition and put all into their names. I sometimes used to think of what I would like to do to him if we met again but, actually, the harm he has done and the pain he has caused are so great he has lost all identity in my mind. He has become part of a morass of evil.

How sad that Jacko didn't survive the journey to England. Don't tell the children. Not yet, anyway.

My health is not too good but I am receiving medication for my heart. Don't tell Victoria, please. What is more worrying is the depression that I keep slipping into, despite my best efforts. The medicines they give me are unpleasant and make me feel drugged, so I am trying to do without them and to fight this battle on my own. I must keep fit for Victoria, Richard and the girls. Life seems so empty without them. Each day is something to be lived through until I receive a letter from one of them. Then the light comes through and I am ready to fight again.

I am glad business is good and that the government still chooses to buy some of its supplies from us – you? It is a relief to know that brother Paul has taken over the overseeing of the southern chain of stores from Chiromo and Port Herald to Sena. Do you think Richard might be interested in becoming involved? Opening up the Swiss branch is keeping me busy and as soon as my health is improved, I shall start finding new customers for our African products.

How ironic that the head office I opened in Hamburg fifteen years ago was one of the most important pieces of evidence against me. Since eighty per cent of our groundnut exports were to Germany it seemed sensible at the time to open the office there, for taking orders and then distributing the goods. Who could have foreseen that Germany would have been the enemy fifteen years thence?

Switzerland's decision to remain neutral in this war does not mean that things are good here. The cost of keeping the army mobilised has resulted in a very high cost to the taxpayer, unemployment is up and vital raw materials have been prevented from coming in, so production has been stalled.

To make matters worse, for the first time I see a split in the population. The French part is solidly behind the French whilst the German speaking section here is behind Germany. You can imagine the tensions and flare-ups. The general strike last month brought the country to a standstill and can you believe that we have food shortages! It is not a good time to start chasing trade for a business, but the war can't last much longer and I would like to be able to proceed immediately once it is all over.

Please continue to keep me informed as you have done. I hope the girls enjoyed their Christmas holiday. How I wish I could have been there!

I send my kindest regards to Ada and my best wishes to you.

Truly yours,
Ludwig Deuss

CHAPTER THIRTY-EIGHT

The years went slowly by as they do when you are young and days are long and sunny.

If the little family did not forget Ludwig, they nevertheless learnt gradually how to live without him. Reminders of his absence eventually became fewer and less painful, and they found within themselves the resources to cope with what had been their dependence on him. Always, though, there was the hope that eventually, he would come home. The nightmare that had started so many years ago would be ended; they would be a complete family again.

Fate, that capricious overseer, did not heed their bruised spirits, their longing for quiet and calm, and continued to push them helter-skelter along the eventful path that their lives had followed thus far, and promised to continue in the future.

Richard married Dina, to everyone's surprise at the suddenness of it. She was a year older than Elsa and no one had had any idea that a love affair had been in progress.

"How strange to suddenly find that Dina is now our brother's wife and our sister-in-law!" was Berta's comment when she heard the news.

"Thank goodness she's nice," was Elsa's and Paulina's immediate reaction.

She was indeed a likeable girl and pretty too, with fair skin, large dark eyes and sleek dark hair. The couple would not have a fixed abode during the first few years, since Richard's work took him all over the country, and they both preferred that she should go with him and stay in rented accommodation. At least, until they started a family.

The family was happy that Richard had married.

A Mayi confided to Elsa some of her concerns: "He tends to drink too much and I do hope that Dina will calm him, especially if and when the children come along."

Elsa shook her head. "I can't help feeling that once a man has developed bad habits, it takes more than a wife to change them."

"I hope you're wrong, Elsa," said A Mayi. "Let's hope and pray that theirs will be a good marriage."

Elsa completed her education and left school at the age of eighteen. The pretty young girl had become a lovely young woman, slim and shapely. Her fine features and slanting eyes were calm in repose; but a rapier wit and her low-voiced asides to Berta on occasion made her eyes shine with merriment and her face dance into life. The accompanying chuckle always took place behind a hand daintily held to her mouth in the African way. Berta's reaction was generally a descent into her well-known giggles, the cause of many a scolding from the nuns.

Elsa's finishing school was a time of crisis because the question arose of what she was going to do. No eligible men whom she liked had presented themselves so marriage, even had she wanted it, which she did not, was not on the horizon.

Strangely, and she would never have admitted this to anyone, random thoughts of Rafael would slip into her mind. As time went on, the horror she had felt faded and she remembered rather that he had tried to prevent the African woman's abduction. And as the angry feelings faded, the memories of him, how he had looked when he said he loved her, his dashing good looks and most of all, how she had felt when he had kissed her, flooded into her mind, making her long to see him again. But that was ridiculous, she told herself. It was all too far in the past and best forgotten. But, said the niggle in her mind, had she let her soul mate slip out of her hands? Was there just one person to whom she had been matched since the beginning of time? Who knew?

Anyway, current thinking was that a girl's destiny was to get married as soon as possible, but it wasn't what she wanted, as she explained to Mother Camille and A Mayi.

"I like a nice home but I cannot make it my passion in life. There is nothing exciting to me about organising a home, making furnishings, having children and so on. I'll do it if I have to and probably enjoy it but, now at least, I want something different."

"Time enough for the family route in the future, my dear," was the nun's pragmatic advice to Elsa, during one of the chats they shared during the last days of her time at the convent.

"Have you any idea what it is that you want, my child?"

The reply was prompt. "Yes. I'd like to run a business."

The nun threw up her hands with a crow of laughter.

"Well, there you go! You're a bright girl and from what you've told me about how you helped your father in his business, you have managed to accumulate some valuable experience. And, from what your mother tells me, she wouldn't have been able to cope without your taking over all the family finances. You know what you want and you're a very determined young woman, so I'm sure you'll get it. There aren't many women business owners around so I'm sure you'll have a very interesting journey to your dream. Good luck and God bless you, my child."

Victoria was privately relieved that she was not to lose her eldest daughter just yet. With Ludwig gone she felt vulnerable. She felt like a mother hen clucking agitatedly as she tried to gather her young ones close to her, as they determinedly ran away to find some succulent corn. It was painful to even contemplate losing another of her family. Yet, she was aware that she should not let this influence her when advising her daughter; she would give her good, objective advice.

"You are young yet," she told her daughter. "Don't rush. Wait with patience and the way will open for you. At the moment I need you here with me; I couldn't manage without you."

Elsa was quick to reassure her mother, "Oh, Mayi, don't ever think I'd leave you. Whatever I plan for the future, you must always know that you are included." And she hugged A Mayi.

Elsa knew exactly what she wanted and she was raring to go. A business of some sort was what she wanted. But what sort?

CHAPTER THIRTY-NINE

Elsa gave a great deal of thought to what business she would enjoy that would also be profitable. Although she had enjoyed helping her father with the retail side of his business, the prospect of working in a shop didn't enthuse her and she certainly wouldn't be permitted to travel around as her father had done. She had, however, thought of a possible scheme when organising the produce of the home farm; after all, her father had made most of his money by exporting agricultural produce to Europe. Surely she could farm, as her grandfather did, for both the local and export markets, she thought with a thrill of excitement.

After much discussion with Ludwig by letter, A Mayi, her grandparents, the sisters at the convent and the Kahns, she decided to buy land in a sparsely populated area, Chiromo, which lay in the lower Shire Valley in the south of the country at the gateway to Mozambique. There she planned to grow cotton, for which there was a growing demand.

"Why Chiromo?" asked her grandfather, who was now showing his age in his slowed movements, and who had travelled up with his wife to see the family and relax with them for a month or two.

"Well, I went there with Papa and Uncle Paul one year when they were touring their chain of stores and I liked it very much. Papa has a factory there, you know," she replied in halting Portuguese. "I mean, had," she added.

"Much of the land in the area is swampy, so there will be a lot of mosquitoes and a greater chance of contracting malaria," he pointed out to her. "And, the weather in the summer is very hot indeed."

"I know," she said. "But cotton is one of the country's major crops and the climate there suits it perfectly. The land that I have been told of that is for sale is a considerable distance from the swamps and is apparently on much higher ground. There is also a cotton ginnery in the town so there won't be any transport costs to speak of."

Roque looked at her thoughtfully and then nodded approvingly.

"Clever girl, "he said with a smile. "You've got a business head on your shoulders. What are you going to do for money?"

"Well, I thought that I might sell my property in town but I've also talked to Mr Kahn about it and he thinks the business might be able to bear the cost of the land. Bear in mind that he undertook to Papa to give each of us what we needed to set us up when we left school, within reason of course.

"Good. Now what about A Mayi?" asked Roque.

"Well, we've had a lot of discussions about it; starting up a farm seems to solve a number of problems."

"Tell me about it."

"We think that it's important that we keep A Mayi with us whatever we do in the future. She still grieves so much for Papa and Fort Johnston holds nothing for us now, only memories. Once Berta has finished school, Mr Kahn has completed his side of the bargain and the agency and the stores are his. I think that this is a good opportunity to make a new start. Can you imagine what fun she'll have organising the new house and property?"

They both laughed.

"And your father?" was Roque's final question.

"He said in his last letter that although it saddened him to think of his home and farm being sold, he had in effect already lost his business, so that when he came back he too would look forward to a new start. I think he's interested in the potential for cotton and its products. He also wants to investigate the possibility of growing other export crops on a large scale. So, yes, he's all right with the idea now. Well, very keen, actually."

There was a pause while Roque sifted through the information Elsa had just given him.

"Elsa," he said finally. "Work out the total cost of your enterprise. Don't forget to include the cost of building the house, barns and so on and of running the estate – and living costs – until you can sell your first crop in a year's time. Then let me know and it will be my gift to you."

Elsa was speechless. Her first reaction was to wonder whether her limited Portuguese had been to blame for not understanding him.

"Did you say a gift, Grandfather?" she asked.

He nodded.

"Are you sure?" she finally stammered.

"Of course I am," he smiled.

"Listen", he said. "When your father married my daughter I wanted to make over a large plantation and a herd of the best cattle over to him for her dowry. He refused to accept it."

He looked at her, eyes wide with astonishment. "Can you believe that? He actually refused the dowry." He chuckled.

"Well, that doesn't surprise me," said Elsa. "He must have had a fit just at the notion!"

"Well, I can tell you that caused a bit of trouble." And he explained to his granddaughter how he had almost fallen out with her father.

"We talked and talked about it but your father wouldn't hear of it. Finally, I suggested to him that I put the plantation into the names of any children that he and my Victoria might have and at last we agreed. So, you see, there is enough there for each of you to buy a farm or whatever else you want."

He smiled at her, very pleased with himself and when Elsa tried to thank him, waved her away.

"Enough of that! Now, I think I need to help you with these calculations; let's sit down and get on with it."

And so it was that a year and a half later, by a combination of train, truck and trek and with the help of their many friends, the family and their menagerie were installed at their new home, Tangadzi Estate, in the area known as the Lower Shire, where the Shire River flowed on its long journey from the lake to where it finally joined the Zambezi river in Portuguese East Africa on its way to the Indian ocean.

Elsa wrote to tell her father of it.

Dearest Papa,
July, 1920
We're here! We've moved in at last!

You will love it. The approach is a long, straight road leading up to the high ground where we have built the house. No surprises there – it's exactly like our home at Fort Johnston. Your study awaits you, sir!

A thousand acres is a lot of land, isn't it? I didn't realise quite how much! We have started clearing the ground for planting and we have also decided where to keep the cattle, sheep, goats and pigs that we plan to buy. A Mayi is busy preparing for the chickens, ducks and geese that she intends to have close to the house. She has the builders building a rather large pond; I daren't ask how many ducks she plans to have. We'll leave the bees until you come – no volunteers for that!

We have planted mango trees along the sides of the drive for about a hundred yards before the house is reached. In between them we have planted oleanders for the colour. It should look lovely when they are fully grown – as well as supplying us with lots of delicious, juicy mangoes. Yes, I am deliberately making your mouth water!

The neighbours seem nice. Mr Watson is from Scotland and Mrs Watson is a local lady. They have a son called Andrew, probably a bit older than I am. Nice looking too. I'm teasing you! No, seriously, they are very helpful and Andrew comes around quite often to help. He has been a great help in getting suitable labourers for us, although they are plentiful now that the war is over, and advising us on the best way to get hold of supplies of all sorts.

Andrew also took me into Chiromo town last week to see the British Cotton Growers Association, the BCGA they call it, cotton ginnery. We went on his motorbike – I in the sidecar, of course – and I had a sad moment thinking of how you used to take us everywhere. Anyway, we met a very nice man, Mr Boby, an Englishman who is in charge of the ginnery and who says that he will visit us at Tangadzi when harvesting time is close and tell us how to go about things. Andrew was a bit annoyed and said, when he dropped me off at the house, that he was quite capable of advising us and who did Boby think he was!

Well, I thought that Mr Boby was charming, but quite ugly. He has such a red face and he is very thin, a bit like a lobster really, and he has strangely pale blue eyes. But he is really nice, with a wonderful dry sense of humour, and I liked him. He lives with an African lady and they have two lovely little boys, Henry and George, who look just like him – only in brown!

The weather is beautiful at the moment, warm, but cool in the evenings and early mornings. We need to be ready to start planting in November, as soon as the rains begin. So exciting!

A Mayi says are you eating well and how is your heart? She thinks of you all the time and keeps wondering how you will like this and how you will like that. She misses you so much, I feel sad for her. Of course we miss you too, but we are starting off our lives in this big, crazy world and we need all our wits about us, which doesn't leave us much time for reminiscing and nostalgia – thank goodness. A Mayi, though, is in her autumn years, which leaves a lot of time for memories and nostalgia.

Tia Francesca and Tia Anania are heaven sent. They help so much with everything but, most important of all, they make it possible for us to have our evening chats on the veranda like we did at home; I mean, Fort Johnston. I think that without them we would just wind up being depressed when the day's work is done.

By the way, we had to leave Sondo and Tanteni behind. They are getting quite old now and it seemed a shame to move them from their home. So the Kahns were delighted to have them and we are happy to know that they went to a good home. We do miss them, though.

I do hope that you will be able to make progress with the British Embassy so that you can come back home at last. We miss you, dearest Papa.

A Mayi and I send you all our love. The two Tias send you their kindest regards.

Your loving daughter,
Elsa

CHAPTER FORTY

What Elsa didn't tell her father was that Andrew was taking a keen interest in her. A day didn't pass but he found some excuse to be at the farm, and she enjoyed his company. He was good looking, made her laugh and openly admired her. He was also an outrageous flirt; his sparkling blue eyes, inherited from his father, made him hard to resist.

"Andrew, you're such a flirt!" she teased him one sunny morning as they strolled through the cotton fields at Tangadzi, admiring the rows of strong green plants and the tiny beginnings of the cotton buds. His banter, however, was in full flow and had little to do with growing cotton, although he tried to make it seem so.

"Aren't these plants beautiful?" he asked, bending over to gaze intently at one by his side. "So strong, yet so graceful and supple. And what a promise of softness in the cotton yet to come."

Elsa glanced at him then looked away, trying not to laugh, trying to edge away from his close proximity, his disturbing smell of young, clean, healthy male. "You are the worst flirt I've ever met and I refuse to take seriously anything you say."

He rounded on her. "Me? A flirt? And who may I ask has the gap between her two front teeth?"

Elsa tried to stop smiling so that the tiny gap would not be visible. "What has that got to do with anything?" she demanded.

"Everything!" he said triumphantly. "It is a well-known fact, and indeed it has been proven again and again, that young ladies with a gap between their teeth are the worst kind of flirts."

"Oh, Andrew," she said in some embarrassment, "you are talking such a lot of rubbish today!"

"OK," he said and stopped, turning towards Elsa and gently gripping her arms: "No more rubbish. Dead serious now." He paused. "Elsa Deuss, will you do me the honour of becoming my wife?"

He still had a playful smile on his lips but his eyes were serious, searching hers and, as she stared at him in shock, he added, "Please."

Elsa looked down. This was much too sudden for her. They had become friends, they had flirted. There had been no indication that anything more serious was intended. She looked up at him. "You're fooling around, aren't you, Andrew?" she asked, ready to fall in with the joke.

"No," he replied, his eyes locking hers, "I don't think I have ever been more serious in my life. Will you, Elsa?"

She smiled up at him. "Andrew, you have taken me completely by surprise. I have no idea what to say. We've known each other for such a short time!"

He smiled ruefully at her. "Well, it definitely isn't 'yes', is it?"

Elsa said nothing.

He squeezed her arms before letting her go. "Poor little Elsa. What an idiot I've been! You're right, this was too sudden. So, I'm not going to say another word – for now, that is! I'm just going to ask you to think very carefully about it all, because I love you and I want to marry you. Take your time. I'm never very far away. All you have to do, someday soon, is say, 'Yes, Andrew' and I shall be a very happy man."

"Thank you, Andrew," she said softly, "whatever happens, thank you."

He smiled down at her, bent and swiftly kissed her on the mouth.

"It's that gap, you know," he said. "Impossibly flirtatious!"

And they both laughed, as they so often did. Andrew had the knack of making ordinary things funny, of making even the dull days bright.

Elsa didn't tell A Mayi immediately about the astonishing proposal. First of all, she was embarrassed to do so. In fact, it would be embarrassing for A Mayi too to have to talk about such intimate things with her daughter, particularly when Elsa had not decided. When the decision was made, then it became easier. It became an announcement of an intended marriage, fitted nicely into the box, and could be opened up for discussion.

In the meantime she went over Andrew's proposal in her mind, replaying every minute: his smile, the way his eyes had darkened to violet with emotion, the kiss on her lips. The reel stalled there. The kiss. It had been very pleasant but it hadn't rocked her, made her sway, made every part of her tingle as Rafael's had done. Impatiently, she brushed the thought aside. Rafael, indeed. She loathed the man, loathed, despised, felt nauseated by the thought of him. Didn't she? How dare he come into her thoughts like this? She headed for the study. Sorting out the fertiliser accounts would stop this nonsense.

Finally, though, it was A Mayi who brought up the subject, one lunchtime, after Andrew had popped in to wish the ladies a good afternoon on his way home from the cotton ginnery. Elsa felt no embarrassment at seeing him. They had been friends for some time now and shared a warm camaraderie which had not been affected by the proposal. As they stood at the top of the veranda steps and waved him off, A Mayi commented that she didn't feel totally comfortable with him.

Elsa was surprised. Turning to her mother, she asked, "Why? I thought you liked him!"

"Indeed, I do. He seems such a nice man, but I hear things about him that make me uncomfortable," Victoria said, as they turned back into the house and she called out to the cook to dish up lunch.

They sat down at the dining room table and waited while the house servant served them before retreating to stand in a corner of the room.

"What do you mean, Mayi?" asked Elsa, puzzled and interested.

"Well, the story goes that he drinks too much."

"Really!" retorted Elsa. "How people talk! I can't imagine it; can you?"

"Well," replied Victoria, "I have to confess that on a number of occasions when he has visited in the morning I thought he looked as though he had been drinking heavily the previous evening."

"Really? How?"

"My dear daughter," replied Victoria looking fondly at her eldest daughter. "You have led such a sheltered existence and I'm glad. Time enough to learn about the unpleasant things in life later. How do I know? His eyes are often bloodshot and I can smell the alcohol on his breath."

"Oh," whispered Elsa, eyes wide in surprise. "But surely that could mean that he had had a drink or two before dinner the previous evening!"

"No," replied her mother gently. "One or two drinks before dinner would not smell on the breath the next day."

Victoria looked at her thoughtfully, and a little sadly, and then seemed to come to a decision.

"There's another thing, Elsa" she said carefully. "I think he plays around with women."

"How do you mean?"

"He doesn't go in for serious relationships with women. I am told that he has two illegitimate children in the area – from different mothers."

Elsa was shocked into silence. She may not know what a hungover breath smelt like but she was perfectly well aware of the facts of life. Her first reaction was to attempt a defence of Andrew, but her pragmatic nature bid her hold her peace. She would try to get to the bottom of this herself.

Has A Mayi guessed that Andrew has proposed to me? she asked herself as the meal came to an end and she helped herself to a slice of delicious papaya grown in their own orchard. *Is that why she is suddenly talking to me of such delicate matters – out of the blue and apropos nothing we have ever discussed in the past?* She suspected so. Everyone knew how astute A Mayi was in her observations. *I need to take what she has said seriously,* she concluded, before urging A Mayi to try the papaya and turning the conversation to the ripe smell of the duck pond in the back yard.

CHAPTER FORTY-ONE

Far away in Switzerland, the news from Ludwig was not good. His physical condition was deteriorating and he was fighting a constant battle against depression. His physician had told him to face up to the fact that he would never be able to return to Africa, that he would not survive the rigours of the journey, and that his resistance against tropical viruses and parasites would be minimal. But he held onto his hope. As he confided to Kahn in one of his letters, without that hope he didn't know whether he would have the will to survive.

His agency business was doing well since the war had ended and Europe slowly and painfully tried to crawl back onto its feet from its ravages. He used his contacts in Nyasaland and Mozambique to the fullest effect but, even here, his physical condition was slowing him down. His enormous energy and powers of endurance were slipping away; at forty-nine he was beginning to feel like an old man. He wrote wistfully to the girls that he was no longer the strong Papa that they had known and that they would have to spoil him dreadfully when they met up again.

"I shall expect to be waited on hand and foot," he teased them.

These tidings were worrying for Elsa, particularly since she didn't want to worry Victoria by sharing them with her. She would sometimes wake up at night full of foreboding, certain that her father was alone and ill, certain that if she didn't do something about it, he would die.

Then daylight would come to chase away the baseless fears. Of course he wasn't alone. He was in the middle of a large, close family and the doctors there were amongst the best in the world. She must learn not to brood, she scolded herself.

But the changes to the bubble that was the girls' environment were not over yet.

To everyone's shock and grief, Grandfather Roque died before he could see Tangadzi farm, and his wife died eighteen months later. They had been a devoted couple and it had been clear to A Mayi and Elsa, who had travelled down for Roque's funeral, that Grandmother Roque would lose the will to live without her husband. Nothing would induce her to move to Tangadzi with her daughter and grandchildren. She wanted to be with her husband, she said. The two aunts stayed with her until she died suddenly and peacefully in her sleep, and it was with great sadness that Berta saw the close of one of the dearest aspects of her young life.

She wept not only for the grandparents she had loved and lost, but also for the pure enchantment of that magical land, where the river ran deep and in its midst their island erupted into green, luxuriant vegetation; where floods ran wild and huge canoes battled against the current; where acres upon acres of land fed crops whose leaves rippled like a green sea as far as the eye could see; where huts perched on stilts, safe from the swirling flood waters below them. It was the end of an era.

The plantations in Portuguese East Africa were bequeathed to the three daughters, Victoria, Anania and Francesca, and Louis, the only son. After much family deliberation and discussion, the plantations were sold and the slaves were sent off with a small sum of money, sufficient to give them a new start. To many of them, this was heart-breaking. They had known no other life than that with the Roque family; they had been born here and their children had been born here too. The outside world could be a hostile place when one's village, the site of their tribe, no longer existed. They could well wind up as slaves to another tribe's members. There were many sad farewells, with Anania and Francesca not hiding their tears as they wished them well.

With their share of the proceeds from the plantations, the two aunts bought a small farm close to A Mayi and Elsa at Tangadzi estate, where they built a comfortable house and busied themselves with rearing fowl and becoming involved in vegetable gardening. This was originally for the family, but then spread to supplying the few expatriate families in the area, who provided an eager market.

Victoria worried that they were tiring themselves out for nothing.

"As if they couldn't get all their food from us," she grumbled to her girls. "We have more than enough. But no, they have to do it themselves."

Elsa reassured her mother that the activity was surely good for them.

"They couldn't sit and crotchet all day, Mayi!" she pointed out.

Her mother replied that she would have liked them to spend more time with her. "I hardly see them at all," she complained.

Elsa thought it prudent not to point out that they came over every evening and stayed until late, when the moon was high in the dark sky, before being carried back home by *machila*. As A Mayi grew older she did seem to enjoy a good grumble!

She had also started to use snuff again. When Ludwig had been around, he had strictly forbidden its use, although most upper-class Africans in Portuguese East Africa indulged. She had plaintively asked him why.

"Because, my dear Victoria," he had said in mock sternness, "I don't like it on you. To me, it isn't ladylike and it is not attractive."

Victoria gave in to him as she did in most things. She adored him. His word was law.

While Elsa thrived and blossomed in her struggles to find her feet on her farm, Paulina and Berta were progressing well at school.

Paulina may have been weak at mathematics and biology, but she was a master at handicrafts and her exquisite embroidery was constantly on display in one context or another. The only problem was that she always seemed to be coming down with unidentifiable illnesses that necessitated her going home.

"I don't know what it is," reported a worried Mother Camille to Elsa. "No sooner is she back at school than she comes down with another ache or pain. The doctor cannot find any physical reason for it and she takes a long time to recover, which is unusual in one so young. So we always feel it best to ask you to arrange to get her home."

Elsa had her own opinion about all this, which she didn't disclose to A Mayi. It was significant to her that as soon as Paulina was back at home, her ills quickly vanished. She just wants to be at home, she confided to Berta, but it's playing havoc with her schooling.

Berta was growing up into a graceful and attractive young woman. She had always enjoyed school, had good friends there and coped well with the academic side, but was known more for her charm and playfulness. Her bubbling vivacity never left her, despite the underlying heartache of not having her father near. Her fits of giggles were frequent and earned her severe reprimands, particularly when they happened in church.

There was the time when a visiting priest performed the sermon and Berta lapsed into silent, shaking laughter, only to choke noisily and have to be taken out, coughing and spluttering, by one of the nuns. Closeted with a stern Mother Camille after mass, there was little she could offer by way of explanation.

"It's just that the priest looked as though his false teeth were about to fall out all the time," she said, earnestly.

"What false teeth? What are you talking about?" demanded the irate and baffled nun.

"The ones that I thought he was wearing," came the lame response. This did not go down at all well.

Although she was becoming used to not having her beloved Papa around, there were many poignant moments when something or someone reminded her forcefully of him and her young heart twisted in pain. But she was young, life was opening up before her and she was moving on.

It was about this time that she decided that she would like to be a nun.

"Why?" asked Elsa, when she confided in her.

"Well, I just would. I love the clothes they wear, all those swishing petticoats and the wimple, and that lovely long rosary that clicks when you walk."

"Berta, that is no reason to become a nun!"

"Oh, no, it's more than that. I love going to chapel and talking to God. It's so beautiful; and I like following the mass in Latin in my prayer book. Oh, and the hymns. I just love the whole thing," she finished off, her eyes glowing.

"All right," conceded Elsa somewhat doubtfully. "You've got a while to go before you can apply, so you have lots of time to make up your mind."

There followed an unprecedented period of exemplary behaviour from the now twelve-year-old girl. She worked hard at all her lessons, did as she was told most of the time and even refrained from spending a good portion of her time in class in a dream world many miles away. Even Mother Camille was moved to congratulate her on her improved behaviour; whereupon Berta earnestly confided to her that she had undergone a transformation and was going to become a nun.

The sister hid her astonishment well; as she told the other nuns that evening, as they sat embroidering and mending in the common room after supper, Berta was the kind of recruit that they wanted, full of life and love and joy.

"She would do very well," she mused.

When Elsa left school, shortly after, Berta was very upset. Having her oldest sister near felt as though she had family close by and that school was an extension of home. But leaving home the following term on the long journey back to school, without Elsa, who had always been her port in the storm, was distressing for her; for a few weeks of the first term she found it difficult to settle down and was inclined to be a little weepy. The nuns were sympathetic. As they said, it wasn't long since she had lost her father and now she had to adjust to being without Elsa.

Paulina was saddened by her sister's misery and, in trying to at least partly fill Elsa's shoes, showed a compassion and tenderness that no one had ever suspected she possessed. Berta was grateful to her, and the two sisters developed an affectionate truce which marked the end of their years of childish bickering.

Three years after Elsa's departure, it was Paulina's turn to leave school, but for her there was no discussion about the future needed. There was only one place that she wanted to be and that was with her mother. So the day came in another January when Berta travelled back to school without any of her family, but with Aleki as escort until Limbe, where they were met by the Storeys and driven to the convent at Nguludi.

Berta had matured considerably in the years since her father had left and the traumas that she had faced and overcome in her young life had given her a resilience and strength of character that were to stand her in good stead in the years to come. She was by then one of the senior girls at

269

the convent and had responsibilities with regard to the younger girls. She had outgrown her desire to be a nun, but the sisters were very keen that she should stay on and be trained as a teacher after completing her education. The idea quite appealed to her. Side by side with her vivacity and sense of humour was a gentle and caring nature. She enjoyed helping others and was extremely good with children.

She felt no sense of urgency to decide; time, she felt, was on her side.

CHAPTER FORTY-TWO

Elsa felt, as she cycled through her acres of sturdy cotton plants, that she had found her niche in life.

She loved her farm and she was supremely happy managing it. She was often very tired, she had to admit, but nevertheless happy. Anyway, it was the good kind of tiredness, the sort that left you weary and satisfied at the end of the day, comfortable to sit and chat with the family at dusk before having a light supper and falling into a deep sleep that left you refreshed when you awoke the next day.

The thrill of the different seasons never left her. The barren drills seemed to her to be hungry for the seed, and planting time had its own special mood of organised activity. Lines of farm workers bent over the tilled and ridged earth, dropping in the seed or seedlings with practised speed and colouring the air with their gay chatter or impromptu songs. When the seeds were in the ground the pump at the river's edge was started up and the river water was sucked up, carried along by pipes and disgorged between the drills. It seeped into the dry earth and made its way to the new life that eagerly awaited it.

Through Andrew and Boby she had been fortunate to find an efficient and experienced farm manager, Alfred Nsoyemi. Of medium height and spare build, he exuded energy and even his rather long hair, crammed under a disreputable felt hat, bounced and twitched as he paced the fields, giving orders, scolding and cajoling. Frequently, the workers would pause to listen, standing up in the melting heat amidst the caked brown earth, and ripples of laughter would float across to Elsa, evoking a grin from her. He knew how to handle people and he also knew cotton very well, and Elsa had learnt to rely on his advice.

He had said, when she had prepared to plant her first crop that first June, "It's too early, donna." He shook his head and his tight little ringlets looked set to hurl his hat from his head. "See, the sun is not hot yet."

He lowered himself onto his heels and grabbed a fistful of soil from the carefully turned earth and handed it to her. She recoiled momentarily and, nodding his head vigorously, he insisted, "Please, donna, feel this earth. It is not yet strong enough."

Elsa opened her hand and, following his example, let it dribble through her fingers.

"Cotton plant is very weak. It needs plenty food and water from the soil. It eat and eat and eat. This soil has not enough for cotton to eat."

Alarmed, Elsa looked down at him. "So what are we going to do, Alfred?"

He rose to his feet and slapped the dust off his hands onto his well-worn and patched shorts. "Easy!" he said, a broad smile emphasising his high cheekbones and wide, finely defined mouth. "We feed the soil."

And they did. Cart loads of animal manure were carried to the acres readied for planting, dug in by the labourers and then watered regularly. Alfred insisted that the land be dug deep because, he said, the root could be as much as twice the length of the plant. By the beginning of August the fields had become acres of compost and planting could begin.

Mr Boby, the manager of the cotton ginnery, who regularly called around to see if there was anything he could do to help, often dropped in unexpectedly, and Elsa was always delighted to see him.

"Not intruding, am I?" he would ask as he walked to her through the lines of cotton plants.

"*Bien sur*, no!" she would respond, pushing her pith helmet up and mopping her face with one of the lace-edged handkerchiefs that she always carried with her.

When he arrived during her first planting season, she could have danced with relief, although she was careful to preserve a proper demeanour as she greeted him with a wide smile.

"I thought I'd pop across and ask how you're doing," he greeted her.

Unsure as yet of both herself and Alfred, she led him to the newly planted acres. She looked anxiously at him.

"How does it look?"

He squatted and took a handful of soil in his hand. He looked up at her in surprise.

"I suspected that the soil was very fertile here, but this is quite exceptional."

Relieved and happy, Elsa told him of Alfred's and her work. She called Alfred across and his delighted nods in being congratulated by Boby resulted in his hair almost bouncing his hat off his head. Smiling broadly, he returned to the workers, a loud catchy song on his lips and hips gyrating to the rhythm.

"There's one happy fella," chuckled Boby, as he turned back to Elsa.

"Now, the main reason I called," he explained, "was to remind you that the plants now need a lot of water, but I see that you have irrigated the whole area. Well done."

At that moment Andrew roared up, parked his motorbike and strode through the field to the little group. Elsa told him excitedly about Boby's approval but to her surprise, he seemed unimpressed. His response was churlish.

"Why do you think we found Alfred for you? What he's doing is simply his job." Then, seemingly making an effort to be sociable, he turned to Boby. "Not at work today, then?"

Boby laughed easily. "Of course I am, in a manner of speaking! Just thought I'd pop out to make sure Miss Deuss was all right. This is a critical season."

Andrew smiled. "Good of you, but I'm keeping a regular eye on things myself."

Boby shrugged and turned to Elsa: "How's your mother, my dear?"

And the conversation shifted onto safer ground. While she chatted with the two men, Elsa's mind was busy. Surely, Andrew could not be jealous of Boby? How funny!

Finally, and in due course, harvesting would begin – the culmination of the year's work, when the cotton was transported by oxcart to the cotton ginnery in the nearby town, Chiromo. Then came the day of reckoning. Had she made a profit? And the excitement when the figures were all entered and balanced and, yes! There was a profit and they could start opening up land for an increased acreage the following year.

How grateful she was to her neighbours for the help they had given her, particularly Andrew, of course and there was Mr Boby. A Mayi's help had been invaluable for the actual rearing of the plants; only first-hand experience such as hers could have filled the yawning gaps in Elsa's knowledge.

The animal stock was doing well, although a few head of cattle had been lost to tsetse fly disease, and vigilance and treatment were required to make the area inhospitable to it.

One of these measures was 'dipping' the cattle and it was a major event at the farm. A shallow trough, roughly chest high to the animals, had been dug and cemented. Leading to it and from it were two fenced pathways that would take only one cow at a time. The animals were herded into one of these pathways and forced along by being prodded with poles, into the trough, which had been filled with water mixed with a strong disinfectant. They would have no option but to swim to its end and clamber onto the exit pathway and thence out to the field. The dipping took the best part of a day and attracted all the farm workers' families, who would laugh and cheer as each unhappy animal ran the medicinal gauntlet.

"What if a cow can't swim?" Berta had asked the chief herdsman, anxiously, during her last school holidays.

He laughed. "Sure, little madam, they are born able to swim!"

Berta was only reassured of this when the entire herd had emerged safely from their ordeal with nothing more, presumably, than a nasty smell in their noses.

Yes, Elsa was happy and she only wished that Papa could have been here to share it with her. And she wished that her grandfather could have been there to see that what he had given her was far more than a piece of land and the money to develop it. He had given her the opportunity to grow, to find out what she was capable of, and she would always be grateful to him for that.

And now, there was Andrew. What was she going to do about Andrew?

She liked him a lot; there was no denying that. But did she want to marry him? Well, yes. Marriage had never been a priority for her, but in Andrew she had found someone whom she found physically attractive, who shared the same interests and who had evolved into a mentor or partner of sorts in her work.

But she felt that she needed to get the bottom of the rumours. If they were true then Andrew was not the sort of man that she wanted to share the rest of her life with. Of this she was certain. She preferred not to tell anyone of his proposal of marriage yet. She needed time to think things through without too much interference, albeit loving, from the family.

She had a more pressing problem on her mind at the moment, though; the problem of marauding leopards and lions.

CHAPTER FORTY-THREE

Life on the farm was not all roses, reflected Elsa, as she surveyed a gruesome tangle of flesh, blood, skin and bone, the remains of a young calf; the problem of predators chasing after the livestock was a case in point.

Periodically, the night watchman would report that there had been a commotion at the far end of the kraal and that by the time he had got there one of the animals had apparently been killed and dragged away. On one occasion Berta was at home on holiday when it happened.

She heard the commotion downstairs just after dawn and tumbled sleepily out of bed to see what it was all about. She pulled on her dressing gown quickly and ran downstairs to find the chief herdsman excitedly telling Elsa what had happened.

"Go back to the kraal," she heard Elsa tell him. "I'll follow shortly. Oh! And tell everyone to bring a spear."

"Can I come?" Berta asked.

"Yes, "answered Elsa, already on her way to her pushbike. "Get some clothes on and hop onto your bike."

Within minutes Berta joined her and they cycled together, Elsa in front, along the narrow path, surrounded it seemed to Berta by massed plants and trees that shifted in and out of human form in the shadowy, misty grey dawn. She remembered the flight from the convent on that unforgettable night long ago and shivered. She glanced back, thinking that she would prefer to go back to the security of the house but, no! The rear was a misty tunnel bordered by the shifting shapes of the shrubs and trees that seemed to lean over and form an arch over their heads. Another tremor went through her and she turned to the front and pedalled faster, to keep as close as possible to Elsa.

Once at the kraal, Elsa left Berta with one of the younger workers by a hut, with strict instructions not to move from that spot. She need not have worried; nothing short of a leopard walking towards her with its fangs showing would have induced Berta to move. Elsa, a few farm boys and the herdsman, together with a small crowd of workers who had gathered, examined the spot where the attack had taken place and then cautiously, spears held aloft, followed the trail of the dragged body towards a thickly forested area, which was misty with the dew from the previous day's heat. The mist, the hanging overhead branches massed with leaves and the heavy undergrowth, combined to make visibility poor and danger from predators ever present.

"Careful, Madam," cautioned the herdsman in a low voice. "They usually leave the remains, but we must go carefully just in case the animal decided to stay with the carcass. Or even maybe it has left and others, like lions, leopards and hyenas, are on their way to taste some food."

The armed party advanced silently, following the clearly marked trail where the undergrowth was crushed and red with blood. About twenty yards into the thicket they found the bloodied and mangled remains of the young heifer. There was no sign of the predator.

Everyone gathered around and tried to deduce what had happened.

"Look, Madam," said the herdsman, pointing to the carcass. "It must have been a lion."

"What makes you so sure?" asked Elsa, with a wary glance at the branches of the trees above.

"If it was a leopard it would have taken the remains up into the tree and hidden it to finish off eating tonight. The lion leaves it down on the ground and hides it in the bushes."

He went closer and pointed out that the inner organs had been torn out and eaten first.

"It is normal that they eat those things first," he explained, "and it looks like it filled up the animal. It will have to return tonight to finish the rest."

"Yes, you are right," replied Elsa pensively. "Now, we have to kill it."

Elsa turned to the farm workers and explained to them that they would return at dusk to poison the carcass, and asked that no one come near it before or after. As she explained to them, she didn't want a villager to meet the lion returning to finish its meal. Further, after she had treated the remains, to leave a toxic piece of meat lying around where there were people and animals created a highly dangerous situation and everyone must stay well clear.

"And," she concluded, "tie up your animals until this is all over."

Everyone was in a quiet and pensive mood as they silently returned to the kraal. Berta emerged and ran to Elsa, wanting to know what had happened. Elsa explained the situation and that the lion would have to be killed.

Berta interrupted: "Why?" she asked. "It was only doing what was natural for it."

"Yes, dear," replied her sister, "but the problem is that normally they chase other animals in the wild. For it to risk its life in coming to hunt our animals, there can only be two reasons."

"Yes?" Berta was wide eyed with interest, her terror of an hour ago forgotten.

"Well, either it's too old to hunt with the others in the wild or it is injured in some way and cannot catch its usual meat. Either way we have to kill it before it starts on humans, who are comparatively easy to catch."

"*Mon Dieu!*" murmured Berta as she went to get her bike, while Elsa called the workers around her and arranged to meet at the same spot later on.

Late afternoon, just before dusk, the girls and the herdsmen returned to the scene with some Arsenic, with which Elsa carefully laced the carcass. The farm workers with their families gathered around, agog with curiosity. She then turned to the onlookers and, the container of Arsenic held up for them all to see, warned them that it was highly dangerous and that if it were able to kill a lion, it most certainly would kill them if they ate it.

"I'm not worried," she confided to Berta. "They know the drill and everyone will be kept away until the lion is dead. Whatever is left of the carcass will then be burned."

As the shadows closed in, everyone was anxious to get out of the thicket before the lion returned for its second feast; the two young women hurried home on their bikes. Now was not the time for humans to be in the bush.

The atmosphere at the homestead that evening was tense. A Mayi, Elsa and Berta sat on the gauzed veranda after dinner, talking in hushed voices, part of their minds some distance away, where a poisoned carcass lay waiting to trap an unwary lion. The two aunts had left early; when lions were hunting in the area, everyone was cautious. Men worked in groups and mothers anxiously called to their little ones to stay near them. By nightfall, everything was eerily quiet; families had shut themselves into their huts and drawn stout bars across the doors.

Several hours later the peace of the night was torn apart by the agonised roars of the poisoned lion as it threshed about in the thickets, tearing the bark off the trees until it finally collapsed in its death throes. Berta climbed into Elsa's bed and tried to shut out the sounds, but there was no escape until the bellows finally faded away.

"I wish there was another way," whispered Elsa, "but the only alternative would be to call one of the men from Chiromo to hunt the animal, and I just couldn't ask anyone to put their lives in danger like that for us."

The next day both carcasses, the lion and the heifer, were burned on a big bonfire, much to the jubilation of the people from the surrounding villages, who came to witness the ceremony and thank Elsa for her protection. For the time being, people could once again walk in safety.

CHAPTER FORTY-FOUR

At the homestead A Mayi was slowly recreating for the family the environment they had enjoyed in Fort Johnston. The vegetable and fruit gardens flourished and already, they were making their own butter and cheese. The honey would have to wait until Ludwig came home though, concluded A Mayi.

"Do you know," she said to her daughters one day, "I now prefer it here to Fort Johnston. I like living on the farm and the cotton growing is really exciting. If only Ludwiki could see it…"

She seemed happier now. The twinkle was back in her eyes, she scolded the servants more in the way that she did in the old days, and the old energy, which the girls had feared was gone for ever, was in evidence once again. Things were looking up.

It was therefore totally unexpected when, in September of 1922, the bombshell fell.

Ludwig wrote to tell Elsa that he was about to share his home and his life with another woman.

My dearest Elsa,

I do not know quite how to write this letter but it has to be written.

I have not told you before but my health has been worsening steadily. I am on medication for my heart constantly now but still become exhausted quite easily. The agency business, which was going so well, has now slowed down, because I find it difficult to keep up with the endless telephone calls and visits. Also, it is difficult for me to travel to find new customers and suppliers. Worst of all, I am ashamed to say that I suffer from bouts of depression. I am being treated for these but they cripple me. This is a sign of weakness, I know, and I hate myself for it.

The family are very good, but since your grandparents died two years ago we don't seem to see one another as often anymore.

The worst blow is that I now know that I shall never be able to return to Africa. It cuts my heart just to say that but it is true and I have to accept it. In the same way I have to accept that I cannot expect you to move and leave your wonderful life in my beloved Africa. There is nothing in Europe to compare with it and, as I said before, A Mayi would never make the adjustment. Even though you might want to make the move, we cannot leave her alone, we cannot separate you from her. It is enough that she has lost me.

Now for the difficult news.

I plan to marry.

I have met a lady banker in the course of my business dealings and we have become fond of each other. She fully understands the situation regarding the state of my health, but she is a good and kind person who assures me that if and when it should become impossible for me to work she will support us both.

How can he do this? you must be thinking. Let me try to explain, please.

I have been so desolate and my life has been so lonely since I left you that the chance to have someone of my own is a temptation I cannot resist. I wonder, can you understand this? Can you understand how I miss you all and my beloved Africa every waking moment?

I have struggled with this decision. In my heart your mother will always be a part of me, my great love, the woman I loved first and for always. We gave each other the best years of our lives, such unforgettably happy years, and she gave me my family, who have been more precious than life itself to me. This lady, Hedwig, understands this because I have been completely open with her. I am not capable of hiding from anyone my love for you all.

Can you find it in your heart to understand me and the situation I am in? Can you understand the loneliness and the ache in my heart? Entering into a serious relationship will not make me miss you less, but it will give me a sense of belonging to a family unit again. And when I am ill, it will be such a solace to have someone who cares for me, and for whom I care, beside me.

This sounds selfish but I hope that I have something to offer her too. My inheritance has permitted me to buy a beautiful home in one of the best suburbs of Zurich. Our family is a fine one and we can trace our antecedents to the sixteenth century. Most importantly, though, we get on well together and have many similar interests, particularly in history and the classics. So, the deal is not one-sided.

So, why do I feel so sad? I ask myself. It is because at last I have to face the terrible truth that I may never see you again. Only if you come to visit me will we meet again. I am in your hands and I beg you to come when you can. You are all comfortably off and are able to do so. I know that it is a long and arduous journey but you are young; you would enjoy it.

Please, never, never, tell my beloved Victoria of this news. She was always the ideal wife and this knowledge would break her heart. She does not deserve that.

I have written to Richard; but I am asking you to please tell Paulina and Berta when the three of you are able to find a quiet spot somewhere during the next school holidays. Or perhaps if you have occasion to go to Blantyre on business you could take Paulina with you and meet Berta at

Nguludi. I have great faith in your intelligence and common sense and rely on you to be my ambassador in this situation.

But maybe you will not understand, maybe I ask too much. Maybe at first you will be stunned, hurt and angry. I won't blame you; I would probably have felt the same. I will just wait and hope that time will allow you to understand me and to forgive me for what must seem to you weakness and betrayal. There is a Russian proverb that says that one shouldn't judge another until he has walked a mile in the other's slippers. I only expect you to fully understand, if not to forgive, when you too have lived some more years in this world, which can be as cruel as it is wonderful.

Hedwig wants very much to meet you and her sister Louisa also takes a great interest in you.

You have always been a family to be proud of in every way and I am so grateful to you for that. I am also grateful for the love that you all showed me every minute of your young lives. Remember that nothing has changed between us. You still have my heart and my dream is to see you again. Don't forget me.

I send you my love, my dearest children.

Your loving father,
Ludwig Deuss

Elsa was distraught when she read the letter and the two months until Berta came home were difficult ones. Even for someone as self-contained as she was, it was difficult to act as though nothing was wrong when her mind and her emotions were in such turmoil. She avoided contact with the family and spent a lot of time out in the fields. She found the cloudless blue skies beaming over the acres a real antidote to the stifling darkness in her heart. When she came home she closed herself in the study or curled up with a book in the sitting room. She even avoided speaking to Andrew, because she felt so close to tears most of the time.

Victoria, who enjoyed her chats with her daughters, grumbled that she didn't see much of her anymore and Paulina looked at her reprovingly and made more of a point than usual of being by her mother's side. Elsa's reticence was straining family relationships, but it was the best way that she could cope in the circumstances; she was trying to hold herself from falling apart.

To her joy and relief, Richard arrived unexpectedly. He had received his father's letter and had made his way to his sister, as much to relieve her feelings as his own. He spent some time chatting with his mother and then turned to Elsa: "From what I saw on my way here, Sis, your plantation is looking good, very healthy plants, I thought. Want to show me around? I'd like you to try out my new motorbike, too."

Elsa leapt up. "Yes, please!" She grabbed her hat and they ran down the steps, settled themselves on the motorbike and roared off down the road leading to the acres of growing crops.

Far away from the house, sitting under acacia trees with the seemingly endless acres of cotton plants before them, brother and sister unburdened their hearts to each other, and struggled to come to terms with an event that at times threatened to shatter their faith in their father and their own feelings of self-worth.

Elsa, in particular, felt that a chasm had appeared at her feet, an unbridgeable gap between 'Before' and 'After'. Before Ludwig left, when she had felt safe in his presence, secure in his love, sure of her worth that was reflected in his eyes and in his words, and after, when the chasm gaped before her, when first his presence and then his love were stripped from her, her worth reduced, left by the wayside as he found better pastures new. How was she going to bear it? She felt like a child, abandoned, left by the wayside, curling itself into a ball, hoping to die.

She turned an anguished face towards Richard: "Did all those years mean nothing to Papa? Did we imagine it all? Did all that happiness exist only in our minds? Did he care about us at all?" She sobbed as though her heart would break, burrowing her head into her brother's shoulder.

Struggling to keep his composure in the face of his sister's grief, Richard held her close. The tears ran unheeded down his cheeks as he tried to reassure her.

"Of course he did, silly. And he still does. He still loves us very much and I'm sure he will always do so."

"But how, Richard? How? How could he do this?"

"I don't know," he replied, wearily. "I wish I did, but I don't."

In actual fact, Richard was more pragmatic and better able to see his father's point of view; but he was deeply shocked that his father appeared to have drawn a line under his previous life.

Fine words he uses, he thought bitterly, *but the fact is that he has moved on, without us.*

Elsa lifted her head abruptly from her brother's shoulder and turned troubled eyes to him. "But, Richard. How can Papa marry when he is already married? It must be against the law."

Richard hesitated, biting his lip, then took his arm away from Elsa's shoulder and turned away. His shoulders slumped as though in defeat and his arms rested loosely on his knees.

"I've thought about it but hoped you wouldn't. You see, my dear, Dad and A Mayi were married by local custom and, probably, because there were no missionaries around at the time, the local chief would have performed the ceremony, or maybe the Chef de Poste. It's as legal as you can get here and totally binding on the couple, but I doubt very much that it would be considered so in Europe."

He turned around to face Elsa and his tone was bitter. "We have to accept, my dear, that it seems that our father does not have respect for the local customs. Although I am certain from the bottom of my soul that had the war not intervened, he fully intended to spend the rest of his days here with us, when it came to it he simply put on his European hat again."

He pulled his weeping sister against him again. "I'm sorry, Sis," he whispered. "I'm so sorry."

Small wonder that at times it seemed that they were coping with bereavement, the loss of the man they had known as Papa. And so they talked, questioning each other, often with tears, until finally they reached some sense of calm, and were able to see beyond their personal pain to their father's.

Elsa raised red and swollen eyes to her brother's face. "Do you know, Richard, sometimes I feel that I don't know Papa any longer." She struggled to find the right words.

"The man I remember was so strong, so full of life. When we were with him it was like being swept along on a flood…"

"Yes, exactly what I'm feeling. He always had a solution to everything. He was so positive, so in control. Now, he seems lost, reaching out for support, at the mercy of every twist of fate. How incredibly sad."

"Poor Papa." And now, the tears that fell were tears of pity. Pity for their father, for their mother, for themselves; now they had to face the fact that it was unlikely that they would ever see their father again. Their father. Papa. With their mother, the love of their lives, their inspiration, their hero, their strength.

They wept in each other's arms. No death could have caused such pain; death was involuntary, a clean cut. This was darkened by the poison of rejection, the loss of someone who was moving away from the centre of their lives to the centre of another's. Someone who had given up his fight to return to them.

They talked until they became calm again, focusing on their father's sense of desolation, his ill health, his loneliness, finding that in understanding his plight, the better they were able to keep a balanced perspective in their own lives.

Richard was remorseful about his earlier, bitter words about his father.

"I take back my words about Dad's not respecting his marriage vows here, Sis. We of all people know how much he loves A Mayi - and us. We now see a side of him that we've never seen before. He has exhausted his resources, his health has failed: he is beaten and reaching out for a situation that must seem like a life saver to him."

The beginning of understanding was difficult, but it was a start on the road to healing. When Richard left a few days later they were both more in command of their feelings, and Elsa was able to look ahead to Berta's arrival with some equanimity.

After Richard had kissed his mother and Paulina goodbye, he left them at the top of the steps and walked quickly down to his motorbike at the bottom. Elsa followed him and kissed him as he sat on the saddle. Leaning close she whispered to him: "Remember, Richard, not a word of this to anyone, not even Dina."

"Of course I won't talk about it," he assured her," but you must understand that I couldn't keep anything like this away from Dina. She is my wife."

Elsa capitulated: "Yes, of course, I'm sorry. It's just that if A Mayi gets to hear it, she will be destroyed." She looked at her brother beseechingly.

"Don't worry, Elsa," he said pausing to give her a hug. "I care as much as you do about A Mayi. I am absolutely certain that Dina will not mention it to a soul."

He rode off down the drive, its hard earth surface framed by the glistening green foliage of the mango trees and the vibrant reds, oranges and pinks of the oleanders that Elsa had planted when she first bought the farm, when hopes and dreams were within her grasp and life was good. *Stop that,* she told herself sternly, as tears began to prick her eyes. *We may be devastated and grief-stricken beyond description, but we all have one another, especially A Mayi, and we have a beautiful home. We have much to be grateful for.*

With a mental squaring of her shoulders and a smile on her face she joined her mother at the top of the steps. A Mayi looked worried and Elsa kicked herself for those final quiet words to Richard, which may have alarmed her mother. She put her arm around A Mayi's shoulders and squeezed her gently.

"Let's have a cup of tea," she said.

CHAPTER FORTY-FIVE

Elsa spent the next two weeks working as she had never worked before. She had to keep busy until Berta arrived, keep a damper on her aching heart. Then the three girls would have their chat, which was inevitably going to be very painful; but she felt that, after that, she would be able to start moving on. She had to stay strong until her sisters had been told. A Mayi was concerned.

"Elsa, what is wrong with you? You work in the fields or in your office until you're ready to drop, come home and fall asleep in your chair. Then you get up and go to bed. You can't carry on like this."

Elsa was immediately repentant. She had been so absorbed in her feelings and her pain that she had tried to hide and that had caused her mother to worry.

"Mayi, I'm so sorry. I do get carried away and forget when to stop. Keep scolding me, please! Tell me when to stop!"

Finally, Berta came home and at the first opportunity Elsa called her two sisters and asked them whether they would like to see how the cotton was progressing. Berta eagerly acquiesced but Pauline glowered.

"Not particularly," she sniffed.

"You're so predictable," scolded Elsa. "However, we are all involved in this farm and I need you to know what's going on. We'll go a little while before dusk, when it is cooler, and I'll show you the stream of which I have often spoken so often."

As the midday heat started to lose its intensity and faint little breezes started to dance through the leaves of the trees, the girls got onto their bicycles and followed Elsa to the little stream that meandered through the plantation. As they cycled along the narrow estate lanes, even Paulina relented enough to be charmed by the little lane that wound through the cotton fields on the left and leafy woods on the right. Luxuriant acacia trees jostled with the slim fever-trees and their roots were blanketed by thick, almost impenetrable undergrowth. Berta was enchanted by the rolling acres of cotton plants, dotted with a small army of labourers, who were weeding and hoeing between the rows in readiness for the rains that were expected at any moment. Many paused to wave to Elsa, who stopped frequently to exchange a few words with them and the *capitao*, Alfred.

Despite the lateness of the hour the sky was still a cloudless blue when they bumped their way to the edge of the stream and dismounted. Berta promptly removed her sandals and started to paddle in the clear waters as they gurgled over the rocky bed.

"I love it here," she called to her sisters on the bank. "I'd like to live here for ever. I know Papa is going to love it too."

There was a slight pause and then, taking the moment, Elsa called back, "Berta, come here please. I have something to tell you and Paulina."

"Can it wait?" she called back, smiling. "There are some interesting stones here in the centre of the stream and quite a lot of small fish. I like the little green plants growing next to the stones as well. Do you remember that Papa sometimes talked about setting up an aquarium? "

"Yes, I do," replied Elsa, "and yes, it is something that we need to think about. But, just now, I really would like the three of us to have a chat about something that has come up."

Berta turned back and looked at Elsa searchingly. She suddenly became aware of a tension that she hadn't noticed previously, and quickened her pace as much as she could without cutting her feet on some sharp stone. She reached the bank of the stream and pulled her sandals back on before walking to where her sisters were sitting. Settling herself on a large boulder she looked questioningly down at Elsa who was sitting at its base.

"Is anything wrong?" she asked.

"Well, you could say that," replied Elsa, drawing their father's letter out of her pocket. "We have had a letter from Papa with some rather unexpected news. Now, I want you both to listen very carefully and not interrupt me until I have finished."

"He's coming home, isn't he?" breathed Berta, her face rigid with excitement.

Elsa glanced up at her, her eyes brimming with pity as she looked at her youngest sister. "No, my dear," she said. "He isn't." And then she read the letter.

There was silence as Elsa read, her rich melodious voice, which she had inherited from A Mayi, rising and falling gently. Only the birds in the trees all around them moved and made sounds. Paulina and Berta sat as though paralysed.

When Elsa finished there was a stunned silence; Paulina and Berta looked at her in disbelief, their faces ashen. Berta spoke first, her eyes fixed on Elsa and her head moving disbelieving from side to side.

"He said he's going to marry someone else. He wants a new family. I thought we were his family..." Her voice broke.

Elsa reached out and held Berta's hand tightly. "No, dear, it isn't that he wants a new family instead of us. It's because he can't have us and he's lonely and sick."

"I could have gone to Switzerland to look after him," volunteered Paulina, speaking tightly, as though her lips were frozen.

"So could I," said Berta passionately. "But he never asked. He just doesn't want us anymore. He's found someone he prefers. He never loved us. He never cared. He just wanted to find someone better." She looked around her wildly. "I hate him. I hate him!" she screamed, clenched fists pummelling her lap.

Then she slipped off the boulder and sank down beside Elsa on the grass. She put her arms around her and cried deep, violent sobs. Paulina sat still on Elsa's other side, the tears streaming down her cheeks, her body convulsing with anguished sobs that she struggled to hold in. Elsa put her other arm around her and sat quietly, tears falling down her face and onto her blouse, while she held her young sisters in their agony.

Finally, the sobs quietened and the sisters talked. They asked the same questions over and over again. "Did Papa not really love us after all?" Berta wanted to know.

She looked beseechingly at Elsa. "How could he do this?" And then the questions came out like an unstoppable torrent. "Was he pretending all those years he was with us? Did he stay with us just to have company until he went back to his home? Maybe it's something we've done?"

Elsa tried to quieten her; to soothe her. She gently stroked her hair. "Shh, my dear. No, don't think that."

But Berta shook her hand away. "You can't really love people and then just throw them away because you've found some others. He won't love us anymore, will he, now that he has a new wife?" Her voice shook and she paused, looking at her two sisters. Suddenly, she rose and with chest heaving as though she was unable to breathe, she walked towards a tree, threw her arms around it and laid her cheek against its rough bark. Her voice came out muffled and shaking. "If he has a new family, who are we now? WHO ARE WE?"

Then, throwing back her head, her mouth turned into an agonised wide circle, a scream like that of a helpless animal trapped and dying, came out of her throat. She screamed and screamed, a terrible sound wrenched out of her unbearable anguish; her body trembled uncontrollably.

Elsa leapt up, Paulina close behind, and put her arms firmly around her. "Come, come, *ma petite*," she crooned in her ear. "It's all right, it's all right."

She rocked Berta in her arms until finally, the screaming died to a thin wail, with silent gasping sobs shaking her vulnerable little frame. Gently, Elsa pulled her down until with quivering lips and tears flowing down her face she subsided once again against Elsa's chest. Finally, they became still, with Paulina echoing in a whisper, "Who are we? Who are we now?"

Exhausted and still at last they began to remember their father's presence, how he had showed them his love in a thousand ways. They recalled the endless occasions when he had sat with them to explain things, the times that they had looked up things together in the encyclopaedias, the games that they had played together.

"Do you remember how cross you got when we played rummy and you lost, Paulina?" smiled Berta through her tears. "Papa said it wasn't ladylike, remember?"

They even smiled when they remembered being woken up in the middle of the night to see some spectacular stellar constellation that was especially bright that night. And who could ever forget those magical trips with him to and from school, when the whole African landscape became an exciting learning game for them.

Slowly Elsa drew their fond memories to the present. She drew for them a picture of a man, separated from the family he loved above all else, a man now in failing health, a man alone. How sad for him this must all be, she said.

"We are in pain," she acknowledged, "but imagine his, too."

Then the reality hit Berta that they would not see him again for the foreseeable future, if ever, and the grief that had been held off by the promise that he would be back overwhelmed her. She cried the heartbroken tears that had been building up since the day her father had been taken away from her. Her two sisters were no less affected and the three clung to one another, shattered by the loss of the man who had, with their mother, been the centre of their lives.

Finally, as the brilliant afternoon sun began its descent into the evening sky, Elsa started to prepare for the return home. As she said, A Mayi would be concerned that they had been away for so long and they certainly didn't want to meet a lion or a leopard out for an early supper. She drew her younger sisters to the stream and together they splashed their faces in the cool, sparkling water, rubbing away the marks of the tears. When they had finished, Berta turned her still blotchy face to her for inspection.

"Mmm," said Elsa as she scrutinised her face, "you look as though you have been stung by a couple of bees, but the ride home should fix that."

She pronounced a similar verdict on Paulina and was then assured by her sisters that she didn't look too bad.

"Just a bit of a red nose," said Berta, encouragingly.

As they picked up their bikes, Elsa turned to them for one last word: "And remember, A Mayi must never, ever know about this. Just remember when you are tempted to tell her that you will break her heart. You will give her the greatest unhappiness that she has ever known, an unhappiness that she will never recover from. I know you don't want to do that, so any time that you feel that you need to talk about it, tell me and we'll find somewhere quiet."

As they rode home in the pink and balmy dusk they discussed what they should say in reply to their father's letter.

"I am very hurt and sad," said Paulina, "but I think we should write and wish him happiness."

Berta was not so forgiving. "I'm still muddled about it all," she said. "I'm not sure who he is any longer and I'm not sure if I love him or hate him. Write if you wish and I'll just write my name at the end. And, you know, I can't call him Papa anymore. Papa is gone. I think the most I can call him is Father."

Finally, it was decided that the letter would be from the three of them, addressed as always to 'Papa', and would simply wish him well. It read:

Dear Papa,

Thank you for your letter. As you can imagine it gave us quite a shock. Anyway, we all wish you much happiness in the future.
Kind regards to Hedwig.

Your loving daughters,
Elsa, Paulina and Berta

They would never know how the cool formality of this letter had driven a knife through their father's heart.

To Berta, this was a decisive moment in her life. She grew up. She emerged from the loving softness of the cocooned existence she had led so far and walked, for the first time, separate from her father's all-embracing love and protection.

Her heart and mind seethed with turbulent, contradictory emotions; a devastating sense of betrayal nestled against guilt that maybe she had been in some way to blame for this catastrophe. At other times she felt her father's pain and loneliness and her young heart ached for him; but soon the painful questions would rear their heads again. How could he do it? Why could he not have called them to him? Just for a little while, just to try things out. But perhaps he was right. A Mayi would never have adjusted to such momentous change, not even to be near her beloved Ludwiki. She would have gone and she would have done her best to settle down for his sake, but she would not have been happy. So it went on, a Ping-Pong battle in her mind, backwards and forwards, never finding any answers.

And always there was an underlying sense of disbelief, of confusion, blending now and then with a hope, a certainty at times, that it had all been a terrible mistake. Life couldn't be this way, lives couldn't be spliced, the past separated from the future. *Please, let it all be a mistake.*

But, as the days, the weeks, the months and then the years went by, she slowly accepted the reality and waited for her broken heart to heal. Gradually, a little barrier arose around her heart, a barrier that she trusted would stop people realising how unworthy she was of their love, a barrier behind which she would crouch when she felt that she was about to give her heart.

CHAPTER FORTY-SIX

Elsa was finding her life a struggle and she reflected ironically how just a few short weeks ago she had been feeling so content, so fulfilled in the new life that she had chosen for herself.

But then her father's letter had arrived and turned all of their worlds upside-down. Probably the most difficult thing was keeping up appearances in front of A Mayi who, thankfully, was going from strength to strength, busy with animals and gardens and happy to have her sisters close by, though she would never admit this.

Elsa's main worry was Paulina's ability to keep quiet about the letter. Paulina thrived on misery, thought Elsa irritably, and was probably bursting to unload onto their mother the unhappy news that had so disrupted their lives. She had to trust that she would not, but A Mayi's vulnerability was causing her serious pangs of anxiety.

Then there was the Andrew situation. Now, more than ever, she wanted the matter cleared up, as she became increasingly sure that she did want to marry him. His presence gave her much comfort and he was able to distract her from the underlying clouds of unhappiness that blotted her view of the blue sky. She decided to confront him on his next visit and steeled herself for what was inevitably going to be a difficult conversation.

An opportunity arose the very next morning. Andrew had popped across to have a look at the new plants in the nursery; he had detected signs of a parasite on his young plants. He clattered up to the house on his motorbike and, after greeting A Mayi, explained to Elsa what had occasioned his alarm.

He looked worried. "I've spotted some burn marks on my plants and, although it may simply be a case of the irrigation not having reached that cluster of plants, I very much fear that it may be an attack of the cotton aphid, Aphid gossypii."

Elsa raised her eyebrows. "Meaning?"

"Not only does it interfere with the plants' ability to photosynthesise, but it's also a carrier of viruses and other insects. Deadly in fact. And very difficult to eradicate. Here in Africa it is the major cause of lost yield."

Elsa's eyes were wide with alarm. "But, Andrew, that's awful," she said. "How soon will you know?"

"Within a week, I should think. If it is merely irrigation failure the plants should recover quickly." He paused and frowned. "I need to order insecticide from Blantyre, just in case." He turned towards her. "I'll have a quick look at your seedlings and then we can make provisional arrangements to get the insecticides here urgently. Shall we go?"

Elsa nodded, explained the problem to A Mayi, grabbed her helmet from the hall and ran down the front steps with Andrew. She got into his sidecar and they rode the mile or so to the nursery acreage her mind churning with the knowledge that there was a possibility of serious damage to her crop. The nursery adjoined the main acreage, with the difference that little straw canopies on stilts covered the seedlings, to protect them from the worst heat of the day.

On their arrival they exchanged greetings with the workers and together with Alfred, Andrew made a detailed examination of random samples of the plants; to everyone's relief, no sign was found of the destructive insect.

"I can tell you, I was worried!" Andrew told Elsa. "Those things can destroy entire fields. On average in Africa, fifteen per cent of cotton yields are lost to this and other pests. The fact that your fields appear to be free of infestation is a hopeful sign that my little problem is one of irrigation."

When they had finished the inspection, Alfred excused himself and returned to work. The two young people stood under one of the towering acacia trees for a bit of shade and Andrew talked about the other pests that they had to watch out for.

"The pink bollworm is another dangerous pest and it's carried in the ball of cotton that we harvest. At the other end is cotton root rot, absolutely deadly and very difficult to eradicate."

His voice droned on but Elsa wasn't listening; she debated silently whether to tell Andrew straight out what she had heard about his behaviour. After all, this was the opportunity that she had been waiting for. She hesitated because Andrew had just had a serious shock and would not be able to relax until the week was over and it seemed unfair to stress him even further. On the other hand, however, she felt that since it was he who had started the marriage discussion he was quite old enough to deal with both issues. And she needed to know. She turned to face him and cut short his monologue.

"Andrew," she said bluntly, "I have heard that you drink too much and that you have fathered illegitimate children. What can you tell me about this?"

Andrew looked pole-axed and, unusually for him, was lost for words for a few moments. Then he tried to laugh everything off and put it all down to gossip mongering, but Elsa knew there was a germ of truth there and she needed to find it.

"Andrew," she said earnestly to him, "this is no laughing matter. You remember you asked me to marry you. Did you mean that?"

"Of course I did – and do!" he protested.

"Well then, you must understand that before I can consider it I have to know the truth. As long as there are doubts in my mind there can be no future for us. Do you see?"

He sighed and nodded his head: "I do see and I do want us to have a future so, much as I hate having to do this, we'll talk. You have to understand that this is very difficult for me. You are such an innocent... how am I going to explain this to you?"

Elsa did nothing to help him. She stood quietly, a few feet away, her gaze calmly on his face.

He was silent for a few moments while he marshalled his thoughts and haltingly, searching for the right words, he told her about the life that he had been leading, the whoring, the drink, everything.

Elsa was horrified, looking at him as though searching for the young man of whom she had become fond, the upright, funny, caring person of whom there was little trace at this moment.

When he finished speaking he gave an embarrassed shrug and looked out at the busy fields, before nervously shooting a glance at her. "That's it," he said. "That's the whole sorry story."

Elsa opened and closed her mouth and then managed to speak: "What about the children? Who supports them?"

"I do, of course. I may have behaved badly but I'm not a fiend. What you must think of me!" He shook his head and half turned from her to look sightlessly across the fields.

"Could you take me home, please, Andrew?" she asked. "I need time to think."

He turned quickly to face her again. "Wait, Elsa," he pleaded. "Please let me try to explain."

"Explain what?" she responded miserably.

"I do believe that this whole thing has been the result of boredom," he said urgently. "Apart from when I went away to school in South Africa, I have lived on the farm with my parents all my life. There is no entertainment in the Lower Shire and my parents don't mix much, mainly because my mother doesn't feel up to it. So, I am ashamed to say that my entertainment has mainly consisted of going out with friends to the African bars in the township or getting drunk at one or other of their houses on *uchema.*" *Uchema* was the local palm wine, a very potent brew. He paused a moment, his eyes on the ground, while he mechanically dug a furrow with his shoe, then continued his explanation.

"You have to understand that women in and around these bars are readily available, indeed competing to give a man a good time. They have been brought up in poverty and sell their bodies for very little. The drink, too, is very cheap so... a few drinks too many, women anxious to please, friends who are all doing the same thing. One thing leads to another and, before you know it, it's become a way of life."

He raised his eyes and looked helplessly at her as she stood before him, ashen-faced, as though she were about to faint.

"Now, in the light of day and with you in front of me, I feel sick at myself. It is all so degrading."

He hung his head.

"Until I met you, I thought nothing of my lifestyle, despite my mother's pleading with me to stop something that couldn't have a good ending." He raised his eyes and a grim smile twisted his mouth.

"And then I met you and suddenly I knew that I wanted to be different. I wanted to be a good person. I wanted to start a new life – with you. With you by my side, I know that I can change. I love you, Elsa, and…" He looked at her like a little boy lost.

"And, I need you. Please don't leave me now."

But Elsa was numb with the shock of the things that he had told her, things that had never existed in her sheltered young life, things that one heard about other people, never about the people one was friendly with.

"Thank you, Andrew," she managed to falter. "I truly appreciate and respect your honesty, but now I need to get back home."

He didn't try to change her mind. He helped her into the sidecar, mounted the motorbike and set off for the homestead. When they arrived he helped her out of the sidecar and they both walked up the steps to the veranda, where A Mayi and her entourage sat in the comparative cool.

He greeted the rest of the family, smiled a little uncertainly at Elsa, and left.

Struggling to appear normal, Elsa sat down with the family to report on her and Andrew's examination of the plants. Her mind felt confused and there was an aching pressure behind her eyes as they talked; she felt as though she would like to cry. She, who was always so pragmatic, so cool.

"Are you feeling all right, Elsa?" asked A Mayi at one point, as Elsa seemed unable to comprehend a perfectly straightforward question.

"No, Mayi, I'm not," she replied. "I have a bad headache. I think I must have stayed out in the sun for too long."

A Mayi was immediately concerned and suggested that she lie down for a while. Elsa needed no second bidding and with hurried apologies fled for the safety of her room.

She closed the door behind her and threw herself onto her bed, pressed her palms against the sides of her head and mouthed a silent scream.

"I can't take any more of this! I can't!" she mouthed, before sobbing distractedly into her pillow.

Was the anguish never going to end? she asked herself wretchedly.

CHAPTER FORTY-SEVEN

In another little world, many miles away, Berta, at eighteen years of age, was preparing to leave school and venture out into the unknown.

The nuns were still hoping that she would consent to remain and be trained to teach, but she felt that she needed a new direction and, if possible, a new environment in her life. Her father's ghost still lingered in all the familiar places and, whilst she had learnt to cherish the happy memories she had of him, she wanted to move on and reach out to the unexplored world around her.

A possible suitor had presented himself in the person of George, a friend of Mona's. She had met him on one of the weekends that she had spent with the Storeys, when she had had Saturday lunch with Mona's family. He was the son of one of the business owners in Blantyre, pleasant and nice looking and, she couldn't help noticing, very well built. Rather than work in his father's transport business, he had found employment as a car mechanic, so as to indulge his passion for that new wonder of transport, cars, and of course motorbikes. They had hit it off immediately because Berta shared the same passions and when she was in Blantyre she and Mona would drop in to see him at his workshop.

How she enjoyed these visits. Before long, and under George's expert tuition, she recognised and knew the functions of most of the tools he had stacked neatly in large drawer units, custom made to be the length of the room. Others were hung on a pegboard wall where he could reach for exactly the right tool that he needed.

Mona was baffled by Berta's interest and told her that as they left George's workshop one day. "What can you possibly find interesting in rooms filled with metal objects which are generally covered in oil, smelly oil?"

Berta tried to explain: "Well, you see, Mona. Every one of those tools does something different and when you look at an engine working and all the parts moving up and down in harmony, it's incredibly exciting. And, in order to achieve that, you have to know which tools to use for the job. I like the smell of the oil, too."

Mona stopped to turn around and stare at her. "You're mad," she said before starting to walk on. She spoke over her shoulder to post a parting shot. "And you'd better watch it. I think he fancies you."

Berta gave a peal of laughter. "Oh, Mona, stop being such an old woman. Of course he doesn't fancy me; we just share a common interest – machines!"

She was unwilling to tell Mona, but she had begun to notice George's attitude changing towards her. It was little things like spending a lot of their time together talking, rather than getting on with examining the vehicle in hand. He also seemed to spend much longer cleaning her hands with a cloth where some oil had lodged than seemed necessary. And, worst of all, the expression in his eyes when he looked at her had become somehow hot, caressing. She had noticed these things but, until Mona's remark, had not given them any significance. When people worked on a project together as they had often done at school with, for example, setting up botanical displays, ideas were shared, help was given to those having a problem and closeness inevitably developed between the team members. If she thought at all about George's behaviour, it was fleeting and easily explained and dismissed.

Things came to a head one day, on a visit to Blantyre, when Berta called at his workshop without Mona, who had planned to go shopping for a few groceries; the girls arranged that they would meet on the road outside the workshop in an hour or so. George hugged and kissed her on her cheek when she arrived. This was unusual behaviour but she disregarded it. They were becoming good friends, after all.

After a tour of his workshop, when she was impressed by the machines and the shelves of new tools and spares he proudly showed her, he put an arm around her and, before she could protest, pulled her to him and kissed her thoroughly on her mouth. She was quite interested, since she had never been kissed by a man and thought she'd be polite and let him get on with it. But that was before she felt his tongue probing her lips.

She broke away in an instant. "Ugh!" she said wiping her mouth and pushing him away with both hands on his chest. "That's disgusting! What on earth do you think you're doing?"

Flight seemed to be the best option in this embarrassing situation; she whirled around, trying to find her bag and doing her best to ignore George, who was looking as though he's been kicked in the stomach. Finally, she found her bag on a motorbike seat, and was by then calm enough to go up to the hapless man and face him.

Her eyes flashed with outrage. "George, I wish you hadn't done that. At least it would have been nice if you had checked first whether I wanted you to kiss me. Goodbye!" And she turned to leave.

George had found his voice: "Berta, please listen," he said, stammering in agitation. "I really didn't mean to shock you, but I've become very fond of you and I've been wanting to kiss you for a long time. The moment seemed right. I'm so very sorry."

Berta turned back and fiddled with her bag strap for a moment, as she searched for words, kind words in the face of such a contrite apology.

"That's really nice of you to say, George, and yes, we have become good friends but please don't ever try to kiss me again. To me it seemed like a lack of respect."

George nodded. "Yes, I see that now. I acted on impulse, foolish impulse. I am so very sorry."

Berta smiled and held out her hand. "That's that, then. Goodbye."

And she walked as nonchalantly as she could out of the workshop, trying hard to resist the temptation to get her handkerchief out of her bag and wipe her mouth again. She made a mental note not to relax and enjoy herself with a member of the opposite sex if she didn't want complications.

She was now getting the attention that Elsa was used to getting. Her skinny frame had filled out into sleek curves, with legs so shapely they were often commented on; but her large brown eyes still danced with mischief over full, curved lips that seemed ever ready to break into an irrepressible smile. What a bore, she sighed, that men would have to be avoided when they were generally so much more interesting than women!

Thinking of Elsa, she felt that a little of the closeness that they had always shared was disappearing. Not in any significant way but, for example, she would have liked to ask Elsa about the tongue thing. But even though it was Elsa who, with A Mayi, had led Berta into puberty, this thing was somehow different. At the time, when A Mayi spoke to her, she was so embarrassed that she could only remember thinking, *Oh, Mayi, please stop!* whereas with Elsa, she was interested, intrigued even, and felt free to ask questions about the physical changes taking place in her body. Now she wasn't sure how she could broach the 'George Event', as it had become in her mind. Would Elsa be shocked that her behaviour had been such that George had felt bold enough to kiss her? No, Elsa was never judgmental. Could her hesitation to speak to Elsa be because there was a man involved? She wondered.

***

"So, what would you like to do?" asked Mother Camille, as they sat companionably in one of the classrooms after lessons had finished for the day.

"I really don't know," said Berta. "I know that, much as I love the farm, I'm not ready to go and live there just yet. I'm not sure what else I can do, though."

"There isn't very much, I'm afraid," sighed the nun. "The problem is that people of mixed race are not really recognised as being on a par with the European, so jobs are almost impossible to find."

"What do you mean, Mother?" asked Berta, bewildered.

The nun proceeded gently.

"You see, Berta, the majority of Africans are not educated and the Europeans perceive them as being inferior in every way. This is why all the missionaries in this country are working so hard to educate and train the African, so that he can take his place in the governing of the country."

"But, Mother," said Berta, too shocked to be angry as she would become later, "my grandfather was an African and he was educated – and rich as well."

"You are perfectly correct, Berta, but the minority such as yourselves may as well not exist. It will probably surprise you to know that there have been an ongoing series of debates over whether people of mixed race should be categorised as 'native' or not. This is important because the result will decide your standing in the community. They seem to be leaning towards racial ancestry rather than culture to decide who is what. Which means that education and background will become irrelevant in deciding who or what you are. People will be what they are named, that is, what the colour of their skin is."

"But that's awful! There are many educated Africans in the country; take John Chilembwe, for example," chimed in Berta.

"Yes," said the nun dryly, "and look where it got him."

"And," continued Berta, outrage making her voluble, "the majority of Africans are educated. Their education is simply different from the Europeans'. I think the Africans could teach the Europeans a lot about the land, the weather and animals. Do you know, I heard the Agricultural Officer talking to Papa one day and he was saying that when he first arrived in the country from England, he was surprised to see that mixed crops were planted together in no particular order. Well, Reverend Mother, you have no idea how difficult it was for him to get the African farmers to abandon that style of farming, which they had learnt from their fathers, and to start to plant the different species separately in rows. Eventually, he succeeded and, do you know what?"

"No, dear," murmured the nun, her pale blue eyes dancing with suppressed humour at the intensity of Berta's explanation.

"Well, the crops were not so good with the new system of planting. And when they analysed the reasons for this, they found that the mix of plants had been just right originally."

"How so?" questioned Camille.

"Well, some of the smaller plants needed the shade of the larger plants and those with shallow roots provided shade for the water to sink down to the roots of those which rooted deeper.

"So," she finished triumphantly. "The African farmers knew best all along. How can the Europeans think that they have it right all the time?

There are other points of view; different doesn't necessarily mean inferior."

Mother Camille sighed and shook her head sadly. "Unfortunately, that is exactly what it has come to mean. Different to the ruling class is always taken to mean inferior, right from ancient times. If it's any consolation, people from the Mediterranean, like the Portuguese, Italians and Greeks and so on, are viewed in exactly the same way. Sadly, it doesn't take long for everyone to become brainwashed and truly believe that the ruling class is superior in every way."

"But," interjected Berta, a little frown between her eyes as she tried to make sense of this new information, "we have always been treated as equals by everyone."

"Yes," acquiesced the nun. "And that is not going to change. However, while he was here, your father's position in the community ensured that you were not discriminated against. Also, you girls were never in a position where you trespassed, as it were, onto white territory. I think it is going to be different now that you want to enter the wider community, simply because memories are short and people move on very quickly."

Berta struggled with these revelations, a bigger frown flitting briefly across her smooth, broad forehead. Mother Camille put out her hand and touched her arm.

"Don't let it upset you, child. You'll find that in your private life people will respect you for who you are. As you said, your family is respected by people of all colours."

'I just can't believe that I never saw all this before," said Berta thoughtfully. "I seem to have been living in a little world of my own, safe and comfortable, but not exactly aware."

The nun nodded. "Of course, Berta. For ten and a half months of the year you girls lived in the convent, and for the remaining six weeks you have been totally absorbed in the lives of your parents in Fort Johnston. I don't imagine you had the time or inclination for interaction with the British officials and their families so, mercifully, you were protected from any unpleasantness that might have arisen. Mind you, I'm not saying that there would have been any; not everyone is the same."

Berta spoke musingly: "Now I come to think of it..." She stopped. She had remembered that long-forgotten incident between her father and Carrain.

"Yes?" prompted Camille.

"I remember a terrible argument between my father and the D.C., Mr Carrain. It was something to do with the fact that my father, a European, had married A Mayi."

She looked at her mentor sadly. "How awful for Papa and A Mayi that must have been."

Mother Camille gripped her arm comfortingly. "Yes, it certainly must have been. But you know, if a person has a certain character they will find something with which to wound others. So, it isn't a question of colour really: it was probably the best thing the man could pull out of the hat for the job."

This kindly assessment, transparently designed to soothe Berta's feelings, lingered not a moment in her mind because, for Berta, things were clicking into place. She could see now that she had been protected from the reality of relationships in her wider environment.

How chilling, thought Berta.

She pulled herself back to the present. "How could I have imagined that there would be judgments made of me based simply on the colour of my skin?" she ruefully asked.

She held out her right arm and looked at it speculatively, gently stroking the silky, gleaming skin with her left forefinger.

"I always thought I was blessed with this colour. I always liked it!"

"And you must continue to do so," broke in Mother Camille. "It's a beautiful colour, the colour of pale milk chocolate. It's a mixture of your father's and mother's skins, an inheritance from your grandparents and great grandparents. It's precious because it's who you are. Whatever you do, don't let some narrow-minded bigots change the way you feel about yourself."

"No, you're right," responded Berta after a pause. She suddenly looked startled and the nun looked at her questioningly.

"I've just remembered something embarrassing," said Berta. "We've looked down on people too. We've considered slaves and servants inferior, and my father didn't like us to play with children that he considered to be of a 'lower class', no matter what their colour. And we've never been allowed to eat *nsima*, because A Mayi considered it suitable only for villagers and servants."

She looked at Mother Camille, her eyes wide and wondering as her mind raced. The nun said nothing but looked at her quizzically, allowing her to follow her line of thought.

"So," she said slowly turning to gaze out the open window, "I didn't like it when it was done to me, but I now realise that I have been doing it to others." Then, with her usual positive turn of mind, she looked at the nun and announced, "I have to change! – no more judging!"

Mother Adelaide smiled with relief that the worst of the crisis seemed to be over. "Yes, of course, Berta, but perhaps not today. Changing the way you perceive life is not as easy as that. You'll have to work at it; but

I'm sure you will succeed. And, do remember that it is human and indeed necessary to make judgments as we go through life. That is how we keep safe and well. It becomes harmful when these judgments are arbitrary and when they're included in laws and influence how society as a whole functions. That is when a lot of people get hurt."

The nun rose and Berta too hurried to her feet.

"Let me give this some more thought," said Mother, as she prepared to turn away. "Don't raise your hopes too high, my dear. It could lead to disappointment. Just trust in the Lord. He really does know best!"

Her forebodings turned out to be justified. The nun made numerous enquiries and although there was general sympathy with the plight of Mr Deuss' daughter, no one was prepared to stand up against the prevailing attitudes and offer her one of the scarce meaningful jobs. It was simply not done. Equally, knowing her and her background, their respect was too great to allow them to offer her some menial position.

Ludwig's old friend, Dharap, an Asian businessman from Blantyre, travelled to Nguludi especially to speak to Mother Camille on the subject.

"It's best if the girl goes home," he advised. "There is a very real colour bar in Nyasaland, but one doesn't notice it until one tries to go into the white domain. And going for one of the very few jobs available to women, for example in the government or local administration offices or one of the shops, will result in a lot of closed doors. It's a shame. She's good-looking, intelligent and educated, an asset to anyone, I would say. Never mind, some fine boy will soon come along and snap her up."

Mother compressed her lips and stood up to her full four feet eleven inches.

"I do not subscribe to the notion that a girl can only fulfil herself if a man comes into her life," she said primly, "but, in this case, I'll grant you that there doesn't seem to be another option. Yet."

After Dharap left, Mother stood by her desk, head bowed and arms crossed and tucked into the voluminous sleeves of her habit. Deep in thought, she crossed the room to the window and looked absently at the clumps of hydrangeas that blossomed, blue, pink and white, in the flower filled beds outside her window.

Should she tell Berta of Dharap's visit? Would it achieve anything? No, it wouldn't, she thought with a little toss of her head. There was nothing new to add to what they had discussed. Why burden the poor girl with thoughts of more obstacles? She needed all her strength and courage for the battle that lay ahead. She'd save her comments for when she had something positive to report and, *dear God, please let it be soon!*

CHAPTER FORTY-EIGHT

For the next few weeks, although Berta was busy with her duties in her final months at school, the matter sizzled quietly on a back burner of her mind. To find the dice so loaded against her and her kind had shocked her and, as each day passed, the sense of helplessness and frustration grew, and with it a pessimistic assessment of her future. She was accustomed to a busy, purposeful life where she was valued; now it looked as though that was disappearing and that she would be left to pick up whatever leftovers were discarded. She did discuss the situation briefly with a few of her friends and it surprised her to find that they were well aware of the situation.

"It's more noticeable if you live in town," offered Mona. "You notice that all the nationalities form their own little groups and all the main institutions like hospitals, clubs, cinemas and so on only permit British people to enter."

This, Berta could well imagine, having Carrain the D.C. as her main example of the British male. She recalled him saying to her father one day when he called past the shop that he had had sixteen white people to dinner on Christmas day a week previously. She had thought nothing of it at the time, but her blood began to boil now at the several kinds of sense the barbed remark now made. Detestable man!

I know, she thought, I'll apply to the shops in Blantyre. Why accept defeat before I start? So in a burst of optimism she penned three letters, two to shops in the main street and one to the Town Hall, in her beautiful copper plate writing.

"...I have completed my education at the Nguludi Convent and have passed in all subjects... I speak French, English, Chisena and Chinyanja," she wrote, finishing off with "...I am hardworking and eager to learn and would be grateful to hear from you whether there is a possibility of my working for you. Yours sincerely..."

She awaited the replies and her mind teased her cruelly, swinging her emotions from dismal fatalism to surging hopefulness that Mother Camille had been wrong and that at least one would say that they would be delighted to interview her with a view to employing her.

The replies when they came were disappointing. They were written with courtesy and the two shops mentioned their respect for her father, with whom they had done business, and their regret that they were not able to accommodate her.

301

"There is a chance, though," she said to Mona, "that there really were no vacancies. I suppose I'll never know."

Mona was thoughtful for a moment. "D'you know," she said finally. "I have an idea that the Limbe Trading Company is advertising for a trainee assistant bookkeeper. I'll find out for sure and let you know."

Two weeks later found Berta standing outside the door leading to the General Manager's office of the company. She had come in through the shop entrance on Blantyre's main street and stood helplessly for a few moments, wondering where the offices were. A pleasant Scots woman serving behind the counter asked if she could help and, when Berta explained whom she wanted, had directed her.

"Ah, yes," she smiled. "Just turn left past the shelves with the bags of sugar, go down the corridor and it's the second door on your right."

Berta thanked her and followed her instructions. She didn't think that the woman had been at all well dressed and wondered uneasily if she was overdressed. She felt that she was simply dressed, in a lime green drop-waisted dress with a long necklace of ivory beads around her slender neck. On her head she wore a beige head-hugging cloche hat and over her arm hung a beige bag, inside which was her carefully written letter of application. No, she was fine. This was typical morning wear for a slightly formal occasion.

Her fingers played nervously with her beads as she paused outside the second door on the right, breathing in deeply and praying for the courage to see this bold step through. Abruptly she straightened her back and raised her hand to knock on the door.

"Come in," floated a voice from the other side of the door.

Berta opened the door and walked in, to come face to face with a middle-aged woman sitting behind a desk covered in neat piles of papers. In front of her was a large, black typewriter. The woman looked up enquiringly. "Can I help you?"

"Yes," came the soft, diffident reply. "I am applying for the job of trainee bookkeeper that you have advertised." She took out her application as she spoke and handed it to the woman, who was staring at her as though mesmerised. Finally, she seemed to recollect herself and reached out for the letter.

"Um," she said as she opened it and read its contents. She looked from the application to the girl standing in front of her and made an indecisive movement with her hand.

"Now, let's see…" Then she came to a decision. "Just wait a moment, please, and I'll speak to the general manager; I'm his secretary."

And she hurried out through a door to an adjoining room. There came the murmur of voices and Berta tried to quieten her racing heart by looking intently at the large portrait of King George V which hung over the door to the manager's office. What, she wondered, were they talking about? Shouldn't they be talking to her? And why had the secretary stared so? Why had she behaved so strangely?

Finally, the door reopened and the secretary beckoned to her to come in.

"Mr Wilson will see you now," she said brightly and Berta walked through the doorway and into a large, airy room with a spacious desk by the open window. Behind the desk sat a middle-aged man, his dark hair slicked back from his face and anchored with Brilliantine, his half-moon glasses perched on the tip of his nose. He looked at her as she approached his desk and smiled.

"Sit down, please, Miss Deuss," he said, with a wave of his hand towards one of two small armchairs opposite him. Berta noticed that he held her letter in his hand; she felt a flicker of hope as she eased herself onto the edge of the seat. There was a moment of silence during which she heard the door behind her close, as the secretary left the room, and then her attention was drawn back to the manager as he started to speak.

"You have impressive qualifications and a glowing reference from the Reverend Mother," he started, as he glanced at her letter. He looked up and smiled. "Useful to have a few languages under your belt!"

She smiled back. "Yes, I suppose."

He continued: "I had the pleasure of meeting your father, you know. Exceptional businessman. He got a raw deal. Something for us British to be ashamed of, I'm afraid."

Berta gazed at him mutely, the stricken look in her big eyes evidence that she was not yet ready to talk about it. The man opposite her twisted uncomfortably in his seat, glanced out of the window and then briefly back at her. She noticed that he was avoiding meeting her eyes. He cleared his throat and hurried on.

"It was good of you to apply for the post that we advertised but I am sorry to tell you that it has already been filled. I do wish that you had written before making the journey."

Berta struggled to control the overwhelming disappointment that swept over her like a nauseous dark cloud, but when she spoke her face was calm and her voice firm and light.

"It's difficult to get here from Nguludi and when I heard that the convent truck was making a trip to Blantyre for supplies, I seized the opportunity to apply in person."

Wilson rose, came around the desk to shake her hand and steered her to the door.

"Such a pity, Miss Deuss; but thanks again for taking an interest in our company."

Then she was in the secretary's office, saying appropriate things while she walked towards the door. Thank God for a strict upbringing, she thought grimly, that stops me sitting on the floor and crying with frustration. The thought brought a little smile to her lips.

As she approached the outer door leading back into the shop, a young woman came in and, after looking hesitantly about her, came up to Berta shyly.

"Excuse me," she said and a blush rose to tint her fair skin, "but you wouldn't happen to know where Mr Wilson's office is, would you?" Berta thought that she sounded Scots.

"Yes! It's the next door on your right," and she pointed to it.

"Thank you," said the woman as she walked towards it. She went into the secretary's office but the door hadn't closed behind her before Berta heard her say, "I'm Mrs Taylor, here for my appointment to see Mr Wilson about the position in the accounts department."

There was a muffled, "Oh, yes, I'll..." before the door closed finally behind her.

Berta froze. Rage washed over her. Her first instinct was to turn back and confront the trio behind that door. Confront them with their stupid, cowardly lies. Confront them with their ignorant, bigoted approach to life. Denounce them for the power they held to hurt and destroy lives. Ridicule them for their little, closed minds and their complacent arrogance. Damn them, damn them, damn them.

She stood in the passage shaking, tears stinging her eyes, fighting the urge to go back into that room. But she had been brought up a lady, with all the constraints that that implied. She straightened her back, furtively wiped her eyes with one of her dainty little lace-edged handkerchiefs and walked out of the building, head in her fetching little hat held high.

Ah well, she thought as she walked away, Mother Camille was right. It had changed none of the important things in her life. *I'm still proud to be Berta Maria Deuss,* she told herself forcefully, her brisk walk and rigid back witness to her turbulent thoughts. *But now I'm angry and I'm determined to fight.* She vowed to herself that she would concentrate on making herself independent of the bigots. She would find her place in society; yes, their rotten, exclusive society. *I'll show them, she thought. I'll stand on my own two feet.*

But how? Where to begin? Oh, Elsa, I need you!

CHAPTER FORTY-NINE

Elsa struggled to come to terms with the reality of who Andrew was, or had been, after his revelations about his past life.

She still felt nauseous, repulsed at the things he had told her, his image tarnished almost beyond repair. But after a few weeks, the shock and horror, yes horror, she had to admit, had started to fade, as all images do sooner or later. She felt fortunate that she had the land and the crops to keep her occupied and that she had A Mayi's soothing presence to greet her when she came home from the fields.

When she and Andrew met in the fields, as they always had done, as partners watching over her crops, Andrew would plead with her to discuss things with him again, not to harden her heart against him by blocking him out. Finally, she relented and agreed to meet him by the corn fields where she would be working the following day. They talked as they stood in the dappled shade of the acacia trees, he earnestly putting his case, she unable to meet his eyes. He appeared to be truly ashamed of his past behaviour and felt that once they were married there wouldn't be any inclination for him to continue it. He told her that he loved her, again and again, but all that this conversation achieved was to reopen the wounds and the horror, and leave her feeling that she wanted to end their relationship.

"Andrew, please," she said, "I can't talk about this anymore and I'm sorry that I agreed to discuss it today. The time will come when I'll feel ready to talk about it; but it's not today."

Elsa spent a lot of time in the fields, speaking to the workers, all of whom she knew by name, and watching with an ever new fascination her plants, brought from the nursery, growing from little seedlings of four or five leaves to sturdy, boisterous plants before branching out, flowering and finally starting to produce the cotton bolls which encased the cotton fibre. A lot like children, she thought more than once, so tender and vulnerable at the start, then reaching for the nourishment they knew instinctively would be at their roots and branching out, flowering and exploring their world before settling down to procreate. *Silly,* she thought with a smile, *whatever will you be thinking next!*

Today, the temperature was relatively cool, the sky an endless arc of blue and the fields an exciting sea of plants, corn and sugar cane mainly at this time of year, rustling in the whisper of a light breeze; looking at her watch, she knew that it was time to think of going home for lunch. It didn't do to stay out of doors too long in the searing heat of the Shire valley, even on a temperate day like today, and even while wearing a pith helmet. She readjusted the helmet, which was starting to feel tight above her ears, and fished for a handkerchief, to wipe her moist face, in the capacious pockets of her summery dress. Pale blue with little white daisies, it was one of her favourite morning dresses; its full skirt let any little breeze in to cool her legs, and the belted waist showed off her figure, though it felt rather sweaty in the present heat. Never mind, she thought, wriggling the belt around, clothes were only worn once before being tossed into the laundry bin for Mzumbo, the dhobi or laundry man, to wash and iron.

Just then she spotted movement a little distance down the road. Peering through the heat haze, she identified Joshua, one of Cook's assistants, running towards her. She turned to walk towards him, wondering what the rush was. By the time he reached her, sweat was pouring down his face, but he still managed to give her his usual wide smile while pausing to get his breath back.

Elsa was concerned. "What is it, Joshua?"

"Madam, "he said, "there is a visitor at the house. A Mayi says that you must come quickly."

"Who is it?" she asked.

"But I don't know. It is a man."

"All right, Joshua. Thank you for calling me. And," as she turned away and headed for her bike, which she had left in the shade of an acacia tree, "there's no need to run!"

Reaching her bicycle, Elsa mounted and started to cycle lazily to the house, waving every now and then to the children who had come to work with their mothers, and who raced to stand by the road and wave, teeth gleaming whitely in dark, dusty faces.

She wasn't particularly interested in the unknown visitor. Of course it wasn't Andrew. She saw him quite often; their relationship had not changed as far as their working together was concerned, but the subject of his proposal was not referred to after the last disastrous effort. She knew, though, that she was starting to mellow and she missed their friendship, a friendship that was already strong before they began to fall in love.

Enough of that, she thought to herself, I'm home now and mildly curious to know who the visitor is. Boby, perhaps? Joshua wouldn't know him as he worked in the kitchens and wouldn't meet guests.

She dismounted and parked her bicycle at the foot of the front steps, giving a curious glance to an unknown motorbike parked by the side of the steps. She could hear the indistinct murmur of voices from the far side of the veranda, the shaded part where the midday sun would have the least effect. She pulled her handkerchief out of her pocket and gave her face a quick wipe, then she tugged off her helmet, smoothed her hair and repositioned the clips on either side. Satisfied, she walked up the steps onto the veranda. She could see Paulina through the railings and hear A Mayi, who was in full flow, sounding animated as she talked to the visitor in Chisena, her native tongue. *Chisena?* thought Elsa, *who on earth...?*

She reached the top of the steps, turned towards the little group and faltered in mid-step. There, talking with her mother, his unmistakable handsome profile in clear view, was Rafael. Her heart skipped a beat. Rafael of Sena, Rafael, friend of the Arab slave traders, the hated and detested Rafael. What a nerve! But how nice to see him!

Before she could turn on her heel and disappear into the house to compose herself, Victoria saw her.

"Ah, there you are, Elsa; look at who's come to visit us!"

Elsa moved forward slowly, willing herself to be neutral as Rafael stood up and extended his hand to her.

"Good afternoon, Miss Elsa. It's good to see you again. How are you?" Still the same voice, she thought, the voice that had haunted her since that woman and her baby had been abducted by him and the slavers. She repressed a shudder, but a traitorous voice in her mind whispered, *He did try to stop the Arabs taking her...*

"I'm well thank you, as I hope you are."

"Come and sit down, Elsa," Victoria said. "We're just having tea."

She chose her seat carefully, since she wasn't sure which was more unsettling, to sit beside him or opposite him, where he would be in full view all the time. She chose to sit beside him. At least she wouldn't have to look at him.

"What brings you here?" she asked, looking at the teapot. "You're a long way from home."

He explained that he had decided to start planting cotton, for domestic as well as foreign markets, and since he had heard that the Lower Shire was the major cotton growing area, he had decided to come and see for himself what was involved.

"I was fortunate to be given an introduction to a Mr Boby, who has very kindly offered me hospitality and who suggested that we meet here to ask your permission to view your plantation, as he tells me that you have been remarkably successful. I told him of my close connection with your grandfather before he passed away and so he thought that you would have no objection."

He turned to look at her with open admiration as he talked and she regretted her choice of chair; his face was now mere inches away from hers.

As if in answer to her prayers, there came the sound of a motorbike climbing up the hill, closer and closer until it came to a stop at the foot of the steps.

"Excuse me," said Elsa. She swiftly rose to her feet and walked to the top of the steps. She was always happy to see Boby, but today she could have kissed him and hugged him. Her mind was seething with contradictory emotions; she felt out of control but, with him around, she began to feel grounded again.

"Hello, my dear," he said, "looking happy and charming as always."

His thin red face under his helmet smiled up at her, his pale blue eyes warm with affection. As always, his trousers and shirt were dazzlingly white; he quickly patted himself to get rid of the dust from the road before walking up the steps to greet her. After they had shaken hands she led him to the group on the veranda, where he greeted A Mayi and asked about her health before smiling a greeting at Paulina and Rafael. Elsa seated him next to Rafael, and sat on his right, where she was partially hidden from Rafael, who looked at her with a little frown between his eyes, but she turned away and started to pour tea for Boby.

The visit was brief. Rafael had already told them the purpose of his visit and it only remained to make arrangements for him to visit the plantation. He leaned over to look enquiringly at Elsa who, feeling trapped, suggested the following morning at seven o'clock, before the sun reached its zenith.

"Will you come too, Mr Boby?" she asked, turning to him.

He shook his head. "Regretfully, no. I shall be in court for the next several days doing my Justice of the Peace bit." He turned to Rafael. "You'll be in good hands. Miss Deuss will tell you all you need to know."

He rose to leave and everyone followed suit. There were greetings all around and Elsa walked the men to the front steps.

"I've just thought of something," Boby said, turning to Rafael. "I'm wondering whether I should arrange for you to borrow a side car for tomorrow. Otherwise, it will be difficult for Elsa and you, one on a motorbike and the other on a bicycle."

Rafael inclined his head. "Thank you, Mr Boby. That is most thoughtful of you."

"Thank you, Mr Boby," echoed Elsa, and stood there as they made their down the steps, got onto their motorbikes and waved before setting off down the drive.

When she returned to her mother and sister, Elsa sat down and tried to gather her thoughts before speaking.

"What is it, Elsa?" asked A Mayi.

Elsa looked at her mother for a moment. "Mayi, I'm surprised that you are so friendly with that man, Rafael. After everything that happened at Sena, I'm still in a state of shock that we have entertained him and that I'm supposed to go out with him tomorrow."

Pauline burst in: "Yes, Mayi, I'm shocked too. I couldn't believe that he was sitting with us and being treated like a guest. That evil man!"

A Mayi held up her hand. "Yes, yes, yes, girls. I do understand what you're saying, but calm down just a moment and let me speak."

Elsa and Paulina sat rigidly in their seats, eyes fixed on their mother, and waited.

A Mayi thought for a moment. "After that slaving incident, you know that we were all stunned to meet him. Your grandfather particularly struggled to believe that Rafael was friendly with and, on that particular day, actually acting with the Arab slavers. Not that he didn't believe you, no, not at all. He just wondered whether there could have been an explanation. You see, he's known Rafael since he was a child; he's seen him transform the run-down plantation that his father left him into one of the most efficient and profitable in the area."

Elsa pulled a face. "Yes, and I wonder how many slaves died in the process?"

Paulina, for once disagreeing with her mother, agreed. "Mayi, although he did try to stop the Arab slavers from taking us, it was only because he warned that there would be huge problems with grandfather, remember. I also recall his telling Papa that we were all hypocrites when there were so many people in the west as well as in the east who were profiting from the slave trade, and made it into such a huge operation."

Elsa folded her arms across her chest and rubbed them with a little shudder. "Papa said that we should try and understand that he grew up believing that slaves are a commodity and that he knows nothing different. Hah!"

"And that he is a good and honourable man otherwise," said Paulina, frowning.

Elsa stood up. "Let's stop talking about him, shall we? I'll try not to dread tomorrow!" She smiled. "And I'm so hungry. Let's have lunch!"

When Elsa awoke early next morning to the sun shining through her bright, floral curtains she stretched comfortably and then remembered something with a slight shock. Goodness, she was to spend the day with that awful man! *Unless I give him a really speedy tour,* she thought, as she got up and hurriedly put on her dressing gown.

After her shower, she attacked her wardrobe, discarding dress after dress. Nothing seemed right. *Stop this,* she scolded herself, it's Rafael, *and the last thing you want to do is to look attractive. But,* she thought, *he is so terribly good-looking and I don't want to look a frump.* And she suddenly realised that she did want to look attractive for him. She finally settled on a pale yellow, short-sleeved cotton dress with a full skirt and deep pockets, and a white leather belt which showed off her neat little waist. It'll do, she told her mirror.

By half past six, she, her mother and Paulina were eating their breakfast, the usual time in hot weather areas, and Elsa was just finishing her coffee when the sound of a motorbike climbing the hill stuttered in through the window. Elsa leapt up, excused herself and ran for her helmet, picking up two hankies from the hall table and stuffing them into one of her pockets.

By the time Rafael reached the house, Elsa was standing at the bottom of the steps waiting for him. He dismounted with a friendly smile and greeted her, handsome in his light tan safari suit, wide-brimmed felt hat and red bandana.

He looked at his watch. "Two minutes late! I do apologise," he said, with a laugh in his voice.

Elsa tried to resist his charm and failed. She smiled and said, as she put on her cumbersome pith helmet, "We've only just finished breakfast, so you're right on time."

He held out his hand for her as she climbed into the sidecar and ensured that she had settled down before walking around to get onto the motorbike.

"Ready?" he asked and, as she nodded, he started the engine. The motorbike roared into life.

"You'll have to direct me," he called out, and she nodded again, shouting "Yes!" to get above the noise.

Elsa was surprised to find that she was enjoying herself. The early morning crispness in the air was refreshing, the sky its favourite shade of Madonna Blue before paling to almost white later on in the day and, before the sun had had time to bleach the green thickets and trees, they gleamed in every shade of green, from the paleness of the young acacias to the dark emerald of the mature ones. Birds rose from the trees in clouds as the engine sound reached them and Elsa noticed a few hawks swooping. *I must remember to warn Mayi,* she thought, *otherwise she'll lose her baby chicks.*

A few hundred yards on, they approached the nurseries and children ran to the road, waving and looking with open-mouthed astonishment at their lady boss, who was arriving in that very rare item, a motorbike, and with a sidecar no less. Elsa waved back and touched Rafael's arm.

"To the left," she shouted, pointing ahead.

He slowed down immediately and turned off where Elsa had directed. The nursery field was now in plain view and she signalled to him to stop.

When he did so, she explained to him that as far as a bamboo fence some fifty yards distant, all the beds were dedicated to seedlings. Several women were busy in the field, weeding and turning the soil. A large barn-like structure, she explained, was where the seeds would be planted before being transplanted into the open fields.

"Come and have a look," she said, as she climbed out of the sidecar, without waiting to be helped, and walked towards the barn. Rafael walked beside her and, as they approached, four gardeners emerged to greet them.

Elsa greeted them in return and explained who Rafael was. "We've come to see the seedlings," she said, and the group moved towards the barn.

Inside, the floor was covered with wooden trays which had been filled with earth and where little seedlings in various stages of growth grew strong and sturdy.

"I notice that the barn only has half height walls," commented Rafael. "Is that to let the sunshine in?"

"Yes. The seedlings need protection from the sun so when they're very young this type of barn will give them that protection while still allowing the light and air to enter. Would you mind if I just take a look at how these are doing?"

"Of course not. I'll come with you, if you don't mind."

"Please feel free."

They chatted while they looked at the seedlings and Elsa tried to answer his questions, although she warned him that she was by no means an expert.

"They'll start to flower about a month or slightly more after we transplant them and will grow to between three and four feet."

"What sort of habit, spindly, bushy or what?" Rafael wanted to know.

Elsa smiled. "Definitely bushy."

"So we need to space them well apart, then. Do they flower?"

"Oh yes. Apparently, they are of the hibiscus family and their blossoms are a lovely delicate shade of pink and white. Flowering lasts about a month."

Elsa went on to explain that when the flowers had been pollinated and had fallen off, the plant formed buds, known as bolls, which contained the fibre known as cotton.

"Would you like to see the transplanted seedlings now?"

Rafael agreed with alacrity. As they cleared the barn a little boy of probably three or four years of age crept behind them, and boldly stuck an inquisitive finger into the calf of the stranger. Rafael spun around and with a mock roar lifted up the child, held him high in the air and tickled him until he shrieked with delight, finally calling to his mother for help.

Laughing, Rafael put him down and watched him scuttle away, looking behind to make sure that the monster wasn't following.

"That'll teach the little monkey to poke strangers in the back!" he chuckled. Standing close to him and laughing with him, smelling that clean smell of freshly washed linen, she suddenly had a vivid memory of the time that he had kissed her, the feel of his lips gently moving on hers. How she had wanted him to do it again and how she had hated herself for wanting it. Flushing, she bent her head and moved away.

"We'll have a look at these seedlings first," she said.

They spent the rest of the morning looking at all the fields and the different crops that were being grown for the local markets, and Elsa found it quite disturbing that she was finding Rafael to be a warm, likeable man, not at all as she remembered him. This was indeed food for thought. As the sun climbed overhead and the midday heat set in, she suggested that it was time that they returned to the house; they mounted their transport and headed back home, grateful for the breeze that the motion gave them.

When they arrived back at the house, Elsa invited Rafael in for a cool drink, which he accepted. Leaving his motorbike at the foot of the steps, he stepped up to the veranda, where A Mayi had thoughtfully prepared a selection of drinks complete with ice in a bucket.

"How cool it is here," he said, as he sank into a chair. "Wonderful!"

"No, thank you," he said, when offered gin or sherry. "I don't drink alcohol during the day and, in fact, very little at any time."

He looked serious for a moment. "My father was a heavy drinker and ruined his life, almost ruining mine and my mother's in the process. She suffered badly but managed to shield me from the worst of it. So, I have no liking for the stuff and am very happy with orange squash, lemonade or whatever you have, thank you."

A Mayi was sympathetic. "I'm so sorry to hear about your father. I met your mother in Sena and she seemed a lovely woman."

Rafael smiled. "Thank you. Yes, she has been a wonderful mother to me, despite all the heartbreak in her life, and I shall always be grateful to her for that."

"Won't you stay to lunch?" asked A Mayi.

"Thank you, but I'm afraid I've arranged to meet Mr Boby for lunch, and later on he's going to take me on a tour of the cotton ginnery. It's kind of you to ask."

He finished his drink and rose to his feet. "Thank you for your hospitality, Mrs Deuss and thank you, Elsa, for a truly delightful morning being shown around your farm."

Elsa rose. "It was a pleasure. I hope that it was useful to you."

"Very much so." And he turned to leave after greeting each of the ladies.

Elsa saw him to the steps and went down them with him. When they reached his motorbike, he turned to face Elsa, intense brown eyes fixed on hers. He looked down and fiddled with the strap of his hat before looking up again. Elsa's breath caught in her throat as she saw the expression in his eyes.

"I just wanted to say that I still feel the same about you as I did the first time I saw you, when I fell in love with you. I hope I am not distressing you by saying this, but if ever you change your mind about me, just let me know and I'll be here for you." He took her hand, kissed it and held it against his cheek for a moment. Elsa hoped that he couldn't see the flame that he had ignited, and that threatened to melt any resistance she had ever had.

She made a huge effort to keep her voice steady and her expression neutral. She looked straight into those eyes that made her think only of how she would like to kiss that generous, chiselled mouth, to hold that muscular chest to her heart.

Her voice astonished her with its cool tone: "Rafael, there will always be a huge obstacle between us. You consider slaves to be commodities to be used and abused. I consider them to be the most unfortunate of human beings, whose very life has been taken from them, leaving them to live as shadows of themselves. How can our minds ever meet? And it is too important an issue to me to be shelved as 'one of our unfortunate differences which we must learn to live with'."

"Oh, Elsa, my lovely girl, how you have misunderstood me! My slaves are treated well. I wish you could come and see the homes that I have built for them, the stores of food that are at their disposal, the tasks which, though heavy, are no heavier than I would expect from a son of mine."

Elsa took a deep breath, looked straight into his eyes and asked, "Would you ever sell any one of them?"

Rafael was a bit taken aback by her question. "Well, it depends." He faltered. "I mean, if the slave were not suited to the work that I required him to do, then I would consider selling him to a more appropriate placement and buying another to replace him."

A shattering disappointment flooded through Elsa, suddenly making her feel very tired and ready to weep. She took her hand from his and looked once again into those eyes, seeing in them something that called out to her that here could have been her soul mate, someone she could have loved deeply and for ever.

"A commodity," she said. "To be used and discarded. I couldn't live with that, Rafael. I am so very sorry."

She reached up to kiss him on his cheek and as they touched they both froze. Slowly, as though in a dream, their faces moved until their lips met, moved against each other, melted in a searing embrace that shook and paralysed them, a hungry embrace that sought to melt them into the one being they were surely destined to be. Elsa's hands went up to caress the hair at the back of his neck, stroking, pulling him towards her, and he pulled her to him as though he would never let her go. Then she pulled away and it was over.

"I'm so sorry," she said again and slowly walked up the steps and onto the veranda without looking back.

"I'm very tired," she said to A Mayi and Paulina. "Please could you start lunch without me? I'll have a nap and eat later. Sorry."

She went to her room, closed the door and lay down on her bed.

As the sound of his motorbike grew quieter in the distance and then disappeared, she felt a sense of loss that frightened her. She realised now that she had felt attracted to Rafael right from the start and that the reason for her flaming hatred had been that, given his beliefs, there could never be anything between them. Her anger was her heart's and mind's protest against a fate that had brought them together, only to brutally tear them apart.

Elsa recognised now that time had mellowed her. What had seemed so black and white on that terrible, never to be forgotten day, was now blurring at the edges. Rafael could not have made a stronger defence of the woman whom the Arabs were abducting without forfeiting his and his mother's safety and, indeed, the safety of his whole plantation. As he had said, the Arabs had known his father and expected Rafael's friendship and the best he could do in the circumstances was to avoid them whenever possible. True, it seemed cowardly, but from her older perspective it was a delicate balancing of his responsibilities that ensured the safety of his own people.

She had always been sensible and even in this sad moment, when tears coursed down her cheeks, she knew that a marriage between them could never have worked. Living in Sena, where her grandparents no longer lived, and at such a great distance from her family, she would have had absolutely no support for her beliefs.

Although the international community was calling to Portugal to live up to its promises and stop allowing and aiding the slave trade in its African territories, how much would things change? There were many forms of slavery and who could say how Rafael would treat his workers in any new climate? She saw clearly that inevitably, at some time in the future, when she witnessed injustice after injustice to the working classes, and being powerless to intervene, she too, like them, would lose herself and become a mere shadow of whom she had been.

Dry-eyed now, she laid her head on her pillow and slept.

CHAPTER FIFTY

In the months following receipt of Ludwig's letter, Elsa had a huge emotional upheaval to deal with, not only her own but also her sisters', particularly Berta's, to whom the blow had been particularly severe because of her young age. Fortunately, all three led busy lives, which left little room for reflection and gave time for the wounds to start healing.

Now, walking through the seedling barn, with its rich aroma of fresh, healthy soil, her thoughts turned to Rafael; his entering her life again had been a bitter-sweet event. She thought of him often, saw his face again and again when she mingled with the crowds in Chiromo town, thought of how she would have loved to run the farm with him by her side. An impossible dream, she knew. She would always cherish the moments they had shared, the feelings they had for each other, the passion they aroused in each other. Her mouth twisted in a sad smile. She supposed that that was what a first love was like and that its memory would grow more and more beautiful until, in her old age, it would bear little resemblance to the reality of what had been.

But now, she thought with a mental shake, it was time to deal with reality. And the reality was that there was an aching void in her heart. Her thoughts turned to Andrew and, all at once, she knew that with him was where her future should be.

Part of her was still repelled by what Andrew had revealed to her, but this was tempered by the knowledge that men generally had different standards of morality to adhere to. A woman behaving in such a fashion was completely outside the bounds of the imagination, unless of course she was known to be a woman of easy virtue. These were not subjects that were discussed at home, particularly with an unmarried daughter, but Elsa had gleaned enough from her friends to know that such women existed.

It seemed to her that these women were actually quite enviable. Imagine knowing all the facts of life so intimately! And not only that. Imagine the power they held over the men who apparently thronged to sample their favours. Heady stuff, indeed, when she herself could only shiver in a welter of strange feelings at a simple touch from Andrew. As for Rafael…

When they next met up for work in the fields she drew Andrew aside at a quiet spot where they were not visible to the farm workers and told Andrew of her decision. He reached out for her and held her tightly as he whispered, "You will never regret this, Elsa. I love you and I want to spend the rest of my life with you, making you happy."

Yes, secure in his arms, she felt that she had made the right decision for her at that particular moment of her life. She pushed Rafael out of her mind and concentrated on returning Andrew's kiss.

She caught A Mayi on her own early next morning as she had her first cup of tea on the veranda.

Elsa sat down opposite her mother and decided to plunge straight in.

"Mayi, I've decided to marry Andrew," she announced.

A Mayi put down her teacup and looked at her silently.

"Why?" she asked.

This caught Elsa on the wrong foot and she stopped and started speaking a few times before managing to say, "Because I love him."

Feelings of this sort were never discussed, and she found it hard to articulate what she wanted to say. She looked anxiously across at her mother.

"I did ask him about the things you told me about, and you were right. It was the truth." And she related to A Mayi what Andrew had explained to her. "I'm sure that that part of his life is over, Mayi. He truly wants to settle down and have a family."

"I remember your saying to me, Elsa, when we talked about Richard's drinking, that one cannot believe that a man will stop his bad habits just because he is getting married..."

"Yes, I remember that well, Mayi," she said with a smile, "but I believe that Andrew's situation is different. You see..."

They talked for a long while and, seemingly reassured, A Mayi looked tenderly at her daughter. "You are a sensible girl, Elsa, and all I and your father want for you is happiness. May God bless you both with happiness and long lives."

And they embraced.

Shortly after this she travelled to the main town, Blantyre, to arrange for some agricultural supplies, and took the opportunity to visit Berta at school at Nguludi and break the news to her.

Before announcing her arrival at the convent to Berta, she had a long talk with Mother Camille, whose main concerns were whether Andrew was a good Catholic and whether he was able to support her. Elsa reassured her on the second point, although she was unsure of the first, except that she thought that he had been baptised.

On the second, she pointed out that Andrew would be moving into the family home at Tangadzi since she, Elsa, had no intention of leaving her farm. It had been suggested that she move onto the Watson's neighbouring estate, but Elsa's view was that since she had a lovely home of her own, a mother and sisters to care for and pressing business interests, it made sense for her to stay where she was.

"And Andrew has accepted this?" asked the nun, looking searchingly at Elsa.

"Oh, yes," was the reply. "He's quite pleased about it, in fact. I suspect that he would like to get out from his parents' shadow and he says that things will be a bit livelier at my place! He will continue to work there, of course, because his father couldn't manage without him. Our business interests will be entirely separate, though, except for the help he has always given me when I've needed it."

"And what do A Mayi and your father think?" pursued the nun.

"Well, my father wants to know what education he has had and is worrying that he might be marrying me for my money." She laughed. "A Mayi has warned me that going to live with my mother-in-law could be a really bad idea! She's not keen on Mrs Watson. Thinks she may be from slave stock. Both think, although they haven't said it in so many words, that Andrew is not good enough for me."

The two women laughed merrily and Mother wryly commented: "Parents haven't changed in thousands of years, have they? No one is ever good enough for one's daughter."

She paused and looked fondly at her ex-pupil. "Although, I must say, Elsa, that you are a very special girl. I do hope that he deserves you."

"Thank you, Mother," said Elsa, smiling happily at the compliment.

When she left the nun and finally broke the news to Berta, the younger girl stared at her sister with her mouth open.

"Getting married to Andrew?" she finally said. "Isn't this a bit sudden?"

"Well, not really. We hit it off right away and it seems the natural thing to do."

"Do you love him?" asked Berta, with her newfound seventeen-year-old wisdom.

Elsa looked uncomfortable, but then smiled. "Of course I do!" she retorted.

"What does A Mayi think about it?" was the next question.

"We have discussed it thoroughly," was the evasive reply.

"Elsa," said her sister earnestly. "This has nothing to do with Dad's new liaison, has it?"

"What on earth do you mean?"

"Well, it was a dreadful shock for all of us. I know that sometimes the thought is so painful I just wish I could run away and stop being myself, if you know what I mean."

"Yes, I do," replied Elsa with a wry smile. "It's all about running away from oneself to try and avoid the pain, isn't it?"

"Yes, exactly. And, Elsa, I would hate to think that that is what you're trying to do. You cannot ever run away from yourself. We all have to fight to face the demons in our minds. We have to overcome them until they no longer have the power to tear us apart, and only then shall we find peace. Another thing, Elsa," she continued a little awkwardly, oblivious to Elsa's look of astonishment as she gazed at her youngest sister, marshalling her perceptive and mature thoughts. "I haven't been able to help hearing stories about Andrew. Are you sure you want to do this?

Elsa thought a moment, looking intently at Berta. Finally she said, fondly and a little proudly, as she stroked her cheek, "Berta has grown up. Our baby sister is now a young woman."

Berta grinned with pleasure but was quick to reply: "Don't change the subject! I won't press you further, but please think about it."

"I already have, dear sister, and I've made the decision. I believe that Andrew is a good man and I owe it to you to tell you his reaction to the stories that have spread about him." She paused for a moment to collect her thoughts.

"I did confront him about what I had heard, Berta," she finally. "I had to. You see, A Mayi told me about what was being said and, if the stories were true, then I needed to reassess my feelings about him."

She fiddled absentmindedly with a small pearl button on her lace and voile blouse and her expression was grave.

"He denied nothing, Berta, and I do admire him for that. He could have lied, and I would never have been able to get to the bottom of the issue, but I would always have wondered. There would always have been this niggling doubt. But he just told the bald truth."

"And how did you feel?" asked Berta, her expression concerned.

"Stunned, actually," responded her sister. "But, let's not dwell on it. Andrew feels that with me as his wife, the old temptations will disappear. He wants nothing more than to start a new life with me. He needs me, Berta."

She stopped and looked sheepishly at her sister, who was staring at her in round-eyed horror.

"It sounds dreadful, doesn't it?"

Berta was speechless. She nodded and Elsa continued: "I thought about it for a few weeks, but Andrew kept on calling and asking me to discuss it with him again, so we did. He is really ashamed of his past behaviour and he feels that once we are married there won't be a reason for him to continue it. He really seems to love me and, yes, I have become very fond of him. He is such good company and he is so protective of me, in fact of all of us, that it feels really reassuring to have him around."

Berta found her voice: "He can't take the place of Dad, you know. We have to learn to depend on ourselves. That part of our lives is gone. Gone, Elsa. To expect Andrew to care for us as Dad did is not realistic. And if all that is keeping him from his past bad behaviour is marriage to you, I feel you are on shaky ground."

"Maybe I see things differently. The older I grow the less black and white I see things. None of us is spotless and I think he deserves a chance."

Berta leaned over to kiss her. "Then, I wish you happiness and a wonderful future with all my heart. Be happy, my dearest Elsa. You so deserve it. I don't think we would have survived losing Dad without your strength and calm good sense."

They hugged, both misty eyed, until Berta drew away. "Your dress! We need to think about your dress!"

CHAPTER FIFTY-ONE

And so it was that a few months later Elsa and Andrew were married in the little brick-built church quite close to Tangadzi, where the Catholic nuns and priests had started a mission station. It was a small affair, with only family, neighbours and close friends invited. As Elsa said, it was too much to expect friends and acquaintances from Blantyre and Nguludi to travel such a long distance on the new, hard, corrugated dirt roads, so they were simply informed of the event.

It was a charming ceremony and the church, which had been built painstakingly and with love by the first missionaries, reflected their care in the intricate brickwork, the mitred windows filled with stained glass and the intricately carved wooden altar. The floor was laid with a gleaming imitation of the quarry tile, which was now brush stroked with the brilliant colours of the windows, thrust through by the streaming sun. The footsteps of the guests rang out as they walked on them to their pews.

Berta and Paulina were responsible for the flowers and every statue, the altar, the communion rail and the path of the bride to the altar were bedecked with a stunning profusion of flowers from the garden. Bowls of engraved brass holding dahlias of every hue from deepest scarlet to the palest of pinks lined the altar, leaving only the opening of the tabernacle free. Each of the statues of the saints had a posy in a vase at its feet, each holding a different flower; cannas, lilies, carnations, asters and zinnias stood proudly sentinel. The communion rail behind which the bridal *prie deux* stood was decked with sweet peas and their penetrating aroma, mingling with the carnations, filled the air as the first guests arrived.

Andrew stood at the altar looking dashing and handsome in a dark grey lounge suit. He was clearly and endearingly nervous, and, hands clasped behind his back, he shifted from foot to foot, turning frequently to see whether Elsa had made her appearance.

Richard, also dashing in a dark blue suit, waited at the entrance to the church, popping out every few minutes to see whether Elsa had arrived. Finally, the rustling and whispering in the back of the church announced to the small congregation that the bride was arriving.

Suddenly she was there. She looked beautiful in a drop-waisted dress in palest oyster satin, which emphasised her slim yet voluptuous lines. Paulina had embroidered pearl florets around the neckline and matching florets formed cuffs on the long, tight-fitting sleeves. On her head she wore a coronet of silk flowers studded with pearls, from which dropped a filmy veil through which could be seen her lovely, fine-featured face, her eyes glowing with happiness. Ludwig had done his best to participate and had enlisted his sister's help in choosing for Elsa the coronet and veil; the pearls were in response to a plea from Paulina.

Richard kissed his sister and whispered, "Good luck, Sis, and God bless you both," before gently placing Elsa's hand on his arm and leading her to the altar where, with a smile and a brief clasp of Andrew's shoulder, he handed his sister over to her future husband. The nuns' little choir sang in their sweet lilting voices and the magic moment touched the hearts of all those present.

Victoria lost herself in the soft cadences of sound and smiled at the recollection of how hasty Ludwig had been when he decided that this girl was the wife that he wanted. He told her later that it was her broad white smile in her dark, shining face and her spontaneous little giggle that had captivated him. He spoke to Roque first, who gave his permission for him to speak to Victoria. In a mixture of Portuguese and Sena, the young couple communicated and Victoria tumbled into a lasting passion for Ludwig. He was to be her first and only love.

Roque had wanted a church wedding and so they had visited the lone priest at the local mission.

Victoria still remembered his ill and emaciated appearance. Hard to forget really.

"Malaria," he explained to them. "No sooner do I get over one bout than another starts."

It seemed that although Catholic missionaries had set up numerous missions across the area, with churches, hospitals and schools, they had been defeated by the hot humid conditions, which nourished the lethal mosquito. The land was littered with abandoned missions and missionaries' graves.

The priest was discouraging about the proposed wedding. "I would have to seek dispensation from the Bishop," he said shaking his head, "but I'm afraid there isn't much chance of getting it. The rules are strict about marrying non-Catholics."

Roque had looked grimly at the young couple. "No point in going to see the bishop in Beira, then," he said. A staunch Catholic, he was not going to see his eldest daughter cohabit in any other than a legal manner.

Victoria was despondent but Ludwig wasn't. He was young and enthusiastic; he would find a way, he announced buoyantly.

"We'll find a Chefe do Posto to perform a civil ceremony," he said confidently to his father-in-law. The Chefe was the equivalent of the British District Collector and each district was supervised by one. He would have the authority to perform civil weddings.

She smiled to herself, warmed by the memory of the love they had shared.

The voices of the couple exchanging vows brought Victoria back to the present. As she heard her daughter say in a perfectly calm voice, "I do," she experienced a moment of shocking recollection as she flew back to the past. Beside her was Ludwig, smiling, helping her to say her vows.

Through the pain in her heart she looked up at Andrew, smiling down at Elsa, and her mind screamed at him: *Don't ever leave her, Andrew! Don't break her heart as mine is breaking. Just love her, I beg you. Just love her.*

A pain in her throat, as she struggled to contain the tears that threatened to swamp her, brought her back to the present. She found herself trembling, her breath shallow and fast and she clenched her fists until her nails dug into her palms. *Be calm for Elsa,* she kept telling herself, *keep calm for Elsa.* Slowly she regained her composure and was able to look and smile at Paulina and Berta as they unashamedly dabbed at the tears on their cheeks as they watched their sister complete her vows.

It was a simple ceremony and Victoria struggled to preserve her stern, aloof deportment when her eyes said everything about her pride in her lovely daughter. If she still had qualms about Andrew, she gave no sign and greeted him as her son-in-law after the ceremony with her usual dignity and courtesy.

Berta stilled her misgivings, hugged him and called him 'brother' as they gathered outside the church, but she experienced a pang of loss that she would never have admitted to anyone. She told herself that she was being silly, but there was no way to still that little ache in her heart that told her that Elsa was now more a wife to Andrew than a sister to her. She knew that it was right that it should be so and she was sincerely glad that Elsa had found her soul mate, but she knew that, no matter how close they had been, there was now an area of Elsa's life that had to be private from her and that she must learn to accept this.

As the guests milled around joyously, kissing and hugging the bridal couple, it seemed to Elsa that this was one of the happiest moments of her life. At last she felt that the pieces of her life, which had danced around haphazardly for so long, had slipped into place and created a harmonious whole. She turned to Andrew and squeezed his arm and he smiled down at her: "I love you," he whispered.

Andrew moved in to Tangadzi Estate and A Mayi insisted that the newly-weds have her bedroom, which was the largest and most pleasant in the house. When they argued against this, she insisted and said with a hint of sadness in her big brown eyes, "If your Papa's health improves enough for him to come home, you can let us have the room back. Until then, it's yours."

The girls exchanged stricken glances and Berta's heart went out to her mother, who didn't know, and must never know, that her husband would never be coming back.

Soon, it was as if nothing unusual had ever happened. Andrew fitted in well with the family and was very much at ease with A Mayi and the girls, who were soon won over by his charming, cajoling ways. Although he left early each morning to tend his own estate, he still popped back at intervals during the day and, when night fell, he appeared happy to be back with his adopted family.

Elsa couldn't quite believe how well things had turned out. In the space of a few months, her life had gone from shock and abject misery to a calm, happy existence with Andrew. The brief episode with Rafael had taught her love, a lost, wild and tempestuous love, and had removed the chains of anger and hatred towards him that had held her soul in bondage for so long. It seemed to her that she at last had a happy and safe future to look forward to.

Things, she reflected, were looking good.

CHAPTER FIFTY-TWO

Berta enjoyed her last days at school. Her seniority meant that she was less constrained by rules and regulations and was able to have a more relaxed relationship with the nuns. She day-dreamed a little, as had always been her wont, and wondered with a frisson of excitement where the future was going to take her. Already she had some ideas, but she needed to discuss them with A Mayi and Elsa.

Mother Camille had soothed her severely depressed spirits on her return from her visit to the Limbe Trading Company.

"I much feared that that would be the result," she said quietly, as they sat on a bench under a jacaranda tree in the garden, "but I am proud of you for taking the plunge and finding out for yourself what goes on out there." And she waved her hand airily in the direction of the world at large.

"The important thing is that you don't let it defeat you. You have simply encountered an obstacle, a large one to be sure, but never doubt that you have what it takes to overcome it."

Strength and optimism surged back into the young girl's heart and she returned to her duties with the glow of her old enthusiasm once again. She was in the warm folds of pleasant reflection when Mother Camille called her from class one morning and took her into her little office.

"Sit down, Berta," she invited her.

Berta sat down a little apprehensively. To be called specifically to see the Mother Superior during class time usually meant bad news. Mother Camille smiled – *that's encouraging,* thought Berta – and waved a piece of paper that she was holding in her hand.

"I've had a most unexpected letter. It's from Mrs Sharpe, a charming English lady whose husband grows tea in the Cholo district. Her father-in-law was Sir Alfred Sharpe, one of the most important British administrators of the last century. His son, Reginald, came out here, loved it and brought out his family with the intention of making this their home."

Berta was familiar with the area, which was not far from the convent and was known for its huge acreage of emerald green tea plants and towering mountains in the background.

"Yes, I've met both of them," she replied. "My father took me to their farm once on a business visit, something to do with exporting sisal string I think. I remember that both she and her husband were very nice."

"Well," continued the nun. "Her letter says that your father has written to them asking if your educational qualifications and background might be useful for mothers on the tea estates, who have to educate their children at home. He asked them for any suggestions as to what sort of work you could find that would suit your qualifications and background."

She smiled at Berta who sat staring at her, shocked into silence.

"Well, it seems that, although Mrs Sharpe teaches her daughter all the usual subjects, she is not sure of her French and particularly, her French accent, or lack of it. It has been causing her some concern so when your father's letter arrived, it was the answer to a prayer. She would like to employ you as a French teacher and governess for Elizabeth. So, what do you think, Berta?"

"Well," she finally stammered, "I need to know more about it." Her troubled mind told her that this job was a far cry from the independence she was determined to build for herself. On the contrary, it would mean tying herself into a subservient role. Would that lessen her chances of achieving her objective, or would it in fact bring her opportunities?

The nun observed her with a puzzled smile.

"I thought you'd be pleased, Berta."

Berta forced herself back to the present and, with a mental shake, addressed her mentor.

"Yes, of course I am, Mother. Just surprised and needing to know about what is involved."

Mother Camille leaned back in her chair, put her hands together at the edge of her desk and smiled more broadly than ever.

"Ask what you will, my child, and I shall try to answer."

"Will I have to live with them?" was the first question.

"Yes," replied the nun. "You will recall that they have a beautiful farm house and you would have your own bedroom, next to Elizabeth's."

"Would I have to eat with them?" was the next question.

"Yes, of course. Mrs Sharpe makes it quite clear that you will be treated as a member of the family."

"Now, that's embarrassing. I shan't be able to eat. Probably waste away to nothing in no time. Mind you, I could sneak off to the kitchen in between meals, couldn't I?"

"And, knowing you and your appetite, Berta, I am quite certain that that is exactly what you would do!" laughed Mother, and Berta joined in, starting to relax at last.

"And what exactly would I be expected to do?"

"Well, first of all there's the French that you'll teach Elizabeth, but Mrs Sharpe seems to hope that you'll also help with general subjects. She has also mentioned embroidery and crocheting. You see, she's educating her daughter herself at home with a correspondence course to help her do it."

Berta was interested. "Really? Why doesn't she send her to school?"

"There are no schools for European children in the country except a very small junior school in Blantyre; it would be impossible to travel to it every day."

Berta smiled wryly. "And, of course, they would not consider sending her to one of the local government schools for African children."

"No," said the nun briefly. She glanced sideways at Berta. "As your father didn't," she said.

Berta nodded. "How old is Elizabeth?" she asked.

"Seven. And her little brother Frederick is a toddler."

"*Mon Dieu*! I wouldn't be expected to help with him, would I?" asked Berta, alarmed.

"No, no. I understand that there are two nannies for him."

"Good. I'm not too keen on babies, but seven sounds like a nice age. I think I would enjoy teaching Elizabeth. She must have been a baby when I visited with Dad, which is probably why I can't remember her." She paused and pondered while the nun waited patiently. The job sounded very pleasant and she knew that she would enjoy the teaching, but what about her ambitions? But then her future plans would take time to come to fruition and she realised that this position was actually heaven-sent, to keep her occupied and broaden her horizons in the meantime. A new environment, many new acquaintances to be made, who knew what might emerge?

She looked up at the nun and smiled. "Well, I've thought about it and, yes, I would like the job."

"Don't be too hasty!" laughed the nun. "You haven't asked about pay."

"Oh, yes." Berta paused. "Pay... I get paid?" Her voice rose incredulously.

"Of course you do, my dear child," said the nun and, looking at the letter, told Berta her proposed salary. This meant absolutely nothing to Berta, who had had rare occasion to handle or be concerned about money. All her needs and most of her wants had always been met. It did seem a novel experience to have money of her own coming in regularly, but since she could think of nothing that she wanted or needed, she thought that she would probably save it.

"Happy?" asked the nun as she finished.

"Oh, yes, Mother," replied Berta, her eyes shining with excitement as the idea took hold of her. "It's something that I have never thought of doing but, you know, I think it could be quite exciting. I just feel terribly shy, moving into a new and strange family just like that, and their being English – and all that!"

"Of course you do. You would have been a very brash, insensitive young woman if you didn't feel that way. Think of Sister Adelaide, the only English sister amongst all the French and Canadian sisters – and we all get along really well! Naturally, you will feel strange in the beginning, but you'll soon find your feet and then they'll have a job keeping you quiet."

"Oh, Mother," replied Berta, squirming. "Do I really talk that much?"

"Yes, you do," was the teasing response, "but we all enjoy it. When you go, it will be like losing a ray of sunshine."

"Thank you, Mother," she responded, embarrassed and pleased at the same time at the pretty compliment. Then she became serious.

"Mother, I feel that I should warn you that I've been thinking very hard about how to become independent. The talk we had about my future prospects and my failing to find a job made me realise that unless I do something quite drastic I face a dull and uninspiring life."

Camille looked concerned. "Have you come up with anything?" she asked.

Berta nodded. "Yes, I think so. You know that my father left me property in Blantyre? Well, I've been thinking that if I build a shop on it I can rent it out in the short-term, while I think of a business of my own that I can open up there some time in the not too distant future."

"But building a shop will cost a lot of money, my dear," cautioned Camille.

"Yes, I realise," said Berta, and went on to explain to the nun the conditions under which Ludwig had signed over his business to Kahn.

"Mr Kahn agreed that the price he would pay Papa for the business was a lump sum to each of us when we completed our education and needed the money to set ourselves up. Of course, there could be a problem with Mr Kahn giving me the money, since the British government confiscated and sold all the Nyasaland business and property, but the Portuguese chain is still doing very well so I think he will be happy to fund me. I'm the last sibling that he'll have to pay out for."

"Well," said Camille, thoughtfully, "this seems to me to be a very good idea; the rents that you collect will give you an independent income. Have you any idea what your eventual business will be?"

"No, none at all!" was the cheerful reply. "But I can assure you that I shall think of something soon. I am absolutely determined to make my own way. Like Elsa! So what I'm trying to say, really, is that much as I welcome going to the Sharpe's, I have other plans in the long term."

Camille was brisk in her response. "Well, I think that that is absolutely acceptable and I don't think that we need to mention your plans to anyone."

As soon as term was over and the last tearful farewells had been said to the nuns and the children, Berta travelled up to Chiromo, where she told A Mayi, Elsa and Andrew of her building plans.

All three were enthusiastic. "You can't go wrong investing in land and buildings," was A Mayi's comment. "Not only will they increase in value with time but you'll have a steady income from them."

Andrew was supportive. "A Mayi's right," he said. "Land and buildings are almost always a rock solid investment. Any idea what sort of businesses you want to attract, or even start up yourself?"

Berta shook her head. "Not yet, but I'm certain something will come up. This is a young, growing country and I just need to keep my eyes open for opportunities."

"I don't think you'll have a problem with Mr Kahn," said Elsa. "He has an office in Blantyre now and I saw him when I was last up there. In fact, he asked about you and I told him that you'd be finishing school soon, so I don't think your request will be unexpected."

Elsa was right that Berta's request was not unexpected, but Kahn proved less than eager to fund the building plans.

He sat behind his desk and looked apologetically across it at the girls, his eyebrows jostling and pushing his brow up into his receding hairline, while his glasses slid down his nose. His arms rested on the desk and the fingers of both hands formed a steeple, over which he peered worriedly. He took off his glasses.

"You know of course, my dear girls, that I am most anxious to do whatever I can to help you with your first steps into the world."

Berta interposed gently. "In terms of your agreement with our father..."

Kahn was thrown. "Er, yes. That's right." He paused.

"Now, as you know, the government confiscated your father's part of the business that was based in Nyasaland, leaving me only the Portuguese operation. As a result, the income from the business has been far less than your father or I had envisaged."

Elsa spoke this time: "I am sure you are right, Mr Kahn, but nevertheless the Portuguese operation has expanded considerably and, from all accounts, you are doing very well indeed financially."

Kahn's response was cautious: "Well, I can't complain, but the profitability is not as healthy as we had imagined when we made the agreement."

Berta saw her dream in danger of receding and when she spoke there was a touch of steel in her voice: "But on the other hand, Mr Kahn, you didn't have to pay out anything for Elsa, because our grandfather paid for Tangadzi farm."

A hard-hitting exchange followed, during which both Elsa and Kahn were startled to see a firm and resolute Berta negotiate her way to a compromise that she felt was fair to both sides. Kahn offered credible evidence of the maximum that he felt able to afford and which he felt honoured his agreement with Ludwig. He addressed the shortfall by accompanying the girls to the local bank, where he used his influence with the bank manager to obtain a loan for the balance on Berta's behalf, at a low rate of interest, and an extended period of repayment. Here, Elsa was able to facilitate the deal by offering herself as co-guarantor with Kahn, in the event that Berta failed to maintain repayments. As she said to Berta later, it was the least that Kahn could do in the circumstances.

With financing assured, the sisters returned in high spirits to Tangadzi Estate and started the process of planning the building, which they envisaged as being a large shop with a veranda the whole length of its frontage. At the rear would be store rooms for stocks, which had to be ordered well in advance and in large quantities, since average delivery times from Europe were in the region of four months from date of order.

Many hot, humid days were spent poring over the drawing, endless glasses of cold water at hand. During the evenings too, while the paraffin lamps hissed in the background and cicadas called gratingly out of the enveloping darkness, the sisters and Andrew could be found bent over the table in the dining room, making notes on the plans; an alteration here, an addition there.

"I really think that the building is large enough to be subdivided into four shops," was Elsa's suggestion.

Berta was dubious. "Surely not! I don't want cramped little rooms. No one will want to rent them."

"You'll be amazed at how much bigger the building looks when it's actually up," said Elsa, who had had a lot of experience with building at Tangadzi Estate. "Trust me, you can comfortably have four shops."

Berta was excited, indeed obsessed with the project. As she looked at the plans she saw not rolls of technical papers with drawings and figures on them, but the fulfilment of a dream, a dream of independence.

A further visit to Blantyre was needed to submit the drawings to the little planning department housed in the Town Hall. There were no problems with this; but there was a chance encounter which astonished Berta and gave her much food for thought over the next few months.

As the sisters left the office they almost collided with an expatriate Englishman who was coming in. He leapt back to make room for them to get through the doorway first, and Berta was thus able to look more closely at him than she would otherwise have done. He looked familiar, a strutting, skinny figure dressed in whites that had been immaculate but were now marked with stains, his skin mottled red from the heat. What threw her, however, was his ingratiating manner.

"Come through, lovely ladies," he said with exaggerated arm movements. "Come through."

They passed through the doorway murmuring their thanks, but the man started to strike up a conversation.

"Have we met?" he asked, and Berta recoiled from the hot interest in his ice-blue eyes and the spirits on his breath.

"No," they replied hastily in unison, but he interrupted.

"I'm sure I know you from somewhere" he said, his hand reaching up to rest on Elsa's forearm. She moved away pointedly and at that moment Berta recognised him. It was Carrain. It was that little man who had brought such destruction onto their family. She stared at him in hypnotised horror, unable to tear her gaze away or say a word. During the early years after Ludwig's deportation she had had many a period of seething recollection, when she had rehearsed what she would say to him if she should ever have the misfortune to meet him. And now, here he was, and all she could do was stare at him with loathing, before turning on her heel and walking briskly away. Behind her she heard Elsa address him.

"Yes, you do know us," she was saying to him, her voice cold and detached. "You almost destroyed our family and you took our father away from us with your cheating and your lies, but you lost much more than we did. Look at you, you seedy little man. Look at your stained clothes, your bloodshot eyes, the liquor on your breath. Drunk at midday, you disgusting specimen. If you ever had any dignity you certainly don't have it now, you hyena, you *filho da puta*."

And with that she turned on her heel and joined Berta where she stood by their car. They got in and drove off noisily, Elsa shaking after the encounter, grinding the gears in her agitation.

They drove in silence for a few minutes then a thought occurred to Berta, "What did you call him?" she asked with interest.

"Oh," replied Elsa airily. "Nothing much. Just something I learnt from my *capitao* Alfred, when he gets angry with the workers."

"Yes, but you must know what it means," persisted Berta, turning around in her seat to look at Elsa.

With a little choke of laughter Elsa managed to blurt out, "It means son of a bitch, or a prostitute, I think. I'm not exactly sure which."

There was a moment's silence. Berta stared at her sister in awe and admiration. "*Mon Dieu*," she breathed before exploding into her infamous giggles. The sisters laughed until they cried, while the little vehicle lurched erratically across the fortunately deserted road.

"But, Elsa," Berta finally said, as she mopped up her tears with a prettily embroidered handkerchief, "what could have caused such a change in Carrain? He looks washed out, finished, kind of unsavoury…"

"Who knows?" said Elsa, thoughtfully. "I do believe that one's sins catch up with one eventually. I can't say I'd be sorry to hear that fate had done to him just a little bit of what he did to us."

"Mm," said Berta thoughtfully. "We must keep our ears open to hear what we can."

They had arranged to lunch and stay the night with Mona, and she had some interesting information for them.

"News is getting around about your planned building, Berta," she said, as she led the girls to the cosy wicker armchairs on the veranda. "I think you already have a tenant!"

CHAPTER FIFTY-THREE

Mona did indeed have exciting news and Berta was agog to hear all the details.

She leapt up from the chair in which she had just lowered herself as Mona spoke and her eyes lit up. "A tenant! No! Really? Who? How?"

"Patience!" Mona said as she settled her guests, and then perched on the edge of her chair, clearly enjoying her moment of importance; even the tight waves that circled her head seemed to quiver. "Well, it was like this," she began, head bent forward conspiratorially. "News gets around so fast in this town; you can't keep anything secret, you know."

Berta interrupted her: "Yes, we know that, Mona. Now please tell us who wants to rent a shop!"

"I'm trying to," said Mona, her eyes glinting reprovingly through her glasses. "Well, there's been quite a lot of interest since you were seen going into the planning offices, and soon everyone knew exactly what your plans were." She settled herself further back in her chair. "Well, the other day I was buying bread from that new bakery that has opened up, you know, the one run by two Greek men at the bottom end of Sharrers Road."

"I think I know who you mean," said Elsa, "but we've had no reason to shop there yet. But go on."

Berta was distracted. "I've never met a Greek," she said.

"Yes, you have," said Elsa. "The bicycle shop that we visited in Limbe, the one owned by the two Vassilatos brothers, Panayis and Vangelis, I think they're called."

"Oh, yes, I remember. And I've thought of another one, from Cholo. Conforzi, I think his name is."

Mona's tone was acid. "He's Italian, actually, and I'm wondering whether you want to hear my news after all, Berta."

Berta's hand flew to her mouth but her dancing eyes belied her contrite apology. "I'm so sorry, Mona. Do forgive me and carry on. Please!"

Mona gave her a final reproachful look and continued. "Well, when he was wrapping up my bread, the younger partner, Nikola Trataris I think his name is, asked me if I knew anything about some new shops that were going up at the top end of Sharrers Road, because he would be very interested in renting one of them." She leaned back in her chair and beamed at the two sisters. "What do you think of that?"

Berta's face broke into a huge smile and she was too excited to say much more than, "No! Would you believe it! It's one thing planning something and dreaming and quite another when things start to happen. Oh, my gosh!"

Elsa's calm voice cut across the excitement: "We haven't thought about the rent, Berta, and we really need to."

After a few minutes' discussion and wild speculation it was clear that they weren't getting anywhere, so Mona offered to ask her father, for some idea of the current rents.

"Oh," she said suddenly, "I've just remembered that Mr Trataris asked if you could meet with him on your next trip to town. Have you got time to see him before you leave tomorrow?"

Berta looked questioningly at Elsa who smiled back. "Of course! *Bien sur!*"

"Tell me what time and I'll send a message to him," said Mona.

"I think nine o'clock," responded Elsa. "That means we can start travelling back to Tangadzi quite early."

Ten minutes short of nine o'clock the following morning found the girls packed and breakfasted, sitting on the veranda with cups of coffee in front of them. "Isn't the garden beautiful?" commented Berta, her artistic eye thrilling to the profusion of brilliantly coloured flowers in the borders, wet now with the morning dew. A gardener squatted at the edge of one of the beds, trowel in hand, weeding and turning up the sweet, dark earth. He wore old khaki shorts and a faded khaki shirt and he quietly hummed a catchy little tune to himself. A man at peace with the world, thought Berta. The only other sounds were the birds chattering in the trees, the buzzing of the bees as they attacked the pollen-rich flowers, and the occasional passer-by calling out a greeting to another.

"Thank you," said Mona. "I can't take much credit though because most of what you see is owed to our gardener, Ironi's, hard work." She sat with them, working on a piece of embroidery, her eyes darting frequently to the little gate at the end of the garden path that opened out onto the quiet pavement with its majestic flamboyant trees.

"He's coming," she said suddenly, needle poised above the fabric. "I can hear footsteps."

"They could be anybody's," retorted Berta, turning to look at the gate in time to see a strange man pause and bend to unlatch the gate, which opened with a squeak. The visitor came onto the garden path, turned to shut the gate and then walked towards the veranda. Dressed in white shirt and trousers, he was of average height and slim; his stride was energetic and jaunty.

He's very sure of himself, thought Berta.

As he approached the veranda steps he removed his Panama hat to reveal thick dark hair that was waved away from a good-looking, fine-featured face.

He reached the steps. "Good morning, ladies." He smiled and bold, dark eyes crinkled above an aquiline nose.

Mona jumped up hurriedly, draping her embroidery on the back of her chair.

"Come on up," she invited, and made the introductions to which he replied,

"No, please, no Mr Trataris, my name is Nikola."

When Mona had seated him within the circle with a cup of coffee in front of him, Elsa opened up the discussion of the shop.

"I believe you are interested in my sister's building?" she asked.

Haltingly, and in a mixture of English, Portuguese and Chinyanja, Nikola said that he was.

"My shop now too much small. Must have more room for foodstuffs and bread."

As they talked, his eyes repeatedly turned to Berta, his admiration clear to be seen. He addressed most of his remarks to her, a smile playing about his lips, his eyes alive with interest. She felt irritation rising but tried to focus on the fact that this was her very first discussion with a potential tenant, a milestone in her young life. When the question of rent arose, however, she spoke quickly, raising the price that the young women had agreed the previous evening by fifty per cent. Both Elsa and Mona glanced at her swiftly, a question in their eyes, but Nikola accepted the figure presented to him with a noncommittal nod.

"When building finish?" was his next question.

Berta's response was firm: "We can't be certain this early on but we'll keep in touch with you," she said, and it was agreed that they would keep him in the picture by calling on him at his shop.

Nikola finished off his coffee, announced that he should be getting back to work and rose to leave. He shook hands all around and clasped Berta's hand for an instant longer than she thought necessary, before thanking Mona for her hospitality and making his way back to the gate. He let himself out, turned briefly, gave a wave of his hand and walked away.

There was a silence until he was judged to be safely out of earshot, and then everyone spoke at once.

"What a charming…" from Elsa.

"I'll buy my bread from him any day…" from Mona.

"What a conceited, arrogant *cochon*! Just who does he think he is?" burst out Berta.

There was another silence while Elsa and Mona turned to stare at the heated Berta.

Elsa couldn't stop the smile that twitched her mouth. "Surely calling him a pig is a bit strong for whatever he might have done? Can't say I noticed anything."

"And raising the rent!" squeaked Mona, reaching for her embroidery.

Berta faltered, her temper cooling as quickly as it rose. "He kept staring at me," she mumbled, "and that really annoys me. Who does he think he is? And who does he think I am? Every time I looked up he was looking at me. I thought he was really bad mannered."

"He certainly admired you, but that's a compliment, you know, Berta. Nothing to get annoyed about!"

"I suppose not," came the disgruntled reply, "but I just hate it when men do things like that. I can tell you," she finished off. "I'll do my best to rent those shops to anyone but him!"

Elsa and Mona gave each other baffled glances, but moved on to discuss their impressions of the meeting. Berta's dislike of her future tenant aside, all in all, it was judged to have been a very useful meeting; particularly since, as Elsa pointed out, word would now get around that not only was a new building going up but that one of the shops was virtually spoken for.

Reluctantly the girls rose to leave for the long journey ahead of them. They warmly embraced Mona, with thanks for her hospitality, packed up the little car and noisily made off down the road, scattering a party of chickens which had been scratching for food at the road's edge. Berta waved to Mona, standing at her little gate, until the blooming flamboyant trees that shaded the pavement blocked her from sight.

In the few days left to her of her holiday, Berta languished at the farm, suffering in the suffocating midsummer heat and dreaming of her shops, yes, the four that she had finally agreed to, that would be her gateway to independence. A Mayi had convinced her that Elsa was right and that the shops would be of ample size.

"The traders want shops that look full," she advised. "It isn't good for business for a shop to look as though there isn't enough stock to fill the shelves. The public will think the shop is not doing well and will shop elsewhere."

The final word about the practicalities was also from A Mayi. "Who is going to supervise the actual construction?" she asked. The idea had not even occurred to Berta, but it seemed that Elsa had given it a lot of thought.

"I had a very brief word with Mr Dharap in Blantyre and he volunteered to keep an eye on the builders for us. I also plan to go up once a month for a detailed inspection."

A Mayi nodded her approval and Berta sent her a grateful smile. What, she thought, would she do without A Mayi and Elsa?

Thoughts of Nikola came and caught her unawares more than she would have liked. She couldn't remember ever having been so antagonised by a man. His open admiration she saw as arrogance; and the fact that it made her unsure of herself, defensive and petulant, made her squirm with embarrassment. Yes, she admitted to herself, she had behaved like a spoilt child with Elsa and Mona, when Nikola had taken his leave that day. Well, she decided, at least she only had to see him when discussing the matter of rent – if he still decided to rent at the inflated price that she had quoted him! – and she smiled with satisfaction at the memory. Chances were that he behaved like that towards any remotely attractive female and she had taken his attitude too seriously. With a mental shrug she reached out for the shop drawings again and immersed herself in happy imaginings for the future. What should the front of the building look like? She'd have to think about a name…

Finally, the day of her departure for the tea plantation arrived and, despite a quivering stomach and a few tears when she hugged A Mayi and kissed her goodbye, she was ready for Elsa to escort her from the farm to Limbe, where they had arranged to meet the Sharpe family, who would pick her up in their new model T Ford and drive her to their home in Cholo, in the Shire Highlands. Both sisters had dressed with care, head-hugging cloche hats, empire-waisted dresses and silk stockings. Three hours later they had reached the agreed meeting point; Elsa drove carefully off the road and parked under the shade of a flame-blossomed flamboyant tree.

"What a pretty area," said Berta, bending to peer through the windscreen. "There are so many fir trees mixed with the flamboyants and the jacaranda trees."

Elsa started to climb out of the car. "It's a much cooler climate here in Limbe, so you'll find that the environment is greener."

"Come on out," she called to Berta, as she walked around stretching her legs. "It'll be cooler than sitting in the car."

Berta climbed out with knees that were beginning to feel shaky and, as the sisters stood waiting, her courage threatened to desert her.

"What have I done?" she asked Elsa, turning her face to her with huge anxious eyes. "I could have stayed at Tangadzi with you and A Mayi. I know I would have been happy."

Elsa smiled, put her arm around her and gave her a quick hug.

"Yes, my dear little sister," she said. "You certainly would – for a month, maybe even two."

She turned Berta around to face her.

"You are far too lively, far too intelligent just to latch onto A Mayi and me as we go about our business. You, my girl, were born to be a success in your own right. Just look at you. Barely eighteen years old and already you are a property owner! And with a charming tenant – sorry! I mean a *cochon* – panting to move into one of your shops."

Berta was momentarily distracted, and her expression darkened.

"He most certainly is a *cochon*, but I suppose if he pays the rent…"

"Exactly!" said Elsa, then with a mischievous smile. "And, after all, he is a very attractive *cochon*…"

She held up her hands in mock fear at Berta's expression.

"No, No. Mercy! I promise not to call him that again."

Fears receding, Berta laughed. "Oh Elsa, you are such a one!"

Elsa laughed merrily. "Yes, I know. And you are such a lucky one. Going to live in a wealthy farmer's home in Cholo, one of the most beautiful parts of the country. Your truly adult life starts today, and may God bless you. You have so much now to look forward to. "

Berta smiled. "I hope so," she said and turned away, her mind's eye reaching out to the emerald landscape to which she was heading. Her new life would bear little resemblance to her past life. Would memories of her father become less frequent? What opportunities might there be awaiting her? Might there be, and she glanced sideways through her lashes at Elsa beside her, might there even be love? But she was too shy to voice this. Time would tell.

Cholo. Berta rolled the name around her tongue. Different, exciting even. A place of tea plantations, soaring mountains, tennis and planters' balls, a bastion of British society in tropical Africa.

So far removed from Tangadzi, A Mayi, Elsa, Paulina and their thriving cotton plantation. She shivered.

THE END

Lightning Source UK Ltd.
Milton Keynes UK
UKOW04f0849010917
308393UK00001B/204/P